SEPOYS IN THE TRENCHES

THE INDIAN CORPS ON THE WESTERN FRONT
1914–1915

by

Gordon Corrigan

SPELLMOUNT

British Library Cataloguing in Publication Data:
A catalogue record for this book is available
from the British Library

Copyright © Gordon Corrigan 2006

ISBN 1-86227-354-5

This edition first published in the UK in 2006 by
Spellmount Limited
The Mill, Brimscombe Port
Stroud, Gloucestershire. GL5 2QG

Tel: 01453 883300
Fax: 01453 883233
E-mail: enquiries@spellmount.com
Website: www.spellmount.com

1 3 5 7 9 8 6 4 2

The right of Gordon Corrigan to be identified
as the author of this work has been asserted by him
in accordance with the Copyright, Designs
and Patents Act 1988

Printed in Great Britain by
Oaklands Book Services
Stonehouse, Gloucestershire GL10 3RQ

Contents

This book is respectfully dedicated to the Gurkha Officers and Other Ranks of the British Brigade of Gurkhas, whose friendship and loyalty I was privileged to be granted.

List of Maps

List of Plates

Preface

It is now nearly 60 years since India became independent of Britain and over 90 years since the outbreak of the First World War. Most Englishmen now alive know nothing of India save that there seem to be a great many Indians working in the National Health Service and the only shop where one seems to be able to buy a pint of milk at a weekend is run by an Indian or a Pakistani. The more affluent may have been on holiday to India, where they will have marvelled at the Taj Mahal, tramped round the palaces of Rajhastan and have been faintly troubled by the lepers and the beggars of Delhi, Calcutta and Bombay. Most Britons will know that there are still Gurkhas in the service of the British Crown, albeit that there are pitifully few of them left, and may have wondered whence the connection arose. It will occur to few now ensconced in the Britain of the European Union that there was a time when the only trained regular soldiers available to prevent a British military catastrophe were those of the Indian Army.

Britain declared war on Germany on 4 August 1914. Four days later two infantry divisions and a cavalry brigade of the Indian Army were ordered to mobilise. Indian soldiers began to arrive in Europe in September, still in their tropical uniforms, and were thrown into the first battle of Ypres in October. Within a month they had won their first Victoria Cross. 23 Indian infantry battalions and 14 Indian cavalry regiments served on the Western Front. The two infantry divisions were re-deployed to the Middle East in November 1915, the cavalry stayed until 1918. India sent 140,000 men to the Western Front, 90,000 in the Indian Corps and the Indian Cavalry Corps, and 50,000 in the Labour Companies. Of the combatants, 8,557 were killed and 50,000 more wounded, many crippled for life. Five thousand of the dead were either never found, or never identified. Drowned and lost in the mud, swallowed up by collapsing trenches, or simply blown to pieces by shells and mines, they have no known resting place.

The old Indian Army was a truly remarkable institution. It had never been structured for all-out European war and its experience lay in frontier raids, punitive expeditions and hill fighting. Battalions had but 12 British officers and there was no system of reserves worthy of the name. The men of the Indian Corps who landed in France were long-service regulars, volunteers all. Even after the unprecedented casualties of the early battles in 1914 and 1915, replacements were all volunteers and remained so to the end, long after Britain had introduced conscription.

This book sets out to tell the tale of the Indian Corps on the Western Front. The official history of the Corps has been set down by its 'Recording Officers'; Lieutenant Colonel Merewether and Sir Frederick Smith ('FE', the celebrated King's Counsel and later Attorney General and lORd Birkenhead). The Corps Commander, Lieutenant General Sir James Willcocks, also recorded his experiences. Apart from these two works published shortly after the war, little has been written outside regimental histories and individual accounts. My purpose has been to examine the activities of the Corps and to look behind the official reports, returns, despatches and citations and seek out what it meant to be a soldier of one of those Indian regiments, thrust into a country of which he knew nothing, subjected to a climate never before experienced, fighting an enemy the like of which he had never imagined, in a cause of which he understood little. I seek too to explain how that old army worked; how it was that men from the Punjab, from the Frontiers, from Nepal, from Madras, from Garhwal, from all parts of India were prepared to follow officers of a different race, religion and culture and from a land far beyond the 'Black Ocean'. And follow they did, often unto death, for it was this partly mystical, partly harshly practical relationship between the British officer and the Indian soldier that made the old Indian Army what it was. When the effectiveness of Indian regiments declined—as it sometimes did—this was directly related to the casualty figures amongst the British officers and the difficulty of replacing them with men who understood their soldiers' customs and could speak their language. The Corps Commander, himself from the British service, was unstinting in his admiration for Indian soldiers, but he was adamant that there could be no Indian substitute for British officers in the field. At the time he may have been right, but the performance of the Indian Army in the Second World War and of the Indian and Pakistani Armies since independence can leave no room for doubt that the sub continent still produces not only soldiers of fine fighting spirit, but good officers to lead them too. The sadness is that the descendants of those regiments which fought side by side on the Western Front and shed their blood in a common cause have spent so much of the last 50 years in fighting each other.

In concentrating on the activities of Indian units I do not belittle the British infantry battalions which fought as integral components of the Indian Corps. Their contribution was immeasurable and they never once failed to support their Indian comrades to the utmost. It is a reflection on successive governments' defence policies that of the ten British infantry battalions that fought with the Indian Army on the Western Front, only two remain on the Army List of 1998. I make only passing reference to the activities of the Indian Cavalry on the Western Front. That contribution, initially a brigade, then a division and finally a corps of two divisions, was immense but one book is not sufficient to examine in detail the activities of both corps. The Cavalry deserves a book of its own.

The Indian Corps came in for criticism on the Western Front. They were said by some to be unable to withstand the cold, to be of low morale, and to have a high incidence of self-inflicted wounds. Some of these accusations were levied at the time, some surfaced much later. In all cases I have returned to the original evidence and have attempted to establish the truth or otherwise of the critics' comments. Some have emerged as total fiction, from either genuine misunderstandings or from more nefarious motives. One published account, which has become part of the mythology of the Western Front, describes Indian troops on the right of a British battalion during First Ypres as refusing to fight. It transpires that the writer's unit was never anywhere near an Indian regiment and the account is entirely fictional.

Published sources for this book are listed. Many of them were produced shortly after the war in the form of regimental histories or regimental records, the majority written by men who were actually there. There are of course lies, damned lies and regimental histories. I found the 47th Sikhs' account to be particularly helpful as a factual record of what happened and when, devoid of hyperbole. The Royal Garhwal Rifles account, written by the Commanding Officer of the 2nd Battalion 1914/15, is excellent not so much for its operational detail (although this is good too) but for its explanations of the administrative difficulties under which the Indian Army of 1914 laboured. Some are less good. No regimental history wants to show its subject in a bad light, and for incidents or actions that were contentious I have relied upon the war diaries, not only of the battalion in question but, perhaps more importantly, of the battalions on either side or in support.

Unpublished sources are also listed. Of tremendous assistance, and a mine of original material in themselves, are the reports of the Censor of Indian Mails held in the India Office Library in Blackfriars, London. The Censor's office produced a detailed weekly report on morale amongst Indian troops as revealed by their letters. The original letters are not there, and the copies appended by the Censor lose something in the translation from Urdu, Gujerati, Hindi or Nepali, nevertheless they give a very full impression of how the sepoys felt, what they were worried about and how they perceived the war. This material has been skimmed in the past, but that research has, in my humble submission, led to incorrect conclusions. Some students have not fully understood what they were looking at. They have failed to realise that most sepoys of the period were only literate in a very basic sense, and that most letters were dictated to the company clerk, who put his own interpretation onto what the soldier wished to say. Previous researchers have concentrated on that small minority of letters held back by the Censor, either because they gave too much detail about operations in progress or pending, or because they showed lack of fighting spirit or resolve. They ignored the vast lode of hum-drum, unexciting domestic trivia which shows the average soldier as getting on with his job without fuss or bother. I have also been able to examine much original material, letters and diaries, held in the Gurkha Museum and all these have helped in giving a clear idea of what people felt at the time.

Cynics say that the best sources are dead sources. Try as I have, I have been unable to trace anyone still alive who served in the Indian Army on the Western Front. I have scoured the hills of Nepal and have interviewed men who were in Palestine, Gallipoli and Mesopotamia, but nary a one who served in France. I have similarly drawn a blank in India. I do not say there are none—even allowing for the Indian and Gurkha propensity to add several years to their age in order to enlist, veterans of 1914/15 would be in their late nineties now—I merely say I have been unable to find any.

In my own reading of military history I have occasionally been irritated by two interdependent factors: the inability to relate some written accounts to the actual ground, and the paucity of maps. While I have in no sense attempted to produce a battlefield guide—that is a separate exercise—the reader should be able to take this book to France, should he or she be so minded, and be able to follow what happened with reference to roads, buildings and geographical features. I have compared all that I have written with contemporaneous accounts, operation orders, war diaries, trench maps and the ground itself. Spending numerous weekends and leaves sleeping in an army tent by night and tramping the plough by day, my long-suffering wife has been the arbiter of 'followability'. Divorce was never mentioned once.

Historical works published earlier this century often included beautiful maps. They were accurate, detailed, folded out and often came contained separately in an envelope at the back of the book. Alas, cost now precludes that happy state, but I have attempted to produce maps and sketches which make sense and which are relevant to what happened and to the ground as it was then, while still being able to be related to today's continental equivalent of the Ordnance Survey map.

The genesis of this book took place in an estaminet in Belgium in the spring of 1996, at the conclusion of a battlefield tour of Napoleon's 1815 campaign organised by the British Commission for Military History. Late at night and after a considerable quantity of the vin du patron, Chris McCarthy, himself a distinguished author of books on the Western Front, opined if I could write like I could talk, I should write military history. He suggested that I should set out to tell the tale of the Indian Corps on the Western Front, and I am especially thankful to him and to the other members of the Commission for their help, support and encouragement in my efforts. I am grateful too to my many friends with far more experience of the Indian Army than I for their help and guidance, and in particular to the officers and men of the British Brigade of Gurkhas, with whom I have spent a large part of my adult life, for allowing me to acquire some insight into the mind of the Indian and Nepali soldier. I owe thanks specifically to Dr Gary Sheffield of the War Studies Department of The Royal Military Academy Sandhurst for his scholarly critique of, and assistance with, a voluminous first draft; to Dr Tony Heathcote for his assistance and advice in matters concerning India and her armies; to Field Marshal Sir John Chapple and Colonel Denis Wood in researching the action fought by the 2nd Battalion 2nd Gurkha Rifles in November 1914; to Brigadier Douglas Wickenden, consultant psychiatrist to the British Army for his advice on the psychiatric casualties suffered by the Indian Corps and their treatment; to Major Martin Kitson RAMC, my Medical Officer, for translating the medical terms used in 1914 into language that is understood today; to Major David Wilson MC for allowing me an insight into Sikhs and Dogras; to Pandit Aitaram Dahal, my regimental priest, for his advice on the religions of the Indian Army, and to Warrant Officer Class 2 Khadkaraj Gurung Queen's Gurkha Signals and Colour Sergeant Indrabahadur Rai Royal Gurkha Rifles for obtaining for me maps of France and Flanders and for photocopying all manner of arcane pieces of paper. It goes without saying that without the help of Brigadier Christopher Bullock of the Gurkha Museum and the ever tolerant staffs of the Public Record Office, The India Office Library and Records, The Imperial War Museum, The British Newspaper Library, The Prince Consort's Library Aldershot and the library of the Royal Military Academy Sandhurst this book could never have been written. For permission to quote from and use documents, papers, reports and photographs in their possession I am indebted to The Controller of Her Majesty's Stationery Office for access to Crown Copyright documents in the Public Record Office and the Oriental and India Office collection of the British Library; The Trustees of The Gurkha Museum; The *Illustrated London News* Picture Library; The *Daily Mail* and Miss Vanessa Harbar of The Imperial War Museum. My especial thanks go to The Honourable Toby Buchan and to Jamie Wilson of Spellmount Publishers and David Grant my editor for their help, advice and extraordinary tolerance exhibited towards a first-time author.

The opinions, and the errors, are mine and mine alone. If I can, in some small measure, bring to the attention of a wider audience the debt that this nation owes to the men of India and Pakistan and Nepal then I shall have achieved my aim.

Gordon Corrigan
Eastry, Kent

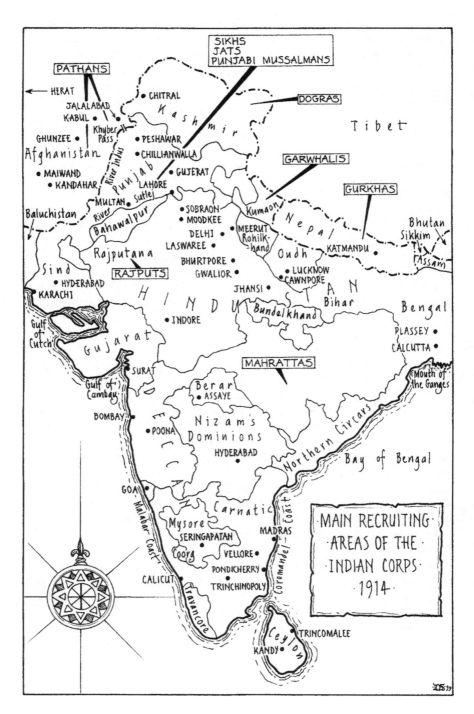

MAIN RECRUITING
AREAS OF THE
INDIAN CORPS
1914

I

A Great Adventure

Throughout the late summer and autumn of 1914 those employees of the French railway system who were too old or too valuable to be conscripted into the army had become well used to the stream of trains moving north and west carrying men, horses, guns and stores. They had watched the moustachioed poilus, some in the red trousers still worn by the French infantry in the early days of the war, pile on to the carriages and go to sleep or light up their pipes as the trains pulled away for the front. They had observed the British Expeditionary Force, still pitifully small, moving east from its disembarkation ports of Rouen, Le Havre and Boulogne and they had seen troops withdrawn from the French North African colonies moving up from Marseilles.

On the night of 18 October 1914 the shunters and marshallers were intrigued to see a series of trains moving from Orléans to St Omer containing what at first glance seemed to be Zouaves, or Moroccans or perhaps Berbers from the high Atlas mountains. On closer inspection at the numerous halts it became clear that whatever these men might be they were not in the French employ, for they spoke no French and were addressed by their unmistakably European officers in languages such as the good citizens of Rouen, Abbeville and Calais had never previously encountered. Some of these men were burly and bearded and wore strangely folded turbans round their heads, some were clean shaven, tall and aquiline in feature and wore a different type of turban. Yet more were short, merry little men with slant eyes and wearing slouch hats, and eventually the whisper went up and down the line that these were 'Les Hindoues' from the British Empire in the east.

Seven hundred or so of the passengers on one of the trains travelling north on the night of 18 October 1914 belonged to the 57th Wilde's Rifles (Frontier Force), and only a minority of them were Hindu. Wilde's Rifles was a regular infantry battalion of the Indian Army and on the train that night was its entire strength of 12 British officers, 17 Indian officers, 729 rank and file (known as IOR—Indian Other Ranks) and 42 Indian civilian 'followers'. There is a perfectly good and direct railway line from Orléans to St Omer but the exigencies of war dictated that the direct route was not taken. The Indian soldier is a past master at the art of snatching sleep when it is available, rumal over his face or balaclava pulled well down he will adjust his position and enjoy a period of unconsciousness until his naik* shouts the stand-to. On this night the frequent halts and the shunting and bumping allowed the passengers little rest, even if there had not been the souvenir hunters who gathered at every halt anxious to swap wine for cap badges, or fruit for buttons, or baguettes for chapattis. Even autographs were eagerly collected.

It was at least a less hazardous journey than on the previous occasion when Wilde's had taken to the iron road. That had been on the journey from Marseilles, the point of disembarkation, to Orléans, the concentration area. Sepoy Zaman Khan, of the Punjabi Mussalman Company, had travelled by rail before, in India, and when a carriage door had become partially opened he had thought little of it and continued to lean against it, his natural balance ensuring that he did not fall out of the now widening aperture. All would probably have been well had not the line been double tracked and had not an express train passed in the opposite direction, removing the partially opened door and hurling Sepoy Zaman Khan far into the night. French trains of 1914 were not equipped with emergency stop chains, nor any other means of communicating with the driver. After shouts and imprecations in Hindustani had failed to reach the ears of the somnolent French engine driver, the company buglers were found in the next compartment and prevailed upon to blow the 'Halt' in unison out the window.

Unfortunately, in an age before NATO standardisation had even been thought of, British and French bugle calls were not the same, and it was only after some minutes of blowing every call that the increasingly frenzied buglers could think of, from 'Take Open Order' to 'Orderly Havildars' to 'Cookhouse', that the driver was prevailed upon to stop. Sepoy Zaman Khan was found several miles back along the line, somewhat grumpy but none the worse for wear. The door was not repairable.

The Indian Army which took the field in 1914 was not in any sense representative of the population of India. The events of the Indian Mutiny

---

*   Equivalent to corporal.

†   Of the 74 regular infantry battalions of the Bengal Army in 1857, 44 mutinied, ten displayed 'Unrest' and were disarmed before they could mutiny, 12 were disbanded on the grounds that they might mutiny in the future and 12 remained loyal. Of the 23 battalions of local infantry, raised for service in a specific area, four mutinied and 19 remained loyal. Of the eight irregular battalions six mutinied and two remained loyal. All 11 battalions of Punjab Infantry stayed loyal. In the Bengal Cavalry all 11 Light Cavalry regiments were disbanded and of the 15 regiments of local and irregular cavalry eight mutinied, one was disarmed and one was disbanded, five remaining loyal. All six regiments of Punjab Cavalry stayed loyal. Thus, of 148 Major units in the Bengal Army 55, of varying capabilities, remained loyal.

of 1857—more properly a mutiny by part of the Bengal Army† one of three armies maintained by the Honourable The East India Company which administered the three provinces of British India on behalf of the British government—had led to a fundamental restructuring of the Indian Armies. Inevitably this reorganisation penalised those who had mutinied and rewarded those who had remained loyal.

All regiments which had mutinied were disbanded, often to the protests, tears and pleadings of their British officers. The gaps left in the Army list by these disbandments were filled by previously irregular regiments, such as the Gurkhas, or by regiments raised from the largely loyal Sikhs and Punjabis.

One aspect of the post-Mutiny reorganisation was to have a direct effect upon the Indian Army in France in 1914. Henceforth artillery, with the exception of relatively low-calibre, short-range pack artillery, would be in British and not Indian hands. This meant that most of the divisional and corps artillery for the Indian Army on the Western Front had to be found from already stretched British resources.

During the post-mutiny reorganisation and subsequently, the theory of the 'Martial Races' began to take hold. Many British officers and administrators had observed that the Prussians were better soldiers than the Italians, the French better than the Spanish and the Swedes better than the Sardinians. Could it be, they wondered, that this self-evident superiority was somehow inherited and a function of race?

Peoples who lived in the northern latitudes, or on hills, seemed to be harder, more outgoing, less devious, more 'manly' than the softer races of the tropics and the plains. Applied to India, the pre-mutiny Bengal Army had been largely composed of plainsmen, many of them high-caste Hindus who had caused problems with their dietary needs and would not serve alongside men of lower caste. These Brahmins had mutinied, whereas the Gurkhas who came from the high foothills of the Himalayas had not. The Sikhs might not be hillmen but they were from the north and they were not Hindu. Much the same argument applied to the other races of the Punjab and the north. If they were Hindu they were not obtrusively so, they were tall or they were fair or they were uncomplicated or (like the Gurkhas) they had a British sense of humour, and of course all of them were brave.

Subsequent reorganisations under Roberts (Commander in Chief from 1885) and Kitchener (Commander in Chief from 1902) created one unified Indian Army and increased the proportion of soldiers drawn from the Martial Races. Within 50 years of the mutiny it was the Punjab which became known as the cradle of the Indian Army. Here were found the Sikhs, the Dogras, the Jats, the Punjabi Mussalmans, men whom the British regarded as excellent military material and who, with the Pathans and the hillmen of Nepal and Garhwal, were to make up the bulk the infantry of the Indian Expeditionary Force of 1914.

Much of the theory of the Martial Races was of dubious scientific provenance. Sikhs, Punjabi Mussalmans, Jats, Dogras, Rajputs and Pathans tend to be tall and impressive looking. Whether or not appearance has any bearing on military ability, men of soldierly appearance (itself subjective) appealed to recruiting officers and were considered by the British to be more like themselves than the shorter, darker races of the south. The theory was unfair to many who had served the British well in the past. In the latter half of the eighteenth century the victories of Arcot and Plassey, against the French and their native surrogates, and the battles of the Mysore wars, were won by largely Madrassi troops trained and led by British officers. The Madras troops were often of low caste, they were black and they were short in stature. A hundred years later they were virtually excluded from the combat areas.

It may be that Martial Races are martial because they believe themselves to be so. The races enlisted into the 1914 Indian Army did consider themselves to be martial and this belief was self-reinforcing and encouraged by the British, indeed often exaggerated by them. British officers would argue long and hard that it was impossible for their men to accept some point or other because it conflicted with their Sanscriti, or culture. Had they not been asked, the men might well have happily accepted whatever the point was, but they would now add this stricture to their bank of folk memory. The Sikh tradition demands that the face is not shaved nor the hair cut. The original Sikh turban (or pagri) was merely a strip of cloth to keep the long hair under control, and even when Sikhs were first enlisted it was of no great significance. A photograph of the Ludhiana Sikhs[*] in 1860 shows their headgear to be a simple cloth wrapped around the head, apparently at the whim of the individual. Thirty years later the turban has become formalised, much larger, tied in a prescribed manner and with a regimental badge affixed. Thus, by the time steel helmets were introduced in 1915 it had become ingrained in the Sikh regiments that no form of headgear other than the pagri could be worn. Strong objections to the helmet were raised. Reminders that the warriors of Ranjit Singh, the Lion of the Punjab and a Sikh hero, wore iron caps fell on deaf ears and the Sikhs never did wear steel helmets.

The popularly recognised authority on the various races and classes that made up the Indian Army was Lieutenant General Sir George MacMunn. MacMunn was an officer of the Royal Artillery but had spent nearly all his service in India and was familiar with most parts of the country and with the peoples who lived there. He was a prolific author who wrote fiction, military history, biographies—including one of Gustavus Adolphus— geographical works and, of course, about India and its religions, customs and peoples. Much of MacMunn's writing is naive and unscientific to the twentieth-century reader[†] but, in that he expressed the beliefs of British

---

[*]   Later the 15th Sikhs, who served on the Western Front.
[†]   But still worth buying for the delightful illustrations by AC Lovat.

4

India of the time, his opinions are relevant. MacMunn wrote one book which was prescribed reading for every newly joined British officer, *The Armies of India*,[1] published in 1911. After the war he published *The Martial Races of India*,[2] and while that volume could not have been read by the British officers of 1914, it nevertheless reflected what they thought.

Not only was the 1914 Indian Army largely recruited from the north, but many of its regiments had originally been raised from erstwhile enemies of the British. Wilde's Rifles had been formed from Sikh prisoners of war in British hands at the conclusion of the Sikh Wars of 1845 to 1849. There was nothing immoral, improper or untoward in this. The idea of nationhood had not yet arisen in India; might was generally right and he who could rule received allegiance. He whose rule failed found that allegiance transferred to someone else. The Sikh soldiers incarcerated in the British camps saw the Sikh dominions overrun and their leaders surrendering their swords. They were trained soldiers who knew no other calling, and it was perfectly natural for them to take up the British offer of enlistment into the East India Company's army, alongside men who had recently been their deadly foes but who had fought bravely and well and, by and large, honourably.

The British Indian Army recruited a great many Sikhs, mainly Jat farmers from the Punjab, and recruiting officers were insistent that only the 'right' sort of Sikh could be enlisted. It has been suggested that Sikhism might in time have been reabsorbed into the amorphous mass of Hinduism whence it had sprung, had not the British insisted on enlisting only baptised Sikhs and on taking care that Sikh custom continued to be correctly observed in the Army. MacMunn saw Sikhs as being tall, aquiline, muscular men whose intelligence and education made them particularly good quartermasters.

The Gurkhas, who would make up the largest racial grouping on the Western Front, with 24 infantry companies, had also first come to the attention of the British as enemies. Unified by the Gurkhas in the last quarter of the 18th century, the nascent kingdom of Nepal continued to expand, first north and east until checked in Tibet by China, and then south into the plain of Bengal where there were rich pickings to be had. Inevitably this brought them into conflict with the East India Company and precipitated the Anglo Nepal war of 1814 to 1816. In this war technology favoured the British, and geography the Gurkhas. Neither side would run, to the admiration of the other. Both sides behaved honourably, treating prisoners well and controlling looting. As a result a mutual respect grew up, and when the Gurkhas sued for peace, fearing that the British had discovered a route through the mountains protecting the capital, Kathmandu, it was agreed that Gurkhas could be enlisted into the Company's army. It was the conspicuous loyalty and competence of Gurkha units during the Mutiny that brought to the attention of the British the fact that Gurkhas were something special. After 1857 the number of Gurkha regiments or regiments with a Gurkha component was increased, and while the Gurkha homeland, Nepal, had never been, and never was to be, part of the British Empire, by 1914 the Indian Army had ten Gurkha regiments, each of two battalions.

To the British general public the Gurkhas, along with the Sikhs, were probably the best known component of the Indian Army. Everyone had heard of the fearsome kukri, and much nonsense was talked about it and its use. The kukri is a broad-bladed, leaf-shaped knife with a single edged eleven inch blade which curves away from the holder rather than towards him, as would a conventional knife. The blade is heavy, affixed to a bone handle and feels unbalanced to the European. The origins of the kukri are obscure but it is probably a Nepali adaption of a Rajput weapon, itself a variation of an Arabic scimitar introduced to India by the Moghuls. Most Gurkhas carried one at home and there was a standard issue version for the Army. The kukri is an all-purpose tool, used for chopping wood, digging holes, butchering meat, opening tins and as a weapon of war. It has no mystical or religious significance and, contrary to the widespread belief of the British public, then and now, once a Gurkha draws his kukri it is not necessary to draw blood—(if necessary his own blood)—before returning it to its sheath. It was and is, however, a most effective weapon in skilled hands. Employed in a combination of a chop and a slice, one blow of a kukri would sever arms and remove heads. It was much feared by the Germans.

Another class from which by 1914 the British recruited a very large number of their soldiers was the Punjabi Mussalman. These Moslem soldiers lived to the north of the river Indus, between the Indus and the Jhelum. Some, probably most, were descended from Rajputs converted forcibly or otherwise by the Moghuls while some—rather fewer than was claimed—were genuine descendants of Moghul soldiers and traders. They were mainly yeoman farmers and peasants with the better off amongst them joining the Cavalry, the rest the Infantry or the Mountain Artillery. MacMunn saw them as being hard working and the backbone of the Army.

The Indian Army of 1914 contained many Pathans. Many of them lived not in British India at all but in the tribal territories where they were subjects of no one; some came from even farther away and were nominally subjects of Afghanistan. The Pathans and their sub tribes had a long history of resistance to the British, while at the same time providing them with excellent soldiers. It was not uncommon for a soldier to go on home leave to a village that was actually in a state of war with the Indian government. Some soldiers were even said to spend their furlough assisting the enemy, although it was universally accepted that a man would not take action against his own regiment.

The British, on annexing the Punjab, had inherited the Frontier problem from the Sikhs. There were those who accused the Indian Army of encouraging the continuation of hostilities for the training value, excitement and adventure that the incessant raids, skirmishes and punitive expeditions provided. There may have been some truth in this, albeit that intent was subconscious, but many British officers found the frontier to be boring, uncomfortable, insanitary and not conducive to good training because it assumed an enemy inferior in weapons and technology. Even without the presence of the British the frontier area was a lawless place, where blood feuds between families, villages and clans could continue for generations, long after the original cause had been forgotten. Havildar Ghamai Khan, a Pathan of the 59th Scinde Rifles, was commended for his conduct at the battle of Neuve Chapelle and promoted to Jemadar. After service on the Western Front he went with his battalion to Mesopotamia at the end of 1915. At the battle of Dujailah he received no fewer than nine bullet wounds which, miraculously, he survived. Sent back to his Frontier village to convalesce, he was killed in a blood feud.

There was always a slight cloud hanging over Pathans in the minds of senior officers. MacMunn considered Pathans to be 'sporting, high spirited, adventurous, jaunty' but added:

> Alas on the Frontier men often think of other things than women, and practices which in the West are the last signs of degeneration and worthlessness are in the East often the trait of the most daring outlaw and Wolf's Head, for East is East.[3]

Whether or not they were any more prone to homosexual practices than anyone else[*], most Pathans had their homes in areas outside British control, where a rifle was worth about four years' pay in the bazaars, and they did have a propensity to desert. Occasionally a Pathan would be seized with religious zeal and would murder a British officer, usually for sleeping with his feet towards Mecca or some such imagined insult. There was only one all-Pathan regiment in the Indian Army, the 40th Pathans known inevitably as The Forty Thieves, and it was regarded by some as unreliable[†]. Nevertheless, Pathans who were prepared to submit to formal military discipline did make exceedingly good soldiers. The first Indian VC of the Western Front went to a Pathan, and four of the original 18 Indian infantry battalions that were to be deployed to France had Pathans in their ranks. In general they did very well, although there were occasional incidents and one embarrassment, when a Pathan officer of 58th Vaughan's Rifles, Bareilly Brigade, took a number of his men over to the Germans.

---

[*]   Attitudes varied. There does appear to have been quite a bit of it about amongst Pathans, and in some Sikh regiments it was tolerated provided the two men were of the same rank (author's interview with Captain P Williams 1970). There was no word for it in the Gurkhali language—they tended to marry very young.

[†]   It did have the second highest number of Indian Army deserters from the Western Front, despite not arriving there until 8 April 1915 as a reinforcement.

While each race had its own traditions and its own religion, and often its own language too, these were not allowed to interfere with the needs of the army. Many in the pre-mutiny armies of Madras and Bombay had said that it was the pandering to religious and caste prejudice within the Bengal Army that had largely contributed to the mutiny. This was not going to be allowed in the new army of the Queen. Racial, and hence regimental peculiarities, idiosyncrasies and eccentricities were permitted, even encouraged, but only so far as they did not impinge on operational readiness. As one typical regimental standing order of 1909 said:

> No pretext of caste or religion can under any circumstances be permitted to interfere with the due and exact performance of any military duties.[4]

Those British officers who advocated their own men's separate identity too vociferously were unlikely to be promoted beyond battalion level: the policy of the army was that the races were different, but equal.

Indian regiments were recruited on a racial (known as Class) and territorial basis. Regiments were either Class Regiments where, apart of course from the British officers, all the men were of the same class, or Class Company Regiments which contained a number of races each in their own company. There was much debate within the Indian Army as to the relative merits of Class Regiments and Class Company Regiments. The proponents of the latter argued that a regiment of different races had available to it the complementary talents of all, and was incidentally less likely to mutiny. Others said that a regiment which was entirely homogeneous fought better and was easier to administer, particularly in matters of Indian officer appointments, religion and diet. The truth was that there was room for both. In 1914 Wilde's Rifles was a Class Company Regiment, having two companies each of Sikhs, Dogras, Punjabi Mussalmans and Afridis (a Pathan sub tribe)[*]. The Subadar Major—the senior Indian officer—of the regiment came from the different races by turn[†] and there was always someone to do guards and fatigues on a religious festival. On the other hand some races—such as the Gurkhas and Garhwalis—seemed to perform better if the regiment was composed entirely of them. There were wholly Sikh regiments and there were regiments where Sikhs served alongside Punjabi Mussalmans, Pathans, Jats and Dogras. Up to 1885 there had even been a regiment, The 42nd (Assam) Regiment of Bengal (Light) Infantry, consisting of four companies of Gurkhas and four of Sikhs.

---

[*]   The Indian infantry battalions were still organised into eight companies and would only adopt the British four-company system on their way to Europe.

[†]   Theoretically the best available subadar was selected, but regiments made sure that all races were regularly represented in the post.

By 1914 the Indian Army had 139 battalions of infantry and 39 regiments of cavalry, with batteries of mountain artillery, companies of sappers and miners and the supporting arms and ancillary services to go with them. All these units had British officers gazetted permanently or seconded to them, having passed out from the Royal Military College Sandhurst for the Infantry and Cavalry, or from the Royal Military Academy Woolwich for the Sappers and Miners and Artillery. Whereas in some other nations' colonial armies the native soldier learned the language of the officer, in the Indian Army British officers were required to learn the language of their men. The official lingua franca of the Army for internal use was Hindustani, or 'Urdu', which had come into India with the traders and soldiers from Central Asia and had been the every day language of the Moghuls. It was written in the Arabic script, although the Army had a Latin version known as Roman Urdu.

During this period all British officers joining the Indian Army were required to pass an examination in Hindustani before being attached to an Indian regiment and then had to pass a further, higher level, examination before their Indian Army probation was confirmed. Having passed in, Hindustani officers going to regiments where the soldiers were not native Urdu speakers such as Sikh, Pathan, Gurkha, Mahratta or Madras regiments, or regiments with companies of those races, had to undergo a further course of study in the language of their own soldiers.

In 1914 the establishment of British officers in an Indian Army battalion was 12, including the Medical Officer, and the establishment took no heed of leave or courses. These officers filled the senior posts in the battalion and under them came a second layer of command, that of the Indian officer. The Indian officers were men selected on merit for commissioning from the ranks after long service—anything between 17 and 20 years—and held not the King's commission like the British officers, but a commission granted by the Governor General of India, hence they were legally known as Viceroy Commissioned Officers or VCOs for short. In the vernacular they were usually referred to as 'Indian officers', or 'IOs' with some exceptions*.

The adjective 'Indian' as applied to 1914 is an inexact term. India was perhaps a geographical entity but the vast majority of its inhabitants considered themselvesas being of the Mahratta or Sikh or Rajput race, or of the Hindu or Bhuddist or Mussalman religion or of Bengali or Madrassi or Punjabi domicile rather than as Indian. Only a few western-educated Brahmins or embryo nationalist politicians tried to encourage a sense of Indian nationhood and called themselves Indians, and in Gurkha and Garhwali regiments VCO were known as 'Gurkha officers' and 'Garhwali officers'. There were three VCO ranks, in the Infantry that of Jemadar, the

---

* After the war, when Indians began to be granted the King's commission, the term Indian officer became confusing and VCOs were referred to simply as VCOs.

most junior; Subadar; and Subadar Major, the most senior. The Cavalry's equivalents were Jemadar, Rissaldar and Rissaldar Major. In broad terms Jemadars did the jobs that would be done by a second lieutenant or lieutenant in a British regiment, such as half company (later platoon) commander or assistant to the adjutant. Subadars filled posts that would be occupied by captains, such as company commander (company second-in-command after the double company system was abolished). The Subadar Major occupied a very special and vitally important niche of his own.

There was only one Subadar Major in an infantry battalion. As the senior Indian officer he was the Commanding Officer's right hand man, adviser in all matters pertaining to custom, religion, welfare, discipline and recruitment. He combined many of the functions that in a British unit would fall to the Second-in-Command, the RSM, the Chaplain, the Adjutant, or the Station Families Officer as well as being prophet, soothsayer, unofficial justice of the peace, marriage broker, historian and a spare company commander when needed. He was the custodian of all that made the regiment what it was. The Subadar Major had enormous power and great prestige. He was selected from amongst the very best of the subadars and those subadars who had been senior to him, but had failed to be selected themselves, were usually sent on pension. As a regimental standing order of 1909[5] put it:

> As the head of the native portion of the Regiment, the position is a most honourable one and should be looked up to by all inferior ranks with the utmost respect.

There does however come a sting in the tail, for after stipulating that the Subadar Major, as the confidential adviser to the Commanding Officer, must bring to the latter's attention any occurrence which might affect the good name of the Regiment, the same order goes on to say:

> It is not possible that such matters can remain hidden from a Subadar Major. The fact therefore of their unreported occurrence would of itself be sufficient proof either that the officer was careless in the performance of his duties, or that he wilfully concealed matters which he was bound by duty to disclose.

All commissions awarded by the Viceroy were, of course, junior to all those emanating from the King Emperor, and so all VCOs, however senior amongst their fellow Indians or Gurkhas, were junior to the most junior British officer, who might be aged 19 and have held a commission for only the time that it took a P&O liner to get from Southampton to Bombay. Some modern commentators have seen this as an example of racial prejudice pure and simple, but this is to fail to understand the purpose of the two types of officer and the way in which the Indian Army worked.

Educated Indians, particularly those from races or classes not eligible for enlistment, often claimed that the men whom the British classified as martial were those who were amenable, unlikely to ask questions and lacking in intelligence. There is some truth in this. A great many of the recruits to the Army between the Mutiny and 1914 were rural peasants, generally uneducated and often illiterate. They were not, however, unintelligent as is demonstrated by the ease with which they learned how to handle complicated equipment and to read and write once they joined the service and had the opportunity to be educated. Many recruits were sons or nephews of men who had themselves served, and although there was some prejudice against the 'Line Boy', who was sometimes regarded as pampered and dangerously sharp, these men did have the advantage of literacy, inherent loyalty to, and some understanding of, the Army.

By 1914 some middle-class Indians were pointing out that while there were Indians at policy making level in the administration and the judiciary, there were none in the Army, where the senior post that an Indian could aspire to was the rank of subadar Major, junior to the most junior British second lieutenant (although it would have been a brave, and foolish, second lieutenant who pressed this point on the subadar Major).

Not all influential Indians agreed. Many saw the British officer corps as a guarantee of neutrality from tribalism and a defence against politicisation. The Sikh of 1914 would have resented serving under an educated Bengali and he would have been worried about nepotism were he to serve under an educated Sikh. Apart from Indian doctors of the Indian Medical Services, the officers of the Indian Army on arrival at the Western Front were British and would remain so.

The Indian Army operated by using the British officer as the instigator and promulgator of policy, while the Indian officer executed it. The British officer was seen as being above tribalism and he had no vested interest in extending favour to one man rather than another. The British officer was educated and could make sense of operational orders written in English. The British officer was impartial. There was a touching—and nearly always justified—faith in the honour and integrity of the British officer who, while he might not always come to the decision that the soldiers would prefer, would at least come to it without fear or favour. While the British officer was not necessarily of more than average intelligence—but then soldiering is not a cerebral profession—in the main he took pains to get to know his men's language and to understand and respect their customs and culture. When Indian or Gurkha soldiers wanted to indicate something that was certain, sure and to be trusted utterly, they often used the expression 'like the word of a British officer'.

The VCOs were men of great ability, naturally highly intelligent, knowing everything that could be known about low-level soldiering and with a deep knowledge and understanding of their men and the background whence they came—a background which they, the VCOs, shared. They were brave, outstandingly loyal and impeccably disciplined. They were not, however, educated men. They had little knowledge of, and less interest in, the Army outside their own immediate regimental family. They had limited technical understanding, they had tribal and kinship interests within the bodies of men they commanded and they had the innate conservatism of men from a rural, subsistence economy where very little changes.

Although technically junior to the British officer, the Indian officer was accorded great status and respect by the British officer. The Indian officer addressed the British officer as 'Saheb' but the British officer addressed the Indian officer as 'Saheb' too and, when he could, always took advice from the Indian officer before coming to any important decision. The Indian officer saw himself as having a vital role to play, as indeed he had, and as having a vested interest in ensuring that the British officer's ideas were correctly put into practice even if they had to be modified into workable common sense along the way. It was not uncommon for a young British officer to complete a long briefing in imperfect and stumbling Hindustani (or Punjabi, or Gurkhali, or Pushtu) and to depart to the British officers' mess having been assured by the assembled company that all was clearly understood. Shortly afterwards a group of men might be seen gathered around their subadar who would address them brusquely in the vernacular: 'What the Saheb really meant—and you are so stupid that you are incapable of understanding him—was …'

British officers led from the front. They had to, even when it was patent tactical nonsense so to do. If you want to lead men who do not share your culture, background or cause you have to demonstrate your own belief in that which you have ordered them to do. Even in 1914 it was becoming evident from the lessons of the South African War that the place of the officer on the battlefield was not five paces in front of his men, cheering them on. The officer must be near the front, he must be able to observe, control, encourage and rally if necessary, but he should not be so close to the action that he is prevented from being aware of the overall situation, nor where he is going to be killed by the first enemy bullet. Officers of the Indian Army, except perhaps for the very young, knew this perfectly well but there was no alternative: sepoys of the Indian Army accepted as a matter of course that their Sahebs would lead them in the literal sense. The very high casualty rate that was to occur amongst British officers would be ample proof that the Sahebs did so lead. In one action around Neuve Chapelle, on 3 November 1914, the 2nd Battalion 2nd Gurkha Rifles lost seven British officers killed and one severely wounded, and this from a total establishment of 12 including the doctor. This action, a relatively minor skirmish meriting but a brief mention in the Official History[6]—and that as a footnote—was by no means untypical within the Indian Corps. Four months later the 1st Battalion 39th Garhwal Rifles lost their entire complement of British officers, including the Medical Officer. The fact was that to function properly an Indian regiment needed both British and Indian officers and neither was capable of doing the job of the other except for short periods[*].

Pre-war recruiting for the Indian Army was very much a regimental responsibility and was usually done by men going to their home village and persuading others to join. In most regiments there was a waiting list and young men considered suitable for enlistment, often very young men desperately trying to look much older than they actually were, would be placed on the list until there was a vacancy. Nepal was a closed country and so Gurkha recruits had to cross the border into India and report to the Gurkha recruiting stations on the Indian border. Recruits were trained in battalions. There were no depots in peacetime, and the Adjutant assisted by the 'Woordie Major', a Jemadar, was responsible for the recruits' basic training. Once he had passed recruit training, and subject to continued good performance, the sepoy could serve for up to 25 years (more for Indian officers) after which he received a pension. Soldiers who for one reason or another did not serve the full 25 years could transfer to the reserve provided they had served a minimum of three years, were under 32 years of age, were recommended and there was a vacancy. Regiments and battalions were each supposed to have 200 reservists who were called back for two months' training every two years. Reservists received a retainer of 3 rupees[†] per month and stayed on the reserve until total service, regular and reserve, amounted to 25 years when they too qualified for a pension.

Here was one of the major problems which was to face the Indian Army in France. The reserve system simply did not work and was universally denounced by officers from the Corps Commander downwards. The Commanding Officer of the 47th Sikhs said that the reservists 'from the first were an incubus which added to the difficulties of all concerned'[7]. It was not the soldiers' fault. The Indian Army was not structured for a war on a European scale, the reserve system was intended to help in the case of war with Afghanistan, or even Russia, on the northern borders, and it was

[*] Much the same applies to the Indian Army of today. On the approach to Independence it was felt that the rank of VCO would not be needed where all the officers were Indian. In fact it is the policy of the Indian Army today that Class Regiments and Class Companies are not officered by men of their own race, and so the VCO lives on as the JCO (Junior Commissioned Officer). A Sikh battalion will have all Sikh JCOs, NCOs and men but will be officered by Rajputs, Mahrattas, Gurkhas—anything but Sikhs. The Deputy Commandant of the Indian Military Academy at Dehra Dun told the author in 1990: 'We are sometimes asked by the politicians whether men would not fight better under officers of their own race. I tell them not necessarily, and I point to the example of the British when they led us.'

[†] About 4/- or 20p in 1914—not a lot even by Indian standards.

consistently underfunded. No soldier left the regular forces if he could possibly help it, and so the men on the reserve tended to be those whom company commanders wanted rid of, or who had left for family reasons or because they had a problem. Even good material quickly lost the skills they had learned once discharged and the climate and hard physical work aged the ex-soldier more quickly than his European counterpart. As battalions had to leave India at war strength plus ten per cent, they took the best of the reserves with them. The remainder were eventually sent to Marseilles where many had to be returned as not fit for service and were eventually remustered into companies for low-priority duties in India.

The situation in regard to officer reinforcements was even worse. At the outbreak of war the Indian Army Reserve of Officers numbered but 47, and the situation was not helped by the British War Office forbidding around 25 per cent of British officers of the Indian Army who were on leave in England from returning to India[8] and directing them instead to training camps where they were to train the recruits for the expansion of the British Army. Given that there were only 12 British officers in an Indian battalion this was a large number of experienced officers who could not be spared. Most of the officers thus snaffled for the New Armies were eventually allowed to return whence they came, once it was realised how long it took to produce an officer suitable for service with Indian troops.

A constant problem throughout the time spent in France by the Indian Army was replacement of the very high rate of British officer casualties. It was relatively easy to replace an officer casualty in the British Army. The public schools, the universities and the Territorial Force produced educated young men with the inherent leadership to command British soldiers after the necessary military training. Later, more and more NCOs would be commissioned and, particularly once the Territorials and the New Armies began arriving in France, there was a good supply of NCOs with sufficient education to assume officer posts. There were no language problems, no difference in dietary requirements and there was a common religious and cultural background. Most British soldiers could see what they were supposed to be fighting for, and despite the post-war talk of a lost generation there was never a serious shortage of officer candidates.

It was different in the Indian Army. Indian soldiers took time to get to know and trust their officers. It took time to train British officers in the language, time for the officers to assimilate the culture and ethos of the men and time for the men to accept them. Once the original British officers who had come with the regiments and battalions from India had been killed or wounded in large numbers the last link with home for the sepoy was gone. It says much for the inherent strengths of the Indian Army that, while the problem never disappeared and was never satisfactorily resolved, the new officers, only some of whom had any experience of India and the Indians, were in the main accepted by the troops.

Indian Other Ranks joined in the ranks of Sepoy, or Rifleman in the
Gurkhas and Garhwalis, and Sowar in the cavalry. Thereafter they could
progress up the ranks as seniority tempered by merit dictated. Ranks and
their British equivalents were:

British	Indian except Cavalry	Indian Cavalry
Lance Corporal	Lance Naik	Acting Lance Daffadar
Corporal	Naik	Lance Daffadar
Sergeant	Havildar	Daffadar
Company Sergeant Major	Colour Havildar	Kot Daffadar

There was no equivalent of Regimental Sergeant Major, for power lay
not in the Sergeants' Mess, as it might in a British regiment, but with the
VCOs. However, there were quartermaster havildars, hospital havildars,
pay havildars and police havildars.

To the Indian soldier the chain of command was all important. Orders
were passed from the British officer to the Indian officer who in turn com-
municated them to the men via the NCOs. That was how the Indian Army
was trained and how the soldiers expected things to be. Every man from
the Subadar Major to the most recently joined sepoy knew his place in the
pecking order and expected to be instructed by his immediate superior. In
the British Army an officer could shortcut the chain of command and give
instructions direct to junior soldiers, but to do so in the Indian Army was
to court confusion. This difference in attitude was to cause problems when
elements of Indian battalions, single companies or platoons, separated
from their own system, were thrown in willy-nilly to support British units
in the early days on the Western Front.

Soldiers joining the Indian Army in 1914 took two oaths of fealty. First
they took an oath to the King Emperor, very similar to that taken by a
recruit to the British Army, and then they took a second oath to their
regiment. While every man of the Indian Army held the King Emperor in
almost mystical awe, he was of course a remote figure whom none had ever
seen and he lived a very long way away. The real focus of a man's loyalty
was the regiment. This was an organisation big enough to offer him a complete life within it, with security and shelter, with promotion and honour if
he merited it. It was also an organisation small enough for the man to know
everyone else in it. Most soldiers served as long as they possibly could and
hardly ever left the regiment except perhaps to attend a course or spend a
tour as an instructor at the musketry school. Every man, however junior
in rank, had his own place within the regimental family. The regimental
system encouraged this family atmosphere. Every regiment had its own
unique individuality whether it was in racial composition, or history, or
exotic lineage, or uniform, or even prowess on the sports field. The modern
term is peer bonding and this took place not just amongst and between the

native ranks but between the soldiers and the British officers too. The sepoys were not the peers of the British officers in terms of education, or wealth or power, but all believed that they shared a common bond of loyalty to, and belief in, the regiment—as the vast majority of them, British officers and sepoys alike, did. Loyalty, then, was personal. Men did their duty because they believed in the honour of the regiment as personified by 'their' Saheb. Consistency was all important for the British officer. Sepoys liked to be able to predict how their Saheb would react. British officers could be draconian disciplinarians or have all sorts of idiosyncrasies provided that they were consistent. As one commanding officer of 1914 wrote:

> It is important for British officers thoroughly to understand and identify themselves with their men, show themselves possessed of a strict sense of duty, and look after the men and their interests without any pampering. With Indian troops as long as you are just you may be as strict as you like. Good discipline is the basis of everything.[9]

In fact discipline was rarely a problem. One regimental standing order said:

> For minor offences it will be better to award extra drill etc. that does not entail an entry in the man's defaulter sheet; in other words the punishment should fit the crime.[10]

It is of course impossible for generalities to be entirely accurate. There were incompetent British officers; there were idle VCOs; there were disloyal sepoys and there were men who misbehaved, but the vast majority were loyal to the system, to the regiment and to their British officers, many of them unto death. When it was announced that the Indian Corps was to leave France at the end of 1915 there were a number of protests from the ranks such as that of a subadar of the 47th Sikhs who complained that: 'We came here to defeat the King's enemies. They have not yet been defeated and we should not leave until they are.'[11]

In India nature was ever capricious and deaths in child bearing, or in infancy, or from accident and disease were normal and regular occurrences. This bred an acceptance of one's lot and a resigned fatalism which was far stronger than any western concept of individual rights. Indian soldiers tended not to complain, tended to accept hardship and misery and were often noted for their stoical acceptance of their wounds in France. This was not because they were supermen, but simply because whether Animist, Shamanist, Hindu, Bhuddist, Sikh or Mohammedan they had an assigned place in the order of things and they had a strong concept of Izzat. This latter is important in understanding why the Indian soldier reacted as he did. Izzat is often translated as 'honour' or 'face' but conceptually it is much more than this. Part of Izzat was external: promotion, rank, medals, a son's successful marriage, wealth, land, all conferred Izzat but it had an internal and individual element too. A man had to be at ease with himself. He had to feel that he was respected for what he did, however humble a post he occupied. There was also an unspoken contractual element. On the frontier regiments had originally made a point of recovering all their casualties, wounded or dead, to prevent torture and mutilation by the tribesmen into whose hands they might fall. In time this became a matter of Izzat, even if the particular enemy encountered no longer subjected slain soldiers' bodies to unspeakable practices. In France if a British officer was wounded in no man's land, Izzat demanded that his men, particularly his orderly, should, if at all possible, bring him back, dead or alive.

On the evening of 26 October 1914 Captain Hampe-Vincent of the 129th Baluch Regiment was leading an attack upon a German trench across open ground. The attack came under shell, machine-gun and rifle fire and Captain Hampe-Vincent fell badly wounded (he was to die shortly afterwards). Watching from the 129th Baluch trenches a lance naik of the reserve company saw the officer fall and immediately dashed out to try to bring him back. The NCO—Nek Amal—was not a tall individual and found Hampe-Vincent impossible to move. He therefore ran back to his own trench and summoned a sepoy, one Saiday Khan. The two men then once more crossed the hazardous killing area and between them succeeded in carrying the dying officer back. Nobody told Lance Naik Nek Amal to endanger his own life and the life of Sepoy Saiday Khan to recover a helpless British officer—there was a clearly laid down system for casualty evacuation by dedicated stretcher bearers—but Hampe-Vincent was their officer and Izzat demanded that it be done. There are numerous instances of soldiers going out to recover wounded or dead British officers at grave risk to their own lives, not just in the early days when the rescuers might not have fully appreciated the dangers, but throughout the time that the Indian Army served in France. Many of them paid the ultimate penalty for this tactical foolishness.

An Indian Army battalion in 1914 was still organised on an eight-company basis. Each company, of about 80 men, was commanded by a subadar with a jemadar as second in command. The company could break down into two half companies, each commanded by a VCO. Each pair of companies was supervised by a British officer, a 'Double Company Commander', normally a captain or Major, with a British 'Double Company Officer' subaltern to assist. The total strength of an Indian infantry battalion at war establishment was only 750, and this included a ten per cent war reserve. British officers were the Commanding Officer (a lieutenant colonel), the Adjutant (a lieutenant or captain) who was the battalion staff officer and commanding officer's representative, four double company commanders (usually captains but sometimes Majors), four double company officers (subalterns) and the Quartermaster (a subaltern). A subaltern was often 'double hatted' as the Battalion Signals

Officer, responsible for instruction in semaphore, telephone and heliograph communication, another as the Machine-Gun Officer and another as Transport Officer. One of the double company commanders, generally the senior, was the nominated battalion Second-in-Command. An additional officer was the Medical Officer, a lieutenant, captain or Major of the Indian Medical Services, and who might be British or Indian.

While on the high seas to France the Indian Army was ordered to adopt the British four-company system. Double companies were to become companies and half companies became platoons. The double company commanders would be company commanders and the Indian officers became company seconds-in-command and platoon commanders. This meant a completely new form of drill and tactical deployment which had to be learned in very quick time indeed, and had been only imperfectly mastered when battalions found themselves in the firing line. Not all battalions conformed and many retained the double company system until well into 1915[*]. To avoid confusion this narrative will use the term 'company' throughout, even if technically some were actually 'double companies'.

In an Indian regiment each officer, British and Indian, had a soldier orderly. The British officer's orderly was emphatically not a servant—although he did carry out some menial tasks for his officer—but rather a helper, unofficial informant, constant companion and, in the field, bodyguard. The orderly's duties included doing all he could to smooth the organisation of his master's life, so that the officer could devote all his attention to that which he was trained and paid to do. The orderly cleaned and prepared his officer's equipment, uniforms and weapons, ensured that on operations his food was cooked and his bivouac prepared. A young British officer learned much of the customs, religion and culture of the men from his orderly, as of an evening the rifleman or sepoy sat cross-legged in the corner of his officer's room polishing the Sano Saheb's[†] boots. Orderlies were usually selected by the Subadar Major personally and were normally young soldiers with three or four years' service who had been earmarked as potential NCOs and had been placed on the *Umedwars'*[‡] list while they waited their turn for promotion. In some regiments British officers' orderlies changed every six months, and in all regiments the relationship was a two-way arrangement. The orderly ensured that his officer was well looked after and untroubled by the minutiae of personal administration, while the officer was expected to teach the orderly such things

---

[*] It was not until the promulgation of Indian Army Order 684 of 1916 that the whole of the Indian Army, rather than just those units on the Western Front, adopted the four-company system.

[†] Literally 'Little Saheb', and applied—not unkindly—to young or newly joined British officers.

[‡] Literally 'candidates' or 'aspirants'.

18

as the sequence of low-level operational orders, telephone procedure and other miscellaneous items of military general knowledge. Whatever their official seniority might be, orderlies considered that they took precedence amongst themselves in accordance with their masters' rank, and discussions amongst orderlies were often settled by the flat statement that 'My Saheb is a Major and your Saheb is only a captain'. Orderlies were regarded with respect by the other soldiers, who thought (usually wrongly) that the orderly was privy to all the secrets of the universe and could influence the Saheb's decisions. While in the British Army the post of officer's batman, or soldier-servant, was not sought after and had little status, the reverse was the case in the Indian Army. Soldiers did not regard their orderly duties as servile, rather they took a pride in helping a more senior member of the family in the execution of his proper role. Officers became very close to their orderlies, often staying in their homes when visiting the regimental recruiting areas.

Stories about orderlies were legion. One orderly, new to the job, decided that his Saheb's civilian suit required cleaning, put it on himself, stood in the shower and gave Savile Row's best a good scrubbing with soap and water. Fifty years later little had changed. This author recalls the first British officer to purchase a pair of suede shoes. The Gurkha orderly examined them with puzzlement mixed with suspicion, took them away, carefully shaved off the nap with a razor blade arid applied copious quantities of brown polish, endeavouring without much success to turn them into the highly polished type of Sahebs' shoes that he had been accustomed to. There were certain tasks which orderlies would insist could be done only by them. India was famous for its 'flying dhobi' whereby dirty clothing left lying about in the morning would be whisked away by the dhobiwalla follower and returned in pristine condition and immaculately ironed the same evening. In Gurkha battalions at least, the orderly would always insist on washing the Saheb's underpants himself. The reason was a belief that possession of a sample of pubic hair allowed a witch to cast a curse on the unwitting donor, so to ensure that the Saheb could not be bewitched the orderly washed those intimate items himself.

Visible signs of honour and glory were important to the Indian soldier. Until 1911 only British officers were eligible for the award of British decorations, there being a separate system of titles, medals and even grants of land applicable to the Indian officer and soldier. In descending order the awards for which Indians were eligible were: The Order of British India; The Indian Order of Merit; The Indian Distinguished Service Medal.

The Order of British India (OBI) had two classes. It was conferred on Indian officers for long, faithful and honourable service and carried with it the titles of 'Sardar Bahadur' (roughly 'gallant leader') for the first class and 'Bahadur' ('gallant') for the second class of the order, as well as an increment to pay and pension.

The Indian Order of Merit (IOM) was given for personal bravery, irrespective of rank. Originally it had three classes, but when Indians were declared eligible for the Victoria Cross (VC) in 1911 the IOM was reduced to two classes, ranking immediately after the VC. Admission to the first class of the order was granted only to those who already held the second class. Like the OBI the IOM carried with it a small, but significant, annual pension.

The Indian Distinguished Service Medal (IDSM) ranked immediately after the OBI Second Class and was also awarded irrespective of rank. It was earned by individual instances of distinguished service either in peace or in war.

In particularly deserving cases a grant of land might be made. Medals and titles were all part of Izzat and men valued them highly as an outward recognition of their bravery or competence. During the frontier campaigns the Army had always tried to award the medal as soon as possible after the deed, but on the Western Front the inevitably long process of vetting and approving—or rejecting—citations for awards meant that the award might be approved after the intended recipient had been killed in a subsequent action.

If a medal could not be awarded instantly then promotion could, especially once casualties began to mount. There were, however, problems, particularly for those regiments which furnished drafts to another regiment. A man might, for example, be part of a draft from Outram's Rifles sent to France to make up casualties incurred in Wilde's Rifles, and after further casualties that man might be promoted, even though there were men in his own regiment in India who were due for promotion before him. Promotion, which meant Izzat and further service, was very important to the Indian soldier. Generally the Indian Army operated a system of promotion by seniority tempered by merit. Merit was seen by the sepoys as a peculiar British invention. No Indian soldier would accept, at least not publicly, that another man who had joined at the same time could possibly be better than he, but happily accepted that a man who had joined before him was his senior and therefore entitled to respect and promotion. Once the casualty lists forced quicker promotion than was normal, and battalions became split between India and the Western Front, anomalies occurred which took years to resolve. Havildar Gajan Singh of the 47th Sikhs was decorated with the Indian Order of Merit for gallantry in rescuing wounded men under fire at Neuve Chapelle. Gajan was wounded and evacuated to the rear. On the conclusion of the battle he was promoted to Jemadar. His wounds were more serious than had first been thought and Gajan Singh was evacuated to hospital in England. There the medical authorities discovered that his injuries would cripple him for life and he was sent back to the Depot in India to be discharged. The Indian authorities would not recognise Gajan's promotion, on the grounds that it had been made after, rather than before, he was wounded and the man was sent off with a havildar's pension. A three-cornered paper battle now ensued between the battalion in France and the Depot in India on the one hand and the Finance Department of the Indian government on the other. Eventually, after many months of wrangling, justice was done, but such incidents were not calculated to boost morale.

Within the Indian Army many of the regulations and much of the equipment were designed for a force which had been engaged largely in frontier skirmishes against enemies small in numbers and armed only with rifles, and many of those of an obsolete pattern. In India British units were rationed by the governments whereas Indian regiments received a cash allowance and made their own arrangements. This was a perfectly satisfactory system within India, given the plethora of racial and religious dietary requirements. It was, however, a cause of resentment amongst British officers of the Indian Army who, when deployed in the field on operations or manoeuvres, continued to pay for their rations, whereas their counterparts in British regiments got theirs free. On arrival in France this system continued, with an officer of an Indian battalion in the trenches, hastily consuming a plate of bully beef stew under fire, having his salary docked to pay for it. After representations this rule was changed, British officers of the Indian Army received free rations and the money taken from pay was refunded. A similar anachronism applied to horses. British officers of the Indian Army received a monthly horse allowance of 30 rupees, or about £2 at 1914 prices, but those who were unable to take a horse to France were charged £5 per month for the use of a government charger once they arrived. Eventually this order too was cancelled and chargers were issued free to those who qualified[*].

A Major grievance amongst officers of the Indian Army was that of repatriation on retirement. An officer of the British service who retired or whose service came to an end in India received a free passage home. British officers of the Indian Army, on the other hand, had to pay their own way back to England, however long and distinguished their service might have been.[†] One exception to this was where an officer was court-martialled and discharged, when he was conveyed home at government expense. Very few officers availed themselves of this opportunity, but some did make use of another loophole, which was to find a friendly doctor who would certify the officer insane and have him committed to a lunatic asylum. As it was out of the question to place an Englishman in an Indian Bedlam, the officer was moved to England under governmental

[*]   Subalterns of the British Army occasionally grumbled that, while they had to march with the men, their equivalents in rank in the Indian Army had horses. Subalterns in the British Army were of course platoon commanders, whereas in the Indian Army they were company officers.

[†]   To be fair, they had volunteered for India, whereas officers of the British service had not, and they got their fare paid when going on leave to England, which officers of the British Army did not.

arrangements. Once back home a miraculous recovery would ensue. This situation was not rectified until well after the war.

Complaints about the administrative system in India were often countered by the riposte that the British had taught the Indians about red tape; the latter had merely refined it into an art form. One commanding officer of 1914 wrote that Indian Army regulations were, 'always delightfully ambiguous and only interpretable by a babu'.[12] The babu was that Indian official who had been lampooned for at least a century. Pictured as a perspiring, overweight Bengali in a dhoti, wearing thick spectacles, perched on a tall stool and surrounded by ledgers, he was seen as responsible for all the ills, frustrations and delays suffered by the Indian Army. In fact he was but the instrument of a governmental system which wanted every rupee and anna accounted for. A reluctance to spend on defence and a fear of corruption led to tortuous regulations and no discretion save at the highest level. The wretched babu, a junior-grade civil servant, could only authorise expenditure if it fell strictly within the rules, and there were a plethora of checks and balances which led to delay, obfuscation, 'objections' when it was thought that some allowance or other had been overpaid, and months, sometimes years, of argument when another allowance had not been paid. The vast majority of babus were industrious and honest men trying to do the best they could, but it was not surprising that regimental officers vented their fury on the head of the babu when the inevitable delays occurred. As a popular saying of the time had it, expressed in the sing-song cadence of babu English, 'daily I am wanting, weekly I am demanding, monthly I am not getting.'

In 1914 not all of India was ruled directly by the British. About one third of the land area was known as 'Native India' or 'The Princely States'. These were areas whose rulers had earlier sided with the British and had either actively assisted them or at least had not opposed them. There were 700 Native states altogether, ranging from vast provinces such as Hyderabad with a population three times that of Ireland, to petty fiefdoms of a few square miles. These Maharajahs, Maharanas and Nizams retained a nominal independence but with British advisers present at their courts to ensure that the standards and methods of government conformed to what the British considered reasonable. Within their borders, and subject to the aforementioned 'reasonableness' clause, these rulers could do pretty well what they liked and could and did maintain armies, although only Hyderabad was trusted sufficiently to be allowed its own artillery. These armies were now of little use for anything but ceremonial, indeed the idea of one of the Princely States actually going to war within India was absurd, but as all the officers were locals they did offer an outlet for Indians to hold more senior command appointments than were available to them in the British Indian Army. States could, if they wished, participate in the 'Imperial Service Scheme' under which the government of India would assist a state to train and equip a portion of its forces to British standards, this portion then being available for military operations with the Indian Army if required. There were 27 states which maintained Imperial Service contingents and during the Great War 21 of them sent contingents abroad, mostly to the Middle East but four to France. Jodhpur was the first state to send its Imperial Service contingent overseas and the Jodhpur Lancers went to France as part of the Secunderabad Cavalry Brigade in 1914. With them went the Maharajah of Jodhpur, who at 70 years of age was an honorary lieutenant general in the British Indian Army and a splendid old potentate whose affection for, and loyalty to, the British never wavered. With him too went a number of other members of the Indian nobility, who while not overworked militarily were of considerable help as advisers to the General Staff and as proof that India did support the Allied cause. Other States Forces to go to the Western Front were The Holkar's Imperial Service Transport Corps from Indore, The Maler Kotla Sappers and Miners and The Tehri Garhwal Sappers and Miners.

Somewhat to the surprise of Germany, whose foreign office had hoped for an anti-British rising, the vast majority of Indian opinion supported the war. Indian opinion of course arose from that minute portion of the population which was sufficiently educated to have an opinion, but expressions of loyalty and support were overwhelming. Even organisations not normally well disposed towards the British rushed to assure the Viceroy of their unwavering desire to assist the war effort. The All India Moslem League, the Punjab Provincial Congress, the Hindus of the Punjab Chief Khalsa, the Mehtar of Chitral and the Parsee Community of Bombay all informed the Viceroy of their wish to support the home government to the utmost. Offers of money, of supplies, of hospital ships, of horses, of ambulances flooded in. Even the Dalai Lama offered 1,000 Tibetan troops, an offer which was tactfully declined. Nepal, never part of the British Empire, placed the entire resources of its army at the disposal of the British, and Nepali troops were to be deployed in India to allow British regiments to be transferred to France.[13]

Britain declared war on Germany on 4 August 1914. Despite Secretary of State for India Morley's pre-war dictum that the Indian Army was not to plan for operations in either Europe or Mesopotamia, both the British War Office and Army Headquarters in India had drawn up mobilisation plans and had studied the involvement of the Indian Army in war 'in a temperate climate'. Units which were earmarked for mobilisation held detailed plans, movement orders and extra equipment, all of which they passed on at the end of their stand-by period to the next unit to be earmarked.

It had been decided that two infantry divisions and one cavalry brigade would be available for immediate despatch, the destination to be decided in due course. In the event the 6th Poona Division was mobilised immediately and sent to the Persian Gulf. The next order for mobilisation was issued to the 3rd Lahore Division on 8 August and to the 7th Meerut Division and the Secunderabad Cavalry Brigade the next day. Both these divisions and the cavalry brigade were warned for foreign operations in an unspecified theatre.

Originally titled 'Indian Expeditionary Force A', the Lahore and Meerut Divisions each had divisional troops and three brigades, each brigade having one British infantry battalion and three Indian battalions. The Secunderabad Cavalry Brigade had one British cavalry regiment, two Indian Army cavalry regiments and the Jodhpur Lancers.* Because the Indian Army still had no heavy artillery, only the Indian mountain batteries and the limited scale of British artillery attached to Indian formations were available for mobilisation, the balance of heavy guns to be provided by the Royal Artillery in theatre. In the event 20 British batteries accompanied the Corps from India. Mobilisation plans demanded that regiments and battalions embarked at full strength plus an extra ten per cent as immediate battle casualty replacements. It was very difficult to find even that number of fit reservists and in the event the number was to prove woefully inadequate.

The Lahore Division, which was to be the first Indian division to reach Europe, was commanded by Lieutenant General HBB Watkis CB. His division consisted of:

The Ferozepore Brigade (Brigadier General RM Egerton CB)
    1st Battalion The Connaught Rangers (British)
    129th Duke of Connaught's Own Baluchis
    57th Wilde's Rifles
    9th Bhopal Infantry

The Jullunder Brigade (Major General PM Carnegy CB)
    1st Battalion The Manchester Regiment (British)
    15th Ludhiana Sikhs
    47th Sikhs
    59th Scinde Rifles (Frontier Force)

The Sirhind Brigade (Major General JHIS Brunker)
    1st Battalion The Highland Light Infantry (British)
    1st Battalion 1st King George's Own Gurkha Rifles
    1st Battalion 4th Prince of Wales' Own Gurkha Rifles
    125th Napier's Rifles

Divisional Troops
    15th Lancers (Cureton's Multanis)
    HQ Divisional Engineers
    Numbers 20 and 21 Companies 3rd Sappers and Miners

---

*   An Indian cavalry brigade was normally made up of one British and two Indian regiments.

Signal Company
34th Sikh Pioneers
HQ Divisional Artillery
3 Brigades Royal Field Artillery each with an ammunition column
1 Heavy Battery Royal Field Artillery

The Meerut Division was commanded by Lieutenant General CA Anderson CB and consisted of:

The Dehra Dun Brigade (Brigadier General CE Johnson)
    1st Battalion The Seaforth Highlanders (British)
    1st Battalion 9th Gurkha Rifles
    2nd Battalion 2nd King Edward's Own Gurkha Rifles
    6th Jat Light Infantry

The Garhwal Brigade (Major General H d'U Keary CB DSO)
    2nd Battalion The Leicestershire Regiment (British)
    2nd Battalion 3rd Queen Alexandra's Own Gurkha Rifles
    1st Battalion 39th Garhwal Rifles
    2nd Battalion 39th Garhwal Rifles

The Bareilly Brigade (Major General E McBean CVO DSO)
    2nd Battalion The Black Watch (British)
    41st Dogras
    58th Vaughan's Rifles (Frontier Force)
    2nd Battalion 8th Gurkha Rifles

Divisional troops
    4th Cavalry
    HQ Divisional Engineers
    Numbers 3 and 4 Companies 1st King George's Own Sappers and Miners
    Signal Company
    107th Pioneers

    HQ Divisional Artillery
    3 Brigades Royal Field Artillery each with ammunition column
    1 Heavy Battery Royal Field Artillery

The Secunderabad Cavalry Brigade was commanded by Brigadier General FWG Wadeson CB and consisted of:

    7th Dragoon Guards (British)
    20th Deccan Horse

34th Poona Horse
Jodhpur Lancers (Jodhpur State Forces)

N Battery Royal Horse Artillery

The organisation of the divisions was thus broadly similar to that of their British equivalents, albeit on a much tighter establishment and short of artillery. The divisional commanders and some of the brigade commanders were of a rank higher than that normally found in command of such groupings, and this was due to those officers' secondary roles as district or area commanders in India. The one asset an Indian divisional commander had which was denied to his counterpart in the British Army until 1915 was a pioneer battalion. These units consisted of men dual-trained in basic engineering skills and as infantry. They were some of the best units of the Indian Army and, while they could not carry out all the highly technical tasks of the Royal Engineers or the Indian equivalent, the Sappers and Miners, they could construct bridges, make roads and prepare defence works and fortifications. It was a shame that their skills were largely wasted, at least at first, where acute shortages of manpower forced the pioneers' employment as infantry pure and simple. Even more wasteful was the use, faute de mieux, of the Sappers and Miners as infantry in the early days.

Another enhancement in an Indian division was the establishment of cavalry. British infantry divisions had only a squadron of divisional cavalry, whereas Indian divisions had a whole regiment.

August in India is the height of the monsoon season. It is rainy, rivers flood and highland regions have landslides. For that reason meaningful military training becomes difficult and it was the leave season for the Indian Army. British officers went on leave to England or on local furlough, usually hunting or to their regimental recruiting areas, and soldiers went home. It was the worst possible time to mobilise for war.111 All regiments ordered to mobilise had a recall scheme ready and waiting. The Adjutant of Wilde's Rifles, many of whose men lived in remote areas, immediately despatched telegrams to all post offices in the regiment's area ordering the regulars to report back and calling up the reservists. At the same time 16 Afridi soldiers were sent to Peshawar to trek into the mountainous areas straddling the frontier and seek out those of their fellows who lived out of range of post offices.

Despite Wilde's Rifles' careful planning, the Indus river was in flood and quite impassable. Men simply could not return to duty and so another regiment of similar composition, 55th Coke's Rifles, were asked to help, which they did by sending a draft of one Indian officer and 80 Indian Other Ranks (IORs) to Wilde's. The now complete battalion, part of the Ferozepore Brigade of the Lahore Division, set off for Karachi by train from Ferozepore and after ten miles halted while a traffic snarl was sorted out. On the opposite siding was a train full of Wilde's own men and reservists who had by now managed to cross the mighty Indus and were on their way to the battalion's barracks in Ferozepore. Seeing their friends in the other train the latecomers attempted to change trains in order to accompany the main body, but rules decreed that they could not, having to return to Ferozepore for documentation and kit issue first.

The 47th Sikhs, a Class Regiment of Jat Sikhs and part of the Jullunder Brigade of the Lahore Division, had rather more luck with the recall of their men and by 18 August all the regulars and the required number of reservists had reported, had been kitted out and were able to entrain at Jullunder. At this point some carriages containing supply and transport personnel were attached to the 47th Sikhs' train and cholera broke out amongst those troops during the journey. On arrival at Karachi the entire battalion was quarantined at a pilgrims' rest house. Fortunately no one in the 47th contracted the disease and the battalion was released from segregation on 20 August. Pro-German agitators in India seized upon this incident to claim that the 47th Sikhs had mutinied and were refusing to embark for the war. The lie to this was shortly to be given.

The 2nd Gurkha Rifles were perhaps at the top of the social pecking order of the Indian infantry. All Gurkha regiments were thought to be exclusive and it was said of their British officers that 'the Gurkhas talk only to each other, and the 2nd Gurkhas talk only to God'. Despite their numerical designation the 2nd Gurkhas were the first all-Gurkha regiment, having been composed of nothing else since their raising in 1815. Six Gurkha battalions were included in the 18 original battalions of the Indian Corps which went to the Western Front. The 2nd Battalion of the 2nd Gurkha Rifles was part of the Dehra Dun Brigade of the Meerut Division and was one of the battalions selected for mobilisation. Stationed in the town from which the brigade took its name, the 2/2nd had a greater problem in recalling men from leave than most. Gurkha regiments had no reservists, and as with all the Gurkha battalions ordered to mobilise, the 2/2nd Gurkhas' leave men were in Nepal, a remote, mountainous land with no roads and taking even longer to get to than the frontier areas in which lived the Pathans. Recalling men from leave in Nepal would have been difficult even if the writ of the government of India ran there, which it did not. Nepal was staunchly pro-British but also determined not to allow western influence to corrupt the country. With the sole exception of the British Resident and his staff, Nepal's borders were firmly closed to all foreigners. When the battalion was ordered to mobilise on 9 August 1914 the only way to recall leave parties was to send men off into the hills to spread the news, a process that could and did take weeks. Gurkha regiments did, however, have one great advantage over most other regiments in the Indian Army—they all had two battalions, and only one battalion of any Gurkha regiment was ordered to the Western Front, thus allowing the shortfall to be made up from the other battalion. The 2/2nd Gurkhas were thus able to organise themselves and entrain for Bombay at full strength on 21 August.

Like the 2/2nd Gurkhas, the 1/9th Gurkhas, also in the Dehra Dun Brigade of the Meerut Division, was able to draw on its other battalion on mobilisation on 9 August and left Dehra Dun by train on 31 August arriving at Bombay on 4 September. Also like their fellow Gurkha battalion, the 1/9th were delighted that the British battalion in the Dehra Dun Brigade was the 1st Battalion The Seaforth Highlanders. Gurkhas did not mix greatly with British troops, although having the privilege of using British canteens* they did so far more than did other Indian soldiers. The differences in language, diet and custom meant that social intercourse was limited, but Gurkhas laboured, and still do labour, under the unshakeable opinion that Scot and Gurkha share a common culture of high hill farming. That there were hardly any genuine crofters left in Scotland since the clearances of the 19th century, and that Scottish regiments recruited far more from Glasgow and other cities than they did from the Highlands, mattered not a jot. Totally unable to understand a word the other said, Gurkha and Jock got on famously. This may have been encouraged by the sharing of a fondness for strong liquor and colourful clothing.

Apart from the Gurkha regiments only the 39th Garhwal Rifles had two battalions, but as both battalions were mobilised as part of the Garhwal Brigade of the Meerut Division, they could not draw on a sister battalion to bring them up to war establishment. In 1914 both battalions were stationed at Lansdowne, 6,000 feet up in the British administered Himalayan district of Garhwal. Garhwal was bordered by Tibet to the north and the Indian plains to the south. To the east lay Kumaon and then Nepal, while to the west flowed the Ganges and then 'Foreign Garhwal', a native state whence recruits for the regiment also came. Prior to 1887, when the 1st Battalion of the 39th Garhwal Rifles was raised, Garhwalis had been allowed to join Gurkha regiments, with whom they have historical links. On the raising of their own regiment the Garhwalis continued to carry the kukri and in ceremonial dress wore a dark green uniform with a Kilmarnock hat, very similar to that worn by the Gurkhas, with whom they were often confused. Their sepoys too were ranked as 'Riflemen'.

The Adjutants of the two Garhwali battalions duly sent out the yellow mobilisation envelopes which reached the few existing post offices in hilly Garhwal and then proceeded onwards carried by postmen on foot. Telegrams were sent to District Officers who sent their staff off to round up the leave men of the regiment. In the event the rumours of war had preceded the messengers and many of the soldiers and reservists had started to trek

---

*   All Gurkhas had been awarded this privilege—denied to other native troops—along with the rank of Rifleman rather than Sepoy as a reward for their performance in the Mutiny.

in before the official news arrived. Within a week most of the Garhwali regulars and reservists had reported in, and on 21 August both battalions marched out of Lansdowne, camping overnight at Dogdadda. The camp site was a field and it was raining heavily, however the Garhwalis were able to borrow some tents from the 2nd Battalion 8th Gurkha Rifles who, as part of the Bareilly Brigade, were also on their way to the railhead. On 22 August the Garhwalis reached the railway station at Kotdwara, to find that because of the reorganisation of the rolling stock necessitated by the move of two divisions, the regiment would have to camp for nine days before a train could be found to take them onward. The monsoon weather was hot and wet, the area was plagued by mosquitoes, and despite a daily issue of five grains of quinine per man, 'fever' (probably a mild form of malaria) broke out. It was not until well into the sea voyage from Karachi that the majority would recover, and a few never did. The two battalions entrained for Karachi on 31 August, suffering further irritation when their train was derailed shortly before arriving there on 2 September, fortunately without injury.

The lst/34th Sikh Pioneers were selected to be the Pioneer Battalion for the Lahore Division. Unlike the Sikh infantry battalions, which tended to be composed of Jat, or high-caste, Sikhs, the Pioneers were formed of Mazbhi Sikhs. Sikhism began in North India in the 15th century when the first Sikh Guru, a high-born Brahmin named Nanak, reacting against the Hindu caste system, began to preach a different theology in which all men were equal. Like all movements which preach equality* the new religion attracted many of low caste or of no caste at all. Although equality was one of the tenets of the new faith the pre-existing social order was too strong and sweepers, animal skinners, shoemakers and metalsmiths remained at the bottom of the pecking order, Sikh or not. When the Moghuls decided that Sikhism was not after all a harmless aberration, persecution began. The ninth Guru, Tegbahadur, having been unfortunate enough to intrigue on the wrong side in a Moghul succession dispute, was executed by beheading in Delhi and his body thrown outside the City Magistrate's office for all to see. A party of Sikh sweepers rescued the body and bore it away so that proper funeral arrangements could be made. In recognition of their action the tenth Guru, Govind, bestowed the title of 'Mazbhi' or 'Religious' on this lowly sub-caste of Sikhs. The Mazbhis continued to be sweepers and labourers, albeit with newly bestowed status, and began to acquire a reputation as particularly efficient road-making gangs. They were also incidentally suspected of following Thugee and banditry as profitable sidelines.

---

*   The Romans called Christianity 'The Slave Religion' due to the numbers of disadvantaged who converted in the hope that they might have a better life than under the state religion.

During the Mutiny the first Sikh Pioneer battalion was raised from Mazbhi labourers in the employ of the government. This was the genesis of a new martial caste for the British and by 1914 there were three battalions of Sikh Pioneers with the regimental motto of 'Aut Viam Inveniam Aut Faciam' which translates appropriately as 'Either find a road, or make one'. 1/34th Sikh Pioneers was stationed at Ambala, in the Punjab, in 1914 and had less difficulty than some in assembling its war strength. The battalion promptly mobilised, embarking at Bombay on 17 August with nine British officers, 19 Indian officers, 806 Rank and file, 57 followers and the first line regimental animals (mules and officers' chargers).

SOURCE NOTES

1. *The Armies of India*, G MacMunn, Sampson, Low, Marston and Co Ltd, 1911.
2. *The Martial Races of India*, G MacMunn, Sampson, Low, Marston and Co Ltd, undated circa 1930.
3. Ibid.
4. Regimental Standing Orders, 6th Gurkha Rifles, 1909, author's collection.
5. Ibid.
6. *Military Operations in France and Belgium 1914*, Brigadier General Sir James Edmonds, Macmillan, London, 1928.
7. Quoted in *47th Sikhs War Record in the Great War 1914 – 1918*, Picton Publishing, Chippenham, reprinted 1992.
8. Sources vary as to the actual number held back, but all agree that about one quarter of the Indian Army officer corps—500—was held back with around 250 actually sequestered.
9. Quoted in *The Royal Garhwal Rifles in the Great War 1914 – 1917* and attributed contemporaneously to the author, Lieutenant Colonel DH Drake-Brockman, who commanded the 2nd Bn 1914/15 and later the amalgamated 1st and 2nd Bns from 1915. Privately published, Charles Clark Ltd, Haywards Heath, 1934.
10. Regimental Standing Orders, 6th Gurkha Rifles, 1909, author's collection
11. *The Indian Corps in France*, Merewether and Smith, John Murray, London, 1919. In effect the Indian government's official history of the campaign.
12. The CO of 2/39th Garhwal Rifles in *The Royal Garhwal Rifles in the Great War 1914 – 1917*.
13. 'Papers relating to support offered by the Princes and peoples of India in connection with the War'. India Office Library and Records, L/MIL/17/5/2385.

II

Across the Kalo Pani

A complaint common to all commanders of armies in war, past or present, is that there are never enough engineers. So it was in India. The Sappers and Miners were elite professional units of the Indian Army. They equated to the Royal Engineers in the British Army and were highly trained in all field engineering skills. They could build bridges, find water, dig, lay and clear mines, construct fortifications, cross obstacles, defuse unexploded shells and supervise wiring. In 1914 there were three separate corps of Sappers and Miners. The oldest corps, the 2nd Queen Victoria's Own Sappers and Miners, could trace its history back to 1759 although its seniority was never accepted by either the 3rd Sappers and Miners or the 1st King George's Own Sappers and Miners*. While the number of Madrassis in the Army had decreased by 1914, they were still strongly represented in the QVO Sappers and Miners, whose members had even created their own caste, the 'Quinsap', to which only those who had served in the Corps could belong, and whose daughters could marry only members of that caste. The 1st Sappers and Miners consisted of a mixture of Sikhs, Hindustani Hindus, and Hindustani and Punjabi Mussalmans while the 3rd contained Mahrattas, Sikhs and Moslems. Unlike the Cavalry and Infantry the Sappers and Miners did not have a permanent cadre of British officers but were led by officers seconded from the Royal Engineers. These officers learned the language and customs of their men and, subject to satisfactory completion of their first tour, would return again and again.

Each of the two infantry divisions warned for France would have with them two companies of Sappers and Miners while the Secunderabad Cavalry Brigade, initially and briefly part of the Indian Corps, would have a field troop. Like every other unit ordered to mobilise the Sappers and Miners had their problems. Missing leave men could be replaced by men of the same trade from other field companies, but there were not

---

* After the war the Sappers and Miners would regain their old Presidency titles. The 1st became the 1st King George the Fifth's Own Bengal Sappers and Miners, the 2nd QVO became the Queen Victoria's Own Madras Sappers and Miners and the 3rd became the Royal Bombay Sappers and Miners.

very many companies to get them from. In August 1914 the QVO Sappers and Miners numbered less than 2,000 all ranks, and had only six field companies. The 1st Sappers and Miners with 1,491 all ranks could produce another six field companies and the 3rd Corps a further six from 1,440 all ranks. In addition to the field companies there were a few pontoon parks and each corps had a depot company. By 1918 the three corps of Sappers and Miners would between them reach a strength of 24,000 Indian ranks serving in 53 field companies and a number of other specialised units, but that time was still far off. Like everyone else they would face almost, but not quite, insuperable problems in replacing the casualties inflicted among those first field companies to arrive in France.

Officers of the Royal Engineers, and those of their number serving with the Indian Sappers and Miners, had a (not always undeserved) reputation for being serious individuals. They were regarded as being either 'mad, married or Methodist'. Neither the Royal Engineers nor the Sappers and Miners had ever allowed the system of purchase, and officers had advanced by seniority tempered by professional merit. The tasks given to engineer units required an officer to know his trade, and in the undeveloped countryside of India he had time to do little else but practise it. In a country where industrialisation had barely started the Sappers and Miners had to use such resources as they could find, and they were already famous throughout the British and Indian Armies for the invention of the Bangalore Torpedo. This device was designed by Brevet Major RL McClintock RE of the QVO Sappers and Miners in 1907. It was intended for clearing a path through a wire obstacle and the latest version, the 1912 model, consisted of a series of thin sheet metal tubes packed with explosive. Tubes were joined together to form the required length and then pushed under the obstacle before being detonated. It was much used in both world wars and is still in service in the British Army of today, albeit in a rather more sophisticated form. McClintock also invented a form of rifle grenade and a bomb that could be thrown by hand, an early forerunner of the hand grenade. In 1914 he extended his extempore activities to a form of star shell and a wire cutter which could be attached to a bayonet. These later contraptions were not accepted by the authorities, but McClintock was clearly ahead of his time for in 1987 the British Army was issued with a wire cutting device which could be fitted to a bayonet and which bears a remarkable resemblance to his design of 1915. The Sappers and Miners were not only inventors of novel weapons, they would meet them too, for on arrival at the front on 23 October at La Gorgue Numbers 20 and 21 Companies were bombed by a German aeroplane, dropping not high explosives, but steel darts eight inches long with feathered ends. They caused no casualties and do not appear to have been used again.

When the order to mobilise was issued to Numbers 20 and 21 Companies of the 3rd Sappers and Miners, the divisional engineers of the Lahore

Division, and to Numbers 2 and 3 Companies of the 1st King George's Own Sappers and Miners who would accompany the Meerut Division, speculation amongst British officers of all three corps was rife. All recognised that attachment to the expeditionary force would be a good career move, and there was much calling in of favours and wheeling and dealing to be allowed to go. By and large entreaties went unheeded and the field companies went with their own officers, although vacancies due to leave or courses in England were filled by officers from other companies. Did they but know it, those who pleaded to be allowed to go and were disappointed would have their chance soon enough.

Every infantry regiment—and most of the infantry were one battalion regiments—selected for foreign service left a small depot behind at their peace-time station. The selection of depot staff was not easy, for everyone wanted to go to the war. Some regiments left their dross behind, which was a mistake as the workload was immense and capable and experienced men were needed.

The depot was required to recruit, train the recruits and send them and reservists on to the battalion or regiment; pay pensions to discharged men and widows; ensure that the property of men killed was passed on to the heirs and administer the sick sent back to India to recuperate. Depot staffs were augmented by temporary babus taken on for the duration, and the implementation of a new system of accounting on the outbreak of war left the Military Accounts Department in a muddle. Such was the chaos that ensued in the early days that the new system had to be abandoned, but an insufficiency of clerks both in quantity and quality did nothing to assist hard-pressed depot commandants in the provision of efficient support to their regiments and battalions.

That the system did not collapse entirely is very much to the credit of these officers, only some of whom eventually managed to be replaced by wounded officers and get to the Front. It was a source of discontent after the war that there appeared to be few awards and little official recognition of the efforts of the depots' staff.

In late August and early September the regiments and battalions of the Lahore and Meerut Divisions and the Secunderabad Cavalry Brigade concentrated in Karachi and Bombay. Contracts were let for rations and fodder, an attempt was made to issue some winter clothing and ships were rounded up to convey the troops to a destination which was still unknown. Rumour was, of course, rife. Optimists thought they would be going to Europe and worried lest the war be over before they got there. Pessimists, remembering the exclusion of Indian troops from the Boer War, opined that their role would be to guard Egypt and the Suez Canal. Overall morale was high and the optimists were given a boost by a message from the King Emperor which was read out to all ranks of the Indian Expeditionary Force:

33

Officers, Non Commissioned Officers and Men:

I look to all my Indian soldiers to uphold the Izzat of the British Raj against the aggressive and relentless enemy. I know with what readiness my loyal and brave Indian soldiers are prepared to fulfil this sacred trust on the field of battle, shoulder to shoulder with their comrades from all parts of the Empire. Rest assured that you will always be in my thoughts and prayers. I bid you go forward to add fresh lustre to the glorious achievements and noble traditions, courage and chivalry of my Indian Army, whose honour and fame are in your hands.[1]

If this sounds to the present day reader more like something addressed to the Army of the Nile by Napoleon than a message emanating from a British king, it caught the spirit of the times and was very well received by the Indian ranks.

At the ports of embarkation regiments were billeted in tents, barracks, goods sheds in the docks and on ships. Two British officers from each regiment stayed with the men while the remainder of the officers were offered four days free board and lodging in the Taj Mahal Hotel, with a reduced rate thereafter.

The great majority of the troops in the force were recruited from the rural Punjab and, like the Gurkhas and the Garhwalis, had never been in a large city nor seen the sea. In the old days Hindus had been forbidden to cross the kalo pani, or black water, losing caste if they did so, but by 1914 there were well-tried systems in place and regimental arrangements for cleansing ceremonies on return. Many of the soldiers were nervous about embarking upon this expanse of water which stretched to the horizon and for all they knew beyond, and that in a huge floating conveyance far bigger than the river steamers they were accustomed to, but none raised any objection.

All regiments organised sight-seeing tours, and the zoo, the traffic and the electric trams were the favourite talking points in Bombay. The Gurkhas attempted to wash in the sea and were much perplexed to find not only that they could not drink the water, but that their soap would not lather. Conversely, the citizens of Bombay, seeing the Gurkhas in their slouch hats, assumed them to be Japanese.[*] When not sightseeing, regiments of infantry went on route marches round the city and into the surrounding countryside and the cavalry groomed and exercised their horses.

---

[*] Little changes. In 1978 and again in 1988 while doing public duties at Buckingham Palace with his Gurkha battalion, the author was repeatedly asked by tourists why Japanese were guarding the Queen, and why the Japanese Army had an English officer!

While the ships which were to take the expeditionary force were being marshalled, one arrival in Bombay harbour was especially welcomed. This was the transporter *Dongola*, which had been chartered to bring back to India army officers not sequestered to train the new British armies and administrators who had been on leave in England when war broke out and which carried officers of many of the regiments due to embark. The passengers were glad to reach Bombay for, as the ship carried no other ranks and only a small crew, officers of the rank of captain and below had been accommodated on the troop decks and had been required to carry out all ship's fatigues.

The first task of the Sappers and Miners at the docks was to assist the Royal Indian Marine in the preparation of the ships that would embark the expeditionary force from Bombay and Karachi. As hardly any of these were designed as troop transports they all had to be modified to take on troops, animals and weapons. The QVO Sappers and Miners sent 267 carpenters and metalsmiths from Secunderabad and Bangalore, where the Sappers and Miners had a workshop, to Bombay, where with 100 artisans from the 3rd Sappers and Miners they constructed stalls for horses and mules, racks for rifles, containers for kit, bunks for soldiers to sleep on, access ramps and all manner of necessary modifications. Similar work was undertaken in Karachi and in all 30 ships were prepared for military use. If some of the ships' captains were unhappy when holes were drilled in the wrong places, the work was finished to a high standard and on time.

The Lahore Division, split between Bombay and Karachi, was the first to board, and despite the dubious condition of some of the ships the embarkation was speedy and efficient. On 28 August the 47th Sikhs boarded the SS *Akbar*, a vessel of the India Persia Steamship Company, which they found crowded and uncomfortable, with poor rations due, the Commanding Officer believed, to war profiteers having secured the contract to provide the food[2]. In Karachi Wilde's Rifles were to share the British India Steam Navigation Company transporter *Teesta* with half of the 9th Bhopal Infantry, who due to delays in getting their men back from leave only just made it in time to embark on 25 August.

Of the Meerut Division the 2/2nd Gurkhas and half of the 1/9th Gurkhas found themselveson the SS *Angora*, while the other half of the 1/9th shared the SS *Arancola* with the 6th Jat Light Infantry. Both ships belonged to the British India Line, but life on the *Arancola* was particularly hard as the ship had been built to carry 500 men but now had to convey 1,200 men and 100 animals. Having boarded the ships on 13 September the passengers remained aboard and in harbour until the 20th, when the convoy was at last ordered to sail. There was a swell in the harbour and as the ship was not under way the effects were exaggerated. Many of the men spent the week being seasick while still having to wash, cook and, most unpleasant of all, muck out the horses and mules.

The system for embarkation was clearly laid down and well known. An advance party of about 50 men would arrive at the docks with the heavy baggage and the machine-guns (two per battalion) which were loaded first. Next would come the machine-gun mules and the officers' chargers and last would come the battalion. The 2nd Battalion 39th Garhwal Rifles were particularly commended for arriving at Karachi dock to board the SS *Coconada* at 11.15 am on 16 September and having all the kit and every man on board by noon. Cavalry regiments took longer to embark, as all the horses had to be loaded onto ships that had not been designed to carry them. In most cases slings were attached round the animals girths and they were hoisted up in the air and down into the hold by derricks. It is a fact that horses treated in this way rarely panic and there were few equine injuries during embarkation.

At last the convoys were ready to sail, the Lahore Division with part of the Secunderabad Cavalry Brigade on 24 August and the Meerut Division on 21 September. Once the elements embarking in Karachi had married up with those who had sailed from Bombay, the convoy headed for the Suez Canal, escorted by ships of the Royal Navy and the Royal Indian Marine. The Official History describes the voyage as being 'uneventful, and the weather perfect'[3]. Not all of those recovering from malaria, like the Garhwalis, or eating bad rations, like the 47th Sikhs, or being seasick like the Gurkhas would necessarily have concurred, but all were agreed that they were off to a great adventure and despite the vagaries of weather and the cramped conditions on most troopships morale was high. The Gurkhas were particularly intrigued as to how a ship could find its way: there were no landmarks, nothing to follow, just a vast expanse of kalo pani that stretched in all directions as far as the eye could see. Some riflemen thought that there must be rails laid on the sea bed along which the ship progressed on wheeled stilts. The conundrum was resolved when one British officer took a party of men to the rear of the ship and pointed out the wake. 'That,' he said, 'is the ship's road, which it follows until it reaches its destination.'[4] The soldiers accepted that. The Gurkha officers knew better, but were too polite to say so.

Probably the most unfortunate passengers were the Lahore Division's Sappers and Miners, Numbers 20 and 21 Companies, who embarked on the SS *Taiyebeh*. The *Taiyebeh* had just been declared unfit to transport pilgrims to Mecca, and to be declared unfit to take the devout but impoverished to Mecca in 1914 meant that the ship was very unseaworthy indeed. It was about to be broken up when mobilisation was ordered, and only the acute shortage of shipping granted it a reprieve. The ship's engines were old and in bad repair. It could only limp along and soon lagged far behind the rest of the convoy. Three days of rough seas, largely avoided by the rest of the convoy, threw the elderly ship about and made cooking impossible, even if the sepoys had been well enough to eat anything. To make matters worse the engines broke down completely and the ship was at the mercy of the waves and the winds for a further day, with engine rooms flooded and a very real risk of the entire vessel, with Sappers and Miners and mules and all, going to the bottom. The weather then changed, the engines were repaired, and the *Taiyebeh* caught up the convoy.

On all the ships every effort was made to keep the troops busy. Besides the necessary chores of keeping themselves, the ship and the animals clean, parties were allowed to descend into the bowels of the ship and take turns at stoking for short periods. Amazingly, the Indian soldiers seem to have enjoyed the experience. Some of the ships had been hastily converted as animal transports and the ramps leading up from the stable decks were so steep as to make it virtually impossible to bring horses or mules up on deck for exercise. Although a horse, unlike a human, will retain its muscular fitness for up to six weeks without exercise[5] it becomes very grumpy if left in its stable and many a Sikh, Gurkha and Pathan received an iron-shod reminder while mucking out or grooming, while mules are bad-tempered at the best of times. As the convoys, reduced to a speed of about nine knots by having to go at the pace of the slowest ship, approached Suez the heat caused discomfort for the animals below deck and ships often had to steam in circles with all portholes open to provide cooling ventilation. Despite the difficulties few animals were lost during the voyage.

Not all the passengers on the convoy were soldiers. Certain castes of the Indian Army could only eat food prepared by men of the same caste and there were some tasks—such as cleaning latrines—which could only be done by low-caste men—'Untouchables'. Similarly there were tasks which could be carried out by soldiers without any problem of religion or caste but which were better and more cost-effectively done by civilian followers. Conversely the British officers would, when they could, eat beef and other items which the sepoys were prohibited by religion from cooking or eating. Whereas in the British Army all officers' servants, mess staff, grooms, cooks and stretcher bearers were soldiers, in the Indian Army many were Indian civilians, usually with years of service in the regiment and often third or fourth generation followers. Wilde's Rifles embarked with 42 civilian followers, made up of 16 cooks, eight sweepers, eight syces (grooms) for the permitted 14 chargers, eight officers' private servants and two British Officers' Mess servants. These men, despite being under no legal obligation to go to war, were to do great work in the trenches and despite eventual strictures from GHQ that civilians were not to be employed in the firing line, most stayed until the end.

The Lahore Division reached Suez on 15 September, still unsure of their final destination. The fact that there appeared to be no British troops there strengthened the case of the pessimists who still suspected that they would be stuck in Egypt for the duration, and this was reinforced when

Wilde's Rifles was ordered to unload the entire Ferozepore Brigade's holding of reserve ammunition. As this amounted to two million rounds, all packed in boxes and having to be carried up from the hold and down a particularly narrow ladder to the quay side, the task took all day. In the event the Sirhind Brigade, much to its chagrin, were ordered to remain in Egypt while the Ferozepore and Jullunder Brigades of the division moved on to Cairo by train that same day, where most units camped on the racecourse, and moved on to Alexandria and Port Said, again by train, on 17 September.

As a means of indicating to the Moslem population of Egypt that, despite their co-religionists in Turkey leaning towards the German camp, there were plenty of Moslems fighting for the British too, route marches through the towns were held, emphasising the presence of Punjabi Mussalmans and Pathans.

The two brigades, Ferozepore and Jullunder, re-embarked on their original ships on 18 September, sailing on the 19th. At this stage the rumour-mongers had changed their predictions and it was now said that the destination was Malta, in order to allow the British garrison there to be moved to France. It was not until they met a convoy full of Territorials coming the other way to take up garrison duties on the canal that the final destination was officially known—Marseilles. The Sirhind Brigade was eventually relieved and moved to France, but arrived just too late to qualify for the Mons Star—a matter of some considerable disappointment.

The Meerut Division had sailed almost a month after the Lahore Division. Their departure had been delayed due to the presence of the German light cruiser *Emden* which was suspected to be prowling the seas off the west coast of India. Between August and early November, when she was sunk by the Australian cruiser *Sydney*, the *Emden* had indeed enjoyed a jolly frolic in the Indian Ocean. She had sunk or taken as prize 21 Allied merchant ships and had even bombarded Madras on 22 September. The Meerut Division was however allowed to sail on 21 September, escorted by HMS *Dartmouth*, HMS *Swiftsure* and HMS *Fox*. Aboard the Meerut Division's ships the destination was now well known to be Marseilles although this was officially confirmed only when the convoy was well out to sea. Conditions were somewhat better than they had been for the Lahore Division as the comforts and welfare system had now begun to operate, with free issues of cigarettes, sweetmeats and other minor luxuries. The Division reached Suez on 2 October, Port Said and Alexandria on 3 October, and sailed again for Marseilles on 6 October.

Marseilles had long been a cosmopolitan city. Phoenicians, Greeks and Romans had all passed through and it was still an entrepot trading port between Europe, Africa and the Levant. Its citizens were well accustomed to the exotica of the East and its streets were thronged with French colonial troops who arrived almost daily on French transports: Algerians,

Zouaves, Chasseurs d'Afrique and Senegalese all poured in and moved on in the direction of the French sector of the Front.

The arrival of the first ships of the Indian Expeditionary Force A—now to be renamed the Indian Corps—was a significant moment. Although the contents of that first ship may have been diverse—part of a Royal Horse Artillery battery, a signal company, a field ambulance and part of a mule corps—what it portended was not lost on the French, for it demonstrated that Britain was prepared to devote all the resources of her Empire to the prosecution of the war. The Lahore Divisions' convoy arrived at Marseilles on 26 September, and the first formed body of Indian troops—Number 20 Company Sappers and Miners—disembarked, not at all sorry to say goodbye to the crew of the now seriously leaky SS *Taiyebeh*. It was a glorious autumn day. This was not, unfortunately, a harbinger of what was to come, for the winter of 1914 was one of the coldest on record, and while the first units to arrive found themselves marching the five miles to the racecourse camp site under clear skies, the Meerut Division arriving on 12 October met sleet and a biting wind as they marched rather farther, to camp at La Valentine, before putting up their tents on a quagmire.

The reception given to the Indians by the citizens of Marseilles was ecstatic. No one in the south of France had yet seen any British or Imperial troops and the natural good manners and dignity of the Indians appealed to the French. Crowds flocked to the docks to see the sepoys arrive and followed them as they marched to their camp sites. Although the war was but two months old the number of young women in widow's weeds was an indication of the scale of French casualties, and the Sikhs in particular were embarrassed by the number of even younger women, not in widow's weeds, who rushed into the marching ranks to embrace and kiss them. One observer remembered a party of British officers of the 129th Baluchis of the Lahore Division leaning over the side of their docking ship, anxious to be reassured that the war was not yet over and that they were not too late to join in the fun. Unloading of the ships was carried out by regimental fatigue parties assisted by French labourers, and by the time it was completed some Indian soldiers, generally natural linguists, were beginning to pick up a few words of French.

Once the units had disembarked and marched to their respective camps on the outskirts of Marseilles, the process of equipping them for the war began. The Indian Army had been issued with the Short Magazine Lee Enfield Rifle Mark II only a few weeks before mobilisation, but the British Army was now equipped with the Mark III, which although essentially the same weapon had a different sighting system and fired higher velocity ammunition. Rather than operate two systems of ammunition resupply, it was easier to withdraw the rifles from the Indian Army and issue the newer model. There would, it was hoped, be time to retrain the men in the use of the new weapon before they would be committed to action.

As it happened, some were only to receive the necessary practice in the trenches, against live targets.

All units, both Indian and British, were allocated interpreters, who might be French-speaking British officers or soldiers, or English-speaking Frenchmen. The 47th Sikhs found themselves with a lieutenant of the British Army and a warrant officer and a private from the French Army, while the 2/2nd Gurkha Rifles found that one of their allotted interpreters was the Commanding Officer's brother, a Major in the 6th Gurkha Rifles.

The units of the Corps were required to leave all surplus personal kit at Marseilles. Apart from what the man carried on his person, all were allowed a limited amount of kit to be carried to the Front in first line transport. The Commanding Officer was allowed 50 lbs, other British officers 35 lbs and the Indian officers were permitted the Indian Other Ranks' scale plus 10 lbs. The kit which an IOR was allowed to put on the transport amounted to one waterproof sheet, one blanket, one length of twine, one pair of spare socks, one spare towel, one balaclava and a small holdall containing the man's personal possessions. Followers were allowed one waterproof sheet, one blanket and a set of cooking pots.

Although the inhabitants of Marseilles became accustomed to 'Les Hindoues' as time went on, they never failed to turn out to cheer the regiments and battalions, whatever the weather. As in Karachi, the people of Marseilles assumed the Gurkhas, four battalions of whom arrived with the Meerut Division and a further two as part of the Lahore Division's Sirhind Brigade, were Japanese, and the loudest cheer was reserved for their followers, who were recognisably Indian.

Marseilles was to be the mounting base for the Indian Corps, while Orléans would be the forward concentration area and supply base. While waiting to be moved up to Orléans the units route-marched, trained on the new rifle and suffered the inevitable inspections by the great and the curious. The 2/2nd Gurkhas were rather unfortunate during a visit by the Corps Commander in October. The Indian Corps had as yet little or no warm clothing suitable for European warfare, but because the nights at Dehra Dun in India were cold, the 2nd Gurkhas were in possession of greatcoats. Gurkha regiments, being rifle regiments, wear black buttons and accoutrements, and because they were a very smart Gurkha regiment the 2nd had dyed their greatcoats black. Unfortunately the General preferred uniforms to be 'as issued' and the black greatcoats were ordered to be withdrawn, to be replaced next day by 'Coats, British, Warm.'[6]

When the order to mobilise had been issued little thought had been given as to how the Indian Army regiments would be employed, or even where they might be used. The Indian government's view was that to employ them as mere garrison troops to release British troops for the Western Front would be wasteful of trained regulars and bad for morale in India. After representations by the Army and the Viceroy to the home government it was decided to employ the Indian Army in France, but there remained the options of using them piecemeal, with units attached to existing corps, divisions and brigades, or as a corps in their own right. Sensibly, it was decided that the Indians would be best employed as a unified corps with their own chain of command, and on 5 September 1914 Lieutenant General Sir James Willcocks was appointed Commander of the Indian Corps and ordered to France.

The announcement that the Indian Expeditionary Force A would hence forth be known as the Indian Corps was promulgated on 27 September, and on 30 September the Corps Commander disembarked at Marseilles from the P&O steamer SS *Malwa*. He was met by the French general commanding the area and by an ADC from General Joffre.

If the government had set out to find a commander who knew Indians and whom Indians knew, they could not have done better than appoint James Willcocks. Although of the British, rather than the Indian, Army he had spent nearly all his service in India or with Indians. He spoke Hindustani and a number of other Indian dialects and was well known by officers and sepoys of the Corps.

Born in 1857, the year of the mutiny, Willcocks had been commissioned into The Leinster Regiment in 1878 and from 1879 to 1880 had served in the Afghan campaign under the great old warrior, Lord Roberts. The next year he took part in the Waziri expedition, where he was mentioned in despatches. He was promoted to captain in 1884 before fighting in the Sudan in 1885. He fought in the Second Burma War from 1886 to 1889, where he gained the DSO, followed by the Chin Lushai affair in 1889 to 1900, and then returned to India to take part in the Manipur expedition of 1891. In 1893 Willcocks was promoted to Major (at 36 he was relatively young for the rank), and in 1897 he was again on campaign with the Tochi Field Force on the borders of India where he was gazetted brevet lieutenant colonel. In 1898 Willcocks moved continents yet again, being appointed second-in-command of the West African Frontier Force (ancestor of the modern Nigerian Army) and then its commander from 1899 to 1900. In this latter appointment he served with the Ashanti Field Force and relieved Kumasi in a bloody battle for which he was granted the Freedom of the City of London, presented with a sword of honour by the Lord Mayor and Corporation, and congratulated by name in Parliament. Having next taken part in the South African War, Willcocks returned to India to command the Zakka Khel and Mohmand expeditions in 1908. In 1914 he was coming to the end of his four-year tenure as Commander of the Northern Army in India and was reputed to wear more campaign medals than any other man in the British Army. Aged 57 when he assumed command of the Indian Corps, a cursory glance at his photograph indicates the archetypal blimp: bristling grey moustache, riding boots and

41

britches, swagger cane and an air of arrogance. A second, more careful inspection shows a sensitivity of feature, a glimpse of humour behind the stern facade and a firm but kindly jaw line.

Although he had spent all his regimental service in the Leinsters, Willcocks had commanded Indian brigades and divisions and had a very real love for the Indian soldier. The sepoy does not care overmuch whether a British officer is clever, or even whether he is particularly competent, as long as the Saheb does his best and leads as the sepoys expect him to lead. The sepoy does, however, care very much that the Saheb should be interested in him and in his welfare. British officers who did not actually like Indian soldiers very much were rare and were smelled out by the sepoys early on. Once the Subadar Major had mentioned to the Commanding Officer that a certain Saheb's face did not fit, the Saheb left rapidly, usually with his papers marked 'Not suitable for service with Indian troops'. James Willcocks, although he was not of the Indian service, did care very much for the sepoys and for their welfare, and the sepoys knew it. As the Corps Commander of the first Indian troops to be employed on mainland Europe Willcocks had a daunting task. While most British Army commanders made real efforts to understand the requirements and limitations of the Indian Corps, some did not. Willcocks had to explain, persuade, convince, cajole and fight to ensure that his sepoys' capabilities and limitations were understood and that they were properly employed and adequately supported. At the same time he had on occasions to be utterly pitiless towards his own men when the exigencies of all out war demanded it. The sepoys knew that Willcocks cared, and they gave of their utmost for him.

'FE', who was recording officer of the Indian Corps until being appointed British Attorney General in the spring of 1915, witnessed Willcocks visiting the remnants of an infantry battalion after the savage fighting round Neuve Chapelle. 'There are very few of you left, Subadar Saheb,' said the General. 'There are twice as many as there were before the General Saheb visited us,' came the reply from the several times wounded Indian officer.[7] Six months later Willcocks was to be abruptly removed and was to hand over command of the Indian Corps. In 1919 he was standing in the crowd, in mufti, watching the Victory Parade march through London. The Indian contingent swung into view and from the ranks a sepoy spotted Willcocks in the crowd. Raising the Sikh war cry 'Fateh' the men broke ranks and ran across the road and into the crowd to shake the hand of their old commander, before returning to the parade.

The Lahore Division entrained for Orléans, the forward base, on 30 September. They followed a roundabout route heading first westwards along the coast to Bezières, then inland to Toulouse and north to Cahors, where cars were provided for the British officers to view the countryside. At the frequent stops firewood was provided for the men to cook, and the by now inevitable sightseers gathered to look at the first soldiers of the British Indian Army ever to come to fight in Europe*.

The units of the Lahore Division arrived at Orléans on 2 October 1914. They marched from the railway station to an artillery practice ground about six miles from the town, where they were to remain for 15 days. As regiments had not been able to bring their full complement of transport from India an issue of wagons and horses was made. Inevitably there were insufficient GS Wagons to go round and so all manner of requisitioned and bought-in carts were issued. In general an infantry battalion could expect to receive around nine of these carts, some obtained from London butchers, which if carefully packed could carry up to 2,000lbs weight. As well as the carts a battalion would receive 34 mules, two water carts, six GS Wagons and a cook cart. With this mixed blessing came 18 draught horses, many of them French Percherons straight from the plough and with no military experience. Unfortunately no Army Service Corps drivers were provided to handle the horses and wagons, and regiments were told to find their own. Most regimental followers had little idea how to deal with a 16 hand high horse, and the soldiers even less. The men of the 47th Sikhs stated that they were unaccustomed to dealing with hattis (elephants!), but made a reasonable job of handling them. The 1/9th Gurkha Rifles, arriving with the Meerut Division later in the month, were less fortunate. Their followers and soldiers were eager to have a go, with disastrous results. A normally well disciplined, smart battalion was reduced to the appearance of a circus with carts and horses galloping in all directions, totally out of control, each with an excited follower or stolid (albeit beginning-to-worry) Gurkha perched on top of the wagon trying, without the slightest result, to control his runaway steeds. One pair of horses with wagon attached and Gurkha aboard, made for the camp perimeter. Swerving neither right nor left, the combination galloped straight over a staff officer's tent. Unfortunately the owner of the tent was inside at the time, trying to make some sense of the plethora of paperwork which is an inevitable concomitant of military operations, when his reverie was interrupted by the crash of hooves through canvas and expletives in Gurkhali. The staff officer escaped from the ruin of his erstwhile home without injury but was displeased. He complained loudly and at length to the Commanding Officer of the 1/9th Gurkha Rifles, who could do little but suppress his amusement and apologise.

The Indian Corps had left India with winter clothing, but most of it was for the winter of the Indian plains, where the sun shines, the humidity is

---

* There were two 'Indian' battalions at Waterloo, in the Dutch service and recruited from the Dutch East Indies. They were stationed on the extreme right of the Allied line and saw no fighting. One shudders for their administrative arrangements.

down and a pullover or a fire is occasionally necessary at night. Uniforms were of Khaki Drill, a thin cotton cloth, and consisted of a bush-jacket type tunic which buttoned up to the neck, long trousers or shorts, puttees which wound to just below the knee, and regimental headgear. This outfit was totally inadequate for the rain, wind, sleet and eventual snow of the French winter, but the thick serge khaki uniforms as issued to the British Army would not be available for the Indians until December. In India regiments had worn their own traditional headgear, slouch hats for the Gurkhas and Garhwalis and various forms of lungi or turban for most of the others. The Gurkha, or Garhwali, hat had originally been issued in 1907 and was a simple broad-brimmed felt hat. As Rifle Regiment drill was abandoned for the duration of the war, the left side of the brim of the Gurkha hat was usually bent upwards to allow rifles to be carried at the slope,* a practice also adopted by the Australians with their slouch hats. The Garhwalis bent their hats up to the right, in an effort to look different from the Gurkhas, with whom they were continually, and to their great irritation, being confused. The British Army wore khaki peaked caps and it was suggested that these might be more practical wear for the Indian Corps. The Sikhs naturally demurred, but the Gurkhas expressed themselves happy and some battalions actually received an issue of caps. The Corps Commander, conservative in such matters, saw a parade of a Gurkha battalion in the new hats, disliked them and directed that the regiments of the Corps would revert to their traditional wear. British Officers could, however, wear peaked caps if they wished, and some did, although most realised that to wear something so conspicuously different from that worn by their men was to make them obvious targets.

Sartorial elegance for British officers was in any case quickly modified in the interests of comfort, at least in the early stages. A photograph of a group of British officers of the 2/2nd Gurkha Rifles taken in January 1915 shows Captain Corse-Scott, the Adjutant, wearing a black greatcoat, presumably saved from the Corps Commander's depredations, and another ranks' issue ammunition bandolier, the whole set off by a Gurkha hat modified to look like an American cowboy's Stetson. Another officer wears a service dress tunic over a civilian pattern muffler and sports a woolly hat with a bobble on top. A third is attired in an ankle-length mackintosh to the belt of which is attached a revolver and a pair of binoculars. Head dress is a rolled-up balaclava. It is not surprising that Indian soldiers sometimes had difficulty in distinguishing between British, French and German officers—certainly the term 'uniform' does not appear to have retained its original definition. A photograph of British officers of the same battalion taken six months later shows them attired in more conventional garb. Captain Corse-Scott wears a collar and tie, tunic and service dress

---

*   i.e. over the left shoulder.

44

cap while only two of the ten shown are wearing Gurkha hats. Admittedly the weather was much kinder in August than it had been in January, but one cannot avoid the suspicion that the officers had perhaps been taken to task, probably by the Subadar Major.

The Indian Corps retained their own pattern of equipment throughout the war. Unlike the British Army's equipment, which was made of canvas webbing, the Indian troops wore leather belts and pouches, a leather bandolier and a webbing pack. Leather took rather more cleaning than webbing, but unlike the latter it did not shrink when wet and could therefore be taken off in wet weather and put on again without having to be re-adjusted.

At Orléans an attempt was made to issue some warm clothing in the shape of British Warm coats, pullovers, balaclava helmets and long underpants. The latter, known to several generations of British soldiers as long johns, were far from sartorial but they were warm, and they were practical in that they had a flap on the seat allowing the soldier to defecate without lowering his drawers and exposing his naked bottom to the biting wind. Unfortunately they were made for (relatively) tall, fat British soldiers and not for short, thin Gurkhas, and the first task given to the interpreters of the 1/9th Gurkha Rifles was to go into the market in Orléans and purchase 3,000 safety pins, so that the men could wear their long johns without them falling about their knees.

Each man was supposed to be issued with an extra blanket, but on the arrival of the Lahore Division insufficient were available, and the men of Wilde's Rifles were to be found wrapped in a variety of eiderdowns, table cloths and even cast-off curtains.

The government now finally took over all private and regimental tentage, and officers' private chargers, for which a price agreed by a board in Marseilles was paid. It was at Orléans too that the men of the Indian Corps caught their first sight of an aeroplane. In general this technological marvel made no impression on the sepoys whatsoever—they expected to see all sorts of wonders once they landed in Europe—but it caused great excitement amongst the British officers, most of whom had never seen one either. If an aircraft failed to spark interest amongst the sepoys, the statue of Joan of Arc in the town square attracted considerable attention, even reverence, and parties of soldiers being marched through the town took to giving the statue an 'Eyes Right' when passing.

Even in winter the farmland round Orléans seemed particularly lush to the men of the Indian Corps. The Sikhs in particular noticed that here things were done differently. The women appeared to do all the work, while milk churns were operated by trained dogs; horses and cows got fat and the men sat around drinking wine. This was not an entirely accurate impression (most of the men were away in the French Army), but many sepoys expressed the view that their own society might be much more fun were they to swap systems with the French.

The provision of rations for the Indian Corps might have been expected to pose problems. Hindus did not eat beef, Moslems did not eat pork, and Brahmins were vegetarian. Many soldiers in the Corps could only eat food prepared by a member of their own caste and meat for consumption by Moslems had to be slaughtered in a prescribed fashion.[*] In peacetime each company in a Class Company regiment had its own cook-house and took its own (civilian follower) cooks with it when deployed in the field. Sikhs and Dogras could eat pretty much the same food, and all would drink each other's tea. Generally Moslems if pressed would eat Hindu rations, although the reverse was unusual.

In fact most soldiers were pragmatic and accepted that in war there might be occasions when they would have to eat whatever was available in order to survive. One British officer of an Indian cavalry regiment quotes a VCO as saying that if there was nothing else available to sustain life they would certainly eat beef but, 'All we ask from you, Saheb, is that you do your best to provide us with food which is not forbidden to us'.[8]

The Indian Army got round all these potential difficulties by providing a standard ration that was acceptable to all: rice or chapattis, dhal (a lentil gravy), vegetables, and meat for those who ate it. Rice was easily imported through Marseilles as was atta, the coarse stone-ground flour used for making chapattis. Chapattis were not easy to make in the conditions then prevalent on the Western Front and the men of the Indian Corps quickly took a liking to the standard British Army biscuit (known irreverently to the British, who did not like it, as dog biscuit).

In India even meat-eating classes only had meat at home on high days and holidays—consumable animals were expensive and the everyday diet was largely vegetarian with the dhal providing the necessary protein. In the Army meat was provided only two or three times a week[†] and this was usually chicken, goat or mutton which was acceptable to the majority of meat-eaters. The weather on the Western Front in October 1914 was far colder than the plains of India and, while not necessarily colder than in the Indian frontier areas, a lot wetter. The Corps Commander, supported by his commanding

[*]   The animal's throat had to be cut and the carcass bled before being butchered, as with the Jewish 'Kosher'.

[†]   1995 recruits to the British Brigade of Gurkhas were trained in the UK for the first time. On arrival from Nepal they were fed Nepali food but with meat twice a day. A plague of boils resulted. The author, then commanding the Gurkha Training Centre in Hampshire, ordered the meat content of the ration to be reduced drastically with a slow build up to the full ration over a period of a month. The boils disappeared. In 1996 when meat was introduced only gradually, no recruit suffered from boils.

officers, felt that reasonable quantities of meat must be provided to give the men the necessary protein to withstand the climate. Regiments were asked whether they would accept frozen mutton. Some were reluctant—Indian soldiers like their meat fresh, preferably on the hoof—but all agreed. The men were then asked whether they would accept tinned mutton and again they agreed. Unfortunately the contract for the provision of tinned mutton was drawn up in haste and perhaps without sufficient attention to detail, for when the first consignment arrived each tin was emblazoned with the supplier's logo: a rampant bull! As most men in the Indian Corps would eat beef only in extremis, and as Indian soldiers, not unreasonably, assumed that a picture on a tin indicated the contents within, the tinned meat experiment was abandoned. From now on flocks of sheep and goats would be delivered to the Indian Corps railhead at Lillers, about ten miles from the Front, and each unit would detach four soldiers to supervise the slaughtering, certifying that the animals were what they purported to be, and that they had been slaughtered in accordance with religious requirements. This system worked very well for the remainder of the war.

By the time that the Meerut Division was arriving at Orléans lessons from the fighting so far were being absorbed and disseminated. One tactical memorandum circulated to all battalions of the Indian Corps said:

Machine-Guns
Troops must be told to keep a sharp look out for enemy machine-guns. These will attempt to creep up ditches and along any kind of approach to positions whence they can bring to bear enfilade fire[*]. Battalion scouts must be used to detect all such movements and the machine-guns should themselves be enfiladed by parties of the strength of a platoon detached for this purpose.[9]

Another memorandum advised British officers not to show themselvesexcept in the assault. In the Indian Army this stricture could not possibly be obeyed, and the skill of the German machine-gunners, the preponderance of enemy artillery, and the absolute necessity for British officers of the Indian Army to be seen to be to the fore were to be the major factors in the very heavy officer casualties that were to come.

By the time the battalions and regiments were arriving at the Front the Indian soldiers had generally decided that they liked France and the French, although the language puzzled them initially. A Sikh sepoy wrote to his uncle in Jullunder:

[*] That is, fire from a flank, always more effective because if the bullets miss the man aimed at they have a good chance of hitting men farther along. Fire from the front is wasted should it miss the men aimed at.

No one has any clue to the language of this place. Even the British soldiers do not understand it. They call milk DOOLEE and water DOOLO ... [du lait and de l'eau][10]

Another Sikh, writing to his brother in the Punjab felt:

This is a very fine country. They have an excellent way of doing things and there is much beauty in the country. There is no doubt about it. Very many people come to see us and one cannot tell the lord from the beggar. All are alike and they do everything with great intelligence and skill. They use dogs to drive their animals, that is cattle, and to extract butter from milk. They grind wheat and do everything by machinery and thresh the straw all by machinery. And they plough with horses. As for the shopkeepers, they are very honest and make no difference to their prices. Whether it be a child or a grown man they ask the same price of everyone. There is no theft or dishonesty. The shops remain open all day long and never a penny is stolen.[11]

At this early stage the sepoys did not entirely understand the culture of France, for the same writer, noting the preponderance of roadside shrines and calvaries went on to say:

And if a man commits theft they inflict a very severe punishment on him. They fix him alive and upright to a stake and fasten his hands with nails and there he dies. So nobody commits theft.[12]

When units—French, British or Indian—were not actually in the line they were generally billeted on French or Belgian civilians, either in farms or in private houses. Divisional Headquarters would allocate a group of villages to each brigade, which would in turn sub-allocate to battalions and regiments. An officer of the battalion to be billeted, accompanied by an interpreter and an NCO of each company, would visit the Mairie and state their requirements. The town officials would then detail individual houses and farms into which the billeting officer would direct his troops when they arrived. Initially the French were wary, even frightened, of the Indian troops, but the latter's natural courtly behaviour and scrupulous regard for property soon made them popular tenants. Most of the sepoys and sowars were farmers themselves, they understood and sympathised with the problems faced by the French peasants and smallholders trying to work their land in a war zone, and they helped when they could. One French wife, trying to cope single-handed while her husband was away with the French Army, described her delight when the men of the 1st Battalion 4th Gurkha Rifles brought her eggs which they had found laid in a barn where they were sleeping. 'Our own men,' said the wife, 'would have had them in their soup in a twinkling.'[13]

Most of the units of the Indian Corps would not stay long in billets in October 1914, for there was work to be done in the firing line farther east.

SOURCE NOTES

1. Quoted in *The Indian Corps in France*, Merewether and Smith, John Murray, London, 1919.
2. Quoted in *47th Sikhs War Record in the Great War*, Picton Publishing, Chippenham, 1992.
3. *The Indian Corps in France*, Merewether and Smith, John Murray, London, 1919
4. *History of the 2nd King Edward's Own Goorkhas (The Sirmoor Rifle Regiment) Vol II 1911 – 1921*, LW Shakespear, Gale and Polden, Aldershot, 1962 (privately published).
5. *The Veterinary Record* February 1996. The definitive answer to an argument that has raged for at least a century—but otherwise how could horses be transported for long distances to the Crusades and to the South African War and still be ready for action so shortly after arrival?
6. War Diary 2nd Bn 2nd Gurkha Rifles, Public Record Office, London, WO/95/3942.
7. *The Indian Corps in France.*
8. *Indian Cavalry Officer 1914 – 1915*, Captain Roly Grimshaw of the Poona Horse, Secunderabad Cavalry Brigade, Costello, 1986
9. Reproduced in *History of the 2nd King Edward's Own Goorkhas (The Sirmoor Rifle Regiment) Vol II 1911 – 1921.*
10. 'Report of the Censor of Indian Mails, France 1914 – 1918, Vol I', India Office Library and Records, L/MIL/5/825.
11. Ibid.
12. Ibid.
13. Quoted in *A History of the 4th Prince of Wales' Own Gurkha Rifles 1857 – 1937*, MacDonell and Macaulay, Blackwood and Sons, Edinburgh and London, 1940 (privately published).

III

First Blood

By the latter half of October, when the Indian Corps was arriving and sorting itself out at Orléans, the short period of mobile warfare on the Western Front was virtually over. The Race to the Sea had ended when the Allies reached Nieuport on the Belgian coast in the first week of October. The tiny BEF* was now sandwiched between the Belgians and the French to the north and the French to the south. The British held the Ypres Salient, its southern extremity being in the area of Messines, about seven miles south of Ypres, and the line then ran south-east to Frelinghien, on what is now the D 945, skirted to the east of Armentières and proceeded south-west to Cuinchy/Cambrin where it joined with the French whose lines continued to the south-east, on down past Sedan and Verdun, to the Swiss border.

The Ypres Salient, which was to figure so largely throughout the war, was at this stage a rough semicircle extending into German-held territory. Its radius was approximately five miles, centred on the town of Ypres itself and the perimeter was 16 miles, give or take a mile or two depending on the ebb and flow of the fighting.

The total British frontage was around 38 miles and was held by I Corps from the top of the Salient to Zonnebeke, about half way round the Ypres perimeter; by IV Corps (actually only Rawlinson's 7th Division and a cavalry brigade) from Zonnebeke to Zandvoorde, by the newly constituted III Corps from the southern end of the Salient at Wytschaete/Messines to Frelinghien, and by II Corps from Frelinghien south to the La Bassée/Cuinchy area. A gap of about five miles between I and III Corps from Zandvoorde to Wytschaete on the Salient perimeter was held by Allenby's cavalry, now expanded to a corps and acting as infantry.

The key to the Ypres Salient in the Cavalry Corps' area was a ridge which runs from Wytschaete, on the southern end of the Salient, due west

---

* Originally four infantry divisions, a cavalry division and an independent brigade. A farther infantry division had now arrived and the cavalry increased to a corps. The arrival of the Indian Corps would increase the size of infantry of the BEF by almost one third. In comparison, the French started the war with 62 infantry divisions and ten cavalry divisions.

for ten miles to Mont des Cats, with the Poperinge to Ypres road to its north and the Lys river to its south. Although the ridge is only 160 feet or so above sea level at its highest and with a maximum width of 3,000 yards north to south, it dominates Ypres and the surrounding countryside. If the Germans could occupy the ridge then Ypres, Poperinge and the surrounding area would become untenable and the British line, if it could be held at all, would be pushed back so far as to give the enemy a good chance of a breakthrough, leaving them less than 40 miles from the Channel Ports and with very little to stop them.

The 'Line' at this stage of the war might more properly be described as 'the forward edge of the battle area'. The complex array of professionally constructed trench lines to be seen later in the war, with saps and bays; traverses and bunkers; support, reserve and communication trenches did not exist, far less were there any fire steps, walkways and concrete shelters. The Cavalry Corps' area was low-lying and boggy. Men dug where they could, improved existing drainage ditches, built breastworks where the height of the water table made digging and standing in a trench impossible, or simply lay on the open ground with banks and hedges for cover. The line was not continuous and there were gaps everywhere, through which German snipers would infiltrate during the long hours of darkness to deal out death and destruction when the light came. At this stage the British had no grenades or trench mortars and the Cavalry had been hastily issued with bayonets and given some brief and rudimentary instruction in their use. There was no wire except what the troopers took from farm fences and even digging implements were in short supply. British artillery, both in terms of guns per mile of front and of shells per gun per day, was considerably less than that of the Germans.

The BEF was holding, but only just. Tiny though it was, it included nearly all the regular units which had been stationed in England. Exhausted by the retreat from Mons to the Marne and then the advance to the Aisne, short of artillery and having taken around 10,000 casualties, the BEF desperately needed reinforcements. There were none to be had. Although two Territorial battalions had been sent to France as part of the BEF, no others were yet ready for war, nor would they be for some time to come. The New Armies were composed of tens of thousands of enthusiastic volunteers, as yet without uniforms or weapons, being instructed in close order drill by instructors many of whom were too old or infirm to be with the BEF. The Canadians, Australians and New Zealanders had not yet arrived, and at that stage of the war were in any case too few to make a difference. The only source of trained regular soldiers anywhere in the British Empire was the Army in India.

At the mounting base in Orléans within the Lahore Division (still minus the Sirhind Brigade) rumour was rife. Although war news was rigidly censored, men and units moved up and down between the front and Orléans, and inevitably stories (usually wildly exaggerated) circulated. There was talk of great British victories and of the British having captured Lille.* Officers and men worried that they might after all have no opportunity to take part in what was still seen as an exciting adventure. They were soon to discover the truth.

On the night of 17 October units of the Lahore Division began to entrain at Orléans, using four stations and numerous sidings. It was dark, it was raining and the horse-drawn transport, the bane of the quartermasters' lives since it had been issued a few days previously, ensured that units' baggage was in complete confusion, with carts arriving at the wrong station, in the wrong order or not arriving at all. The men had to march through mud and over broken pavé but eventually the Division was on the move, and on 20 October arrived at Arques and Blendercques, satellite villages of St Omer and about 25 miles west of the southern end of the Ypres Salient. From their arrival stations units then dispersed to billets, either in public buildings or in private French houses. Having de-trained, Wilde's Rifles, in one of those quirks of military planning which defies logic, marched four miles in the opposite direction to the Front to Wizerne, where they spent the night. The 47th Sikhs had less far to go and from Arques were directed to the monastery at Lembernesse where the sepoys tried to make sense of the statues of the twelve apostles. Told that they were the gurus of the Christians, the Sikhs obtained some amusement from being billeted at the feet of the Saints. The 9th Bhopal Infantry, the third Indian battalion of the Ferozepore Brigade, were in Wizerne with Wilde's Rifles and had two companies billeted in a brewery and two in a girls' school. This battalion was considered to have won the billeting stakes.

On the morning of 21 October the Ferozepore Brigade was ordered to concentrate at Wallon Cappell, while the rest of the Division would be deployed farther south. The Brigade marched the 12 miles to Wallon Cappell getting there in the afternoon. At 2100 hours that night Wilde's Rifles were told to be prepared to get onto motor vehicles at 0300 the following morning, later changed to 0600. Each man was issued with 200 rounds of ammunition and put one day's cooked ration to be eaten cold, with a further day's emergency ration (biscuit and raisins) in his haversack.

Exact timing in regard to transport is rare in any war, and it was not until 0830 hours on the morning of 22 October that the transport for the Brigade actually arrived. To the great amusement of the British troops, it consisted of 36 London buses, still in their red livery and still with advertisements for Glaxo—'the Food that Builds Bonnie Babies!', Buchanan's Black and White whisky at 54 shillings [£2.70] a dozen, Carter's Little Liver Pills 'for billiousness, torpid liver and constipation', emblazoned on the sides. Ever

---

* This would not happen for another four years!

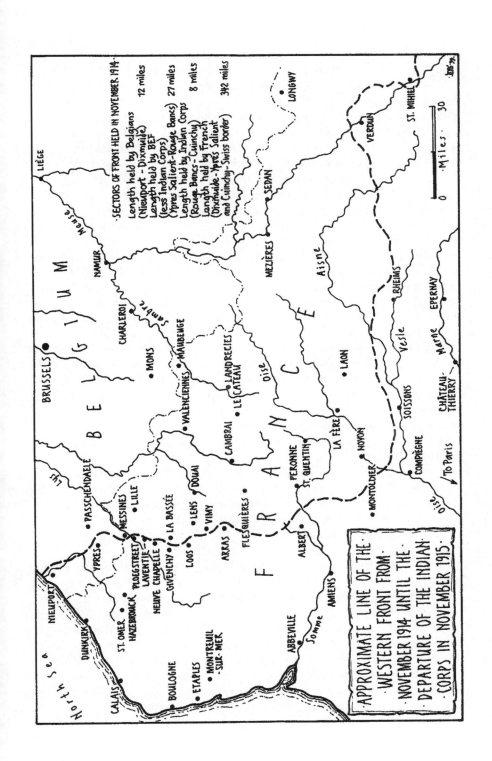

SECTORS OF FRONT HELD IN NOVEMBER 1914.

Length held by Belgians
(Nieuport - Dixmuide)   12 miles

Length held by BEF
(less Indian Corps)   27 miles
(Ypres Salient-Rouge Bancs)

Length held by Indian Corps
(Rouge Bancs - Cuinchy)   8 miles

Length held by French
(Dixmuide - Ypres Salient
and Cuinchy-Swiss border)   342 miles

·APPROXIMATE· LINE· OF· THE·
·WESTERN· FRONT· FROM·
·NOVEMBER·1914· UNTIL· THE·
·DEPARTURE· OF· THE· INDIAN·
·CORPS· IN· NOVEMBER· 1915·

since, the British and Indian Armies have referred to the process of getting onto transport—whether road, air or water—as 'embussing'.

The 1st Battalion The Connaught Rangers, the British battalion in the Ferozepore Brigade, were the first to embus while the remainder marched. The buses took the Connaughts to Wulverghem, about a mile and a half from the Front, turned about and, meeting Wilde's Rifles on the road, delivered them to the same place. Despite roads which had not been designed for London buses, the manoeuvre was repeated with the 129th Baluchis, and the only battalion of the Ferozepore Brigade which had to march to Wulverghem was the 9th Bhopal Infantry, who were detailed to escort the brigade and regimental horsed wagons. The 9th Bhopals were then detailed as corps reserve for the Cavalry Corps, moved hither and thither being given all sorts of contradictory orders, and were never actually deployed in the Salient until at last, on 26 October, they were sent south with the Connaught Rangers to rejoin the rest of the Indian Corps.

Armies are formalised institutions. A division and a brigade is constructed so as to work as one formation. This is even more so at regimental and battalion level where the establishment of officers, men, equipment and especially communications, are not such as to allow a sub unit (a company or a squadron) of a regiment to operate away from its parent body for long. General Watkis, commanding the Lahore Division, would have preferred to concentrate his entire division, less of course his Sirhind Brigade which was still in Egypt, and then commit it as a division. Even more so would Brigadier General Egerton, commanding the Ferozepore Brigade, have preferred to fight his battalions as a brigade, and it would certainly not have entered the heads of the lieutenant colonels commanding the Connaughts, Wilde's Rifles and the 129th Baluchis that their first experience of European warfare would be as anything but formed battalions. The situation then prevailing simply did not permit this ideal. The British defences were under severe pressure, the regiments of the Cavalry Corps were tired, there were weak spots all along the Front, and men simply had to be thrown in as they were needed, regardless of the normal chain of command.

Once the Indian troops reached Wulverghem (and the entire Ferozepore Brigade was there by 1100 hours on the morning of 22 October, even if some of their baggage was strewn out on the road behind them), they came under the command of the recently promoted Lieutenant General Edmund Allenby, commanding the Cavalry Corps. The Connaught Rangers were allocated to the 1st Cavalry Division (Major General Beauvoir de Lisle) who ordered half the battalion to relieve a battalion of the Essex Regiment just to the east of Messines, while the other half battalion took over from a cavalry regiment to the north-east. By the morning of 23 October the Connaughts were the first British battalion of the Indian Corps to be in the firing line.

Shortly after arriving at Wulverghem, Wilde's Rifles were ordered to march a mile north to Wytschaete and on arrival there found themselves under the 2nd Cavalry Division, commanded by Major General H de la P Gough. Gough's regiments were exhausted and desperately needed relief, so he ordered Wilde's to provide a company to each of the 4th and 5th Cavalry Brigades. On the afternoon of 22 October the Afridi Company of Wilde's relieved the Scots Greys and the Dogra Company the Carabiniers, allowing those two British regiments to come out of the line to rest and re-fit. The Sikh and Punjabi Mussalman Companies were ordered to improve the second line trenches east and south-east of Wytschaete while the Machine-Gun Section (2 Maxim guns) was sent off to the 4th Cavalry Brigade and Battalion Headquarters remained at Wytschaete itself. Once darkness fell the companies of Wilde's Rifles moved up to occupy their allotted positions. They moved in file, using what cover they could find, and met officers of the regiments they were to replace behind the forward defence line. Wilde's men moved silently up to the line, the Scots Creys and the Carabiniers stood to with every man alert in his allotted firing position, and the sepoys lay or crouched beside them. Reference points and the direction of German positions were hurriedly pointed out, the Wilde's company commander agreed with the cavalry commanding officer that relief was complete, and the British cavalry troopers withdrew as silently as their replacements had arrived.

The night of 22/23 October was a quiet one with only sporadic German shelling and sniping, but even so five sepoys of Wilde's Rifles were wounded. All day on 23 October the companies in the forward position worked to improve their firing positions while the two companies employed in developing the second line of defence carried on digging, until in the evening these too were ordered into the line, the Sikh Company to relieve the Household Cavalry Regiment on the northern end of the Cavalry Corps' area, and the Punjabi Mussalman Company the 12th Lancers to the east of Oost Taverne. That night there were relatively minor German attacks on the Afridi and Dogra Companies' areas which were easily repulsed but not without nine men being wounded, some seriously. Sepoy Usman Khan, a member of the Afridi Company, won the first gallantry decoration awarded to an Indian in France for his conduct that night. Usman Khan was not a member of Wilde's Rifles at all, but one of the men attached from Coke's Rifles when Wilde's had been unable to get their leave men back. He was, however, an Afridi so had no difficulties in fitting into the company, despite the different cap badge he wore. Usman Khan was wounded twice during the night and was ordered back to the Regimental Aid Post at Wytschaete. He refused to go, on the grounds that, in his opinion, his wounds were slight and he could fire his rifle perfectly well as long as he remained in the lying position. He was again wounded, rather more seriously now, for a bullet removed a sizeable portion of both his thighs, causing serious bleeding. This time he was not given the choice and was dragged off the field, protesting feebly that he could still fire his rifle. He was subsequently awarded the Indian Distinguished Service Medal.

The 24th and 25th October were what the communiqués describe as 'quiet': that is there was no major movement on either side but there remained a steady trickle of wounded from sniping and shelling. By this time the men of Wilde's had eaten the cooked ration and emergency ration they had brought with them; getting further supplies of food was difficult and there were no replacements for the wounded. On 26 October Battalion Headquarters at Wytschaete was shelled and the Commanding Officer, Lieutenant Colonel Gray, was wounded and evacuated. Command now devolved upon Major Swifte, the company commander of the Punjabi Mussalman Company whose place was taken by Lieutenant Forbes, hitherto Company Officer of that company. Although Wilde's were not aware of it at the time, Colonel Gray's shell was but a small component of the German bombardment of the British line prior to a drive for the Channel Ports which the enemy was then preparing.

At the time that Wilde's Rifles had been attached to the 2nd Cavalry Division, the 129th Baluchis had once again embussed, this time for St Eloi, where they too were placed under the 2nd Cavalry Division and directed to support the 3rd Cavalry Brigade. On 26 October orders were issued for an attack on that portion of the German lines which formed a wedge from Gapaard running north-west to Wambeek and then bending north-east to Houthem. The attacks would be carried out by the 1st and 2nd Cavalry Divisions. The 1st Division would hold Messines and provide fire support for the Connaughts on the right and Wilde's Rifles on the left attacking towards Wambeek/Gapaard, while the 2nd Division would assault Wambeek/Houthem with the 129th Baluchis as the right-hand battalion of the assault brigade, the other two brigades in the division remaining in close reserve. It was to be the first offensive action undertaken by units of the Indian Corps on the Western Front.

The attack began at 1500 hours. It achieved little, other than perhaps a delay to the Germans' own plans, but as the Indian Corps' first taste of offensive action it is significant. They suffered very few casualties, received a relatively inexpensive teach-in to warfare on the Western Front and showed that they were able to operate in conjunction with British units and formations. Perhaps most important of all they showed the British Army, in the shape of the Cavalry Corps, that their vaunted fighting spirit was not just legend: they had gone forward with alacrity, had come under enemy artillery and machine-gun fire and they had stood it well. It was but a gentle introduction to what was to come.

The night of 26 October was 'quiet' and on the 27th Wilde's Rifles was relieved and took up a position between Wytschaete and Oost Taverne.

On that date the Connaught Rangers were with the 1st Cavalry Division, the 129th Baluchis with the 3rd Cavalry Brigade, half of Wilde's Rifles with the 4th Cavalry Brigade and the other half with the 5th, while Battalion Headquarters was still in Wytschaete. On the 28th a further distribution took place. The Connaughts were replaced in the 1st Cavalry Division at Messines by two companies of Wilde's Rifles and sent south with the Ferozepore Brigade Headquarters to rejoin the Lahore Division. By the end of that day Wilde's Rifles was spread over five miles of front with one company and the Machine-Gun Section in support of the 4th Cavalry Brigade, one company in support of the 5th Cavalry Brigade and two companies operating under the 3rd Cavalry Brigade. The 129th Baluchis remained with the 3rd Cavalry Brigade whose Indian strength now exceeded that of its British component. During this period the German artillery bombardment continued. Messines was heavily shelled throughout and the Germans made a number of what appeared to be faint-hearted (but were probably feint) attacks all along the front. The British guns, considerably inferior in numbers to those of the Germans, made answer as the shell supply situation allowed. There was a wind from the east which brought with it a ground mist, and British air reconnaissance—the only arm in which the British could mount a local advantage over the Germans—was unable to see anything. On the night of 28/29 October sentries, patrols and observation posts all along the Ypres Salient reported sounds of massive enemy movement; horses, horse-drawn and motor transport and marching feet. It was evident that something serious was in the offing.

At 0600 hours on the morning of 30 October a very heavy bombardment was opened on the positions of the 2nd Cavalry Division, and on those of the 3rd Cavalry Division in Zandvoorde. Messines, from which the civilian inhabitants had now been evacuated, received shells in all parts of the town and many of the buildings were destroyed. Shortly after this bombardment the Germans attacked with infantry along the axis of the Menin Road, which leads from Menin north-east towards and through the Ypres Salient. Two squadrons of the Household Cavalry Regiment were effectively obliterated. The 2nd Cavalry Division was forced back to the ridge of Klein Zillebeck, about two and a half miles nearer Ypres, where it managed to hold until nightfall. While this was going on the 1st Cavalry Division, in whose 2nd Brigade were the 129th Baluchis and two companies of Wilde's Rifles, was also being subjected to increasingly heavy artillery fire. The brigade staff calculated that, whereas previously there had been but six guns firing upon their section of front, there were now 40. By mid-day it was clear that the Germans were preparing a major attack on the 2nd Cavalry Brigade, and at 1230 hours the 5th Lancers, the British cavalry regiment in the line and numerically weaker than an infantry company even before the casualties of the past few days, were attacked by two German battalions. The Lancers held on until they had lost 30 out of only

90 men present. They then withdrew. The Cavalry Corps had now become so weak that the defence consisted of a thin scattering of isolated posts, which allowed the enemy to capture one post and then enfilade others in turn. It was clear that the present positions could not be held and a general withdrawal was ordered. The troops were fortunate in that the Germans had halted briefly to regroup and resupply and, although the line fell back in daylight with the enemy belatedly continuing their attack, most units reached their secondary defensive positions satisfactorily. Most, but not all. The Punjabi Mussalman Company of Wilde's Rifles under Lieutenant Forbes, defending the area near Oost Taverne, did not receive the order to retire in time. Perhaps the enemy artillery had cut all the telephone wires and runners had been shot trying to get through. We shall never know. In any event, by the time the order did get through Forbes and his men were isolated, enfiladed by machine-gun fire on both flanks and with the enemy infantry upon them. Forbes now attempted to retire by half companies, the Company Officer, Lieutenant Clarke, taking the first two platoons back. It was of no avail. Shattered by machine-gun fire from close range, Clarke and most of his men were killed or wounded. Forbes eventually managed to withdraw the remnants of both half companies to Wytschaete where he took up a position a quarter of a mile north-east of that village. Of the 140 men with whom Forbes had started the day only 60 were left and he himself was wounded.

Wilde's Sikh Company was luckier. It was composed largely of recruits who had not long emerged from basic training but their position, farther south, was not so heavily shelled. The Company Commander, Major Williams, began to withdraw them by half companies, two platoons moving back 40 yards or so and then lying down to give covering fire to the other two platoons who would leapfrog back and give covering fire in turn. They had got a few hundred yards back into a shallow valley when the Germans, accompanied by a great deal of shouting and blowing of bugles, reached the Sikh Company's old position. The Germans were now silhouetted against the sky and the whole company and the 9th Bhopal machine-guns (detached to Wilde's) opened up and caused considerable damage and a stop to any further bugle blowing. Williams then withdrew the company to the east side of the Wytschaete/Messines road.

In the same brigade as Wilde's Punjabi Mussalman and Sikh Companies, the 129th Baluchis too had a trying day. On the morning of 30 October Numbers 1 and 2 Companies had gone into the forward positions while the other two companies were relieved by cavalry and ordered back to billets in rear. Despite fairly heavy enemy fire, Number 4 Company was withdrawn intact to the reserve trenches, such as they were, but Number 3 Company was the object of heavy shelling. While one platoon reached the reserve line safely, the other three had to take shelter behind a farm just to the rear of the forward positions. At about 0630 hours the German bombardment which had been falling on Wilde's Rifles for the past half hour was extended to the 129th Baluchis' position and Number 4 Company, in the reserve line, took some casualties including the Company Commander, Major Humphreys, who was killed. This was, of course, a good time to begin an attack as the relief in the line was still taking place and there were men moving about who would otherwise have been under cover. Many British officers were of the view that it was the Germans' 'elaborate system of espionage'[1] which informed them that a relief was taking place, and this paranoia with spies is a constant theme in contemporaneous accounts. In fact it is much more likely that it was the German use of the Mark I eyeball and ear which told them that a relief was imminent. Most Frenchmen had a real hatred for the Germans, born of the humiliation of 1870, and any French assistance to the enemy, or Germans disguised as Frenchmen and spying behind the lines, would have been quickly detected and dealt with.

At around 1200 hours the men in the firing line were being hard pressed by German infantry and machine-guns, in addition to continuing shelling, and all available men of the 129th were ordered into the forward positions. While on the way up the 129th men met the whole of the line retiring. Now began an untidy series of manoeuvres whereby one company of the 129th went into a wood which they held to cover the withdrawal of the remainder, before retiring itself. This retirement was assisted to some extent by the battalion's two machine-guns, under Captain Dill. Dill was badly wounded in the head and one gun was put out of action by enemy fire. The crew of the other gun fought on until all except one were killed. The survivor, Sepoy Khudadad Khan a Pathan, was himself severely wounded and when the Germans finally rushed the position he feigned death, later crawling away and rejoining the rest of the regiment. For his gallantry that day Khudadad was later awarded the Victoria Cross, the first to an Indian soldier, and it was presented to him by King George V personally in hospital behind the lines in December 1914. By the end of the war he would be a subadar Major. At about 1600 hours on 30 October the 129th Baluchis were ordered to take up a defensive position in some trenches to the north of their original position. This they did, and by dusk the battalion was reunited and ready to face what the night might bring.

The night would bring tragedy, although it would fall not upon the 129th Baluchis but on the Afridi and Dogra Companies of Wilde's Rifles farther south, where they had taken up position between two cavalry regiments covering Messines. The Afridi Company had one British officer, the Company Commander, Captain Gordon, while the Dogra Company was commanded by Major Barwell with Lieutenant Molony as Company Officer. Just after 0300 hours on the morning of 31 October Messines was assaulted by nine German battalions. The enemy was described as coming on in a jog trot and making 'raucous, guttural sounds'. Supported by artillery and then machine-guns, the German infantry closed on Wilde's defensive positions. Major Barwell was killed almost immediately, as was Captain Gordon when he attempted a counter-attack on Barwell's company's position which was being overrun. This left one British officer, Lieutenant Molony, erstwhile company officer and now commander of two companies. As the Dogra Company had managed to hollow out firing positions and dig trenches along a hedge line, they were able to fire on the enemy without the latter being able to see them, despite part of the Afridi Company's area, to Molony's right, having been captured by the enemy. A fire fight between Indian and German went on for about two hours until the Germans managed to bring up a machine-gun and bring fire to bear on Molony's men from the captured trench on his right. Molony pulled his men back 20 yards to where they could lie down in a small depression from where they continued to fire on the enemy. By now it was about 0600 hours, and Molony was badly wounded in the arm. As it was still dark his men decided to drag him back to where medical attention could be applied, but before he was taken off the field Molony instructed his two Indian officers that they were to hold the position and only to retire should the British cavalry on either side do so. The cavalry, also under attack but not at the point of the assault as were Wilde's men, did not retire and the fast reducing remnants of the Dogra Company fought on, preventing the Germans from breaking through. Eventually only the two Indian officers, Jemadars Ram Singh and Kapur Singh, were capable of firing their weapons, command having devolved upon Kapur Singh when Ram Singh was badly wounded. At this stage the ammunition was about to run out and there was nobody to go back to get some more. Jemadar Kapur Singh, the commander of the post and the only man not dead or wounded, used his last round to shoot himself.

Why did Kapur Singh find suicide necessary? Nobody today would blame him if he had surrendered or retired—he had no men and no ammunition, he had done his best and there was nothing more that he could do. Even in 1914 few would have held him culpable for the collapse of the defence, certainly not any British officer. While we cannot say what went through Jemadar Kapur Singh's mind before he rolled onto his rifle and blew his brains out over the grass in the wet, cold darkness of a winter morning in France, we can surmise that faced with the impossibility of the situation, Izzat demanded that he must follow his dead sepoys as the only way to reconcile two opposing imperatives. Dogras in the Indian Army of 1914 came mainly from the hills between the Punjab and Kashmir, some from Jammu, a princely state, and from Kangra, a British Himalayan territory. They were members of the old Aryan Hindu stock who had avoided Islam and had resisted the blandishments of Sikhism. MacMunn, the pre-war authority on the Indian races, described Dogras as 'of good behaviour, courtly manners, high courage and physical endurance'[2]. Others described them as stolid, even priggish, and one of their British commanders felt that 'worthy' was the most appropriate one-word description of a Dogra. Whatever adjectives may be applied to Kapur Singh's unnecessary waste of his life in the midst of so much waste, his action secured for him a place in the mythology of his village and his regiment which endures to this day, and perhaps that is what he most wanted.

At this point there was no British officer anywhere in the Wilde's two companies' area, confused fighting was still going on, no one was quite sure exactly where the forward positions were, ammunition was running short, no reinforcement was imminent and it was beginning to get light. The senior Indian officer, Subadar Arsla Khan, a Pathan, led a counter attack of such men as were available in the support line, but he was driven back with heavy losses. Arsla Khan realised, in the rapidly growing daylight, the utter hopelessness of his position and effected a skilful withdrawal of what was left of the Afridi and Dogra Companies back to the ruins of Messines itself, where they took up improvised defensive positions. For his presence of mind and tactical good sense, Subadar Arsla Khan was later awarded the OBI Second Class, with the title of Bahadur.

While the Afridi and Dogra Companies of Wilde's Rifles were fighting for their lives at Messines, the wrath of the enemy was to fall once more on the remnants of Captain Forbes' Punjabi Mussalman Company, which had spent the night of the 30th to the north-east of Wytschaete. Forbes' band held on as long as they could, but superior numbers and weight of fire told and the Germans managed to penetrate the position, actually getting into some of the trenches. One trench, more properly a ditch, was held by a Havildar Ganga Singh, who when not employed in more martial duties, was a Physical Training instructor and incidentally the Ferozepore District bayonet fencing champion. Havildar Ganga Singh probably did not know a great deal about the theory or history of bayonet fighting, but that he knew the practicalities of the art is evident by his killing of five Germans with his bayonet before it broke. He then picked up a sword (probably German—officers of the Indian Army had abandoned their swords even earlier than their British counterparts) and fought on until he collapsed through pain and loss of blood from no fewer than five wounds. He survived, was recovered when the trench was eventually retaken, and was awarded the IOM Second Class. Shortly afterwards a counter-attack was delivered by the 5th Dragoon Guards and what was left of Wilde's two companies, which succeeded in reinstating Wilde's in their original positions.

The night of 30 October had passed reasonably quietly for the 129th Baluchis and a number of French units were fed in to support the sector, a move which was to cause some confusion. In the early hours of 31 October three companies of the 129th were sent into the line to support the 18th Hussars, taking over a number of their trenches.

The fourth company of the 129th Baluchis under Major Potter had been holding a small farm when, at about midnight, the sentries saw a party of men marching towards them. The newcomers made no attempt to conceal themselves and showed no aggressive intent. They were clearly not British, but as the enemy would not approach with such confidence they must surely be French. It was only when the advancing party was almost in the farm that the truth was realised: these were Germans! It was too late—Major Potter's men killed ten or so but were forced to withdraw to a trench 50 yards to the rear of the farm. At about 0300 hours the 129th counter-attacked the farm, drove the Germans into the buildings and then pursued them with the bayonet. Here again the defender could not avoid hand-to-hand combat and many were bayoneted by the sepoys. In all ten Germans were killed, three wounded and 14 surrendered, the rest having retreated at speed. This action was the last for the 129th Baluchis in this sector, as they were now ordered to hand over their trenches to French dismounted cavalry, rejoin the Ferozepore Brigade and proceed south to be reunited with the Indian Corps. Referring to the confused movements and happenings of the period 21 October to 1 November, the Commanding Officer of Wilde's Rifles wrote in a report to Brigade Headquarters:

It is not possible to submit a detailed report or make special mention of individuals, owing to the fact that six out of seven British officers employed with my companies were killed or wounded.[3]

The 129th Baluchis' Commanding Officer wrote in similar vein:

Owing to the casualties amongst the officers of Numbers 1 and 2 Companies I find it very hard to get any information regarding individuals.[4]

The confused fighting around Ypres in that last week of October 1914 cost Wilde's Rifles three British officers, two Indian officers and 80 Indian Other Ranks killed, and three British officers, two Indian officers and 196 IORs wounded. Of the 750 all ranks who had entered the Salient, only 460 remained. The 129th Baluchis too had been sorely tried. Their losses amounted to three British officers, three Indian officers and 64 IORs killed and four British officers, two Indian officers and 100 IORs wounded with 64 initially posted as 'missing'. The missing were at first thought to have been taken prisoner, but as portions of the abandoned line were regained, it was found that the majority had been killed, some by shot or shell, some by trenches collapsing on them and others by drowning in the dark, water-filled ditches.

While the Ferozepore Brigade had been fighting piecemeal in the Ypres Salient, the remainder of the Lahore Division—effectively the Jullunder

Brigade, to be joined by the headquarters of the Ferozepore Brigade and the 9th Bhopal Infantry—had moved south to where the men of Smith-Dorrien's II Corps (the heroes of Le Cateau) were holding from north to south the line Ratinghem/Aubers/Neuve Chapelle/Givenchy. The 3rd Division was on the British left (north) and 5 Division on the right (south). Also in that area were some French cavalry, who held a gap between two of the brigades of the 3rd Division.

On 21 October the Jullunder Brigade with the Lahore Division headquarters and divisional troops marched four miles to Renescue, and on the 22nd continued east for 15 miles to Metern. The men still had no real idea of where they might be going, a situation made even more mysterious by the issue of great piles of maps optimistically showing the ground as far east as the Rhine. On 23 October the march continued for another ten miles, south this time to Estaires via Berquin; a seemingly unnecessary jink which added several miles to the journey.

Shortly after Wilde's Rifles and the Connaught Rangers had been committed to action in the north, the 1st Manchesters and the 47th Sikhs were ordered south to take over from some French units and link up with the Gordon Highlanders of the British 8 Brigade. The Sikhs relieved a regiment of French chasseurs and were given a hurried tour of the positions before the French departed. The line here was a series of unlinked shallow trenches. There was no wire and there were no communication trenches nor a support line. The French commanding officer was most anxious to tell the 47th Sikhs that some French dead had been buried in the parapet of one of the trenches, and he would be most obliged if the bodies could remain undisturbed. The Sikhs would know where the burials were, as an arm had been left sticking out of the ground! According to the orders given to the Jullunder Brigade the French, once relieved in the front line, were to remain in reserve until replaced by British or Indian troops, but they departed to be seen no more. The trenches confirmed all the worst prejudices held by British officers about the French. No attempt had apparently been made to keep them clean, rubbish was strewn everywhere and although there had been some attempt to construct latrines the former occupants had elected to discard their waste products apparently at random.* Indian sepoys are by nature clean in their bodily habits (they washed far more often than did British soldiers), and this first experience of French trenches was to colour the opinions of the fastidious Sikhs for months to come. As it was, the 47th began to improve the position.

---

* To be fair, some British trenches were not much better. For the first part of the war at least, German defence works were far superior to those of their adversaries. The British attitude was that it was pointless making trenches comfortable as they would shortly be advancing.

Digging was difficult as heavy rain had made the ground waterlogged, but the men did what they could. The Quartermaster moved his empire up to the rear of the positions and food was prepared and carried up to the forward companies along with a rum ration for the sepoys and cigarettes for the British officers.* The British Officers' Mess staff, civilian followers, prepared a huge pan of ham and eggs and scurried from trench to trench, officers seizing what they could from the out-thrust container.

During the night there were numerous alarms but no attack materialised. The 47th Sikhs officers and NCOs kept strict fire control, the sepoys being allowed to fire only when there was a clearly identifiable target. Just before first light on the morning of 24 October, the Manchesters and the Sikhs were relieved without incident by the other two battalions of the Jullunder Brigade, the Scinde Rifles and the 15th Sikhs. It soon emerged that this was far too wide a frontage to be held by two battalions, each having to hold 1,200 yards of front with around 600 effectives, and so during the day of the 24th the divisional pioneer battalion, 1/34th Sikh Pioneers, was also fed into the front line.

The process of disintegration of the Lahore Division continued, for the Manchesters were now detached and rushed into the line at Festubert to support the British 5th Division, while the 47th Sikhs spent the day being moved north to south and back again, here being told to dig a trench line, there being placed in support of various British and French units. At last, well after dark on 24 October, the 47th were ordered to split into half battalions. One half was ordered into the line to support the rest of the Jullunder Brigade, while the other half was told to move to Croix Barbée where they would act as a reserve. In a puzzling diaspora of the command element the Jullunder Brigade headquarters first accompanied the Manchesters to Festubert, before returning and reverting to its proper role of exercising command over the rest of the brigade.

The portion of the line for which the Jullunder Brigade was responsible now ran about 300 yards east of the Rue Tilleloy from Picantin on the left to Fauquissart on the right. It was held from left to right, or north to south, by the 59th Scinde Rifles, the 1/34th Sikh Pioneers and the 15th Sikhs. The divisional cavalry regiment, 15th Lancers (Pathans and Border Moslems), were in brigade reserve at Locon while the brigade headquarters were one and half miles back at Laventie. This was too far back to exercise direct command and, as a telephone line had not yet been laid, the task of co-ordinating the activities of the three and a half battalions fell largely on the shoulders of Lieutenant Colonel Fenner, commanding the Scinde Rifles. The half battalion of the 47th Sikhs were directed to take up a position about 50 yards in rear of the 15th Sikhs, and on arrival the two companies began to dig a trench line. The 47th were instructed that they

---

* Sikhs do not smoke, but they are prodigious drinkers.

were there to counter-attack should any portion of the line be overrun: on no account were they to reinforce the front line otherwise. The battalions of the Jullunder Brigade carried on the work of improving the trench line started on the 23rd, and although the cold and the heavy rain made digging difficult, the night of the 24th was relatively quiet. It was not so quiet for the Gordon Highlanders on the right, however, for they were assaulted in strength, the Germans breaking their line and capturing a large number of prisoners before eventually being driven back.

Some humour was provided during the night when an unknown European was frog-marched before the company commander of Number 3 Company of the 47th Sikhs. Spy mania was at its height and the sepoys had observed this person skulking in rear of their position. Despite wearing a turban he was not one of the 47th Sikhs' Sahebs; he was wearing a non-regulation overcoat, and when the sepoys pounced on him and knocked off his turban, he was found to have close-cropped hair. Certain confirmation, in the Sikhs' eyes, of their prisoner's Teutonic origins was provided when he was unable to speak Punjabi. It transpired that the prisoner was in fact a British officer of the 1/34th Sikh Pioneers, on his way back to Brigade Headquarters. He explained that when he was suddenly jumped on by four burly Sikhs, he had so lost his temper that he was unable to express himself in any language, far less in Punjabi. He was given a large tot of whisky and sent on his way.

It will be recalled that on 26 October the 9th Bhopal Infantry, after escorting the baggage of the Ferozepore Brigade to the Front, had been sent south. They had first been moved to Voormezeele on 25 October and placed in 'Corps Reserve' (nobody was sure which Corps) destined to relieve Wilde's Rifles in the line on the morning of 26 October. On that morning they duly fell in on the road when at 0830 hours fresh orders arrived informing the battalion that it would move by bus to Vieille Chapelle for an as yet unspecified task. The buses did not arrive until 1700 hours, just as it was getting dark, and the battalion duly set off. While the distance from Voormezeele to Vieille Chapelle is but 23 miles, the need to negotiate shell holes and damaged buildings meant that the 9th Bhopals did not arrive at Vieille Chapelle until 0700 hours on the morning of 27 October, when they were able to cook a hurried breakfast. At 1100 hours the battalion were ordered to move to Rouge Croix, where they found the half battalion of the 47th Sikhs which had been detached on the 25th. Both units were now warned for an attack on Neuve Chapelle.

The 9th Bhopals were something of an oddity within the Indian Corps in France. They had a company of Sikhs and a company of Punjabi Mussalmans, as had many of the battalions in the Corps, but they also had a company of Rajputs and one of Brahmins. Rajputs are of pure Hindu Aryan stock and, although many of them were peasant farmers and small landlords, they were traditionally the aristocrats of their race. They were found mainly in Rajhastan and in the Dogra hills. Many of the Indian nobility were of the Rajput race, and Rajputs made up the bulk of the armies of the northern princely states. Those that joined the British Indian Army tended to join the cavalry, but there were some in the infantry. They were by tradition a warrior race—they would claim *the* warrior race—and generally made good soldiers.

There were many Brahmins in the pre-1857 armies of the East India Company, and very large numbers of them had mutinied. By 1914 there were only two all-Brahmin single-battalion regiments, the 1st Brahmins and the 3rd Brahmins, with a few in other Class Company regiments. MacMunn claimed—somewhat unfairly—that the Brahmins had all been put into their own regiments so that they could intrigue together without corrupting anyone else. The problem with Brahmins was not their martial prowess—there was no lack of that—but their insistence upon observing caste restrictions even in the field. They would only eat food cooked by Brahmins and be tended by medical orderlies who were Brahmins. Due to their position in the Hindu hierarchy they demanded—and were usually given—respect and deference by other Hindus regardless of rank. On occasions newly joined British officers had unwittingly entered the cookhouse when, their shadow having fallen upon the rice, the food had to be thrown away. Replacing casualties was a problem because Brahmins could not easily be mixed in with non-Brahmins. Some even insisted on removing boots and leather equipment before eating, hardly a practical proposition on active service. Prior to going abroad at the beginning of the war, Brahmin soldiers had been asked, and had agreed, to relax caste restrictions while at the front. At first the Brahmins conformed, but as time wore on they reverted to type which meant that although hungry they often could not be fed, and although wounded they could not be tended. It was a pity, for many were big, strong men and they were generally better educated than other Indians. They fought bravely, but it was just too difficult to administer them in a multi-racial war and after 1918 their numbers were reduced still further.

The movements of the 9th Bhopals and the 47th Sikhs had now outrun their administrative tail and both units had exhausted what little food they carried with them. Fortunately for them many of the farms in the area had been abandoned by their occupants. Potatoes and wine in plentiful quantities were stored in the outbuildings, and pigs were running around in the fields. As the pigs were not being fed it seemed an act of kindness to catch them and convert them into rations for those who could eat pork, while the Brahmins and Punjabi Mussalmans were able to supplement potatoes with maize found unharvested in the fields. As looting was forbidden, requisitioning was authorised and lists of everything taken were compiled and left in the kitchens. This situation was to continue for the next few days until quartermasters could eventually make contact with their charges.

The section of the Front opposite the village of Neuve Chapelle was held by 7 and 8 British Brigades who had originally occupied a trench line running east of the village. The area had come under increasingly heavy pressure from the Germans who on 26 October had managed to occupy a corner of Neuve Chapelle itself. After desperate close-quarter fighting for most of 27 October the British managed to push the enemy out, but in the afternoon further reinforced enemy attacks forced evacuation of the village. The situation was now critical. Isolated British battalions were hanging on at the north and west of the village, but there were reports that the Germans were moving through the buildings to the south. At 1700 hours on 27 October the Lincolns were holding north-west of Neuve Chapelle and the Royal West Kents, isolated and with Commanding Officer and Adjutant both killed, to the south-west. In between these two battalions were a battalion of the Wiltshire Regiment and one of the South Lancashires. The Wiltshires and the South Lancashires had taken heavy casualties and had been pushed back to the west. They were now fighting a rearguard action trying to check the enemy prior to withdrawing farther once it became full dark. It was clear that unless something was done, and that quickly, the Germans would force a gap between the two British brigades and then break out to the west, thus endangering the whole of the British 2nd Corps.

The 9th Bhopals and the half battalion 47th Sikhs were now told by an agitated staff officer to move forward for a counter-attack. With the Sikhs as advance guard the little force set off from Rouge Croix in column of platoons with the right flank on the La Bassée road, now the D947. Although the distance was only 3,000 yards, progress was slow because of the rain-filled ditches, the boggy ground, German artillery fire and the farmers' wire fences which had to be negotiated. Halting short of the British forward positions, just west of what is now the D170, the force had to split. The commander of the 47th Sikhs half battalion, Major Davidson, moved forward to make contact with the British troops when he met Lieutenant Colonel Smith, commanding the Lincolns. Smith explained that his battalion was exhausted and that the Germans had driven a wedge into the middle of his line; he had no local reserves and an immediate counter-attack was required. Davidson ran back to his force and brought forward the three other British officers of the 47th Sikhs, Major Browne, Captain McCleverty and Captain Brown. They crouched behind a haystack while Colonel Smith of the Lincolns began a hurried explanation of the situation. Half way through the briefing Colonel Smith, in the grip of total exhaustion as were most of his men, fell asleep, but Major Davidson was able to find out from other officers of the Lincolns where the enemy and friendly positions were, and had heard enough to concoct a quick plan for the counter-attack. Major Browne was to take Number 1 Company, move up a ditch and attack the left of the Lincolns' erstwhile position, while Captain

McCleverty was to attack straight ahead with half of Number 4 Company. The other half of that company was to remain in reserve under Captain Brown. There was no artillery available—the time had not yet come when the guns could provide instant local fire support—and the advance had to be made over 200 yards of open ground. As soon as the 47th Sikhs got up to advance they came under German artillery, machine-gun and rifle fire but, amazingly, they reached the German occupied positions with the loss of only seven killed and 28 wounded. Amongst the wounded was Major Browne, hit almost as soon as he stood up, command of his company being assumed by Subadar Thakur Singh. Thakur Singh led his company with great gallantry and determination until he too was wounded. He was later awarded the Military Cross.[*]

The 47th Sikhs drove the Germans out of the Lincoins' trenches, stabilised the position and set to work digging an improved set of trenches on the Lincolns' right. Major Davidson returned to the battalion headquarters of the Lincolns where he found that an order from the British brigade had arrived telling him on no account to become involved in the fighting unless it was 'absolutely necessary'. It was bit late, but in any case there can be no doubt that his actions were 'absolutely necessary' if the integrity of the British defence was to be maintained.

While the 47th Sikhs were assisting the Lincolns, the 9th Bhopals were ordered to bolster the Royal West Kents at the other end of the fast developing gap. The Kents had continued to hold their positions but, due to the withdrawal of the Lancashires to their left (north), the Germans had been able to get round their northern flank. The Kents were now subjected to fire and probing attacks from their front (east), from their left and from behind. The 9th Bhopal arrived on the left flank of the Lincolns, which was also the right flank of the Germans, and were able to drive the enemy off and re-establish the Royal West Kents' left-hand positions. The Indians now began to entrench on the left of the Royal West Kents, this being made more difficult by the lack of proper spades and the sepoys having only the small Sirhind entrenching tool which each man carried as part of his equipment.

The situation had been stabilised, but only temporarily as there was still a gap between the 47th Sikhs' half battalion to the Lincolns' right and the 9th Bhopals on the Royal West Kents' left. To fill that gap the 20th and 21st Companies Sappers and Miners, the engineer units of the Lahore Division, were moved up into the line. They were absolutely the last available reserve, and indeed had they not been, they would never have been used, as infantry, for they were too few and their skills too precious to be squandered in such a way.

---

[*] By now Indian officers were eligible for the MC like British officers, although as it carried with it neither a title nor an increment to pay and pension, Thakur Singh would probably have preferred the OBI.

Enemy shelling continued into the night and a German searchlight played on the British and Indian positions, making reorganisation particularly difficult. As dawn broke on 28 October the line was held by the Lincolns on the left and then, running north-east to south-west, by Number 20 Company Sappers and Miners, the half battalion 47th Sikhs, Number 21 Company Sappers and Miners, the 9th Bhopal Infantry and the Royal West Kents. During the night Major General Sir Colin MacKenzie, the divisional commander responsible for that sector of the front, had been making strenuous efforts to scrape together enough troops for an attack on Neuve Chapelle in order to remove the dangerous salient which the Germans had created by their capture of the village. At 0800 hours Major Davidson, commanding the detachment of the 47th Sikhs, Captain Paris RE, commanding 20 Company Sappers and Miners and Captain Richardson RE, commanding 21 Company Sappers and Miners were summoned to Richebourg St Vaast where they were given orders for an attack on Neuve Chapelle. Lieutenant Colonel Dobbie, Commanding Officer 9th Bhopals was also summoned, for he was to command the attack, but he did not receive the summons and was only made aware of what was to happen when written orders were delivered to him some hours later. Dobbie was much loved by the men of the 9th Bhopals. He was 51 years old, having been commissioned in 1885, had been promoted to lieutenant colonel in 1910 and was already a sick man before the battalion left India. Despite this he held on in order to command his beloved regiment in war. The stress of battle on the Western Front was already taking its toll of his faculties and this, coupled with his absence at the conference at Richebourg St Vaast, did contribute to the confusion which was to accompany the assault.

The attack was to be spearheaded by the half battalion 47th Sikhs and the Sappers and Miners, with the 9th Bhopal in close support. The right of the attack would be supported by the 2nd British Cavalry Brigade, while the left would be assisted by a battalion of French chasseurs, a detachment of French cyclists (dismounted), a battalion of The Royal Scots and a battalion of The North Staffordshire Regiment. The artillery would open the attack with a 15-minute bombardment at 1100 hours. The verbal orders stated that, as a control mechanism, the advance was to be 'By the right', the written orders[5] said that units were to keep in contact on both left and right and Colonel Dobbie thought that units were meant to advance independently.[6]

At 1100 hours the artillery duly opened up, firing on the village and on the German-occupied positions to the east. At 1115 hours the half battalion 47th Sikhs flanked by the two companies of Sappers and Miners moved off towards Neuve Chapelle, about 700 yards away. Despite the lack of cover and fierce enemy fire the 47th Sikhs and the Sappers and Miners got to within 100 yards of the village when they saw the Germans leave their outposts and run back into the buildings. The Indians charged and caught some of the fleeing enemy, before finding themselves on the outskirts of the village where they came under very heavy fire from houses which the Germans had spent the night putting in a state for defence.

As the 47th Sikhs' half battalion fought its way towards the centre of the village, Captain McCleverty, who had commanded Number 4 Company in the operation to stabilise the Lincoln's position on the night of 26 October, was shot through the head by a sniper hidden in a house. Amid the close-quarter fighting Major Davidson, commanding the half battalion, attempted to stalk the sniper with drawn revolver, to no avail. A group of Punjabi Mussalman sappers, observing this, shouted to Davidson to stand aside and leave the sniper to them. Kneeling in the middle of the main street, with bullets whistling about him, one sapper waited calmly until the sniper popped his head out to take another shot, when he shot him dead. His task complete the sapper moved off to re-join his company. In the heat of the battle no one ever did find out who this sapper was and he was denied the decoration that would undoubtedly have come his way.[*]

By now the 47th Sikhs and the Sapper and Miner Companies were well into the centre of the village, but the carefully sited and concealed German machine-gunners were taking their toll. Captain Paris of 20 Company was wounded, refused to be taken to the rear and was taken prisoner. Captain Richardson led a charge of some of his 21 Company men which actually penetrated to the far (east) side of the village when he too was killed. Lieutenant Rait Kerr, one of the two subalterns of 20 Company attempted to go back to find some more men to bring up. He was shot and wounded before he had got 100 yards. A group of Germans attempted to take the helpless officer prisoner but Rait Kerr's orderly, Sapper Dulit Singh, drove off the would-be captors, dragged his officer into the shelter of a ruined building and continued to defend him against other attackers before eventually carrying him off the field. The bitter fighting continued until at last most of the village was in Indian hands. It was now mid afternoon. Major Davidson, seeing that there was now no second line behind him, sent a message back to the 2nd Cavalry Division telling them to come forward. No one appeared. It transpired that the message was received but someone (no one knows who) countermanded it.

There was no second line behind Davidson because the 9th Bhopals had passed either side of the village and had succeeded in reaching the trench

[*]   In 1921 Davidson, by now a Major general commanding the Jhansi Brigade Area, recognised one of the sappers who had taken part in the incident. He was now Subadar Shah Nawaz Khan of the 2/107th Pioneers. Davidson had the immense satisfaction of ensuring that the man received the OBI which he had earned seven years before.

line previously held by the Wiltshires.[*] Scrambling into the trenches the Bhopals attempted to defend them against German counter attacks. At first they held the line, while behind them the remnants of the 47th Sikhs and the Sappers and Miners tried to reorganise their scattered forces and consolidate their hold on the village. Had reinforcement been available they might have succeeded but there was no one immediately available to come to their aid: the 2nd Cavalry Division and the French chasseurs and cyclists with the Royal Scots and the North Staffords were fully occupied on the flanks, and when the German strength opposite began to build up and a particularly heavy counter-attack supported by artillery began, withdrawal became inevitable. The 9th Bhopals withdrew by companies from the left with the Commanding Officer and a few men being the last to pull back.

Poor Colonel Dobbie; the strain was just too much for him and, a brave man unable to cope with the loss of so many of his soldiers, he broke down completely and after the withdrawal had to be evacuated sick[†]. Captain G A Jamieson, the senior surviving British officer, took over command of the battalion, regrouping near Pont Logis at about 2100 hours.

The 47th Sikhs and the Sappers and Miners withdrew from Neuve Chapelle over the 800 yards of open ground in good order. It was dark except for the light of burning buildings and they moved back to the Rue Tilleloy by bounds[‡], groups providing covering fire for each other.

Of the 280 men of the half battalion of the 47th Sikhs who had been detached on 24 October, only 68 were fit to fight by the night of the 28th. The 9th Bhopal casualties since the 25th amounted to six British officers (of whom three were killed), five Indian officers (two killed) and 262 rank and file. Every single British officer of the Sappers and Miners was killed or wounded and a third of each company became casualties.

The German counter-attack reached the village, lapped beyond it to the west, and then ran out of impetus. It was probably a mistake for the British to try to re-take the village of Neuve Chapelle on 28 October. There had been only just sufficient troops to stabilise the fast crumbling British line the day before, and to expect those same troops, deprived of rest or proper food for the past two days, to go on to capture the village against determined and growing opposition was surely asking too much. They did capture the village, at fearful cost, but to capture a position and then

---

[*] This was the line of trenches known as 'The Smith-Dorrien Line' and was to feature prominently in the March 1915 battle of Neuve Chapelle.

[†] He never returned to active service and retired in August 1915.

[‡] In military terminology a tactical bound is that distance, or portion of ground, which can be covered by a man or group of men without pausing. While covering that bound another man or group of men will give covering fire.

to hold it are two different things. Nevertheless, the gap in the British line had been closed and would not be broken in this sector again; some British soldiers captured on the 27th had been recovered and the Indian regiments had shown that they could hold their own on the Western Front.

A naik of the 47th Sikhs, wounded and evacuated to hospital in England wrote to a relative in Amritsar:

> If it be the will of God I will some day tell you the whole story. In the meantime I write this much. On 28th October in the evening while in the act of charging I was wounded by the enemy's machine-gun bullet. My company suffered heavy loss and inflicted the same upon the enemy, many of whom were taken prisoner and many killed. Before this too we had heavy fighting and our troops had proved their fidelity to the government, so that our renown was very great. Well, when I was wounded I came to England and many men of the Indian troops have come to England. Now I am all right again. My wound healed very quickly. The fighting is still going on just the same. I hope we shall soon be victorious. So you are all well and happy, but our brothers who are in the trenches have endured sufferings beyond the powers of words to describe. When God grants me to see you again I will tell you the whole story. I think you will not believe what I tell you of the fighting, of our ships and of our fights with the bayonet. I have seen such sights that my wits are still amazed … [7]

During what came to be entitled the Battle of First Ypres such of the Indian Corps as had arrived at the Front was still scattered in penny packets, thrown in where reinforcement was desperately needed and acting as the equivalent of damage control parties. It was at this stage (29 October) that the Corps Commander, Sir James Willcocks, wrote in his diary:

> Where is my Lahore Division?
> Sirhind Brigade: detained in Egypt.
> Ferozepore Brigade: Somewhere in the north, split up into three or four lots.
> Jullunder Brigade: Manchesters gone south to [British] 5 Division. (This disposes of only British unit).
> 47th Sikhs: Half fighting with some British division; half somewhere else!
> 59th Rifles and 15th Sikhs. In trenches. 34th Pioneers (Divisional troops) also in trenches.
> 15th Lancers. In trenches. Two companies of Sappers and Miners fighting as infantry with British division.
> Divisional Headquarters. Somewhere?
> Thank heaven the Meerut Division will get a better chance.[8]

One cannot but sympathise with the Corps Commander's frustrations, but there was simply no alternative. If the Marne was the critical battle of September 1914—critical in that had the Germans not been stopped the Allies could have lost the war—then First Ypres was the critical battle of October. Had the German assaults down the Menin Road succeeded, or had they been able to break through at Neuve Chapelle, then the whole of the BEF position might have been rendered untenable, with the Germans being able to reach the Channel Ports and force British withdrawal—if not from the war at least from the continent. The Lahore Division's contribution was perhaps peripheral, in that they had not faced the main German onslaught, but it was vital in bolstering up the Cavalry Corps and in closing the gap at Neuve Chapelle. While it was perhaps hyperbole to say that they had 'Saved the Empire', it was certainly true that they had saved the BEF.

SOURCE NOTES

1. Stated in *The Indian Corps in France* (2nd Edn), Merewether and Smith, John Murray, London, 1919.
2. *The Armies of India*, G MacMunn, Sampson, Low, Marston and Co Ltd, 1911.
3. Quoted in *With the Indians in France,* Lt Gen Sir James Willcocks, Constable & Co, London, 1920. The Indian Corps Commander's own account of his tenure.
4. Ibid.
5. Quoted verbatim in *47th Sikhs War Record in the Great War 1914 – 1918,* Picton Publishing, Chippenham, 1991.
6. *Solah Punjab, the History of the 16th Punjab Regiment*, Lawford and Catto, Gale & Polden, Aldershot, 1967.
7. 'Report of the Censor of Indian Mails France 1914 – 1918 Vol I', India Office Library and Records, L/MIL/5/825
8. *With the Indians in France.*

IV

A Sector of their Own

The Meerut Division and the bulk of the Secunderabad Cavalry Brigade had arrived at Marseilles on 12 October, the infantry getting to Orléans on 21 October and the cavalry on the 23rd. The pleasant weather which greeted the Lahore Division's arrival in France was not repeated, and even with their long johns and extra pullovers the men were quickly wet through. Ideally the Division would have had ten days or so at Orléans to accustom themselves to the horse-drawn transport and new weapons issued to them, but time was not to be had: the British line was under severe pressure and every rifle was needed. The Division embussed on a series of trains on 26 October and arrived at Lillers and other stations in the vicinity on 28 and 29 October. Half of the Dehra Dun Brigade, consisting of the 2/2nd Gurkhas and the 1st Seaforths, detrained at St Thiennes at 0400 hours on 28 October and marched the eight miles to Merville, arriving at 0940. At 1700 hours they were ordered to Vieille Chapelle and covered the five miles in seven hours, being hindered by the dark and by the propensity of their recently acquired horse transport to depart from the line of march at speed and in whichever direction individual equines seemed to think fit.

The other half of the Dehra Dun Brigade, the 6th Jats and the 1/9th Gurkhas, arrived at Merville at 0230 hours on 28 October and were billeted in a school, where they remained for the rest of the day, marching to Vieille Chapelle to be reunited with the rest of the Brigade on the afternoon of 29 October. The Garhwal Brigade had arrived at Lillers at 1400 hours on the 28th and had then marched seven miles to Colonne Sur Le Lys. With all four battalions of the brigade on the road, followed by four battalions' worth of transport, the equine confusion was even greater than that of the Dehra Dun Brigade, and the seven-mile march was not completed until 1915 hours when the troops were distributed to various public buildings and a mill for the night. Early next morning the Brigade was on the road again. After ten miles they had a short halt at Les Glatignes, a group of houses about three miles from the Front, before arriving at Les Facons.

The Bareilly Brigade left Orléans on 26 October and detrained at Hazebrouck on the 28th, whence it marched the 15 miles to Gorre, pausing to round up errant transport wagons on the way. The Brigade was without the Afridi Company of Vaughan's Rifles, as some of that company's sepoys had contracted chicken pox in Marseilles and had to be placed in isolation, not being reunited with the battalion until 9 November.

So far such units of the Indian Corps as had reached the Front had been thrown into the battle as they arrived. The normal chain of command had virtually ceased to exist, and the plugging of gaps and local counter-attacks were often the results of commanders of hard pressed units begging support in person from other units less heavily involved. Once battalions began to deploy, communications to brigade headquarters were not sufficiently responsive to allow the brigade commander to exercise much influence, and battalions were simply grabbed and placed under command of whoever happened to be the senior officer in the sector. Great Plan there was none, and that the haphazard local arrangements and old boy network co-operation worked (and insofar as the Germans did not succeed in forcing a breakthrough they did work) says far more for the flexibility of junior commanders on the ground than it does for any overall strategy.

The battle that would come to be known as First Ypres would not come to an official end until 11 November. If the crisis had not yet passed, then at least by 28 October it looked as if it would pass. Some order could now be imposed upon expediency and the Indian Corps was ordered to take over its own section of the front, a total length of about ten miles from Rouges Bancs (a mile north of Fromelles) in the north, and running south to Givenchy. It was not the most salubrious portion of the British line. Mainly farm land interspersed with man-made drainage ditches, small orchards and wire fences, it was low lying and with a high water table. A major crop was sugar beet, which gives off a particularly unpleasant smell when being processed; a smell which many soldiers considered to be worse than that of rotting bodies. The Indian Corps was to take over from II Corps, now exhausted and short of men, and would remain in this same area until November 1915.

A point which had perhaps not been fully appreciated by the Commander-in-Chief of the BEF was that, although on paper the Indian Corps was constructed like any other corps (it had two divisions each with three brigades, each brigade with four battalions), it was in fact much smaller numerically than its British equivalent. A British battalion at war establishment numbered 1,000 all ranks, the increase over the peacetime strength being accomplished by the recall of reservists on mobilisation. An Indian battalion numbered only around 750. Additionally, the six British battalions in the Indian Corps came to France at their Indian, peace, establishment* which meant that even if all six

---

* Theoretically the establishment of a British battalion in India was increased to take account of the impossibility of its reservists joining speedily in time of war, but in fact all the British battalions of the Indian Corps seem to have been well under strength.

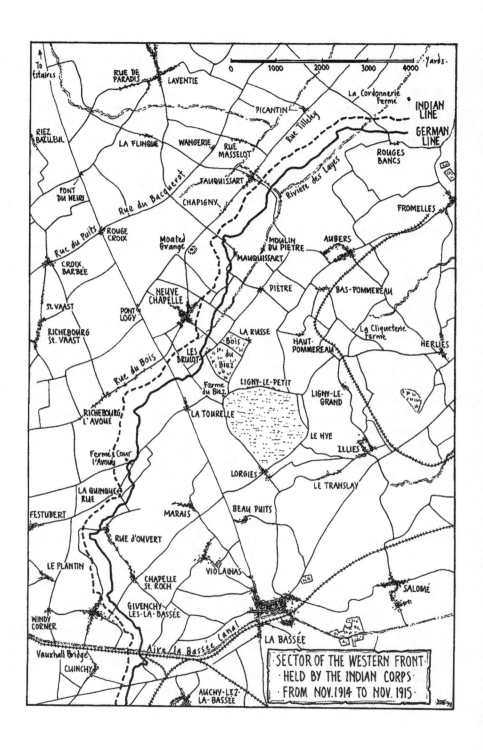

To Estaires
RUE DE PARADIS
LAVENTIE
PICANTIN
La Cordonnerie Ferme
INDIAN LINE
GERMAN LINE
RIEZ BAILLEUL
LA FLINQUE
WANGERIE
RUE MASSELOT
Rue Tilleloy
ROUGES BANCS
PONT DU NEIRI
Rue du Bacquerot
FAUQUISSART
Rivière des Layes
CHAPIGNY
FROMELLES
Rue du Puits
ROUGE CROIX
Moated Grange
MOULIN DU PIETRE
AUBERS
CROIX BARBEE
MAUQUISSART
BAS-POMMEREAU
ST. VAAST
NEUVE CHAPELLE
PIÈTRE
PONT LOGY
La Cliqueterie Ferme
RICHEBOURG St. VAAST
LA RUSSE
HAUT-POMMEREAU
HERLIES
Rue du Bois
Bois du Biez
LES BRULOT
Ferme du Biez
LIGNY-LE-PETIT
LIGNY-LE-GRAND
RICHEBOURG L'AVOUE
LA TOURELLE
LE HYE
ILLIES
Ferme Cour l'Avoui
LORGIES
LA QUINQUE RUE
LE TRANSLAY
FESTUBERT
MARAIS
BEAU PUITS
RUE D'OUVERT
LE PLANTIN
CHAPELLE St. ROCH
VIOLAINAS
SALOMÉ
GIVENCHY LES-LA-BASSÉE
WINDY CORNER
Aire la Bassée Canal
LA BASSÉE
Vauxhall Bridge
CUINCHY
AUCHY-LEZ-LA-BASSEE

yards.
0   1000   2000   3000   4000

SECTOR OF THE WESTERN FRONT
HELD BY THE INDIAN CORPS
FROM NOV. 1914 TO NOV. 1915

brigades had been present (and the Sirhind Brigade was still in Egypt), there were around 6,000 men fewer in the Indian Corps than there would be in a fresh British corps. This is before taking into account the casualties which the battalions of the Lahore Division had already suffered.

The Indian Corps took over its portion of the line on the night of 29 October. The Lahore Division lacked not only its Sirhind Brigade but also the Ferozepore Brigade which had not yet rejoined from the north, so two British brigades were lent to the Corps as a temporary measure. Most of the Jullunder Brigade was already in the line so they took charge of the northern sector, spread between Rouges Bancs and Fauquissart, with the Meerut Division being responsible for the line Rue des Lurons down to Givenchy. The gap between the two divisions, from Fauquissart to Rue des Lurons, was held by 8 British Brigade, while the second borrowed brigade was used to bolster other thinly held sectors of the Indian Corps' front.

The Meerut Division put all three of its brigades into the line, the Dehra Dun Brigade linking up with the British Brigade and covering the west of Neuve Chapelle as far as Port Arthur, as the junction of the D171 and the main Estaires to La Bassée roads came to be known, while the Garhwal Brigade line ran as far as Verte Feuille, south of Richebourg, and the Bareilly Brigade took the line on down to Givenchy.[1] The Meerut Division was fresh, up to strength and keen to get going. All along the line on the night of 29 October small parties from the Meerut Division's battalions moved forward and made contact with the British units they were to relieve. It rained heavily all night which was unpleasant but did at least mask any noise made by the movement of troops up and down. Some battalions were luckier than others. The 2/2nd Gurkhas, the left-hand battalion of the Dehra Dun Brigade, were to take over from the Northumberland Fusiliers. The Fusiliers had only taken over their trenches the night before during the reorganisation consequent upon the loss of Neuve Chapelle. It was a particularly exposed part of the line, being only 500 yards from the German-occupied village at its nearest point. As much fighting had taken place in the vicinity, the trenches, those few which had been dug at all, were badly battered and offered little protection. The approach was across open ground upon which the Germans would regularly fire a salvo of shells on the off chance of catching somebody. Despite this the 2/2nd Gurkhas occupied their portion of the line with only four men and a mule wounded.

The 1/9th Gurkhas were to take over their 500 yards of line from the Lincolns, and would be on the right of the 2/2nd. Moving up in the dark along the D170 from Pont Logis towards their rendezvous with the Lincolns, the battalion was led by their chief interpreter, a French officer known to all as Monsieur Penon. M. Penon was a rotund officer, and in keeping with his appointment as interpreter to a Gurkha battalion he had taken to wearing a brown uniform of his own design and yellow field boots, the whole ensemble crowned with a Gurkha hat. Added to the fact that M. Penon wore pince nez and spoke English with a strong accent it was perhaps not surprising that when the battalion met the Royal Scots Fusiliers on the road, an officer of the latter battalion assumed M. Penon to be an enemy spy and rugby-tackled him, sending him sprawling in the mud. Having rescued their interpreter the battalion occupied their allotted positions with two men and a mule being wounded by shellfire. M. Penon shortly thereafter reverted to wearing French blue and a kepi.

On the right of 1/9th Gurkhas were the 6th Jats and on their right, holding the area around Port Arthur and linking up with the Garhwal Brigade, the 1st Seaforths. The Garhwal Brigade were allocated the stretch of front from Port Arthur running just south of the D166 to west of La Quinque Rue and occupied it from left to right with the 2/39th Garhwalis, the 1/39th, the 2/3rd Gurkhas and the 2nd Leicesters. The 2/39th Garhwalis were to take over from a battalion of The King's Own Yorkshire Light Infantry and the reconnaissance party duly reported to an estaminet on the Rue de L'Epinette, where they were treated to a very fine dinner of roast goose, no doubt liberated from one of the farms near about. As the men of the Garhwal Brigade were moving into their assigned positions, heavy rifle fire broke out from the German trenches. It was a moonlit night but misty, so the Germans could not have seen anything, but their fire went on for half an hour, causing few casualties to either British or Indian soldiers. The Bareilly Brigade held the right of the Indian Corps front in the order 2/8th Gurkhas, 2nd Black Watch and 41st Dogras, with Vaughan's Rifles in Brigade reserve.

Meanwhile the units of the Ferozepore Brigade, who had been plugging gaps on the Ypres Salient to the north, were being extricated and moved south to join the rest of the Indian Corps. On 29 October the 9th Bhopals were withdrawn to Estaires where they were able to have their first proper meal since the 26th, after which they marched down the main La Bassée road to Pont du Hem where they arrived at 2200 hours. Next morning the battalion marched to Rue de Paradis, just west of Laventie, where they were to form a reserve. In the next few days they found themselves moved around and placed under command of a bewildering array of higher formations, the record being four different brigades in one day. Wilde's Rifles had been involved in the fighting around Messines right up until 31 October, and had lost about a third of their strength. They reorganised themselves into a two-company battalion and now found themselves as reserve for the Lahore Division. Within the Jullunder Brigade the 47th Sikhs had lost not far short of 50% of their strength, so Nos 1 and 4 Companies were amalgamated into one, and the battalion with Major Davidson now in command*, relieved

---

* The original Commanding Officer, Lt Col Richardson, had been wounded and evacuated during the battalion's action on 26 October.

the 59th Scinde Rifles on the left of the brigade front. As the 47th Sikhs had insufficient men to cover the whole of their allotted area, one company of the 59th remained behind with one of their machine-guns, two more guns being borrowed from the 15th Lancers. The 1st Manchesters returned to the brigade on 30 October and were able to relieve the 15th Sikhs.

The 2/8th Gurkhas were particularly unfortunate in the lines that they took over. As the left-hand battalion of the Bareilly Brigade they had relieved a British battalion who had occupied a drainage ditch in the triangle formed by La Quinque Rue and the D72 from Festubert, situated about a mile east-north-east of Festubert village. On the Gurkhas' right was a battalion of The Devonshire Regiment, one of the borrowed British battalions. While this ditch had a number of brick culverts which made useful shelters, it was quite unsuitable as a defensive position. It was between 12 and 25 feet wide, making it easy for the enemy to lob shells and mortar rounds into it, and it had been adapted, by digging down, for occupation by British troops. The average British regular soldier of 1914 came from an inner city slum and, despite regular exercise and wholesome if unappetising army food, he was shorter in stature than his modern counterpart. Shorter than today's British soldier he may have been, but he was a lot taller than the Gurkha of 1914 whose height rarely exceeded five feet two inches. The riflemen of the 2/8th Gurkhas could not see over the parapet of the line they now occupied, and as soon as they arrived in the trench on the evening of 29 October they had to begin to dig firesteps—which widened the already too wide trench—and scurry about to find ammunition boxes and ration crates to stand on. It was as well that they did set to immediately, for they were not to be given much time to improve their lot.

The 2/8th had only been in their new trenches for a few hours when the German artillery opened up. The enemy appeared to have calculated the range to the Gurkha trenches exactly, and owing to the width of the ditch many shells fell into it, exploding amongst the men and beginning the attrition of dead and wounded which would continue for 24 hours. A number of infantry attacks were also made, but these were not pressed home and were probably launched in order to seek out weak spots and gauge the determination of the defenders. At first light the last of these probing attacks was beaten off, the Gurkhas straining desperately to fire over the sides of trenches constructed a foot too deep for them. All telephone lines to the rear were now severed, and as fast as the battalion signallers attempted to re-lay them, they were cut again by artillery.

At 0800 hours on 30 October the German guns once more began a bombardment of the 2/8th Gurkhas' and the Devons' positions and at 1100 hours the infantry attacks began again. Lieutenant Colonel Morris, commanding the 2/8th, found himself having to feed more and more men into the firing line, and this without any communication trenches to provide cover. By 1330 hours the entire battalion was in the firing line and ammunition, originally issued on a scale of 200 rounds a man, was beginning to run low. Messages were sent back by runner to the headquarters of the Bareilly Brigade, asking for reinforcements and more ammunition, but either the messages never got through or there was nothing to be had, for none arrived. The enemy attacks increased on the right of the 2/8th and on the Devons' left, and by 1530 hours the line had started to crumble. Morris sent successively more and more men over to help the right-hand company, but the portion of ditch in which the fast dwindling band fought furiously had now collapsed in places, burying many of the men in mud and debris. Captains Davidson and Stack took groups over to help but both were wounded, Stack mortally. Davidson was wounded, was last seen lying on the ground firing his revolver at the advancing enemy and was later posted as missing. Major Barlow tried to get into the right-hand portion of the ditch with 15 of his men, but was badly wounded and by the time his little group had managed to get themselves into the path of the oncoming Germans, there were only ten Gurkhas left alive and unwounded in that portion of the line. The Germans were now through the gap between the 2/8th and the Devons and in the gloom of the approaching night they were able to get in behind both battalions, rendering the positions still held untenable. The Devons' left and the Gurkhas' right had been turned and the enemy infantry were into parts of the support line, such as it was. By last light the brigade commander was desperately trying to cobble together a counter-attack with such units that he could scrape up. The 2/8th Gurkhas had by now lost five British officers killed, three wounded and one missing, with 212 Gurkha officers and Other Ranks dead, wounded or missing[*] in their first action of the war. The battalion was now without a single British officer in the battle area.

By midnight the headquarters of the Bareilly Brigade had succeeded in finding some reinforcements: the Bedfords and the West Riding Regiment were sent forward, the former to occupy the support line of the 2/8th Gurkhas with what remained of that battalion, and the latter to the support line of both the 2/8th and the Devons. The German flood had been temporarily stemmed, but it was only a matter of time before it flowed again, and action to retake the firing line was now imperative.

At last a counter-attack force was mustered and Lieutenant Colonel Griffiths of the Bedfords was instructed to take half of his own battalion, half of the West Ridings, Vaughan's Rifles and half of the 107th Pioneers, the Meerut Division's pioneer battalion, and retake the lost trenches. The force moved up to the rear of that portion of the line now held by the

---

[*]   111 Gurkha ranks were posted as missing but most were later found to have been killed by shellfire or by the sides of the ditch collapsing on top of them.

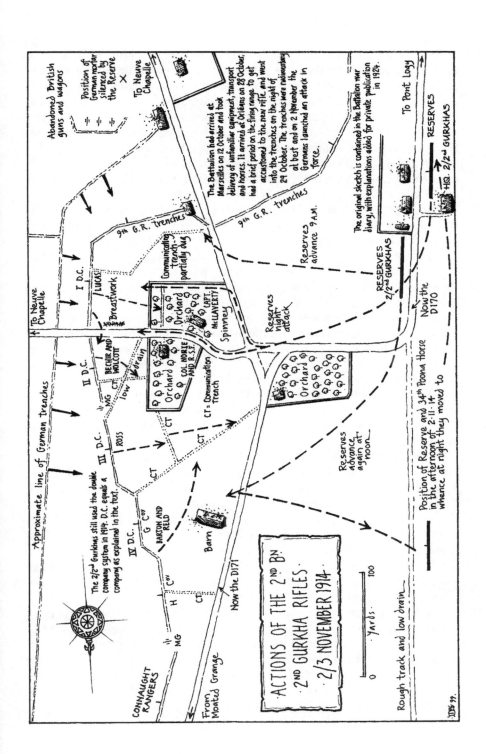

ACTIONS OF THE 2ND BN.
· 2ND GURKHA RIFLES ·
2/3 NOVEMBER 1914

Abandoned British guns and wagons

Position of German mortar silenced by the Reserve ✕

To Neuve Chapelle

The Battalion had arrived at Marseilles on 12 October and took delivery of unfamiliar equipment, transport and horses. It arrived at Orléans on 28 October, had a brief period on the firing range to get accustomed to the new rifle, and went into the trenches on the night of 29 October. The trenches were reconnoitred at dusk and on 2 November the Germans launched an attack in force.

9th G.R. trenches

9th G.R. trenches

Reserves advance 9 A.M.

The original sketch is contained in the Battalion war diary, with explanations added for private publication in 1924.

To Pont Logy

RESERVES
HQ. 2/2nd GURKHAS

RESERVES 2/2nd GURKHAS

Now the D170

Reserves night attack

9th G.R. trenches

Communicating trench partially dug

To Neuve Chapelle

I D.C.

LUCAS

Breastwork

II D.C.

BECHER AND WALCOTT

MG

low drain

Orchard

CAPT. McLLAVERTY

Spinney

COL. NORIE AND R.S.F.

Orchard

CT

CT

CT = Communication trench

ROSS

III D.C.

Reserves advance again at noon

Orchard

Approximate line of German trenches

The 2/2nd Gurkhas still used the double company system in 1914. D.C. equals a company as explained in the text.

IV D.C.

G Coy

BARTON AND RELD

Now the D171

Barn

KZN

From Montd Grange

CONNAUGHT RANGERS

MG

H Coy

CT

Position of Reserve and 34th Poona Horse in the afternoon of 2·11·14 whence at night they moved to

0   Yards   100

Rough track and low drain

JDS 99.

enemy. Despite heavy rifle and artillery fire the atrocious weather was now an advantage, for the force was able to approach with few casualties. At 0230 hours the support line was rushed and Vaughans' Rifles simultaneously attacked the German-held firing line. Some of the enemy were killed, some simply melted away, back whence they had come. With the exception of a few forward outposts which remained in German hands, the line was now re-established and the troops hastened to prepare for the expected German counter-attack. It never came, but as dawn was breaking Lieutenant Colonel Vennour, commanding Vaughan's Rifles, was shot and killed while peering over the parapet to see what the enemy was up to. Throughout the whole of 31 October shells rained down on the Bareilly Brigade front line while a steady rifle fire prevented any movement. Some parties of Germans were even able to get close enough to Vaughan's Rifles to throw bombs into the trenches, and by midnight on the 31st, when the regiment was relieved by the 41st Dogras, the butcher's bill amounted to three British officers, including the Commanding Officer, and five sepoys killed, four Indian officers and 79 sepoys wounded.

The 2/8th Gurkhas were now without a British officer of sufficient seniority to assume command of the battalion, and the Corps Commander despatched Major Tomkins, hitherto Assistant Military Secretary at Corps Headquarters, to take over command. Tomkins was an officer of the 28th Punjabis, and spoke not a word of Gurkhali, but as all VCOs were required to be able to speak Urdu, the lingua franca of the Indian Army, Tomkins was able to issue his instructions through them. He served the regiment well until a commanding officer from a Gurkha regiment could be found.

Soon another Gurkha battalion was to be the object of the Germans' attention. The 2/2nd Gurkhas in the Dehra Dun Brigade had taken up a position to the north-west of Neuve Chapelle with the 2nd Connaught Rangers on their left and the 1/9th Gurkhas on their right. The 2nd Connaughts were one of the regular British battalions lent to the Indian Corps, the first battalion of the same regiment being in the Ferozepore Brigade. The 2/2nd were in their new positions well before midnight on the 29th and began to improve their trench lines by extending them, digging communication trenches to the rear and connecting up with the battalions on their left and right. The battalion's trenches ran roughly north to south before the line crossed a ditch and then turned west before connecting with the 1/9th. To begin with all four companies were in the firing line. The battalion continued to work at improving their trenches, despite desultory German shelling and sniping which wounded ten Gurkha Other Ranks on the 31st and a further four on 1 November. On the right of the 2/2nd's line where they linked up with the 1/9th, the German positions were only 30 to 40 yards away and it was clear that the enemy was not being idle by the sounds of digging and prodigious amounts of earth

82

being thrown up. As in other parts of the Indian Corps' line communications were difficult, with telephone lines being regularly cut. By first light on 2 November much work on the 2/2nd Gurkhas' positions had been done and battalion headquarters was now established about 400 yards back in a farmhouse, just across the road from another building used by the 1/9th as their headquarters.

On the morning of 2 November the Germans began an artillery bombardment of the 2/2nd Gurkhas' trenches, concentrating on the right-hand company, No 1 Company. Particularly effective was a mortar which lobbed high explosive shells into the trenches from a position 150 yards away by the Neuve Chapelle road. By 0900 hours parts of No 1 Company's trenches were collapsing and men were being blown up into the air while others were being buried as the sides of the trench fell on top of them. Soon the survivors began to extricate themselves, some filling to their left and crowding into the portion of trench held by No 2 Company and some escaping to a shallow ditch some way behind their own trench. Lieutenant Lucas, of No 1 Company, trying to gather his men together to re-occupy their now empty line was killed, and as the artillery shifted its attentions to No 2 Company, German infantry leapt into the abandoned trench line. The left of the 1/9th Gurkhas was now in danger of being outflanked and two platoons of that battalion's reserve were sent up under Lieutenant Baille, who doubled as the battalion signals officer, to try to restore the line. Baille was killed by machine-gun fire and the party never reached the firing line.

The 2/2nd Gurkhas had established a battalion reserve of six composite platoons by taking men from all the companies in the firing line. It was located with battalion headquarters where also were the Commanding Officer Lieutenant Colonel Norie, the Adjutant Captain Corse-Scott, Major Norie of the 6th Gurkha Rifles (interpreter and the Commanding Officer's brother) and Captain McCleverty whose brother had been killed with the 47th Sikhs in the attack on Neuve Chapelle a few days before. Led by Colonel Norie[*] the reserve managed to find the German mortar and put it out of action but, realising that they could do nothing to restore the position on No 1 Company's front, they returned to battalion headquarters to replenish ammunition and prepare for a counter-attack on the lost line.

Back in the 2/2nd Gurkhas' firing line No 2 Company was now being shelled as well as coming under fire from the enemy infantry occupying No 1 Company's trench. Major Becher, commanding No 2 Company, decided that he could hold his position no longer and attempted to evacuate his men and the survivors of No 1 Company back along a communication trench. Becher was killed, as were a number of his men, the survivors taking cover in the ditch to the rear and behind a breastwork which had

---

[*] He had only one arm, the other having been left on the Frontier. See plate section.

been built on the south side of the road, while yet others crowded into No 3 Company's trenches.

The machine-gun officer of the 2/2nd Gurkhas was Lieutenant Innes. His two Maxim guns were in the firing line, one between the Connaught Rangers and the left-hand company of his own battalion, and the other between Nos 2 and 3 Companies. When this latter gun was destroyed by shelling, Innes went into No 2 Company's trench where he found 12 men under two subadars still holding on to the left-hand portion. Taking those 12 men and Lieutenant Walcott (the company officer of No 2 Company), Innes worked his way along a drain which ran back from No 3 Company's line to the Neuve Chapelle road and from there to the breastwork. Innes and his party now charged the No 1 Company trench. They got into it and killed some of the occupants before both British officers and both subadars were killed, the survivors taking shelter once more behind the breastwork and thence into the drain.

There was now a gap of 150 yards between the 2/2nd Gurkhas and the 1/9th, in which the German infantry was trying to establish a firing line. Major Ross, commanding the next 2/2nd company along (and also now the battalion second-in-command after the death of Major Macpherson on 30 October), realised that something had to be done. With Ross was the battalion's Subadar Major, Mansing Bohra[*], and taking a platoon of No 3 Company the pair charged the gap, actually getting into the trenches, setting about the occupants with bayonet and kukri. Gurkhas are by nature a gentle people, but when their temper is roused the whites of their eyes redden and they can present a terrifying appearance[†]. Some of the Germans, faced by a group of furious Mongolians wielding their kukris which can take a man's head off in a single swipe, took to their heels and ran, but others were made of sterner stuff and there were simply not enough Gurkhas to hold the advantage they had seized. Ross and the subadar Major were both killed and, when only ten men were left standing they had no alternative but to run back to their own trench.

The 2/2nd Gurkhas' war diary says of this stage of the action: 'By this time a number of men had managed to escape to the rear and got away altogether from the trenches'. In blunt terms, some of the men had taken it upon themselves to retire without orders. One cannot but sympathise. There was hardly anybody left to give them orders, but for a proud battalion it was to attract some—largely uninformed—criticism later on.

---

[*] Bohras are a sub clan of the Thakurs, or Khas, and are regarded as being particularly intelligent. Mansing came from a distinguished family: his father had been subadar major of the same battalion and his three sons also became subadar majors, two in Mansing's own regiment and one in the 9th Gurkha Rifles.

[†] The author long believed this to be an old wives' tale, until he saw it for himself!

The 2/2nd Gurkhas' left-hand company, No 4 Company commanded by Captain Barton, was also coming under pressure and Barton was shot dead while standing in his trench. The Company Officer, Lieutenant Reid, seeing that the whole battalion was in danger of being routed, sent a runner to the Connaught Rangers on his left, asking for help. Reid then moved into No 3 Company's line shouting to the men to hold on as help was at hand. With the men rallied, Reid went back to his own company and met a party of Connaught Rangers coming to his assistance commanded by a sergeant. In the act of leading the Connaughts and a group from his own company with three Gurkha Officers to No 3 Company's trench, both Reid and the Connaughts' sergeant were killed. The party did manage to get into the trench, but were unable to occupy it against intense German resistance which easily outnumbered the combined Connaughts and Gurkha force. The group now attempted to withdraw down the No 3 Company communication trench, but the Germans had set up a machine-gun firing straight down it, which caused very heavy casualties to the Connaughts and the Gurkhas.

The relevant entry in the 2/2nd Gurkhas' War Diary reads: 'Meanwhile more parties under Gurkha officers and NCOs had managed to retire out of the trenches and get away to the rear'[3]. Fortunately in the rear was the battalion Quartermaster[*], Lieutenant Scoones, who scooped up these lost souls and sent them to join the battalion reserve.

It was now mid-day and the Dehra Dun Brigade headquarters was aware that a very dangerous situation had developed and that the line must be restored by a counter-attack, as all local measures had failed. The Brigade Major ordered the Poona Horse (dismounted) and a squadron of the 7th Dragoon Guards (also dismounted), both of the Secunderabad Cavalry Brigade, a company of the Royal Scots Fusiliers and the reserve company of the 6th Jats to report to the Commanding Officer 2/2nd Gurkhas. Colonel Norie and the Commanding Officer of the Poona Horse, Lieutenant Colonel Swanston, were old friends and Norie briefed his ad hoc force on the situation. Led by Colonel Norie, with his own reserve and the Poona Horse as the vanguard and with the other units following up, the counter-attack force advanced in three lines towards the Gurkhas' Nos 3 and 4 Companies' positions. They came under severe shelling and

---

[*] Quartermasters in today's Army are commissioned rankers, usually with considerable service. In 1914 the Quartermaster of an Indian battalion was a regimental officer, usually fairly junior. Along with that of Adjutant the post of Quartermaster carried with it extra pay, and was regarded as a valuable grounding in logistics for British officers. Nevertheless it was not a job that everyone wanted to do—there was always the chance of kit being lost and the Quartermaster being ordered to pay for it.

machine-gun and rifle fire from the Germans in the old trenches. The sowars of the Poona Horse, in dismounted action within 12 hours of arriving at the railhead, refused to lie down and take cover, suffering unnecessary casualties because of it. Eventually the whole line was forced to halt and get down about 150 yards from the trenches. Neither commanding officer was sure which part of the line was held by the enemy and which part was still occupied by Gurkhas, and Swanston, attempting to scrutinise the trenches through his binoculars, was shot dead. The counter-attack force managed to get into some of the 2/2nd Gurkhas' support trenches but were unable to make any further headway in the face of determined German resistance. The Poona Horse and the 2/2nd's reserves stayed where they were until 1430 hours when a well directed artillery barrage forced them to pull back 200 yards where they found cover in a ditch. The Poona Horse were instructed to stay there until arrangements could be made to close the gap in the Dehra Dun Brigade front. By now the German attack had lost its impetus. They were in the 2/2nd Gurkhas' old trenches in strength but they were unable either to advance farther or to extend their gains to right or left. The 1/9th Gurkhas, whose left flank was now in the air[*], withdrew their left-hand company into reserve and filled in the trench vacated by it.

At about 1730 hours, just after dark, Lieutenant Colonel Norie decided to have one more try to re-establish his battalion's old line. The attack would be on the No 1 Company position on the battalion's right and would be two pronged. Colonel Norie with his brother, the interpreter, and Captain Corse-Scott would take the squadron of the 7th Dragoon Guards, the company of the Royal Scots Fusiliers and the company of the 6th Jat Light Infantry and assault the northern, left-hand, portion of the trench where it met the Neuve Chapelle road. Captain McCleverty with the 2/2nd Gurkhas' reserves would attack 100 yards farther south just before the trench turned west to link up with the 1/9th Gurkhas. The attack got to within 50 yards of the German-held trenches when fire was opened on them. The Scots Fusiliers' company commander was killed with a number of his men, and both Major Norie and McCleverty were badly wounded. The attack could make no further progress and, under covering fire from the 6th Jats, Colonel Norie withdrew. The entry in the 2/2nd Gurkhas' war diary, timed at 0300 hours 3 November says, rather laconically:

> The battalion had a severe engagement in the trenches today, losing seven British officers, four subadars and 33 Gurkha Other Ranks

---

[*] A technical military expression which simply means that the flank did not join up with anybody and was therefore open to being turned by enemy getting behind it or attacking it from the side.

killed, one British officer, one jemadar and 57 Gurkha Other Ranks wounded. 40 Gurkha Other Ranks missing.[4]

Captain Grimshaw of the Poona Horse thought that the 2/2nd Gurkhas had behaved badly, and in his published diary[5] says that the counter-attack with the Poona Horse was only put in 'to save the face of the 2nd Gurkhas'. He also says that the attack was carried out only because Colonel Norie prevailed upon his friendship with Swanston (not true—it had been ordered by the Brigade Commander, and in any case a counter-attack had to be put in if the Germans were not to exploit their breach of a very thin line) and that Colonel Norie had said nothing about his men 'quitting their trenches'. Grimshaw was not however involved in the counter-attack—his squadron was in reserve at the time and the first he knew of the action was when he met some wounded coming back—and his diary is constantly critical of any unit other than his own Poona Horse squadron. His information is partly surmise and partly what he heard from others during the next few days. Grimshaw does say that some men of C Squadron Poona Horse (Grimshaw commanded D Squadron) had also absented themselves, and that he and the Adjutant of the 2/2nd Gurkhas spent the next day rounding up stragglers. While doing this Grimshaw 'found 2nd Gurkha men in all kinds of places. Ditches, ruins and even under the culverts, and I regret to say one or two men of C Squadron among them'.

Although the total casualties of the Gurkha battalion were not excessive by later standards (44 killed and 99 wounded or missing), they were very significant. Every British officer in the firing line was killed and the death of the Subadar Major, the senior Gurkha and revered by all, must have had a particularly shattering effect on morale. The battalion had only been at the Front for four days, having had but half a day on the range to familiarise themselves with their newly issued rifles. The devastating attack resulting in the sudden loss of the British officers whom the men knew and trusted left them confused and shaken.

The war diary of the 2/2nd Gurkhas, written just after the affair, lists the reasons for the battalion's failure to hold its positions as being:

1. The salient created by the evacuation of Neuve Chapelle [on 27 and 28 October] was too pronounced.
2. No Sapper officer visited the 2/2nd trenches to advise regimental officers.
3. The Indian Army had no experience of mortars and grenades.
4. The Artillery support was entirely inadequate due to the battle raging to the north. The battery in support had changed the night before, the new battery did not know the ranges or the likely targets.
5. The Connaught Rangers had relieved the Royal Scots Fusiliers [on

the 2/2nd's left] only the day before and did not know the ground. There were no communication trenches to the Connaught Rangers, and the 2/2nd's own trench lines had not been completed.[6]

The diary gives the impression of scratching around for excuses, when perhaps none was needed. The salient was too exposed, and in hindsight the British line should have been established farther west, but in 1914 to suggest giving up ground not actually occupied by the enemy would have been regarded as heresy. There was no sapper officer to advise because the few sappers available were being used as infantry. Certainly the Indian Army had no experience of mortars or grenades, but the 2/2nd Gurkhas' reserve under Colonel Norie dealt very efficiently with the mortar that was troubling them. The artillery support was inadequate for the entire BEF—there was simply not enough of it—and the main effort had to be in the north where the Germans were still trying to force the Menin road. The Connaught Rangers were new to the ground—as was every other battalion of the Indian Corps—but when help was asked for they responded as best they could, and to a personal request from Lieutenant Reid rather than as a result of any order from on high. The points made by the keeper of the 2/2nd Gurkhas' war diary, Captain Corse-Scott, would be repeated time and time again by all the units of the BEF as the war wore on, but this was the first time they had been recorded in writing. They were all true, but there was little alternative in 1914.

Contrary to what Grimshaw says the battalion did not 'abandon their trenches', but undoubtedly some men did seek safety when there was no one to turn to for Orders and succour. They were quickly rallied, largely through the actions of the Quartermaster and Lieutenant Colonel Norie, whom even Grimshaw admits 'gallantly exposed himself unmercifully'[7] and in the next 12 months the battalion was to recover whatever part of its reputation they may have lost on that fateful November day. Norie himself, aged 49 in 1914, was a very experienced officer. He was twice mentioned in despatches and promoted brevet Major in the Tirah in 1897, awarded the DSO and twice more mentioned in despatches in South Africa. In this war he would be awarded the CB, the CMG and the Serbian Order of the White Eagle as well as being mentioned in despatches a total of five times. He would command the Bareilly Brigade and retire as a major general. Norie's battalion quickly recovered from their appalling introduction to European warfare and on 5 December 1914 Norie wrote:

People have said awfully kind things about the behaviour of the Regiment, and I am awfully proud of it, I can tell you. But oh! I mourn Stuffy [Lieutenant Innes] and Hamish and Walcott and Lucas and the four Gurkha officers killed. These were my best. It will take years for us to make good the work of the Germans that day.[8]

Despite Sir John French's comment, in his despatch of 20 November, that 'The situation was prevented from becoming serious by the excellent leadership displayed by Colonel Norie of the 2nd Gurkha Rifles'[9] the Army has a way of damning with faint praise, and that the high command were not entirely happy with the 2/2nd Gurkhas was demonstrated by the award of nothing more than the mention in despatches to the surviving British officers of the battalion. Lieutenant Colonel Norie at least was surely deserving of a bar to his DSO.[*]

It was clear that the original line could not be restored, and to plug the gap between the Connaught Rangers and the 1/9th Gurkhas, the Royal Scots Fusiliers and a composite battalion made up of men of the 1/34th Sikh Pioneers, Vaughan's Rifles and the 9th Bhopals dug trenches to the rear of the old 2/2nd Gurkhas' line during the night of 2/3 November. The old line would be recaptured later in the month, but being exposed and badly sited for defence was not re-occupied, but filled in and abandoned. The 2/2nd Gurkhas themselves were pulled out of the line at dawn on 3 November to refit.

Now began a period when the Indian Corps could consolidate their positions and adjust to life in the trenches. At this early stage of the war the Germans were without question far better trained and equipped for European warfare than were either the British or the Indians. While British personal weapons (rifles) and machine-guns were as good if not better (in the case of the rifle) than those used by the Germans, the latter tended to have more ammunition and more machine-guns available. The British and Indian Armies were short of all manner of equipment. Offices and businesses in England were asked to make gifts of typewriters to equip battalion orderly rooms, whilst the Lord Roberts Appeal for Field Glasses robbed bird watchers to ensure that infantry officers could take the field properly accoutred.

The British artillery of 1914 was well handled and equipped, with superb horses to draw its Field and Horse Artillery guns, but there was far too little of it and some of its guns were verging on obsolescence and with barrels shot out (the grooves of the rifling worn away) from use in the South African War. The Germans appeared to have no shortage of either guns or ammunition and, from the point of view of the infantry in the trenches, had one great advantage over the British and Indians—they had trench mortars. A field gun fires a high velocity projectile over a relatively flat trajectory, which means that if the person being fired at gets behind a bank of earth, or behind a building or into a trench he is relatively safe. A field gun cannot lob. A mortar can lob, and was designed for exactly that

---

[*]   His brother, Major Norie the interpreter, did get a DSO and Lieutenant Colonel Norie
       was promoted brevet colonel, which was some compensation.

purpose. The mortar round could be much heavier than that fired from a conventional gun and was fired from its mortar at a high angle, virtually straight up in the air. It therefore came straight down on its target. The higher the angle at which the round was fired the shorter was the range, but a trench mortar could be fired from inside a trench and only needed to be able to reach the enemy trench, a few hundred yards away. If the range was calculated correctly it would drop its shell into the opposing trenches, killing the occupants and collapsing the trench itself. The Germans were well equipped with Minenwerfer, or trench mortars, as the Indian Corps had discovered. One shell fired at the Seaforth Highlanders on 7 November made a hole 15 feet across and eight feet deep, burying a colour sergeant and several men. While it would be some time before an official issue mortar was provided for British and Indians, units searched around for some way to reply to the daily German bombardments. Some units even raided museums and obtained century-old French mortars, last employed to bombard British infantry at Waterloo. Others made their own.

The Indian Sappers and Miners were great improvisers and they began to manufacture mortars, using whatever materials were available. The first mortars were made from lengths of cast iron piping and used black powder to fire a home-made shell a few hundred yards. They were highly inaccurate and tended to blow up after a few discharges, causing more damage to their own side than to the Germans, but eventually Major Patterson of the Royal Field Artillery, attached to the Indian Corps, came up with his own design, which he had manufactured by No 3 Company Sappers and Miners of the Meerut Division. Known as 'Patterson's Pills for Portly Prussians' the mortar shells were made from cut-down 18-pounder shell cases filled with three and a half pounds of explosive packed round with stones, horse shoe nails and anything else that came to hand. The first two prototype dischargers were tubes made of wood and cast iron respectively, later versions being made from steel piping. The propellant was black powder which also ignited the shell fuse, the length of which was calculated to explode the shell when it landed in the enemy trench. The first live trial was held on 19 November with Lieutenant Robson of the Sappers and Miners as the chief gunner. Robson had only joined his unit the day before and was presumably given the task on the old Army principle of giving particularly risky jobs to the latest subaltern to arrive, on the grounds that he was unlikely to realise the danger and would not argue anyway. Robson fired 20 rounds, and to the great delight of the watching sepoys, two exploded in the German line. The Sappers and Miners now went into full manufacture of Patterson's brainchild and soon battalions of the Corps were able to make some reply to the enemy.

At first this novel method of inflicting damage on the enemy from a distance was highly popular and attracted large audiences of sepoys. It very shortly became apparent, however, that the black powder used to propel the pill gave off a large cloud of smoke, indicating to the enemy where the weapon had been fired from, and attracting a retaliation in kind. The bomb gunners, as they were known, adapted their tactics whereby they would set their weapon up in a trench, fire five rounds or so in quick succession and then vacate the area with their contrivances as fast as possible. This was all very well for the mortar crews but diminished their popularity with the other occupants of the trench who were unable to decamp, and one British battalion even put up a notice in their trench which said 'No Hawkers or Trench Mortars Allowed'. Eventually, but not until well into 1915, the trench mortar designed by Sir Wilfred Stokes would come into service, capable of firing a 10-lb projectile 1,200 yards from a three-inch diameter tube.

It soon became apparent that some means of projecting high explosive was needed for short-range engagements, particularly when fighting along or around an enemy trench when the enemy was in the next traverse only a few feet away. The Germans were well provided with hand grenades, mainly of what became known as the 'Potato Masher' type, which had an explosive head attached to a wooden handle. A string attached to the handle was pulled, igniting the fuse, and the grenade was lobbed by hand into the opposing trench or round the next corner. At this stage the British and Indians had no grenades and so again improvisation was called for. The first grenades consisted of empty tins packed with explosive with a fuse inserted in the top. They were known as 'jam tin' or 'jam pot' bombs, and the thrower had to light the fuse and then throw the grenade. The sepoys were quite happy to employ these devices against the enemy, but were unhappy about having to go to the rear to practise with them, owing to a tendency for them to explode as soon as the fuse was lit. In time the fusing improved and on 5 November the 47th Sikhs had their first issue of no fewer than three jam tin bombs, being instructed that they were to be kept under the supervision of an officer and only used in dire emergency.

If the first home-made trench mortars were not greeted with total enthusiasm by those in their immediate vicinity, the re-invention of the catapult for hurling jam tin bombs at the enemy was more acceptable. Made of strong elastic it was claimed to be able to hurl a bomb up to a range of 300 yards, the range being dependent upon the number of strands of elastic employed for each discharge. Also tried, with some success, were an adaptation of the clay pigeon trap and a modern version of the medieval crossbow. The issue of the Hales Rifle Grenade on 9 November 1914 was generally welcomed, albeit that battalions of the Indian Corps received only eight each. This weapon consisted of a grenade affixed to a rod. The rod was inserted in the barrel of the rifle which was then loaded with a blank cartridge and fired at high angle towards the enemy. The cartridge propelled the grenade from the rifle and forced the rod into the body of the grenade, igniting the fuse. The range of the Hales grenade was about 200 yards but its accuracy was far from being pinpoint. It was replaced later in the war with a cup discharger fitted to the end of the rifle and firing the Mills bomb, with less range but much more accuracy.

All sorts of items of equipment which were in plentiful supply in the German Army had to be improvised by the British and Indians. Searchlights, widely used in defence by the Germans, were improvised by the Sappers and Miners from motor car headlights (which in their intended role worked by paraffin or carbide) into which electric bulbs were inserted and the whole connected up to an electricity supply from the rear. They were nothing like as effective as the German purpose-built version, but were better than nothing. Sandbags, to help with building trench parapets and strongpoints, were only slowly to come into service and being all of one colour were regarded as inferior to those of the Germans which were multi-coloured and merged into the background when viewed from afar. The German artillery had observation balloons, which were surprisingly difficult to shoot down, whereas in 1914 the British had none.

Once the Indian Corps line had been occupied on 3 November 1914 a routine began to be established. Despite the propaganda put out in the Allied press that a major advance was imminent, it was beginning to dawn upon the military that the war might last rather longer than anyone had imagined*, and that presently held positions should be put into a state where they could be defended against massive attack. The battalions of the Indian Corps began to dig and extend their lines. The firing line was improved, communication trenches were dug to the support lines and reserve lines were constructed. The area had a high water table and the winter of 1914 was a wet one. Trenches collapsed due not only to German shelling but also because the earth was waterlogged, and it was obvious that trenches must be revetted. Revetting is the process of shoring up the sides of a trench with planks, sandbags or corrugated iron to prevent them from falling in. At this stage no revetting material could be provided, and so abandoned houses for miles behind the lines were scoured for doors, tables, window frames and anything that could be pressed into service to protect the trench walls.

Men kept in the line for long periods inevitably suffered from the effects of the weather and the lack of sanitation. Although the 1/9th Gurkhas were in the line for 20 days without relief, the period spent in the line was more usually a week or ten days, and sometimes only two or three days. Battalions were then moved to brigade reserve and later to billets in rear

---

*   Kitchener, the Minister for War, had maintained right from the beginning that the war would last three years, and the future Commander-in-Chief, Haig, was also to realise this early on.

before being sent forward again. Billets varied. Some were evacuated public buildings in various states of repair, some were private houses which might or might not still be occupied. Most battalions tried to establish an officers' mess, and the 47th Sikhs considered themselves exceptionally fortunate to be able to set theirs up in a farmhouse behind the lines just east of Picantin. The occupant was an old woman, who took the officers' rations and in return provided superb meals for those who could escape from the trenches long enough to eat them. She also did the officers' laundry and generally appeared to do her utmost to alleviate the hardships of the winter. The 47th Sikhs' suspicions were first aroused by their noticing that, while every other house in the area became a target for German shelling, their mess remained inviolate. When a flanking battalion reported that the old woman's dog had been seen making regular trips to and from the German lines, arrest was inevitable and the old woman, and her dog, were removed by the Gendarmerie. Next day the house was shelled and the 47th Sikhs had lost not only a good cook but a comfortable officers' mess as well.

While the question of meat for the Indian Corps had been resolved to everyone's satisfaction and supplies of other foodstuffs arrived regularly through Marseilles, the men in the trenches could only rarely eat a properly cooked meal, except at night when it would be carried up. As cooking in the trenches produced smoke which attracted the attention of enemy artillery the sepoys often had to resort to eating pre-cooked meals cold, or mixing atta with gur (coarse Indian sugar) and eating the result accompanied by raisins and biscuits. Things were better by night when not only cooked meals but additional extras could be supplied.

The ration issued was drawn from a list of acceptable items, not all of which could be regularly obtained, but except in dire emergency Indian troops were able to receive their own foodstuffs throughout their time on the Western Front. In the early days British troops were forbidden alcohol in the trenches. The Indian Army took a more liberal line, probably because excessive drinking was a very real problem in the British Regular Army of 1914 whereas it was not in the Indian Army. Rum was sent up to the line for those who could drink it, and for the Moslems and high caste Hindus who could not, extra tea was supplied.

With no improvement in the weather and warm clothing still being in short supply, life for the men in the trenches was far from pleasant, although Corps headquarters and battalions did their best to alleviate conditions. Charcoal braziers were carried up by the civilian followers and placed at intervals along the trenches. Men often had to stand in a foot of water and, as duckboards were yet to be provided, straw was put in the bottom of trenches. Soldiers on duty at night were provided with whale oil to rub on their legs and feet, provided initially through the generosity of the Maharaja of Gwalior and eventually at government expense. Men wore sandbags stuffed with straw tied round their boots to keep their feet warm. Despite these precautions, and the sepoys' natural tendency to keep themselves and their equipment clean, troops quickly became verminous and lice-infested. Drills were devised to get rid of lice, with irons being heated up on charcoal braziers and applied to the seams of clothing, but it was only when battalions were rotated back through billets in the rear that they could disinfest themselves and be really clean again. Latrines had originally been dug any old how, but as the lines became more organised designated latrines were dug to the rear. It was important that these were properly sited and under cover from German view. In the early stages of the war an ordinary soldier might not shoot an enemy in the act of performing his natural functions, but a sniper would delight at the chance to catch a man 'with his trousers down', and the Germans had many very competent snipers armed with hunting rifles equipped with telescopic sights. Even when defecating the Army retains its rank distinction and there were separate latrines for British officers, usually with seats, for Indian officers and for IORs, the latter without seats.

Kit lost in action was gradually replaced, although this was not made easy by the Indian Army system of 'Half Mounting' under which only some items were government issue and the regiment received a cash allowance to have other items made locally. Many of the men of the 2/2nd Gurkhas had lost their Gurkha hats in the fighting of 2 November. French contractors do not as a matter of course manufacture Gurkha hats, and it was some time before these could be replaced by borrowing from other Gurkha battalions.

At this stage there was no question of the Indian Corps, or of any part of the BEF, making a major attack on the German lines. The Germans were still trying to break through to Ypres and the Indian Corps' task was to hold as many of the enemy as they could on their front, to prevent enemy divisions being moved north. Too long in a defensive posture breeds a defensive mentality, arid it was important for morale that units could see that, while they might not be advancing, they were at least achieving something. The policy was one of aggressive defence, and this meant covert reconnaissance of the enemy lines, patrols in no man's land and raids on enemy trenches. The Germans too conducted an aggressive defence, which in their case took the form of sapping. A sap was a small narrow trench dug out, usually at night, from the main firing line towards the opposing defences. Progress of 50 yards a night was not uncommon and sometimes the Germans would dig a number of saps and then join them up, thus advancing their firing line. Otherwise a sap would have a sniper in it, firing from a metal loophole or through the narrow end of a pyramid-shaped box dug into the parapet.

Indian soldiers were good at patrolling—they were countrymen and accustomed to moving around in the dark—and the information that they acquired on their nocturnal wanderings was particularly useful to the artillery who were so short of ammunition that they could not fire at anything other than a clearly identified target. While the British and Indian trenches and rear areas were subjected to regular shelling, British guns were tightly rationed and a telephoned request from the infantry for a German-occupied house or observation post to be bombarded was often answered with an apologetic: 'Can't—used up my allowance'. The allowance in some cases was only 18 rounds per battery, or two rounds per gun per day, as the battle in the Ypres Salient was given priority for such stocks of ammunition as existed. All this would eventually lead to recrimination in Press and Parliament but it would be well over a year before the Allies could match the Germans in both guns and shells.

Up to 3 November the Indian Corps losses had amounted to 1,550 killed, wounded and missing from the Indian units. The British battalions had also taken their share and altogether the Corps had lost the equivalent of three battalions in less than two weeks. Of particular significance, the 15 Indian Battalions had lost the equivalent of four and a half battalions' worth of British officers. Some officer reinforcements now began to trickle in. The 2/2nd Gurkhas received Captain Bayley of their own regiment, just released from the Staff College at Camberley, and Captain Duff of the 1/1st Gurkhas on 5 November. Duff was the son of General Sir Beauchamp Duff, Commander-in-Chief India and was placed in command of No 2 Company of his new battalion. On 6 November the 2/2nd Gurkhas were ordered to send a company to reinforce the Seaforths and on the principle of last in gets the first dirty job, Duff and his new command were sent. On 7 November Duff was killed.

To conform with the policy of aggressive defence, it was decided that a raid should be mounted on a part of the German line which was only 50 yards in front of the Garhwal Brigade. The night of 9 November was fixed as the date and the operation was to be carried out by 50 men from each battalion of the 39th Garhwal Rifles, under command of Major Taylor of the 2nd Battalion. It was to be a silent[*] attack and the aim was to seize a portion of the enemy lines, capture some prisoners and fill in the trench before retiring. Emerging from their own forward trench line in the dark the men crawled through the mud towards the opposition. Close to the enemy trenches and so far undetected, Taylor gave the signal to assault by firing his revolver. The men sprang to their feet and jumped into the trenches. They had achieved complete surprise and the Germans fled. Soon 75 yards of the German trench line were in Indian hands. Six prisoners were taken and the riflemen began to fill in the trench. Even with the extra shovels they had taken with them they found the task impossible.

[*]   That is, it would rely on surprise, with no preliminary artillery bombardment or covering fire.

The German trench was eight feet deep, with a firing step, and was stoutly revetted. Doing as much damage as they could, the Garhwalis made a quick search for maps and documents and withdrew, taking their prisoners with them. As they retired a searchlight from the German support trenches began to play upon them but they managed to regain safety with only four casualties. It had been a successful little operation and a welcome change from standing in mud and water in their own trenches. The prisoners were escorted to brigade and then divisional headquarters for interrogation.

Flushed with the success of their first attempt, it was decided to launch a more ambitious raid on the enemy trenches on the night of 13 November, also to be carried out by the Garhwal Brigade. This time artillery would be used and the raid would be carried out by men of the 2/3rd Gurkhas and the 2/39th Garhwalis, again under Major Taylor, with the Sappers and Miners following up to demolish the captured trenches. The Poona Horse and a company of the 1/9th Gurkhas would be available in support. The whole operation would be commanded by Lieutenant Colonel Ormsby of the 2/3rd Gurkhas.

At 2115 hours, after a 15-minute artillery bombardment, the attackers moved off over the shell-pocked plough. Alas, the Germans were not to be caught napping twice, and the sepoys did not help their own cause by beginning to cheer—contrary to orders—as they approached. Carefully sited machine-guns and fire from the German support line dealt out death and destruction and save for one subadar, all the British and Indian officers on the right-hand flank of the attack were killed, including Major Taylor. Despite repeated attempts, the only penetration of the enemy trenches was by a group of Gurkhas under Lieutenant McSwiney. They killed thirty Germans and captured four in hand-to-hand fighting but could make no further progress. When German artillery opened up and searchlights began to play on the struggling sepoys, most of whom were still trapped in no man's land unable to go forward, there was no alternative but to withdraw to the Indian trenches. The company of the 1/9th Gurkhas, which had now arrived in the Garhwal Brigade firing line, could do nothing but go out and attempt to recover as many of the wounded as possible, at considerable cost to themselves.

The escapade cost the 2/3rd Gurkhas 61 casualties out of about 200 engaged, and the Garhwalis 40 out of 72 engaged. It was time to lick wounds and re-think tactics for raids.

Corps headquarters was at this stage located in a château at Hinges, about six miles from the Front, while the Lahore and Meerut Divisions' headquarters were at Estaires and Locon respectively, each about four and a half miles back. Whatever may have been written and said about 'Château Generalship', Sir James Willcocks, commanding the Indian Corps, was one senior officer who spent a great deal of his time on the road, visiting his divisional and brigade headquarters and battalions in the line and, despite his age, he did most of it on horseback. His example was infectious, for the war diaries show that commanders and staff officers of the Indian Corps were frequent visitors to the forward positions. It is clear from the entries in the war diaries listing visits to the trenches that both divisional commanders and their staff officers were intensely interested in the welfare of their troops and were in no sense remote from what was happening at the Front. Partly this was due to the regimental and staff officers of the Indian Corps all knowing each other, which was not the case in the BEF once it became diluted with Territorial and New Army men, but also to the very close relationship that existed between British officers and Indian ranks of the Indian Army. Some—and to be fair only some—officers of the British Army looked upon Indian Army officers as colonial curiosities, and their men as native cannon fodder, and this tended to make the Indian Army contingent draw closer together.

On 12 November Field Marshal Lord Roberts arrived at Corps Headquarters in Hinges. He had been appointed Colonel in Chief of the Indian Corps and despite his age (he was 82) and the bitter weather, he had insisted upon going to France to welcome the first Indian soldiers ever to fight in Europe in the British service. Roberts visited Corps headquarters and the headquarters of both divisions and the Secunderabad Cavalry Brigade as well as touring the rear areas. As far as they could every Indian unit sent representatives, British and Indian, back to meet him, and the fact that the revered 'Bobs Bahadur' had made the journey to see them was an undoubted help to morale. The Indian Army of 1914 was very much a family affair. There would have been many sepoys who stood along the road to cheer the Field Marshal on that wintry day whose fathers, grandfathers and great grandfathers would have served alongside him from the Mutiny onwards. It was the coldest day of a very cold month, and Roberts, who insisted on getting out of his motor car at each stop to meet the troops, caught pneumonia*. On 14 November he died. For a while his body lay in state at St Omer, guarded by men of the Indian Corps, and he was subsequently buried in St Paul's Cathedral, beside that other great soldier of Imperial England, and Roberts' rival, Garnet Wolseley.

SOURCE NOTES

1. *Military Operations in France and Belgium 1914 – 15*, JE Edmonds, Macmillan and Co, London, 1928. Map 19, Operations of the II Corps

* It was said that he refused to wear a greatcoat, on the grounds that this item had not yet been issued to the men of the Indian Corps.

BEF 25th Oct – 2nd Nov which accompanies the Official History is wrong, as it shows the Bareilly Brigade holding the centre of the Meerut Division front with the Garhwal Brigade to the south. All other authorities, from the Corps Commander's memoirs to the brigade and battalion war diaries and histories, say it was the other way round.

2. War Diary, 2nd Bn 2nd Gurkha Rifles, Public Record Office Kew, WO/95/3942
3. Ibid.
4. Ibid.
5 *Indian Cavalry Officer 1914 – 15*, Captain Roly Grimshaw (ed Wakefield and Weippert), Costello, Tunbridge Wells, 1986.
6. War Diary, 2nd Bn 2nd Gurkha Rifles.
7. *Indian Cavalry Officer 1914 – 15*.
8. Private letter published in the 'Joumal of the 2nd KEO Gurkha Rifles (The Sirmoor Rifles)', 1955.
9. Supplement to *London Gazette*, HMSO, Nov 1914.

V

Trench Raids and Trench Foot

After the fighting near Neuve Chapelle on 2 and 3 November 1914, the next three weeks or so in the Indian Corps' area were officially considered to be 'quiet', and compared to the fighting still going on around the Ypres Salient, they were. Whatever the Battles Nomenclature Committee[*] may have thought, however, the sepoys had not suddenly entered an era of peace and tranquillity. There was a steady drip of killed and wounded from sniping, shelling, mortaring and in patrolling and raiding. From 3 to 23 November the average rate of casualties within the Indian Corps was 90 a day, few of these as a result of any dramatic action. The 9th Bhopals, who relieved the Royal Scots Fusiliers on the night of 4/5 November, had 55 men killed and wounded as the result of a chance German shelling on 7 November, which lasted but ten minutes. During the same night another short bombardment caused 15 casualties. Within the space of three days the 1/9th Gurkhas' battalion headquarters was forced to move out of a ruined farmhouse to take cover in the farm's dung heap, subsequently being forced to move into another dung heap a few hundred yards away. A French midden was not the most salubrious location for a tactical headquarters, but the smell was perhaps compensated for by the capacity of heaps of old manure to absorb blast and shell fragments.

It was not only the enemy who inflicted casualties. Despite the infantry's impolite name of 'dropshorts' for the gunners, it was unusual for the Royal Artillery to score an own goal. On 15 November however, the British guns dropped three shells on the 2/39th Garhwal Rifles' trenches, killing four men including the company bugler. Fortunately the telephone lines to the rear were intact and the gunners were called off.

The Indian Army reserve system, such as it was, was calculated to replace casualties at the rate of 10% a month, or 85 men a day. There were never that number of reinforcements available—although even if

---

[*] A committee convened by the War Office which meets as required to decide what was a battle, for what period it lasted, what it should be called, whether a battle honour should be awarded and if so to which units. It met to consider Falklands War battle nomenclatures and honours and most recently battle honours in Iraq 2003.

there had been it would have been insufficient—and the strength of the Indian Corps continued to decline. There was also a drain on manpower because of sickness, much of it due to the now very cold weather which caused numerous cases of frostbite, particularly in the 41st Dogras. The 2/3rd Gurkhas had never really shaken off the malaria which they had contracted while waiting in the middle of an Indian swamp for trains to take them to their port of embarkation, and it now began to recur. All in all, though, the health of the Indian troops was remarkably good, and significantly better than that amongst the British units of the Corps. In the month of November 1914 the British sick rate within the Corps was 114 men per thousand compared to the Indian rate of 40 per thousand. This figure surprised Corps headquarters, as Indian troops were considered less able to withstand cold and wet than their British comrades, and was thought to be due to the debilitating effects upon the British soldiers of the time spent in India before transfer to the Western Front. In fact the rate of sickness amongst the Indian troops was no worse than that amongst units of the original BEF, who were accustomed to cold and rain.

The effects of the cold were not all bad, however. The ground now frequently froze which made the home-made grenades manufactured by the Sappers and Miners and issued to the Indian battalions much more likely to explode amongst the enemy, rather than having their fuses extinguished by sinking into the mud. Hard, frozen ground enabled patrols and raiding parties to scamper from one bit of cover to another, rather than having to wade through mud into which men sank to their knees. On 14 November two German soldiers emerged from a house on the outskirts of Neuve Chapelle and gave themselves up to the 2/2nd Gurkhas. They were suffering from hypothermia, having been hiding in a cellar ever since the fighting of late October, originally living off a dead cow which had now become inedible.

On the night of 15/16 November the overall tactical situation had improved to the point where the Lahore Division—the Ferozepore and Jullunder Brigades—could be taken out of the line and placed in corps reserve, their place being taken by the British 8 Division. Partly as a diversion to cover the relief and partly because the Indian Corps would now have a sufficiency of reserves, it was decided to mount a raid on the German lines the same night. The 107th Pioneers had been holding the Quinque Rue area of the Meerut Division's front and for the past few days two German saps had been steadily approaching their line. About 100 yards apart they had snaked their way closer and closer and were now a real threat to the Indian positions. The saps could not be shelled by artillery because they were too close to the Indians' own trenches, and not enough mortars had as yet been manufactured for the Pioneers to do the shelling themselves. Whether the saps were purely to cover the approach of bombing parties or whether they were to be used to project the German line forward was not known, but it was time that they were dealt with.

The raid would be carried out by 125 men of the 6th Jats, who were in Bareilly Brigade reserve, and a half company of No 3 Company Sappers and Miners, the whole to be under the command of Major Dundas, 6th Jats. The plan was for the Jats to enter the saps and work their way down them until they came to the main German firing line. They would then clear and hold that portion of the firing line while the Sappers and Miners filled in the saps. The Indian Corps had learned a lesson or two from their previous french raids, and this time the attack would rely on surprise, with no preliminary bombardment. Once the 6th Jats were in the German front line however, the guns would open fire on the enemy support and reserve trenches, to prevent a counter-attack and to allow the raiding party to withdraw unscathed.

Jats come from the Punjab, Rajputana and Oudh. They are Hindu, but not obsessively so,* and the majority recruited into the army were from agricultural stock. They should not be confused with Jat Sikhs, also farmers from the same area but whose forefathers had embraced Sikhism. Jats were generally tall, large limbed and handsome and were considered to be stoical and capable of putting up with extremes of privation. MacMunn considered that the Jat was 'stolid and unimaginative, but never forgets what he has once learned'[1]. The 6th Jat Light Infantry, which was to be awarded the sobriquet 'Royal' for its performance in the War, was a Class Regiment with four companies of Jats.

The raid was a model of what such an operation should be. At 2055 hours the assault group crept out of the 107th Pioneers' trenches and moved off towards the heads of the two saps. They achieved almost complete surprise: the enemy in the left sap took to their heels, while those in the right sap, although of stouter heart, were soon put to the bayonet. The Sappers and Miners set to in order to fill in the saps, and the whole force was able to withdraw after an hour of profitable work. Despite some Germans having got in behind the withdrawal route the whole enterprise cost only 29 wounded amongst the 6th Jats, and three killed and one wounded amongst the Sappers and Miners. The latter, having to work on top of the saps in order to render them untenable, were more exposed to enemy fire than were their infantry comrades. An efficient and inexpensive action, the raid raised confidence amongst the men of the Bareilly Brigade and brought a DSO to Dundas, the IDSM to a jemadar and a colour havildar of the Sappers and Miners, and an MC, an IOM and two IDSMs to the 6th Jats.

The two brigades of the Lahore Division could now at last get some rest well behind the lines. The 47th Sikhs were billeted in an abandoned farm in Lacouture, the men in large, weatherproof barns with a plentiful

---

*   The Jats permitted widows to remarry, a practice abhorrent to most other Hindus.

supply of straw for sleeping on, and the officers' mess in the house itself. A well stocked and comprehensive wine cellar was soon uncovered, the contents of which assisted in the recuperation of the battalion which had been constantly in action from 21 October to 16 November.

Officer replacements continued to arrive in ones and twos. For the Gurkha regiments there were the second battalions to draw on, whose British officers spoke Gurkhali and understood the customs of the men. It was more difficult for the single battalion regiments. The posting authorities would try as far as they could to send to a Sikh regiment someone who had some experience of Sikhs, and to a regiment with Pathans an officer who could speak Pushtu, but it was not always possible and even when it was, there could be problems of assimilation. Lieutenant Colonel Gunning of the 35th Sikhs had arrived on 13 November. He had originally been sent to France to take command of a different battalion altogether but was sent in error to the 47th Sikh lines. As he was in situ and as the 47th did not have a lieutenant colonel, the normal rank of a battalion commander, since the wounding of Richardson on 26 October, Corps headquarters told Gunning to assume command. Despite Gunning's coming from a Sikh regiment the 47th Sikhs were unhappy about this arrangement. They did not know Gunning and they had assumed, not unnaturally, that Major Davidson who had commanded the battalion with some distinction since the evacuation of Richardson, would be confirmed in command. Armies do not work like that, however, and even in wartime seniority rules. Gunning was in fact an excellent soldier, but he had to work hard to overcome the initial resentment of a battalion which had bonded under fire and which regarded him as an interloper.

Although soldier reinforcements were still not arriving at more than a trickle, Vaughan's Rifles did at least manage to recover its Afridi Company, now fully recovered from chicken pox, on 9 November and with them came Captains Baldwin and Bale, who had been retained in England to help in the training of the New Armies. Baldwin would last but a fortnight, before being killed at Festubert.

On 21 November the Prince of Wales, later to be King Edward VIII, visited the Front. For reasons of security his visit was kept a closely guarded secret until the last minute, but those units not actually in the firing line sent a few men to meet him and those who could be spared lined the route behind the reserve trenches. Whatever Edward's merits as a man and as a future King may have been, he was 'good with people' and he genuinely cared. His brief meetings with soldiers of the Indian Corps reinforced their belief that the King Emperor was concerned about the welfare of his Indian subjects and the visit was talked about for weeks.

The length of front held by the Indian Corps, with one division in the line, was now about three and a half miles, running from Port Arthur, the junction of the D171 and the D947, on the left, to Givenchy on the right.

Battalions continued to conduct an aggressive defence, and patrols and small-scale raids continued. On 21 November snow fell for the first time. Most of the sepoys had seen snow on the far Himalayas, but few had actually experienced it. Battalion quartermasters hastened to provide makeshift smocks made from old sheets commandeered from French houses, and these provided some measure of camouflage for men on patrols in no man's land. The first periscopes began to make their appearance. These were manufactured by the Sappers and Miners and consisted of a small mirror on a stick. The user stood in the trench with his back to the enemy side and pushed the mirror up above the parapet. Inevitably these made fine targets for bored enemy snipers, but they were better than nothing and very useful for sentries, who need not now keep their heads where they might be shot at.

The Battles Nomenclature Committee would recognise two battles of Festubert, both of which are battle honours for those regiments that were there. The better known of the two, Festubert 1915, would be borne on the colours of numerous British and Indian regiments, but Festubert 1914 would be carried only by the regiments of the Indian Corps, for it was upon them, and upon them alone, that the next German onslaught would fall. There was some warning that something was up. German sapping activities increased all along the Indian Corps' front and on 21 November there was a severe mortaring of the 6th Jats, followed the next day by a further mortar bombardment which fell on them and on Vaughan's Rifles. It was planned that the Meerut Division would be relieved in the line by the now rested Lahore Division, the changeover taking place in two phases, on the nights 22/23 and 23/24 November.

It was a good time for the Germans to launch an attack: newly arrived units were still adjusting themselves to the trench systems they had taken over, and command was in the process of changing from one division to the other. It is reasonable to assume that the enemy knew a relief was taking place, and they might have had more success had they attacked around midnight, when units were still moving up and communication trenches were crowded, rather than, as they did, just before first light.

All along the Indian Corps front the enemy saps had been getting closer and closer, despite patrolling and trench raids to try to eliminate them, and at about 0715 hours, just before dawn, on 23 November the Germans launched a major attack in at least divisional strength against the centre part of the Indian line, east of Festubert. It began with a torrent of bombs thrown from saps at the junction between the Connaught Rangers company and the 1/34th Sikh Pioneers, just south of the D72 and 12,000 yards east of the Festubert cross-roads. Subadar Natha Singh was in charge of this section, where there was also a Maxim machine-gun of the 1/34th. The enemy were so close, and still largely able to take cover in their sap head, that the gun could do little. The crew hung on as long as they could, but when all had been killed or wounded, a havildar whose post was nearby picked up the gun (no light weight) and carried it back to the support line. The German artillery was not up to its usual standard and there was less shelling than had preceded previous attacks, but the combined Regimental Aid Posts of Wilde's Rifles and the 129th Baluchis, in Festubert village, received a direct hit killing both battalions' Medical Officers, Captain Kunwar Indrajit Singh of Wilde's Rifles and Major Atal of the 129th. Both were of the Indian Medical Services, were the only Indians in their regiments to hold the King's commission, and were well liked and good doctors.

As the German infantry continued to come on, preceded by bombers with a seemingly inexhaustible supply of grenades, to which the Indian Corps had only a very inadequate answer, Subadar Natha Singh pulled the remnants of his men out of the forward line and reorganised them in the rear. This allowed some Germans to get into the trenches and the gap once opened, began to widen. The 1/34th Sikh Pioneers were literally bombed out of their trenches, as were the 9th Bhopal on the Pioneers' right. The Germans were now able to enfilade the Connaughts, on the north side of the gap, and Vaughan's Rifles on the south. The Connaughts, not helped by the Garhwal Brigade trench mortar which was supporting them bursting its barrel, began to crowd into the trenches of Wilde's Rifles and those of the 129th Baluchis. On the other side the left-hand company of Vaughan's were also driven back.

At about 0900 hours the German effort appeared to be slackening somewhat and the 1/34 Sikh Pioneers attempted a counter-attack to regain their lost trenches. It came to nothing. The Germans now occupied about 800 yards of the Indian line, running from the D72 south-south-west to a point 500 yards north-east of Les Fontaines. Although the entire centre section of the Indian line was in the hands of the Germans, the gap was getting no wider and the mixed force of the 129th Baluchis, Wilde's Rifles and the Connaughts were able to hold on the left, where Lieutenant Colonel Southey, Commanding Officer 129th Baluchis, had ordered some of his men into a line of ruined houses to the rear of the firing line. From these buildings the men could fire down on the advancing enemy while remaining under cover themselves. On the right three companies of Vaughan's Rifles and the Black Watch held firm.

At noon the 6th Jats had arrived in the support trenches and were thrown into a hasty counter-attack. It failed, beaten down by the machine-guns which the Germans had succeeded in establishing in the captured Indian trench line. Any unit available was now ordered up for a counter-attack which would be organised by Brigadier General Egerton, commanding the Ferozepore Brigade. Battalions moved up from billets or reserve were the 1/39th Garhwalis, the 2/8th Gurkhas, the 2nd Leicesters, the remainder of the Connaught Rangers and the 107th Pioneers. The Secunderabad

Cavalry Brigade, dismounted, was moved up to Essars to provide further support if required.

The counter-attack to seal the gap was planned for 1600 hours. The Corps Commander had ordered that the lost trenches were to be recovered 'at all costs', an expression that was to become depressingly familiar as the war went on. It was a different situation from that which had prevailed when Neuve Chapelle had been lost earlier in the month. Then the British could simply abandon the village and pull back to an equally good defensive posture farther back and buy time until resources allowed its recapture. Now this portion of the firing line could not be abandoned, for to do so would eventually render the whole of the line untenable and might allow a German breakthrough. Perhaps equally important, in the mind of the Corps Commander, was the knowledge that this was the Indian Corps' first solo action. In blunt terms, however many casualties might be sustained, the position had to be restored.

The orders given to Lieutenant Colonel Grant, commanding the 2/8th Gurkhas, who would command the counter-attack, were for a frontal attack straight into the gap. The Gurkhas, the 6th Jats, the 9th Bhopals and the remainder of the Connaughts moved off, with the 107th Pioneers in support. It was an advance of the type later to be described as a partridge drive—up, into one line and walk or run towards the enemy. There was snow on the ground and most of the men were still wearing Khaki Drill. Despite French artillery support the sepoys were easy targets for the Germans, and made little progress except on the right. There, the 2/8th Gurkhas managed to pick up groups of men of the 9th Bhopals and Vaughan's Rifles, who were still sheltering behind their old line, and recapture a portion of the lost trenches. The gap had been reduced, but it was still there.

Captain Buckland, 2/8th Gurkhas, now ensconced on the south of the gap, took Havildar Hariparsad Thapa and tried to extend his hold by moving along the trench towards the other side of the gap. Between them they bombed and bayoneted their way along but were soon held up by stout resistance from behind a traverse. Buckland tried to find more men to exploit his success, but found that of the other two British officers with the 2/8th Gurkhas one was dead and one badly wounded. Such riflemen as had established a lodgement were busy trying to defend it, and there were no more men to be had.

By this stage it was 1930 hours and full dark. The Germans still held 600 yards of the British line, although there was now a crescent of sepoys just east of Festubert and west of the gap. Brigadier General Egerton now had the services of the 1/39th Garhwalis, just arrived in the area. A further attack must be made and this time it would be carried out by the 1/39th Garhwalis on the left and two companies of the 2nd Leicesters with two companies of the 107th Pioneers on the right. The whole would be commanded by Lieutenant Colonel

Grant, who had received his orders from Egerton at the Ferozepore Brigade headquarters in Festubert village. Grant returned to the battle area and called his subordinate commanders together. The orders were for the attack to be made frontally, and included the snippet that intelligence suggested that the Germans had in fact abandoned the captured trench. On hearing this gem, Lieutenant Orchard, of the 2/8th Gurkhas, opined that this was simply not so. The line was strongly held and there were numerous machine-guns in place—he knew, he had only just returned from the last unsuccessful attack. Lieutenant Colonel Swiney, commanding 1/39th Garhwalis also demurred: three frontal counter-attacks had failed, surely there must be another way? Orchard added that in his opinion the only method which gave a reasonable hope of success was to launch a pincer attack from the left and right of the gap, still in Indian hands, coming in from behind the enemy. With the views of the conference so firmly expressed, Colonel Grant went back to Brigade headquarters to try to persuade the Brigadier to change his mind. He returned with the news that there was to be no more argument: the attack was to be conducted as ordered and immediately.

After the war the high command was to be accused of ordering impossible missions from miles behind the lines after a good dinner. There is of course nothing wrong with a good dinner, but it does appear that in this case such criticism was justified (more often it was not) for while many of the accounts are vague and contradictory, it does seem that Egerton never actually looked at the ground across which he was launching so many of his troops. On that night the men on the spot concocted their own plan of action.

The troops moved off, ostensibly to a Brigade-dictated start line in the support trenches at the end of a road 400 yards east of Festubert and 800 yards west of the objective. The official accounts say the 1/39th Garhwalis, not being familiar with the ground and having arrived in the dark, got lost and somehow found themselves in touch with the 129th Baluchis to the north of the gap—just where they would have gone had the Brigade Commander accepted the conference's recommendations! A message went back to Egerton to the effect that the left of the attacking force was out of position but could attack from the flank. Egerton obviously accepted the situation and replied that the plan would now be at the discretion of the commander on the spot. This made far more sense, and at 0230 hours a two-pronged attack was launched. On the right the 107th Pioneers were repulsed but the 2nd Leicesters effected a lodgement and held. On the left the 1/39th Garhwalis now began to bomb, bayonet and shoot their way along the trench, actively encouraged and assisted by Lieutenant Robson of the Sappers and Miners and lately the prototype mortar officer. Although a full company was attacking down the trench, the frontage could only be two or three men, owing to the narrowness of the trench, and small groups of men took turns at the point of the advance. The company commander, Major Wardell, was soon killed, and his place at the front of the company working its way down the trench was taken by Naik Darwan Sing Negi. The naik must have had a charmed life, no one knows how many Germans he killed personally, but he worked his way from traverse to traverse until at last the 1/39th were able to join up with the 2nd Leicesters at the other side of the gap. Darwan Sing was eventually badly wounded, but survived to be awarded the Victoria Cross. No one ever found out exactly how Major Wardell was killed—his body was never found—but it was known that he was very short-sighted and the battalion believed that he had come to a sap and blundered down it, towards the German positions, thinking it was the original Indian line.

By dawn the Indian line was back where it had been 24 hours before, and more and more men of the Lahore Division were being pushed up in support. The gap had been closed, but at a cost of 40 British officers and 1,150 Indian all ranks killed and wounded. Vaughan's Rifles had three British officers, one Indian officer and 53 IORs killed and two British officers, one Indian officer and 61 IORs wounded, with 11 missing. The 2/8th Gurkhas lost three British officers, three Indian officers and 14 GORs killed and two British officers and 57 GORs wounded. The Official History makes little mention of the action, but it was a gallant little affair fought out in the dark in filthy weather and caused even heavier casualties to the enemy. The 1/39th Garhwalis alone captured two trench mortars, three machine-guns and four German officers and 100 Other Ranks as prisoners.

By 25 November the Indian Corps could resume an aggressive defence, but trench foot was now causing serious concern in some units. Trench foot is caused by reduced circulation in the feet and legs brought on by continuous standing in cold water and mud. It starts as chilblains, then the feet go white, feeling is lost in the toes and eventually the entire foot becomes numb. At this stage there is damage to the nervous system and even on recovery hot and cold twinges may persist. It becomes very painful to walk. If the condition is not treated the feet become blue-black, gangrene develops and the feet may eventually require amputation. The condition was not helped by the tendency of the men to wrap their puttees round their legs as tightly as they could, in order to prevent them being sucked off when moving through knee-deep mud. The medical services were well aware of the dangers and issued regular instructions about its prevention. They pointed out that men's feet should be kept dry, socks should be changed regularly and recommended the provision of warmth, shelter, hot food, and facilities for washing the feet and drying wet clothes for men leaving the trenches—which was all good stuff, but rarely possible at this stage of the war.

In regiments where officers insisted on regular feet inspections and where men were able to care for their feet, cases of trench foot were few—the 47th

Sikhs had hardly any—but in units which had to wait in support or communication trenches for long periods, or whose trenches were below the water
table, large numbers of men fell prey to it and suffered accordingly. The
Poona Horse, who had been ordered into the firing line on 24 November,
took one and a half hours to walk one and a half miles when coming out
again on 26 November, so bad was the state of the men's feet.

A short thaw now set in, making the conditions in the trenches worse.
Parapets slid to the trench floor and loopholes carved out of frozen earth
collapsed. There was more work for the Sappers and Miners, and patrols
in no man's land could no longer skip lightly over the frozen ground.
That peace-time standards of equipment management still held good in
some battalions was demonstrated on 27 November, when the 47th Sikhs
despatched a patrol of Havildar Lachman Singh and Sepoy Rur Singh to
examine a German sap in front of the 47th's trenches. The pair got to the
sap but on their way back were fired on, Rur Singh being wounded and
unable to run. Havildar Lachman Singh picked up the wounded man and
got him to safety in his own trench, when he noticed that Rur Singh's rifle
was still lying where it had been dropped. Leaving Rur Singh to the care
of the medical orderlies the havildar scrambled back out of the trench,
retraced his steps as fast as he could and recovered the lost rifle—returning without a scratch despite fire being directed at him from the German
trenches. It was a terrible thing—a disgrace—to lose a rifle on the frontier
and in 1914 even in France izzat demanded its recovery.

The strength of the Indian Corps, including the Secunderabad Cavalry
Brigade, was now down to around 14,000 effectives, or about the strength
of a British division. Despite the Corps Commander's request for the
Indian Corps to be taken out of the line for a short period to recuperate
and receive reinforcements, there was nobody to replace them and they
had to stay in the line.

Some help was at last on the way, however, for on 1 December the Sirhind
Brigade arrived at Marseilles, and the 1st Battalion The Highland Light Infantry,
the 1st Battalion The 1st Gurkha Rifles, the 1st Battalion The 4th Gurkha Rifles
and 125th Napier's Rifles disembarked. They had been retained in Egypt to
guard the Suez Canal, where the insistence of a sentry of the 1/4th Gurkhas
in ordering a British warship passing through the canal to halt and give the
password has gone down in legend. Asked later what he would have done
had the ship not stopped—which at considerable expense and loss of time it
did—the rifleman said that he would have fired at the bridge where he knew
the captain would be. On 2 December the Brigade entrained for Orléans and
subsequently for Merville, whence on 7 December the battalions marched to
billets at Les Lobes, five miles west of Neuve Chapelle.

Reinforcements from India began to arrive too. Previously there had been
a few individual British officer replacements and a number of reservists had
been sent up from Marseilles. Many of these latter were quite unfit for life in

the trenches, either because of age, poor physique or, in at least one case, due to having no teeth! All of this should have been recognised in India before the men were sent, and that it was not was an indication of just how anti-quated the reservist system was. Now at last some regular soldiers began to arrive, although in many cases not from the regiment to be reinforced. Regimental depots were recruiting as hard as they could, but the system was still very much ad hoc. Apart from the Gurkhas all regiments in France had only one battalion, except for the Garhwalis, both of whose battalions were there, and drafts had to be from other regiments of similar racial composition. Initially reinforcements were sent as groups of individuals but later formed companies would be sent complete with their own officers and NCOs which was much better for the morale of the new arrivals.

In early December the 9th Bhopals received four Indian officers and 180 men drawn variously from the 1st Brahmins, the 21st Punjabis, the 96th Infantry and their own depot, while on 9 December they received two British officer replacements in the shape of Lieutenant Taylor of the 1st Brahmins and Captain Jardine of the 96th Infantry. Even with this reinforcement the strength of the battalion was now so low that the Commanding Officer reorganised it into a two-company battalion, one company being composed of Sikhs and Rajputs and the other of Mussalmans and Brahmins, which must have given the cooks something to think about. After three weeks at the Front the 2/8th Gurkhas had only one of their original complement of British officers left, Captain Buckland, and until British officer reinforcements arrived he found himself looking after the firing line by day and acting as both adjutant and quartermaster at night.

The 47th Sikhs received one British officer from the 35th Sikhs, and one British officer, two Indian officers and 187 IORs from their own depot on 8 December. On the same day two British officers, two Gurkha officers and 131 GORs arrived from Dehra Dun and reported to the 2/2nd Gurkhas while the two battalions of the 39th Garhwalis got two British officers and 158 IORs between them. Vaughan's Rifles had the luxury of five new British officers—they needed them—with two Indian officers and 204 IORs from the 91st Punjabis.

The 129th Baluchis were not quite so fortunate. Their linked regiment, the 124th Baluchis, had arrived back in India from China in September 1914 and were then sent on leave prior to standing by to reinforce the 129th. A rumour swept round the Pathan Mahsuds of the 124th Baluchis that the Indian government was planning a punitive expedition into their tribal territories once the cold weather of 1914 arrived,[*] and 22 Mahsuds

---

[*] I can find no evidence to support this rumour and it is unlikely that the government would have embarked on such a frolic when so many Mahsuds were fighting in France.

failed to report back from leave, electing to stay at home instead. A draft was nevertheless cobbled together and the 129th got some men.

Most units of the Indian Corps received a draft and at last most of the battalions could once more parade at something like their correct establishment. Warm clothing began to make its appearance, khaki serge jackets and trousers, as issued to the British troops and more pullovers, gloves and flannel shirts. Greatcoats too began to emerge from the logiscal machinery. It was only just in time for the 1/9th Gurkhas, whose men were still in khaki drill shorts, many of them now in rags. A well meaning attempt to find clothing sizes to fit the Garhwalis went wrong when the first consignment of jackets had to be taken away as being too small to fit even them.

Even with the reinforcements and the arrival of the Sirhind Brigade the Corps was still well under strength and there was an acute shortage of British officers. In the first week of December Corps headquarters ordered that no British officer was to go 'over the top' in any action involving fewer than 60 men. While the logic of this order is unarguable, it was totally out of the question as far as the British officers themselves were concerned. Their men expected them to lead, and lead they would. The order was largely ignored, and in most battalions not even promulgated.

By 1 December the casualties of the Indian Corps had amounted to 61 British officers, 27 Indian officers and 546 IORs killed, 100 British officers, 58 Indian officers and 3,148 IORs wounded, with 26 British officers, ten Indian officers and 1,041 IORs missing. Many of the missing were later found to have been killed. With the arrival of the Sirhind Brigade from Egypt on 7 December the Corps Commander hoped to have the Corps relieved from duty in the trenches and moved back to billets in the rear area to rest and refit. It was not to be, indeed given the enemy pressure it could not be. On 9 December Field Marshal Sir John French's Chief of Staff ordered the Indian Corps to extend its line even farther, and on 11 December the Corps took over the Givenchy sector from the French. Both divisions were now in the line, Meerut to the left and Lahore to the right, linking up with the French on the Bethune/La Bassée road.

The weather gave no respite. It was cold and there was constant rain. The drainage ditches which criss-crossed the area became blocked up for want of maintenance and this made the already waterlogged ground worse. Some trenches were 18 inches deep in glutinous mud which covered everything and got into rifle bolts, compasses and field glasses. Despite efforts to keep clean everyone by now was caked with wet mud, and while Indian troops could generally be distinguished by their headgear, it was impossible to tell Germans from British at any distance. Bundles of straw littered the fields, propped up on slicks in a vain attempt to allow them to dry, and at night these looked deceptively like men, causing many a false alarm amongst the sentries.

This would be the Sirhind Brigade's first experience of European trench warfare. The initial deployment saw the Highland Light Infantry, the 1/1st Gurkhas and Napier's Rifles all in the line, with the 1/4th Gurkhas in Brigade reserve in the Rue de Bethune, about a mile west of Festubert. With the arrival of Napier's Rifles a further racial group was introduced to France, for the regiment had, in addition to three companies of Rajputs, a company of Mahrattas—the only Mahratta company to serve in the Indian Corps infantry, although there was one company in the 107th Pioneers and half a company in the 3rd Sappers and Miners. Mahrattas, like so many of the groups which made up the Indian Army, had originally been enemies of the British. The Mahrattas and their allies the Pindaris—nomadic mounted reivers and scallywags—had caused the British considerable trouble in the eighteenth and early nineteenth centuries. They had only been brought under the control of the East India Company at the end of the Third Mahratta War in 1819. Mahrattas come from Central India and the Deccan and most were peasant farmers or small landlords. They are Hindus and tend towards a slim, wiry physique. They were conspicuously loyal during the Mutiny and by 1914 there were six Class Regiments of Mahratta Light Infantry, each of one battalion, and Mahrattas were also represented in other Class Company regiments.

Although the 1/4th Gurkhas were in reserve, their introduction to what many of them still called 'The Game' was not to be delayed, for on the battalion's first day at Rue de Bethune their billets were heavily shelled. The men took shelter in ditches and few casualties were caused, but one shell came through the roof of the house being used as an office by the Adjutant and the Quartermaster, destroying most of the accumulated paperwork. This was a godsend to two harassed young officers struggling with the myriad reports and returns required by regulations. For days the reply to any letter, directive or reminder from Brigade headquarters was 'It is regretted that the correspondence was destroyed by shell fire'[2]. Eventually a letter from the Brigade Major of the Sirhind Brigade, Major Ridgeway, also a Fourth Gurkha, said starkly: 'The effects of the shell referred to must cease after the 10th inst.'[3] On 16 December the battalion relieved Napier's Rifles just north of Givenchy.

On 12 December the Corps Commander, Sir James Willcocks, attended a conference at General Headquarters. Here he heard that the Commander-in-Chief intended to mount an offensive from the Messines area with II and Ill Corps beginning on 14 December, the objective being the line Le Touquet/Warneton/Holbeke. The Indian Corps and IV Corps would not be directly involved but would carry out 'other local operations with a view to containing the enemy now in their front'[4].

On 16 December the Ferozepore Brigade was accordingly ordered to carry out an attack in the Jullunder Brigade area just west of Givenchy. Here the Germans had been digging two saps towards the 15th Sikhs. The left-hand sap had got to within about 25 yards of the Sikhs' line while the right-hand excavation stopped about 50 yards short. The plan was to attack both saps simultaneously and then to advance down them and seize the portion of the German main line between the two saps. The assault would be carried out by the 129th Baluchis, one company attacking each sap head. Wilde's Rifles would follow up, the 1st Connaught Rangers would be in support while the French 142 Territorial Battalion, lent to the Ferozepore Brigade for the operation, would be in reserve.

At 0520 hours on the morning of 16 December the 129th Baluchis and Wilde's Rifles got into position for the assault and at Zero Hour, 0830 hours, the assaulting parties doubled across the open round towards the objectives. On the left the company commanded by Major Potter got into the sap and began to shoot and bomb up it towards the German main line. On the right the company led by Lieutenant Browning also reached the sap head but seemed to the watchers in the 15th Sikhs' trenches to be making little progress. Follow-up action now turned out to be impossible as the Germans had woken up to what was happening and were bringing a heavy fire down on both saps and on the 15th Sikhs' lines. This possibility had been foreseen, and it had been realised that reinforcement would depend upon a communication trench being dug to link the captured saps with the 15th Sikhs' trenches. Two parties each of ten men of the 15th Sikhs had moved out with the 129th's companies and now began to dig from the sap heads back towards their own lines. At the same time men from the 1/34th Sikh Pioneers and the Sappers and Miners began to dig out from the Indian trenches towards the saps.

Despite the short distance it was very difficult to see from the 15th Sikhs' trenches what was happening to their front and in the saps. It appeared that the right-hand attack was making no progress and the decision was taken to tell Major Potter, with the left-hand party, not to attempt to press on any farther. The problem was how to communicate with him, the eventual solution being to write a message on a piece of paper, tie it to a stone and throw it into the left-hand sap. If the message ever got to Potter he ignored it, for after about an hour it was discovered that both attacks had in fact progressed to within a few yards of the German main line. By mid-afternoon, however, both assault groups had become bogged down and were just holding their own, with Browning and all the Indian officers in the right-hand group wounded. Digging of the communications trench in both directions was going well but it was beginning to become obvious that speedy reinforcement in the face of heavy German rifle and machine-gun fire across the intervening open ground was not an option. The 15th Sikhs did their best to assist. At one stage the Adjutant, Lieutenant Barstow, spotted a German firing over the enemy parapet down into the right-hand sap. Barstow grabbed a rifle from the nearest sepoy and proceeded to kill or wound no fewer than ten Germans. Although the range to the target was not great, this was a near incredible feat: the rifle was not zeroed[*] to Barstow and he was himself under fire the while. The Germans now began throwing bombs into the left-hand sap, but as they had miscalculated the length of the fuses, the sepoys were able to pick most of them up and throw them back.

Just before last light the diggers of the 15th Sikhs met those of the 1/34th Sikh Pioneers and the communication trench to the left-hand sap was complete. The task on the right-hand side was much more difficult, however. There the distance was greater and the Germans had a good field of fire across and into the sap and the communication trench. It was found necessary to dig the latter much more deeply and to construct a parapet along it so that some fire could be returned. Nevertheless, by last light only 12 yards remained to be dug, and hopes began to rise that a significant reinforcement might yet be effected.

Unfortunately for the optimists the men of the 129th Baluchis in the right-hand sap were now in a perilous situation. They had fought all day with no officers, they had taken a number of casualties and they were being subjected to bombing, with the correct lengths of fuse this time. After dark, at about 1800 hours, those left on their feet attempted to withdraw back to their own lines. Not a single man got back. The Germans now re-occupied their sap and began to fire down the still incomplete communication trench. There was no option but to evacuate the communications trench, build a barricade and cease operations on the right-hand side.

On the left Major Potter held on for a while but eventually had no option but to withdraw his men. The losses of the two companies of the 129th Baluchis involved were considerable: one British officer, one Indian officer and 53 IORs killed, with two British officers, two Indian officers and 57 IORs wounded. While the attack had not been a success, it had at least prevented the Germans from moving troops from that part of the Front to anywhere else.

On 17 December the Commander-in-Chief of the BEF announced that he intended 'attacking all along the front'[5] on 18 December, using II, III, IV and the Indian Corps. In a later paragraph in the same written order Sir John French said 'these Corps will demonstrate and seize any favourable opportunity to capture any enemy trenches in their front'. Here was potential confusion, as Sir James Willcocks was quick to realise. To attack is quite clear—it implies a deliberate offensive against the enemy line. To demonstrate, on the other hand, implies a feint or a show of force, usually intended to divert attention from operations elsewhere. At 0245 hours on 18 December Sir James issued his own orders to the commanders of the

---

[*]   Each man holds his rifle slightly differently and this affects the fall of shot. Each man's
       rifle therefore had its sights adjusted to that individual. Someone else firing the rifle
       would have to watch where the first shot landed and adjust his aim accordingly.

Lahore and Meerut Divisions, telling them to prepare local offensives. At 1015 hours on the same day an addition to the original operation order arrived from GHQ which stated: 'the efforts of II, III, IV and the Indian Corps should be directed only on such objectives as are reasonably feasible'[6]. A further codicil at 1615 hours said: 'The II, III, IV and Indian Corps are to demonstrate on 19 December along the whole front and seize every favourable opportunity which may offer to capture any of the enemy trenches.'[7]

Despite the uncertainty as to exactly what Sir John French wanted the troops to do, the Commander of the Indian Corps was clear that local operations of limited extent were required. He left the details to his divisional commanders with the proviso that he would finally approve or reject divisions' plans. Lieutenant General Watkis, commanding the Lahore Division, produced a somewhat grandiose scheme which involved an attack on a frontage of 1,000 yards. This was far too ambitious for the number of men and the artillery support available, and the Corps Commander restricted the division to an attack on a 300-yard frontage. It would be an assault on the German trenches opposite the junction of the Ferozepore and Sirhind Brigades, in front of and just north-east of Givenchy.

Sir James approved the Meerut Division's plan as it stood, which was for an attack on the German trenches near the wood known as The Orchard at La Quinque Rue opposite the 6th Jats, the left-hand battalion of the Dehra Dun Brigade.

Zero Hour for the Lahore Division's attack was 0534 hours on a dark, wet and stormy morning and was preceded by a short (four-minute) artillery bombardment. Shells were still in short supply and it was felt better to retain the majority of the available ration to deal with any German counter-attacks, rather than to fire it all off in the initial stages. On the Division's left the jumping off point would be just behind the front line trenches. They would then have to advance and negotiate the wire which protected the German positions. This wire was not the sophisticated barrier which would appear later in the war, but merely a few strands slung between posts. It was nevertheless an obstacle and gaps in it would be cut by Captain Inglis, the Adjutant of the 1/4th Gurkhas, who would then guide the attacking troops, the Highland Light Infantry and the 1/4th Gurkhas, to the gaps. Inglis crept out with a small group of battalion scouts, soldiers specially selected for their ability in field craft, who took with them a reel of telephone wire which they would use to guide the main body and as a means of communication later. Having cut gaps in the wire the little group returned to the main line and brought the assaulting troops forward as soon as the artillery bombardment started. In four lines, the whole commanded by Major Nicolay 1/4th Gurkhas, the assault group arrived at the wire, about 120 yards from their own lines. The men

1. British Officers, sepoys, followers and dockyard coolies loading a troop transporter at Bombay in August 1914. The medallions round the necks of the two men leaning on the rail in the foreground indicate that they are official regimental followers, who accompanied the troops.

2. Embarkation points for Indian troops bound for Europe were Karachi and Bombay. Here regimental baggage is being unloaded from goods wagons prior to being loaded onto the ships at Alexandra dock in Bombay. Baggage mules travelled too, and as equine bowels move eight times a day the men would have had to take care where they placed their feet.

3. Men of the 39th Garhwal Rifles arriving at the Front from Marseilles, 2 November 1914. Frequently mistaken for Gurkhas, with whom they are racially and linguistically linked, they turned their hats up on the opposite (right) side to effect a distinction.

4. Men of the 129th Baluchis near Holobeke, 28 October 1914, during First Ypres. The Indian Officer in the lead is carrying an obsolete pattern cavalry or light infantry sabre. As the Indian Army did not bring swords to the Western Front this is probably a family heirloom.

5. A sowar of the Indian cavalry near Messines, 4 October 1914. He is armed with a lance and has affixed his sword where the rifle would normally be. As left-handedness was regarded as unlucky, the exchange of rifle and sword is probably a personal affectation, generally tolerated in what was still mainly Silladar cavalry until the outbreak of war. He carries an extra bandolier of ammunition round the horse's neck, standard practice for cavalry. The man is a Pathan so probably from the 15th Lancers, the Lahore Divisional cavalry regiment.

6. Indian cavalry on the Western Front, besides the divisional cavalry squadrons, grew from one brigade to two divisions and remained in France until early 1918 when an urgent requirement for more cavalry to pursue the Turks led to their redeployment to Palestine. Probably

the best light cavalry in the world, the conditions of the war in Europe prevented them from showing all that they could do, but they were a very useful adjunct to the BEF nevertheless.

7 & 8. Having been detained in Egypt to guard the Suez Canal pending the arrival of Territorial units from the UK, the Sirhind Brigade of the Lahore Division landed at Marseilles on 1 December. They reached the front on 7 December and had their first taste of action in the Battle of Givenchy on 20 and 21 December. The plate above shows men of the 125th Napier's Rifles, Rajputs and Mahrattas, leaving the trenches with a home-made regimental flag and, with an eye to Allied solidarity, a French tricolour. They would not receive winter clothing until early 1915, such was the pressure that rapid expansion placed upon the British textile industry.

9. The Punjabi Mussalman company of the 129th Baluchis behind breastworks near Wytschaete, October 1914. Although the photograph is obviously posed, it shows the khaki drill uniforms in which the Indian Corps would spend the winter. The British Officer in the rear rank has attached a non-regulation chinstrap to his turban to prevent it being knocked off. The sepoys were more practised at tying turbans securely.

10. *Opposite above:* A trench mortar improvised by the Indian Sappers and Miners, winter 1914. This is an early prototype made of wood bound with wire, but could propel a limited number of 6lb projectiles 400 yards. The next versions were made of steel piping and copied by the whole of the BEF. While the Germans had a plentiful supply of trench mortars, the BEF had only the Indian invention until the arrival of the Stokes trench mortar in early 1915.

11. Gurkha pipers, probably those of the 2/3ʳᵈ Gurkhas, playing in billets in 1915. With the exception of the 2ⁿᵈ Gurkhas, all Gurkha regiments had pipe and drum bands for no other reason than they were originally raised by Scots officers. The 2ⁿᵈ Gurkhas, having been raised by an Anglo-Irishman, had a bugle platoon. The soldiers now have serge uniforms and while retaining their black chevrons, have had to accept general issue brass buttons instead of their normal black.

12. The 2/3rd Gurkha Rifles being inspected shortly after the issue of serge uniforms in 1915. The left marker of the front rank is very young and probably well under age. Many Gurkhas claimed to be 18 in order to enlist but some were as young as 14 or 15. The same applies today.

13. A company of the 15th Sikhs coming out of the line August 1915. The British Officer leading them is Lt J G 'Jackie' Smyth who had been awarded the VC for his bravery on 18 May.

14. A battery of Indian artillery moving up to the Front in August 1915. While the infantry divisions of the Indian Corps would leave France in November 1915, much of the Indian artillery would remain, formed into the 'Indian Artillery Group' and be used to support a variety of British corps until the end of the war.

15. Neuve Chapelle before the battle. This is the Rue d'Eglise with the cemetery behind the brick wall on the left.

16. House-to-house fighting, Neuve Chapelle. As one Sikh wrote home to his wife, 'When we met the enemy hand to hand my heart exulted'.

17. Neuve Chapelle after the battle. The remains of the cemetery can be seen where shelling by both sides opened up old graves, scattering the remains of long dead bodies.

18. *Above left:* Previously published, purporting to be Gurkhas reversing a captured trench, this is actually the 2/2nd Gurkhas training behind the lines on a mock-up of a German trench in early 1915. The British Officer to the left, walking towards the camera, is Lt Col Norie, the CO who lost his right arm in the Tirah before the war.

19. *Above right:* A soldier of the Indian Corps dressed and equipped for trench duty late in 1915. As he wears a balaclava he is probably a Gurkha. His greatcoat has the skirts buttoned back in the French style for ease of walking. Rubber trench boots, a periscope and a bell to warn of gas are attached to his pack. The item in his right hand appears to be a roll of barbed wire.

20. Kulbir Thapa, 2/3rd Gurkha Rifles, who was awarded the VC and promoted to naik for his actions at Loos. He enlisted in 1906, aged 16 but claiming to be 18, and was already a relatively old soldier when he arrived on the Western Front. He survived the war, retired as a havildar and died in 1958 aged 68.

21. The Indian Memorial at Neuve Chapelle was designed by Sir
Herbert Baker and formally opened on 7 October 1927 by Lord
Birkenhead, one time Recording Officer of the Indian Corps. Present
were Marshal Foch, Rudyard Kipling and a representative contingent of
all ranks of the Indian Army.

22. King George V, despite his German relatives, was as patriotic as any Englishman and took a great interest in his dominion and colonial troops, particularly those of India, whose emperor he was. They in turn revered the King, whose simple and straightforward manner helped to put them at ease, despite neither speaking the other's language. Here the King visits lightly wounded Indian soldiers somewhere in France. Those more seriously wounded were evacuated to Indian Military Hospitals in the UK, the largest of which was in Brighton.

lay down for a few minutes until the artillery lifted and then charged through the wire. Not content with getting the men to the right place from which to attack the enemy trenches, Inglis now insisted on staying with them and accompanying them in the assault. This was achieved with remarkably few casualties, but the few nevertheless included Captain Inglis, killed in his first battle of the war and with no business to be there anyway. Seizing the German first line, and taking 70 prisoners in the process, the men pressed on and attacked the support line. The Germans were now thoroughly roused and the British artillery had ceased fire. The Highlanders and the Gurkhas could make no impression on the second line of trenches and had to be content with consolidating their hold on the first line.

On the Division's right progress was less satisfactory. One company of the Scinde Rifles veered off its axis and got mixed up with the Highland Light Infantry to its left, while a platoon of the right-hand company lost direction and wandered off to its right. As a result only a few men actually reached the German firing line, while other small groups got into two German saps which ran out almost to the Indian trenches. The Sappers and Miners set to in order to join the saps to the Indian trenches, and eventually the right-hand sap was so joined, allowing the 129th Baluchis, who were holding the main Indian line at that point, to push reinforcements up. Despite the dark and the rain, German machine-guns on fixed lines kept up a heavy fire and the main enemy line could not be captured.

On the left the captured trenches were straight, and had no traverses in them. The reason for this now became clear as German enfilade fire began to take its toll from a firing position on some high ground near Givenchy village. Enemy local counter-attacks from the front and the flanks began, with bombs being widely used. Although all these attacks were beaten off throughout the rest of the night and the day, casualties began to mount. The jam tin bomb then issued to the Indian Corps consisted of a charge of gun cotton in a tin, with a fuse attached. To light the fuse it first had to be cut to expose the core, after which a match head had to be held to the end of the fuse before being ignited by the matchbox. Fuses, matches and boxes became soaked and an entire boxfull might have to be used to ignite one bomb. In any case the men of the Highland Light Infantry and the 1/4th Gurkhas quickly exhausted their own small stock of bombs, replenishing them from the much more effective German versions found in the captured trenches. The telephone wire had long since been cut by enemy fire and visual signalling was impossible. By last light it was evident that the position could not be held and Captain Cramer-Roberts 1/4th Gurkhas volunteered to take a message back to the Indian Corps trenches asking for artillery support to cover a withdrawal. By a miracle he actually reached the Sirhind Brigade line, but just as he was about to jump down into it he was caught by a burst of machine-gun fire which shattered both legs and an arm. The message got through, however, and the British guns opened up with a short salvo sufficient to allow the Highlanders and Gurkhas to get back to their own trenches bringing their wounded with them. Cramer-Roberts survived to be awarded the DSO, but he would never soldier again.

On the right a bad situation was becoming worse. The 129th Baluchis were unable to force the saps to the German main line, and as night drew in there was confusion and mounting casualties. The order to retire was given and the men of the Scinde Rifles began to withdraw back to their own line, all except one group which refused to withdraw as the body of their British officer, Lieutenant Bruce, had not yet been recovered. Every single man of this party was killed.

As an adjunct to the Lahore Division's assault an attack on a German sap head to the left of the Sirhind Brigade by two platoons of the 1/1st Gurkhas had been planned for 0530 hours on the morning of 19 December. The terrible conditions of the route to the jumping off point—mud, water and shell holes, crowded and collapsing communication trenches—meant that there was a long delay, and instead of the attack going in under the cover of darkness, it began at 1000 hours in broad daylight. It must have been obvious that there was no chance of success, and the operation should have been called off, but in it went, led by Captain Burke and Lieutenant Rundall. The party were easy targets for the enemy machine-guns and when both British officers had been killed and over 50% of the Gurkhas had been killed or wounded, the remnants withdrew back to the Indian line.

Shortly after dark the Lahore Division was back in its original trenches, the gains of the day having been lost. During the night no fewer than 30 German machine-guns kept up a heavy fire on the Highland Light Infantry trenches and it began to dawn on the Corps Commander that the Germans might have plans of their own.

The attack by the Meerut Division began at 0330 hours on the same morning, 19 December. Despite heavy enemy machine-gun fire a company of the Leicesters captured parts of a German advanced line on the left and penetrated as far as the main line. They were unable to hold however, as the main enemy position was not only stoutly defended but also under friendly artillery fire. On the right another company of the Leicesters had also seized and were holding a portion of the advanced line. At about 0400 hours a company of the 1/3rd Gurkhas under Major Dundas attempted to close the gap by bombing along the trench from the Leicester's right-hand company. At first good progress was made, but then a machine-gun opened up from a concealed position only 100 yards away. As dawn broke this machine-gun was able to enfilade the whole of the captured trench. Enemy mortars opened up and the Leicesters' right-hand company and Dundas's Gurkhas were forced to withdraw. On the left the company of

116

the Leicesters held on all day, but when they too came under increasing enemy retaliation, and when British aircraft reported German troop concentrations forming up opposite, they had no choice but to withdraw.

By nightfall everyone was back in their original positions. No objectives had been held, but the enemy had been heavily engaged and prevented from reinforcing other parts of his line.

For some time there had been rumours of German mining circulating amongst the Indian Corps. Outbreaks of tunnelling and counter-tunnelling, with dedicated companies of tunnellers on both sides often composed of men who had been miners in civilian life, would come later, and at this stage the Sappers and Miners had not yet tried their hand at it. The sepoys would shortly discover, to their cost, that the rumours were true.

The night of 19/20 December was relatively quiet, but it soon became clear that the Corps Commander's suspicions and the inferences drawn from the aviators' reports had been well founded. Torrential rain fell throughout the night, fire steps were washed away and, despite the efforts of the sepoys, rifles became clogged with mud and many would not fire. As the first glimmer of dawn appeared German artillery and trench mortars began a bombardment along the whole of the Indian Corps front, followed by Infantry assaults on Givenchy village and along the line Givenchy/La Quinque Rue. These assaults were repulsed, albeit with difficulty and with numerous casualties amongst the by now exhausted and hungry defenders.

At 0900 hours on 20 December there was a series of ten terrific explosions along the Sirhind Brigade front. Earth, revetting materials, bodies and bits of equipment flew twenty feet into the air. The rumours were true and the enemy had succeeded in tunnelling under the Indian trenches. Everyone in the vicinity of an exploding mine was killed outright while anyone within 50 yards was knocked senseless, dazed or otherwise rendered incapable of action. On the right of the brigade front a company of the 1/1st Gurkhas and half a company of the Highland Light Infantry were simply blown to pieces or buried in the collapsing trench. Very few survived, except for a small group on the extreme left and right of the mined area who held on as best they could. The enemy now followed up his mining success with an attack on the gaps created. Each group of German infantry, supported by bombing parties, was led by a man holding up a staff to which was fixed a black, wooden German Eagle intended to show artillery observers the extent of their advance as well as to give the men a rallying point in the poor visibility caused by the smoke and the rain.

The two companies of the 1/4th Gurkhas which were in the firing line put up such resistance as they could, but clogged rifles and the preponderance of enemy bombs allowed the German infantry to get into the Sirhind Brigade's trenches. The Gurkhas now abandoned their useless rifles and vicious hand-to-hand fighting ensued, kukri against bayonet. Casualties began to mount, including Captain Rundall who was killed leading a bombing party. He was the elder brother of Lieutenant Rundall of the 1/1st Gurkhas who had been killed in the abortive attack on the German sap head the day before. The defenders' small stock of bombs was soon used up, many of them failing to explode in the mud. Soon the 1/4th Gurkhas' trenches were under enfilade fire from German machine-guns, and at 1300 hours the remains of the battalion were ordered to withdraw. The two companies began to pull back under cover of their own two machine-guns and those of Napier's Rifles, until suddenly another series of buried mines were detonated. Of the machine-gunners all were either killed (in some cases simply blown into bits so small that nothing remained for identification) or wounded and captured. The officer commanding the machine-gun detachment, Captain Wylie 1/4th Gurkhas, was rendered unconscious and made a prisoner with some of his men when they were attacked from the rear while trying to move up into a more advantageous firing position[*]. Of one of the companies of the 1/4th Gurkhas, under Captain Yates, no trace has ever been found.

Despite fierce, albeit uncoordinated, resistance by those small groups and individuals who were capable of standing and fighting, it was eventually obvious that the situation was hopeless. After prolonged and bloody fighting the enemy were in possession of the Indian firing line.

On the right, what remained of the 1/4th Gurkhas and Napier's Rifles withdrew through the village of Givenchy, helped by their own artillery which managed to slow the German pursuit somewhat. On the left the Highland Light Infantry and the 1/1st Gurkhas pulled back to their support trenches, but they found no respite for the Germans had penetrated here too and eventually the Indians had no choice but to fall back in the direction of Festubert. A few isolated parties did manage to hold out in the support trenches, including Lieutenant Stewart with 80 men and two machine-guns of the Highland Light Infantry, who managed to resist all attempts to evict them until relieved 24 hours later.

By mid-day it was clear to Corps Headquarters that the situation was very serious. With the exception of the 9th Bhopals and one company of Wilde's Rifles, who were still holding east of Givenchy, virtually the whole of the Sirhind Brigade had been driven back and was now conducting a tenuous defence from the reserve trenches, such as they were, and from along the Festubert road. On their right the Ferozepore Brigade too was under heavy attack and that brigade's left, occupied by the 129th Baluchis,

[*]   The semi-official history *The Indian Corps in France* says that all the machine-gunners were blown up and killed, but the account was written shortly after the event and before the full details were known. My account is taken from *The History of the 4th PWO Gurkha Rifles*, Blackwoods, Edinburgh, 1940.

was unsupported and unlikely to hold. South of the La Bassée Canal things were a little better and the Connaught Rangers and the territorial battalion of the Suffolks were holding firm. There were few reserve troops left at the disposal of General Watkis, commanding the Lahore Division, and these included the Scinde Rifles, which having taken a severe mauling the day before was unable to muster much more than a company. The Corps Commander now allocated the Secunderabad Cavalry Brigade and the 2/8th Gurkhas of the Bareilly Brigade to the Lahore Division, to which was added the 47th Sikhs, the Lahore Division's own reserve, the whole to be under command of Major General McBean, the commander of the Bareilly Brigade.

By 1400 hours the Germans were in possession of the whole of the Sirhind Brigade front apart from isolated pockets which were still holding out, had occupied Givenchy village and had forced back the left flank of the Ferozepore Brigade. Givenchy had to be regained: it was a strongpoint and was only just north of the junction between the Lahore Division and the French. The Jullunder Brigade, less the 47th Sikhs, was accordingly ordered to recover Givenchy while McBean's force was to make contact with the Sirhind Brigade and counter-attack as necessary, the aim being to regain the lost trenches. Further assistance would be given by two French battalions placed at the disposal of the Lahore Division by the GOC French X Corps.

The recapture of Givenchy was entrusted to the 1st Manchesters and one company of the 4th Suffolks. They were to clear the enemy out of the village after which the two French battalions would assault the 129th Baluchis' old trenches. The attack began at 1500 hours, and on reaching the outskirts of the village, the Manchesters found it to be strongly held by a determined enemy. Fierce house-to-house fighting took place, and it was not until after dark that the village was in the hands of the Manchesters, by which time it was impossible to distinguish where the 129th Baluchis' old trenches were. The second phase of the attack was therefore postponed until the next day.

Farther north General McBean's force began to move into position in order to launch an assault along the Sirhind Brigade's abandoned support and firing lines. Although they began to move at 1400 hours, progress was painfully slow, and it was not until 1700 hours that the 7th Dragoon Guards and the 47th Sikhs, both under the command of the Dragoons' Commanding Officer, Lieutenant Colonel Lemprière, were ordered to attack on the right of the Sirhind Brigade. Eventually both units managed to reach the trenches held by the 1/4th Gurkhas from which point the attack was to start, and were told that a French battalion would co-operate on the right and would provide guides to the objective. Lemprière and Walker, commanding the 1/4th, discussed the situation and came to the conclusion that the ground over which they were to advance was flooded, visibility was nil, the trenches which they were to capture were by now almost certainly destroyed by shelling, and German machine-guns were firing across the entire area on fixed lines. The whole operation was pointless and should be called off. Lemprière managed to get through to Brigade headquarters on one of the few working telephones and recommended cancellation. He was told to get on with it.

Again there was delay: cut telephone wires, crowded and collapsing communication trenches, confusion as to exactly where the enemy were, all contributed to the attack not starting until 0100 hours on 21 December. Moving off in two lines, with two squadrons of the 7th Dragoon Guards and half the 47th Sikhs in the first wave, with one squadron 7th Dragoon Guards and the remainder of the 47th Sikhs following on, the force failed to meet any French guides. The French commanding officer had decided that the operation was a waste of time and lives and had declined to play. Lemprière's band came under enemy fire but reached the old support lines about 600 yards east of Le Plantin. Here they paused, but quickly came under fire from both flanks. The objective now was the old firing line, but it was pitch dark and the state of the ground and the weather made it impossible to recognise any landmarks or features. Lieutenant Colonel Lemprière stood up on the parapet to try to distinguish the objective and was shot dead. Command now devolved upon Lieutenant Colonel Gunning, 47th Sikhs.

Gunning was faced with a hopeless task. It was impossible to keep direction, the enemy positions could only be identified by the muzzle flash of their rifles, Gunning's force was enfiladed from both flanks and the ground across which they must advance was now being shelled by their own artillery, which was trying to break up the German strongpoints. Wisely, Gunning decided to withdraw and pulled his force back to Festubert, reaching there about 0400 hours, whereupon he asked for further instructions from the Bareilly Brigade headquarters.

General McBean was quite clear that the lost ground must be regained and he ordered that a second attack should be made, this time under the command of Lieutenant Colonel Grant 2/8th Gurkhas. Zero Hour was 0500 hours on 21 December and was preceded by a seven-minute artillery bombardment, after which the counter-attack force moved off in two lines. In the first line from left to right were one squadron Poona Horse, 20th Deccan Horse, a further squadron Poona Horse, half the 2/8th Gurkhas and the 47th Sikhs. They were followed by the third squadron Poona Horse, the Jodhpur Lancers, the other half of the 2/8th Gurkhas and all three squadrons 7th Dragoon Guards. The cavalry were, of course, dismounted and a squadron was roughly equal to a platoon. The infantry battalions were well below their established strength. The rain still fell in torrents, no one could see anything, men fell into ditches and shell holes and the direction was but an approximation. Sporadic German shelling hindered the advance, and machine-guns on fixed lines kept up a steady attrition of Grant's force, but the first wave reached the support trenches and, incredibly, began to cheer.

The Gurkhas got into the enemy trenches and sent patrols down it. The patrols reported that 500 yards or so of the trench to the left was unoccupied. It was unoccupied because it was flooded to an extent that no one could remain in it, and two Gurkhas had just drowned trying to move along it. To the right, however, the trench was strongly held and German machine-guns were able to fire along it. Captain Padday, 47th Sikhs, took a bombing party off to the right to try to force a way along, but he and most of his men were killed to no avail. At first light it was evident that the lodgement could not be held and a retirement to Festubert was ordered. The withdrawal was accomplished under heavy enemy fire, assisted by their searchlights, and was not complete until well after daylight.

Meanwhile the Manchesters were holding grimly onto Givenchy village, having been reinforced by one company of the 4th Suffolks and a company of French infantry. At 0630 hours on 21 December the postponed attack on the 129th Baluchis' lost trenches was put in, but as the men attempted to advance they were silhouetted against burning haystacks and were easy prey for the German rifles. Little progress could be made and casualties were beginning to reach alarming proportions when at about 1100 hours, after a 45-minute bombardment of the village and the trenches occupied by the Manchesters and their allies, the Germans put in a strong infantry attack. The French were forced back and the Germans began to work their way round the village with the aim of outflanking the defenders. Lieutenant Colonel Strickland, commanding the Manchesters, managed to hold for the time being, but when a further assault came in at 1500 hours he was forced to withdraw his force through the village and back to Pont Fixe on the main road. There were only three officers left with the whole party, and in some companies hardly any NCOs were still on their feet.

With the withdrawal from Givenchy, pressure on Wilde's Rifles and the company of the 9th Bhopals, who had held their original position throughout, increased. German infantry got into ruined houses in the rear, and the force was in danger of being completely surrounded.

The Meerut Division, holding the northern half of the Indian Corps line, had not escaped the fury of the Battle of Givenchy, as the fighting of 16 to 22 December 1914 later became to be designated. At La Quinque Rue the 2/2nd Gurkhas had part of their firing line blown up by a German mine, and despite stout resistance and local counter-attacks by them, the Seaforths, the 6th Jats and the 1/9th Gurkhas, the Dehra Dun Brigade was driven out of their orchard and had to establish a new defence line farther back.

Battered, tired, hungry, with very heavy casualties, with many rifles incapable of being fired and with little artillery support and virtually no bombs, the Indian Corps had been pushed back, but it had taken an enormous toll of the enemy and it was still holding. Help was at hand, for I Corps under Sir Douglas Haig had been ordered up from reserve to support the beleaguered Indian Corps. At 1600 hours on 21 December 1 British Brigade attacked Givenchy and The Scots Guards made contact with Wilde's Rifles, while that night 2 British Brigade relieved the Dehra Dun Brigade and counter-attacked the orchard[*].

At mid-day on 23 December 1914 Haig's I Corps took over the whole of the Indian Corps front, and by 27 December all the Indian units were in reserve in billets for rest and refitting. Of the actions of the Indian Corps during the Battle of Givenchy Field Marshal Sir John French said: 'The Indian Troops have fought with the greatest gallantry and steadfastness whenever called upon'.[8]

SOURCE NOTES

1.   *The Martial Races of India*, G MacMunn, Sampson Low, Marston and Co Ltd. (undated, circa 1930).
2.   Quoted in *A History of the 4th Prince of Wales' Own Gurkha Rifles 1857 – 1937*, MacDonell and Macaulay, Blackwood and Sons, Edinburgh and London, 1940 (privately published).
3.   Ibid.
4.   *With the Indians in France*, Lt Gen Sir James Willcocks, Constable and Co, London, 1920.
5.   Ibid.
6.   Ibid.
7.   Ibid.
8.   Quoted in *With the Indians in France*.

•

---

[*]   They were unable to hold it, being driven out again on 23 December with one battalion of The Northamptonshire Regiment taking nearly 800 casualties.

VI

Recruiting, Reinforcement and Warm Clothing

Between 22 and 27 December 1914 the Indian Corps was relieved by units of the British I Corps. The Indians had been in the line for two months, for most of the time still in their tropical uniforms. They had suffered severe casualties without sufficient reinforcement and were in any case expected to hold the same length of Front as a British corps but with only about two thirds of the manpower, reducing to about half by the end of December. Some of the men's feet were in a terrible state and many of the 2/8th Gurkhas came out of the trenches barefoot, carrying their boots in their hands. Asked if it did not hurt to march without boots they replied that it did, but it was much more painful to march with them.

The 1/4th Gurkhas, in their first experience of European warfare, had been standing in their trenches in front of Le Plantin for two days until they were relieved on 22 December by the 1st Battalion The Irish Guards. The trenches were six feet deep and a crude fire step had been constructed from greasy planks and ration boxes. The fire step was difficult to stand on and many a riflemen ended up in the three feet of mud and water at the bottom of the trench from the recoil of firing a rifle with its barrel half clogged with mud. The Gurkhas had collected mangel worzels lying about in the surrounding fields and had placed them in the bottom of their trench, but as mangel worzels have an irritating tendency to float this was not much help.

The Irish Guards battalion taking over on 22 December was composed very largely of young recruits and reservists. They had a not unnatural tendency to duck when they heard a shot and were not yet accustomed to gauging where an enemy mortar shell would fall. Noting their nervousness the Subadar Major of the 1/4th suggested to his Commanding Officer that perhaps the Gurkhas should stay in the trenches until the Guardsmen were used to life in the firing line. This was not passed on to the Guards, probably wisely, and the Gurkhas marched back to Auchel, taking six hours to cover the nine miles, so bad were the men's feet.

The 2/39th Garhwalis were still in the firing line on 22 December when they noticed that the water level in their trench was rising rapidly. They attempted to dig drainage ditches to the rear, with little effect as the whole of the area was already waterlogged, and tried to dam the worst affected parts of the trench line. Despite working bare-legged all night and digging a further trench line behind the existing one, the Garhwalis could achieve little and the water level in the trenches was still rising. Lieutenant Robson, of the Sappers and Miners, then appeared, and after a careful inspection of the trenches and the ground between them and the enemy—about 300 yards—gave as his opinion that the Germans had pumps and were pumping the water out of their own trenches and into those of the Garhwalis. Robson reckoned that he could hear the pump and knew where it was. Going forward to try to pinpoint the exact position from where the enemy were conducting this schoolboy jape, Robson was shot and killed. The men of the Indian Corps were by now used to sudden death, but that of Robson was keenly felt. By his constant presence around the forward positions, his introduction of the homemade trench mortar and his bravery at Festubert he was well known to all the battalions. After little more than a month on the Western Front his cheerful presence would be felt no more. On Christmas Day an artillery officer came up to the Garhwali lines and directed fire onto the position of the German pump, which ceased operations.

The extraordinary and unofficial truce of Christmas Day 1914, which seems to have been initiated by the Germans, went unobserved by most of the Indian Corps, even by those who were still in the firing line. The 2/39th Garhwalis were an exception however, for on Christmas Eve the Germans opposite them placed small Christmas trees on the top of their parapet, some with candles on them, which the sepoys said reminded them of their own festival of lights, Diwali. During the night singing and the noise of celebration was heard and this went on into the following day. The 2/39th were due to be relieved on 27 December by the 2nd Battalion the Worcestershire Regiment, of Gheluvelt fame. In the afternoon of Christmas Day the Commanding Officer, Lieutenant Colonel Drake-Brockman, had just said goodbye to the Worcesters' recce party and was returning to his dugout when the adjutant informed him that 'the Germans were out of their trenches'[1]. The German soldiers had emerged from their own lines in groups, one or two men at first and then more and more and were now standing in front of the Garhwali trenches trying to communicate with the sepoys and offering them cigarettes, cigars and chocolate. Drake-Brockman spoke German and conversed with the visitors. He found that most of them had consumed a considerable amount of alcohol and were convinced that they were winning. One told Drake-Brockman that Russia was now out of the war and produced German newspapers to prove it. The Garhwalis took the opportunity to search no man's land for their own dead, and a number of bodies, including those of two British officers, were recovered and buried. At 1545 hours, as it was beginning to get dark, whistles blew from the German trenches and the German soldiers were shepherded back to their own lines by their NCOs. Not a shot was fired throughout the night.

The Christmas truce caused great displeasure amongst the high commands of both Allies and Germans. It would not be repeated, and an unauthorised attempt to arrange another at Christmas 1915 would lead to the court martial of the Commanding Officer and a company commander of the Scots Guards.*

Those units of the Indian Corps which were safely back in billets on Christmas Day celebrated the festival as best they could. It meant nothing to the sepoys, of course, but they were delighted with the small gifts sent out by Queen Mary: sweetmeats, cigarettes, postcards and the like, each present contained in a small, flat, square tin. Even today homes in India and Nepal will produce the tin with great pride to show to visitors. Most of the British officers managed some Christmas fare, although one unit met with a disappointment when the mess yakdan†, containing Christmas dinner, a plum pudding and 200 cigarettes, was stolen.

With the whole of the Indian Corps out of the line it was time to take stock and review the lessons of the past three months. The Corps had arrived in France largely unprepared for the type of fighting they would encounter. They had been issued with brand new rifles with very little—in some cases no—time in which to train in their use. They had been flung into the firing line piecemeal as and where reinforcement was needed, and they had subsequently been allocated a portion of the Front far longer than the Corps' numbers warranted. They had been greatly outnumbered by a better equipped foe and up to the end of December had suffered nine and a half thousand casualties.

Battered as they had been and on occasion pushed back as they had been, they had held on and were never routed, nor did the Germans ever effect a breakthrough. Despite being in Khaki Drill uniform throughout most of the dreadful weather of the winter of 1914, morale remained high. A Garhwali rifleman wrote to a relative in Garhwal in January 1915:

> And our regiment has made a great name for itself and its bravery has been published. But what will happen later in the war I do not know. Anyhow, the name of the Garhwali has been made. I am not allowed to write any description. We are all comfortable and well looked after. The English will win, but the Indian troops will be finished first.[2]

---

* The Commanding Officer, Captain Barnes, was found Not Guilty and the company commander, Sir Ian Colquhoun, Guilty and awarded a reprimand. This punishment was later quashed by Haig, now Commander-in-Chief, in regard for Colquhoun's previous gallant conduct.

† An Afghani saddlebag, made of hide and which could be slung on the back of a mule.

That the writer thought the Indian troops would be finished first is hardly surprising, for the major problem which was to dog the Indian Corps throughout its time in France was manpower. A system of single battalion regiments and a recruiting organisation which depended mainly on individual regimental effort simply could not meet the requirements of the Western Front. This had been recognised by the Indian Army and by the Indian government. The Adjutant General of the Indian Army, Lieutenant General (later Sir) Havelock Hudson CB CIE, set up a Recruiting Directorate as part of his staff as early as 15 August 1914, with extra funds being authorised for the provision of more recruiting officers. At the outbreak of war the total reserve strength of the Indian Army was 30,000 men but, as we have seen, many of these were unfit for active service. Pre-war the annual recruit requirement was around 15,000 men and with some augmentation of the existing system a total of 2,100 men were recruited in August 1914 and 2,803 in September. By early October it was obvious that this would not be sufficient to meet the needs of the Indian Corps in France, much less that of all the other Indian Army expeditionary forces, and so a radical reorganisation was carried out. Recruiting Officers reporting to the Recruiting Directorate were established in each province, under whom were placed Assistant Recruiting Officers and Assistant Assistant Recruiting Officers. In addition to these there were Special Recruiters, who looked for men in remote areas where there could be no permanent presence, and Regimental Recruiters who were detached from their parent regiments and recruited only for them. As the Army was reluctant to employ too many regular officers and men on recruiting duties—men who would otherwise be at the Front—pensioners, provincial governments, district administrations and the police were roped in to help. The use of policemen as recruiters was not popular with the administration due to the propensity of the police recruiters to enlist themselves, and indeed some good material was obtained in this way. Whoever did the recruiting, some form of military presence was considered vital, even if it was only a man recently out of recruit training, for only he could be presented to potential recruits as the finished product.

In October 1914 the number enlisted had gone up to 8,067 and to 8,486[3] in November, when a bonus of 14 rupees 'bringing in money' was authorised. Many of those who brought in recruits refused to accept the bonus, so Recruiting Officers were able to amass an unofficial fund with which to entertain those who were particularly good providers of recruits, and give them presents of guns, watches and robes of honour.

Recruits were still enlisted for a specific regiment or arm of the service. This was considered inefficient, as when sufficient recruits were enlisted for a regiment to bring it up to its established strength, recruiting had to cease, regardless of the number of remaining applicants. General enlistment, that is enlistment into the Army with recruits then being drafted to regiments as required, was considered but rejected, as was a milder proposal to enlist into branches, Infantry, Cavalry, Sappers and Miners and so on.

Most young men had definite ideas as to what they wanted to join and would not accept an alternative. This was particularly so in the Punjab, whence 42% of all the combatants enlisted during the war came. Eventually regiments were allowed to recruit above their authorised establishment, and authority was given for one extra havildar and a naik per 20 men, and an extra jemadar per 114 men thus enlisted.

If men could not be persuaded to join the Army, rather than a particular regiment, then the recruiting base had to be widened, and as time went on some regiments had to change their class composition and classes not previously enlisted were considered. Later in the war Kumaonis, Coorgs, Hill Brahmins, Gaurs and Mahars were all tried, Kumaonis and Mahars finding themselves a permanent place in the Army List. The difficulty in enlisting classes not previously considered was the provision of Indian officers and NCOs to command them, and one of the Adjutant General's subsequent recommendations was that as many classes as possible should be included in the Army in peacetime, a move away from the Martial Classes policy.

In some areas pre-war recruitment had become more and more incestu-ous, with specific small villages, sub clans and families providing most of their menfolk to one or two regiments. As in England with the formation of 'Pals' battalions territorially recruited, this was later to enhance the myth of a 'lost generation'.* Now regiments wishing to recruit in those areas had to have the permission of the District Assistant Recruiting Officer, who would refuse if the area had recently been trawled.

The Indian Army saw no need to reduce peace-time standards for enlist-ment, which were maintained throughout the war except for a reduction of the height limit for all races to five feet two inches in 1917. As fully qualified medical officers to carry out pre-enlistment medical examina-tions were in short supply, there was too much hanging about before recruits dould be passed as fit to begin training. Assistant surgeons (who ranked as Indian officers but, while highly qualified as combat medics,

---

* In 1973 the author was in an area of East Palpa, Nepal, and noticed that while there were plenty of old women there were hardly any old men. He was vociferously attacked by two old women who told him that they did not wish any of their young men to join the Army. They remembered when the British had come once before, they said, and all the young men had gone away. None had ever come back. A conversion from the Nepali to the Western calendar indicated that the ladies were referring to 1914. Five of the six Gurkha battalions which served on the Western Front had recruited heavily from that area. They still do.

did not have medical degrees) and sub assistant surgeons (warrant officers) were therefore permitted to carry out medical examinations, to be confirmed later by a doctor.

Once enlisted, recruits received their basic training at the regimental depot, one month for the Infantry and rather longer for the cavalry (who had to be taught to ride), before being posted to a regiment or battalion. This was not long to turn a largely uneducated peasantry into soldiers capable of surviving in the highly technical world of the Western Front[*], and that the men coped as well as they did says much for the inherent quality of the material enlisted. In some cases regiments set up temporary depots in a remote area, carried out basic training of a recently enlisted batch of recruits and then closed down. In other cases the small depots left behind by the battalion on overseas service ran the training. The exception was the Gurkha depot at Gorakhpur, on the India/Nepal border, which was properly established with a commanding officer and a permanent staff, and which examined and enlisted or rejected Gurkhas for all 20 Gurkha battalions and then conducted recruit training. There was of course no official recruiting inside Nepal, and all volunteers for the Gurkha Brigade had to make their own way down from their hill villages, as over 55,000 of them did.

As a move to prevent regiments poaching each other's recruits, Pathan tribes were now allocated to regiments, and in Bombay and the United Provinces geographical areas were also so designated. It was considered that the allocation of regimental areas in the Punjab was not yet practical, but a recommendation was made that this should be instituted after the war.

During the period 1914 – 1918 the recruiting organisation in India recruited 1,272,460 combatants, the largest racial groups recruited being Punjabi Mussalmans (136,126), Sikhs (88,925), Gurkhas (55,589), Rajputs (49,086), Jats (40,272), Hindustani Mussalmans (36,353) and Pathans (27,857).[4] These numbers do not include those recruited under purely regimental arrangements, and the figure for Gurkhas is probably too low, as while they were officially only enlisted into Gurkha infantry regiments there were also Gurkhas in the Guides, the Assam, Lushai, Naga Hills and Burma Military Police and the Sappers and Miners, as well as the battalions of the Nepal Army stationed in India.

It was not only combatants for whose recruitment the Adjutant General's Recruiting Directorate was responsible. Bearers, muleteers and followers were also its responsibility. Prior to the war the Army Bearer Corps, largely stretcher bearers, was mainly composed of Nepalis, including those of

---

[*]   Today, 1999, Gurkha recruits for the British Army receive 40 weeks' basic training. The modern Indian Army recruit training is of roughly the same duration.

non martial clans. There had been no difficulty in recruitment but the Nepal government had never been happy about this arrangement—they wanted their citizens to be combatant soldiers—and in 1917 recruitment of Nepalis as bearers was stopped. Eventually the Army Bearer Corps grew from 3,500 in 1914 to 25,708 by the end of the war, the enlistment criterion being 'all classes from whom Hindus will drink water'.

Muleteers, on the other hand, had always been a problem. Despite the skills required to care for and manage a sometimes difficult animal, and the dangers inherent in transporting rations, stores and machine-guns right up to the firing line, muleteers had been classed as followers and their pay was low. The pay was increased and in 1917 muleteers were granted combatant status, after which there was no difficulty in obtaining sufficient men.

Before the war followers—sweepers, bhisties (water carriers originally), cooks and mess servants—were entirely a regimental responsibility, but on deployment to France the Indian government assumed responsibility for their recruitment and pay: sweepers at 5 rupees 8 annas a month (40p in 1914 values, very roughly £300 today), bhisties and cooks at 6 rupees 8 annas. In May 1915 pay was increased, and a further 50% field service allowance and cash in lieu of rations was authorised. Eventually all followers were formally enrolled 'for the duration' and a central followers' depot was set up in India. In 1914 officers' servants had been a matter for the individual officer, but this responsibility too was assumed by the government, although the numbers were reduced and they were placed on half pay when not actually employed, which was bad luck when an officer was killed, or wounded and evacuated.

The provision of British officers was also addressed by the authorities in India. Officers in regiments not deployed in one of the expeditionary forces were posted to France as reinforcements, and the Indian Army Reserve of Officers was expanded. British businessmen, planters and administrators living in India were granted reserve commissions and after basic military training were shipped off to the Western Front[*]. In England too, suitable young men were asked to volunteer for the Indian Army, as were British Other Ranks. These latter had much more to learn, linguistically and culturally, than had residents of India and it was not until much later that their numbers could be significant.

In reviewing the action of the Indian Corps in 1914 one is struck by the ad hoc arrangements for command and control that existed. Many operations were directed and co-ordinated by the individuals on the spot and operational direction from brigade, divisional and corps headquarters was loosely exercised. In the defensive posture perforce adopted by the

[*]   The Indian Army Reserve of Officers expanded from 47 in August 1914 to 2,600 in December 1916 and to 4,500 in November 1918.

Indian Corps throughout most of 1914 there was of course little initiative that could be exercised by the higher commanders, and the fact that most of the British officers in the Corps knew each other enabled a system which operated largely by word of mouth and mutual understanding to work. If the staff officers at the various levels were not overly detained in running operations, they did ensure that the administration of the Corps worked as efficiently as was possible given the overall situation. The arrangements for the supply of rations, ammunition and equipment was their responsibility, as was the mass of reports and returns required by the often tortuous system. The Corps, divisional and brigade Commanders themselves spent much of their time visiting units, being seen and jollying the men along. At this stage of the war there was probably little else they could do.

For the Indian Corps the priorities now were the provision of winter clothing for all, the absorption of reinforcements, the sorting out and replacement of damaged and defective equipment, and training. This last included a great deal of route marching, for the long periods spent in wet, cold trenches had softened the feet of all, including those men who had not suffered from frostbite or trench foot. The battalions also trained in the use of bombs, rifle grenades and in the assaulting of enemy trenches, mock ups of these being constructed in rear areas.

During the two to four weeks that the Indian Corps was in reserve in billets, most battalions received reinforcements. The 2/2nd Gurkhas, now down to a total strength of 531 all ranks, received two British officers, two subadars and 48 GORs from India, being either their own recruits or men from their 1st Battalion, and 43 GORs from the Lushai Hills Military Police Battalion. The 1/4th Gurkhas took on strength four British officers, three Gurkha officers and 241 GORs from their own depot in India, two Gurkha officers and 150 GORs from their own 2nd Battalion and a draft of volunteers from the Burma Military Police. In addition the 1/4th welcomed a British officer from Outram's Rifles and one from the 69th Punjabis. Vaughan's Rifles were sent four British officers (none of their own regiment) and 204 IORs of the 82nd Punjabis. These were not as yet to be of value to Vaughan's as most had contracted mumps on the voyage. The 2/8th Gurkhas got 11 British officers, 14 Gurkha officers and 710 GORs, the 2/3rd Gurkhas three British officers (one from the 1st Battalion 10th Gurkha Rifles), two Gurkha officers and 121 GORs of their own and 44 volunteers from the Naga Hills Military Police. In addition the 2/3rd had returned to them the company of their own 1st Battalion which had earlier reinforced 2/8th Gurkhas. Originally of 215 all ranks, only 102 of that company were left.

While it had initially seemed that reinforcements for Gurkha battalions could come from the battalion of the same regiment not in France, it soon became apparent that these Indian based battalions would be needed elsewhere and could not be denuded to keep the battalions in Europe up to strength. News travelled very slowly in Nepal; it took time for it to be known that more recruits than usual were needed and for the volunteers to trek down to the border. The Burma, Assam, Lushai Hills and Naga Military Police battalions were paramilitary units which were indistinguishable from infantry. They were almost exclusively composed of Gurkhas but they could not be ordered to serve outside the states where they had been raised to keep the peace. They were asked to volunteer for the Western Front and it is to their enormous credit that they did so in large numbers. Without them the reinforcement of Gurkha battalions in late 1914 and early 1915 would have become impossible.

Wilde's Rifles received a draft of one British officer, four Indian officers and 211 IORs of the Guides Infantry, and 1/9th Gurkhas got one British officer, one Gurkha officer and 135 GORs, consisting of their own recalled leave men and 29 volunteers from the Assam Military Police. To the Scinde Rifles came four British officers and 250 IORs including a complete company from the 52nd Sikhs, and to the 9th Bhopals one British officer, four Indian officers and 155 IORs from the 11th Rajputs.

Reinforcement of the 47th Sikhs took rather longer, as they had been sent a jemadar of their own and the reservists of the 35th and 36th Sikhs. On arrival the jemadar reported that in his opinion the reservists were not good enough to join a battalion at the Front, and after inspections by the Subadar Major, the Commanding Officer and the Brigade Commander himself it was agreed that, with one or two exceptions who had only recently left the colours, the reservists were physically and medically quite unfit for war. They were returned to Marseilles and replaced by a further draft of one British officer, one subadar and 123 IORs of the 35th Sikhs.

Most battalions now began to receive men back from hospitals in France or England, as many as 331 Indian Other Ranks in the case of the 47th Sikhs. One of the rules that caused considerable complaint amongst the men of the Indian Corps was that sepoys discharged from hospital and certified fit for duty were asked to sign a certificate stating that they returned to the Front of their own free will. Indian and Gurkha soldiers were suspicious of documentation, particularly when asked to sign something which they could not read by an officer not their own. When it was explained to them what the paper said, many of them considered it insulting and either tore up the paper or refused to sign, complaining bitterly on return to their regiments in France. The instruction was regarded as particularly offensive when it was discovered that it was only Indian soldiers, rather than all BEF wounded, who were required to sign, and the rule was quietly dropped.

Despite the increase in the rate at which reinforcements from India were now arriving, the Indian Corps was still well below the strength of an equivalent British formation and in January five British Territorial battalions and one Special Reserve[*] battalion joined the Corps. In future there would be one British regular battalion, one British Territorial or Special Reserve battalion and three Indian battalions in each brigade. Despite this and the fact that the Territorial formations had now received the training and equipment to fit them for front line service, many of them were under strength and in January 1915 the Indian Corps numbered only 21,000 infantry, 900 cavalry and 120 guns.

The pace of training moved up a gear and the Lahore Division established a divisional bombing school run by Captain BC Battye of the 21st Company Sappers and Miners. Grenades were still in desperately short supply, and despite Sir John French asking in October for a minimum of 400 bombs[5], the issue in November 1914 for the whole of the BEF was less than 300. The Sappers and Miners transport made daily rounds of billets to collect empty tins for the manufacture of 'jam pot' bombs, already described and with which the sepoys were familiar, to which they now added the 'Battye bomb' and the 'hairbrush'. The Battye bomb, named after its inventor,[†] was made in an ironworks in Bethune and consisted of a small cast iron cylinder four inches long and two inches in diameter, closed at one end and with serrations on the outside to facilitate the break up of the case when the bomb exploded. The bomb was filled with shredded gun cotton or ammonal and sealed with a wooden plug, in which was a hole for the detonator and the fuse. Eventually the fuse would be replaced by the Nobel fuse igniter, obtained from the coal mines in the Pas de Calais. The Battye bomb was considerably more reliable than the jam pot and soon superseded it.

The hairbrush bomb consisted of a slab of gun cotton wired to a piece of wood shaped like a hairbrush, thus providing a handle for throwing. Again, a detonator and fuse were attached. At this stage all three types of bomb required the fuse to be lit by match, cigarette or pipe and, although improvements were being made continuously, they were far from reliable. During a demonstration for senior officers of the BEF a hairbrush bomb was ignited and thrown. Unfortunately the gun cotton fell off and only the wooden handle reached its target. The very senior spectators scattered, seeking what cover they could, and when no explosion occurred the offending gun cotton slab was found beneath one of the spread-eagled generals. All these inventions were soon adopted by the rest of the BEF

---

[*]   The 'Special Reserve' was the old Militia, by 1914 almost indistinguishable in practical terms from a Territorial battalion, except for the rules on call-out. Most SR battalions were used as drafting units and very few ever went to France.

[†]   Battye's normal occupation was the superintendance of hydro-electric schemes in India. He was a member of a famous Indian Army family.

and the Official History credits the Indian Corps as being the leaders in improvisation. With the realisation of the importance of bombs in trench warfare, brigade bombing companies were now formed. These were to consist of 30 men from each battalion and would be trained and employed under the central direction of the brigade head quarters. In operations each battalion would be allocated 20 men from the bombing company, while the remainder would be held in reserve or deployed as the brigade commander saw fit.

It was during this period that short leave to England for British officers was instituted, and many took advantage of the opportunity to get home for three or four days. A further enhancement was a grant of 1,400 French francs to permit every officers' mess to buy a horse and cart, thus allowing the mess staff to forage farther in search of extra items, paid for by the officers who consumed them.

There was now a reorganisation of the BEF, and a 'general post' within the Indian Corps itself. The BEF had originally been organised as a General Headquarters commanding the divisions direct, but had then introduced the corps level of command to conform with the French. Now it would be reorganised into armies. The First Army would be commanded by Sir Douglas Haig, newly promoted to general, and the Second Army by Smith-Dorrien. The Indian Corps was to be part of the First Army, which rather rankled with Sir James Willcocks who felt that, as he had been senior to Haig as a lieutenant general, but junior to Smith-Dorrien, the Indian Corps should have been placed under the latter. It was a minor personal niggle and does not seem to have occurred to anyone else.

The British Army rarely finishes a war under the same generals with whom it starts, and there were now a number of senior commanders who were sent home or retired, usually because they were too old or too inflexible for high intensity warfare, but in some cases as part of the normal career progression of senior officers. Within the Indian Corps Lieutenant General Watkis was replaced as commander of the Lahore Division by Major General Keary, until now commander of the Garhwal Brigade. Of the brigade commanders only Egerton, commanding the Ferozepore Brigade, was to remain in post (he would continue to command his brigade both in France and later in Mesopotamia). Lieutenant Colonel Blackader, Commanding Officer 2nd Leicesters, succeeded Keary in command of the Garhwal Brigade. In the Jullunder Brigade Lieutenant Colonel Strickland, Commanding Officer 1st Manchesters, took over from Major General Carnegy who was invalided out. Command of the Sirhind Brigade passed from Major General Brunker to Lieutenant Colonel Walker, Commanding Officer 1/4th Gurkhas, and that of the Bareilly Brigade from Major General McBean to Lieutenant Colonel Southey, Commanding Officer 129th Baluchis. In the Dehra Dun Brigade Colonel CW Jacob assumed command from Brigadier General Johnson. Jacob had hitherto been Chief of Staff of the Meerut Division and was the latest of a renowned family to serve in the Indian Army (an earlier member of the family had raised Jacob's Horse). He would later command the Meerut Division, and a British corps when the Indian Corps left France for Mesopotamia. He would eventually rise to Field Marshal and Commander-in-Chief India.

The new Army Commander, Haig, visited the Corps on 4 January 1915 and said a few encouraging words to each battalion. On 7 January a brigade from each division of the Corps, the Sirhind and Garhwal Brigades, marched to Burbure to be inspected by the Commander-in-Chief, Field Marshal Sir John French. It was a wet and windy day and the great man was late. Eventually the Field Marshal arrived by motor car. He alighted from his vehicle and walked with the Corps Commander slowly down the line of men. He spoke not a word to anyone, despite being introduced to each commanding officer in turn, nor shook a single hand. At the end of this inspection Sir John simply climbed back into his car and was driven away, leaving the Corps Commander to tell the men how well they had done. It was felt that, while the Commander-in-Chief spoke no Indian dialect, he might at least have said a few words to the British officers.

The billets that the Indian Corps were now in varied in quality, but at least they were dry, and as the battalions settled in their reinforcements, received new clothing and equipment, took advantage of the baths and laundries that had been established for them and route marched and trained, they quickly took on the appearance of seasoned troops once more. Charges for billets had now been standardised for the whole of the BEF, and these were laid down as being one franc per night for officers, 20 centimes for Indian Other Ranks with beds, five centimes without beds. The charges were paid from regimental funds and later reclaimed from the government. Now that the troops had access to French tradesmen and estaminets, there were some cases of drunkenness amongst the Sikhs and a few men contracted venereal disease from French women—not all of them prostitutes, although that trade too flourished behind the lines. French law forbade the sale of spirits in the war zone but this was easily circumvented, and most of the British officers and many of the Indians developed a taste for the occasional glass of cognac.

Discipline had never been a problem in the Indian Army. The men took easily to a structured life and discipline was largely self-imposed and often quasi-legally enforced without men having to be arraigned on a formal charge. The ultimate sanction of the law was there, however, should it be needed. Officers and soldiers of the Indian Army were subject to the Indian Articles of War, as enumerated in the Manual of Indian Military Law of 1911, which was itself based on British military law and adapted for Indian troops. The manual, to be found in every orderly room, explained the law as it applied to soldiers, defined offences and laid down punishments. The possible punishments were draconian, and included the death penalty for:

Shamefully abandoning a post (only applicable to the officer or NCO in command of the post)
Casting away arms and ammunition in the presence of an enemy, or inducing others to do so
Cowardice
Communicating with the enemy and not reporting it
Treacherously giving away the password
Assisting the enemy with victuals or money
Giving a false alarm on active service
Spreading reports calculated to create alarm or despondency
As a sentry, sleeping at a post in time of war
As a sentry, quitting a post in time of war
Leaving a post to go in search of plunder in time of action
Leaving a post without being regularly relieved
Looting in time of war
Mutiny, including failing to suppress it and failing to report it
Assaulting a superior
Disobeying a lawful command
Allowing, assisting or permitting a prisoner to escape
Desertion in the face of the enemy.

All these offences (and indeed any offences) could be tried by court martial, which in wartime had to consist of only one officer, with two others in attendance. In practice the one officer would usually, but not always, be a British officer, while those in attendance would be Indian officers. The court had the power to award death, transportation for from seven years to life (to the Andaman Islands), imprisonment for up to 14 years, dismissal from the service, reduction in rank and a variety of minor punishments. Where the death penalty was awarded the method of execution, shooting or hanging, was decided upon by the court.

Many of the offences for which the death penalty could be awarded are self evidently serious—that a soldier, particularly a volunteer, regular soldier, should be put to death for cowardice, assisting the enemy, mutiny or desertion needs no justillcation. Other punishments may, on the face of it, seem over drastic. It is often asked by those who have not themselves experienced war why a sentry, possibly hungry and exhausted, should be put to death just because, however hard he tries to keep alert, he falls asleep at his post. The fact is that the wakefulness of sentries was and is fundamental to the security of an army in the field. Men resting or sleeping, or working where they cannot see forward of their own trenches, had to rely totally on the sentry to warn them of an enemy approach, particularly at night when patrols and trench raiding parties would attempt to creep up unobserved and kill as many of the opposition as they could. The lives of everybody relied on the sentries and this was why sleeping on sentry duty had to be regarded in the most serious light.

Despite the gravity of the offence men did occasionally fall asleep while on sentry duty and were caught by officers or NCOs and brought to court martial. Within the Indian Corps, however, no one was ever executed on the Western Front, because the Indian Articles of War contained a proviso denied its British equivalent. Section 45 of the Manual of Indian Military Law allowed a court martial to order flogging for any offence committed on active service, and permitted any sentence of death, transportation, imprisonment or dismissal to be commuted to flogging. For an Indian or a Gurkha to be flogged was a terrible disgrace. At the time of the Mutiny in 1857, it was said that one of the reasons why Bengal troops had little regard for British soldiers was because at that time the latter could be publicly flogged whereas the former could not. By 1914 up to 30 lashes could be awarded to soldiers of the Indian Army and the punishment was inflicted in public, traditionally by the Drum Major, and witnessed by the man's own comrades and any other units which were in the vicinity. It was used rarely, but at least one rifleman of the 2/3rd Gurkhas was flogged in France for being found asleep on sentry. The Corps Commander, Sir James Willcocks, was concerned that, as flogging was such a degrading punishment, and as it could not be applied to British soldiers of the Corps but only to Indians and Gurkhas, it should be used sparingly. In January 1915 he ordered that all sentences of flogging were to be referred to him for confirmation, and, where he agreed that flogging could be inflicted, it was not to be carried out in a public place.

The official statistics of the war[6] show that no sentence of death on a member of the Indian Corps on the Western Front was ever carried out.[*]

A constant worry of the Indian government at this time was the risk of soldiers being seduced from their allegiance, either by the machinations of Germany or by agitators at home. While the mass of articulate Indian opinion was pro-war and anxious for India to be seen to be putting all its resources at the disposal of the King Emperor, there were embryo nationalists who saw the deployment of Indian troops to Europe as an opportunity to stir up anti-British sentiment. The government saw its fears confirmed by the arrest in Toulouse of a member of the Indian Revolutionary Party at the time when the Indian Corps was passing through that city on their way to the Front. This individual was in possession of a large quantity of what was considered to be seditious literature which he had apparently hoped to distribute amongst the sepoys.

[*] A sowar (trooper) of the 16th Cavalry, then part of the combined British/Indian Cavalry Corps, was shot by a firing squad of his own regiment in 1917 for the murder of an Indian officer.

To ensure that seditious pamphlets and broadsheets were not circulated amongst the soldiers the authorities proscribed a number of publications, most of them produced in India itself or in America. While it is not difficult to understand the banning of such titles as *Hindustan Student, Justice, Spur* and *Indian Sociologist*, the inclusion on the list of the *Gaelic American* is perhaps curious, but forbidden it was.

With the entry of Turkey into the war in October 1914 the government's fears were increased. The Sultan of Turkey as Caliph of the Faithful held a theoretical religious authority over all Mohammedans, and the Indian Army had very large numbers of Moslem Punjabis and Pathans. In the same month a proclamation,[7] inviting all Moslem soldiers in the service of the British to come over to the Germans, was issued under the name of the Kaiser, copies of which were dropped from aircraft, put on notices raised above the German parapets and left lying about in no man's land.

The proclamation was regarded as a joke, and Moslem soldiers derived great amusement from creeping over to the German lines at night and leaving rude messages on the notice boards, while the leaflets were used for a variety of purposes from rolling bidis (Indian cheroots) to wiping bottoms. Some soldiers were sent letters in the mail urging them to change their allegiance. One, unsigned and written in an educated hand in Gurumukhia, the Punjabi script, was posted in Canada on 4 November 1914 and sent to a subadar in the 15th Sikhs:

I pray to all my brothers, Hindu and Mussalman, to join together and break the English rock. There is no withstanding Germany. Germany burns up all who come against her. Let no army come from India. Soon there will be a mutiny in India. Let all men join and put an end to the English. Germany marches forward dealing death. She has put Belgium to death and the half of France. Very soon she will be the death of the English too. The bombardment of England began on 2 November. The first German gun carries 18 miles. The second 25 miles, the third 30 miles. Where its ball falls kills men all round for a distance of 4 miles. Very soon the whole world will come under the German sway. India will come next year. On our side you have Germany, Austria, Turkey, China and Holland, these five. Germany is a giant in strength and in religion. On the other side are England, France, Russia, Serbia, Belgium, these five. But giant Germany is attacking, destroying the whole five. She has captured and imprisoned four lakhs [400,000] of their men. She has sunk 80 British men of war and has taken 70. Countless soldiers perished in the ships which were sunk. The name of Germany is breathed throughout the world like the name of Harankash [a demon]. Hail Germany. Hail. Tear off the veil and listen. Verily my words are true.[8]

All this had no effect on the vast majority of the sepoys. One Punjabi Mussalman Indian officer wrote to his home in India:

What better occasion than this to prove the loyalty of my family to the British government? Turkey, it is true, is a Moslem power, but what has that to do with us?[9]

At the same time a Shia Moslem wrote to his family:

You should pray to the God of mercy that the victory may be given to our King, Jar Panjam [George the Fifth][10]

Even in India the German and Turkish propaganda had little effect. In November 1914 a resident of Garhwal wrote to his son serving in the 39th Garhwal Rifles saying:

... it appears that the Turks have got ready an army near the Suez Canal to attack our government. Our Mohammedan brothers however are quite unmoved and all is quiet here.[11]

On the other hand a Sikh sepoy serving in a Garrison Artillery battery in China wrote to a relative serving in France on 2 February 1915:

We hear that our King is taken prisoner. Germany said that if she were paid a lakh of rupees by 5 o'clock on the first of the month she would release the King. The money was paid but Germany refuses to let him go ... [12]

The German attempts at propaganda directed at the Indian Corps confirmed the authorities in their decision to censor mail coming to and from Indian troops, as had already been implemented for the BEF and the French Army. Initially the concern was that soldiers might inadvertently give away information useful to the enemy, and the men were told not to write anything about the war, with their letters being censored by their own officers. It was quickly realised that this ad hoc arrangement would not work—the officers had better things to do and the level of censorship would depend upon individual whim—so the post of Chief Censor of Indian Mails was established with Second Lieutenant EB Howell of the Political Department of the Indian Civil Service selected to fill it. Howell, an intelligent and politically aware young man, had been sent to France as an interpreter with the Secunderabad Cavalry Brigade and he had a thorough knowledge of Indian dialects. Promoted to captain and provided with a staff to assist him, he set up his office in Boulogne through which all mail to and from Indian troops passed.

Initially the sepoys wrote very little, largely because they were unaware that letters could be sent to India, but inward mail soon reached an average total of 200 items a week per infantry battalion and cavalry regiment. After a few months on the Western Front, when soldiers had been made aware that not only would letters despatched from France reach India in a few weeks but that postage would be free, outward mail went up to around 600 items per unit per week with inward mail about the same. On top of this were letters from one unit to another within the Indian Corps and letters from wounded men in hospitals. Howell's burden of work soon became intense, as he was responsible for spot checking all regimentally censored letters for the entire Corps, and for censoring all inward mail and mail to and from men in hospital.

Howell reported to Colonel Strachey, an officer of the Indian Army based at the India Office in London, and the two quickly realised that censorship not only prevented the inadvertent passing of information to the enemy, but that it also provided a guide to the morale of Indian troops and an indication of worries which the men might not express to their officers. Howell produced a weekly report as to the general tone of the mail which his staff saw. In the report he described what soldiers were saying in their letters home and looked for any signs of sedition or of lowering morale. This report was read by a wider and wider audience—eventually a copy even went to the King—which often led to agitated correspondence between Howell and Strachey. One such exchange, conducted in copperplate longhand and preserved in the India Office Records and Library[13], occurred when Howell's staff intercepted letters from men recuperating in English hospitals to their comrades in France which described sexual encounters with British women, some of whom clearly preferred the generally handsome and polite young sepoys to what British male company was not at the Front. Strachey and Howell debated as to whether these matters should be included in the weekly report, and it was eventually decided that, as the report might be seen by the Queen, all reference to amorous dalliances with the ladies of England would be excised.

In those early days on the Western Front morale was high, despite the weather, and Howell had little to worry his superiors about. There was a fundamental difference between letters written from and to the Front by Indians and Gurkhas, and those written by and to British soldiers. The British soldier knew his letter would be read, but only by one of his own officers who would not repeat anything in it provided it did not breach security, and he could therefore express his innermost thoughts. Many sepoys, however, were illiterate and even if they were not, most of those to whom they wrote were. This meant that letters from the Indian Corps were often dictated to the company clerk, or some other literate person, who expressed in writing what the originator wanted to say. When the letter reached home it would be taken to the village letter writer who would read it aloud, often to an audience of the whole village, and it would be the village letter writer who would pen the reply. These writers had been educated in the classical style and they would often dress up what the sepoy wanted to say in flowery language and with an emphasis not always intended. Sepoys generally wrote for the world, while British soldiers wrote for their loved ones.

At this period the vast majority of letters out and in contained domestic chit chat, descriptions of France and talk about weather and crops and, in the case of inward mail, the extreme patriotism of the elderly relative well away from shot and shell. Some showed a distinct sense of humour familiar to any parent whose child is away at school. An Indian officer of the 4th Cavalry, in the Meerut Division, heard from his uncle in Loharu, near Delhi:

> Since the writing of long letters is forbidden by Army Regulations, and rightly so, for soldiers are not journalists and what have they to do with the writing of voluminous letters? What they have to think of is to keep their weapons in good order, to look after their horses and to maintain a sharp watch for the enemy. That is what they have been sent to the Front to do and that is their business. It is not for them to spin long yarns to their relations. It is enough if they write two lines once a week so that those at home may know that their son or husband or brother or whatever it may be at the Front is alive and well![14]

One of the restrictions enforced by the BEF, which caused resentment and bewilderment amongst the men of the Indian Corps and in India itself, was the strict censorship of news. Cameras were not allowed in the battle area and newspapers were forbidden to mention specific units. This meant that people in India had no idea as to the doings of Indian soldiers in France. While British newspapers could circumvent some of the regulations by referring to a 'Highland Regiment' or a 'Brigade from the Midlands', the mixed class composition of most Indian regiments prevented this ruse from being employed. While the rules would later be relaxed, for the moment it was impossible to tell the people of India of the deeds of their sons on the Western Front and this was considered to have an adverse affect on recruiting. Some news did filter through, however, and on 5 January 1915 a message was received from the Indian National Congress:

> This Congress rejoices to place on record its deep sense of gratitude and pride in the heroic conduct of the Indian troops, whose deeds of valour and conspicuous humanity and chivalry in the great war are winning the respect of civilised mankind for the mother country,

and resolves to send a message of hearty greetings to them and their comrades in arms, with fervent prayers for their well being and success.[15]

While warm serge uniforms were being issued by the Army, gifts of clothing from civilians in England now began to flood in. Many were quite unsuitable for military wear, particularly the large quantities of body belts which arrived. The sepoys did not wear them as intended but used them as scarves. One well meaning lady sent out quantities of bright, multi-coloured waistcoats for 'our dear Sikhs' which caused great amusement amongst the recipients as they puzzled how on earth they could wear them in the firing line. Coats, pullovers and scarves continued to flood in, and on one occasion when the Poona Horse had been fallen in on the road to march from one billet to another, it was noticed that one sowar, normally a wiry, slight youth, appeared to have put on a considerable amount of weight and to resemble nothing so much as a great fluffy football. Ordered to strip he was found to be wearing no fewer than seven layers of clothing. Meanwhile worn out articles of clothing were not entirely useless, and most battalions took to using old socks with the toe removed as bolt covers for their rifles. These protected the bolt and breech from mud and could be easily rolled down the small of the butt when the rifle had to be fired. Eventually a purpose made bolt cover of canvas would be issued.[*]

On 15 January 1915 the Jullunder and Sirhind Brigades moved back into the line, relieving part of the British 2 Division of I Corps, the Sirhind Brigade in the firing line with the Jullunder Brigade in reserve behind them. On 24 January they were relieved in turn by the Garhwal and Dehra Dun Brigades and on 2 February the entire Corps relieved the British I Corps and was back in its old trenches, stretching from west of Neuve Chapelle in the north to Givenchy in the south, the Meerut Division in front with the Lahore Division in reserve.

The weather in January and February was still appalling, so much so that most of the trenches were flooded to the top and could not be occu-pied. The Corps constructed lines of breastworks, rather like grouse butts, behind the firing line and placed piquets of an NCO and six men behind each while the remainder occupied the cellars of ruined houses ready to deploy to the breastworks if required. The cellars varied, some being open to the sky while others provided reasonable shelter, but even this could be a mixed blessing and the 47th Sikhs lost a jemadar who went to sleep in a closed cellar with a charcoal brazier and died of carbon monoxide poi-soning. So bad was the weather that neither side could conduct offensive operations, but even so snipers, shelling and patrolling took their toll. In the month of January 1915 the Indian Corps had three Indian officers,

---

[*]   And would remain in service for 50 years!

141

nine BORs and 20 IORs killed, nine British officers, one Indian officer, 47 BORs and 72 IORs wounded, with one Indian officer, ten BORs and 2 IORs missing.

The deficiencies in machine-guns had long been recognised and it was now announced that battalions would receive a further four, making six in all, and that brigade machine-gun companies would be formed*. Trench mortars, still manufactured by the Sappers and Miners and their British equivalents, would henceforth be grouped together under brigade head-quarters. This decision made sense as the combined mortars of a brigade could now be used in a co-ordinated fashion, and in truth many of the sepoys were glad to see these magnets for enemy counter-bombardment removed from the vicinity of their own trenches.

While offensive operations above ground on any scale were out of the question owing to the weather, operations below ground might be profitable, and the Sappers and Miners, taking the lead from their ene-mies, began to consider the possibility of tunnelling under the German trenches. One of the first attempts was carried out by a party of the 1st King George's Own Sappers and Miners of the Meerut Division from the Indian trenches opposite Festubert, the target being a German sap which ran out towards the Indian lines. The Sappers and Miners managed to find a relatively dry trench from which to begin their tunnel and dug a vertical mine shaft from where they began to burrow towards the enemy position. Later in the war tunnelling would become a highly technical operation, with men issued with stethoscopes specially detailed to listen for enemy counter-mining, but at this stage all the men could do was to dig in the direction of the enemy, keeping direction by compass, measuring by string and shoring up the tunnel as they went along. At last the miners arrived at a point which they calculated was directly beneath the German sap head, and they began to ferry down explosives. The charges had been placed in position but the fuse had not been connected when a new type of German medium trench mortar began to shell the trench from where the mine originated.

Part of the tunnel collapsed, burying some men and killing others. The NCO in charge, Havildar Sucha Singh, withdrew his men until the shelling ceased and then entered the mine shaft himself. Pulling out the dead and wounded he forced his way past the collapsed portion of the tunnel, reached the charge and set the fuses, despite the trench mortar having renewed its shelling. Sucha Singh then returned to the Indian lines from where the mine was detonated once it was confirmed that the sap head was occupied. Havildar Sucha Singh was awarded the IDSM for his coolness in what was a highly dangerous and claustrophobic escapade. It

---

* In fact only a further two machine-guns would be issued, in February 1915. Six remained an aspiration for some time to come.

takes little imagination to picture the courage needed to move alone, in the dark, 30 feet below the ground, along a tunnel three feet high and partially collapsed, with the threat of the remaining roof collapsing at any time and with no possibility of rescue if it did.

SOURCE NOTES

1. Quoted in *The Royal Garhwal Rifles in the Great War 1914 – 1917*, Lt Col DH Drake-Brockman, Charles Clarke Ltd, Haywards Heath, 1934 (privately published).
2. Report of the Censor of Indian Mails, France 1914 – 1918, Vol I, India Office Library and Records, L/MIL/5/825.
3. 'Recruiting in India before and during 1914 – 18', AG Dept Indian Army, IOL L/MIL/17/5/2152.
4. Ibid.
5. *Military Operations in France and Belgium 1914 – 1915*, JH Edmonds, Macmillan and Co, London, 1928.
6. Statistics of the Military Effort of the British Empire during the Great War 1914 – 1920, HMSO, London, 1922.
7. Proclamation by the Kaiser to Indian Other Ranks to Desert and go over to Germany (Oct 14), India Office Library and Records, L/MIL/5/828.
8. Printed Reports. Censor of Indian Mails, France, Dec 1914 – June 1918, India Office Library and Records L/MIL/5/828.
9. Report of the Censor of Indian Mails France 1914 – 1918, Vol I.
10. Ibid.
11. Ibid.
12. Ibid.
13. Op. cit. L/MIL/5/828.
14. Op. cit. L/M1L/5/825
15. *The Indian Corps in France*, Merewether and Smith, John Murray, London, 1919.

VII

Neuve Chapelle

By the spring of 1915 the BEF held a frontage of about 21 miles, sandwiched between the French 8th and 10th Armies. The French now held most of the Ypres Salient whilst the British line ran from the Ypres / Zandvoorde road to the La Bassée canal. The 2nd Army held the northern sector while the 1st Army, including the Indian Corps, was responsible for the southern sector from Bois Grenier to La Bassée. The Indian Corps line ran from Pont Logis, where it joined the British IV Corps, to La Bassée where it linked up with the French. The village of Neuve Chapelle lay 1,000 yards to the East of Pont Logis with the German forward positions 100 to 400 yards from those of the Allies.

Neuve Chapelle had changed hands several times. On 16 October 1914 Smith-Dorrien's II Corps had captured the village, establishing the 'Smith-Dorrien Trench' between Neuve Chapelle and the Bois de Biez, a wood to the south-east which was 1,000 yards long and 800 yards deep. On 27 October the Germans had retaken the village. An attack by the Indian Corps on 28 October had briefly returned ownership to the British, but the assaulting troops could not hold what they had gained and had been pushed back to the present line. The Neuve Chapelle area now formed a German salient pushing west into the Indian line, and since the end of 1914 had been relatively quiet.

Since the end of the 'race to the sea', the BEF had undertaken no major offensive action against the German armies, indeed both the Germans and the French paid little heed to the tiny British presence, beyond allowing that such British troops as were present[*] were effective. From the French point of view a large part of their country was in German hands. They saw the withdrawal of German forces from the west[†] to deal with Russia as being an opportunity for offensive action by the Allies. Joffre, the French Commander-in-Chief, wanted this to happen as soon as the weather and

---

[*] The BEF still consisted of only 11 infantry divisions, two of them Indian, and five cavalry divisions, two of them Indian.

[†] The Germans moved eight infantry divisions and six cavalry divisions from the Western to the Eastern Front in November and December 1914.

the ground permitted. The French High Command, Joffre himself and the French public were all under the impression that the British Empire was not playing its full part in the war, as so far it was the French who had borne the brunt of the fighting and had taken most casualties. All this was at least partly true, but the BEF, reinforced by the Indian Corps, was the only army that Britain had in 1914. It had escaped destruction at Mons, had held on the Marne and had just avoided being routed at Ypres. Ideally the British would have liked to wait on the defensive until the New Armies were ready and sufficient supplies of artillery shells, trench mortars and bombs became available, but Sir John French had been instructed by the British cabinet to do his utmost to conform to and assist the French, and he was under constant pressure from Joffre to do something to aid the planned French efforts farther south.

The British Commander-in-Chief decided to attack at Neuve Chapelle. His reasons for attacking here were mixed. In the immediate term it would be useful to pinch out the German protuberance into his line and the enemy might be caught off guard and made to take casualties out of proportion to those which would be suffered by the attackers. At the operational level it was tempting to go on beyond Neuve Chapelle and capture the high ground of the Aubers Ridge. This feature, a 20-mile long ridge with a flat arable top, ran across the British front at a distance of between one and four miles, from La Bassée through Aubers to the west of Lille. At no point does it rise more than 40 feet above the surrounding plain but it had allowed German artillery observers to dominate the British line and particularly that occupied by the Indian Corps. If Aubers Ridge could be captured by the Allies it would render a large portion of German-held territory untenable, and might even force an evacuation of Lille. Perhaps as important as any purely tactical factors, a successful attack would be good for the morale of Sir John's men who had spent an uncomfortable and largely unprofitable winter in the trenches when the initiative lay very largely with the enemy.

On Christmas Day 1914 the BEF had been re-organised into two armies, and now the First Army under General Sir Douglas Haig was given the task of attacking Neuve Chapelle. It was to be a two-corps attack, with IV British Corps attacking from a start line along the D170 road and advancing south-east, while the Indian Corps would attack north-east from the D947. At first glance the plan was a good one, and like all good plans was simple in its concept, although at second glance it was perhaps not so simple in its execution. The two thrusts, British and Indian, would take the forward enemy positions, press on and meet up at the northern end of Neuve Chapelle. The whole force would then swing round to face east and capture the Bois de Biez, about 1,000 yards south-east of the village. It was at this point that aspiration began to overtake practicability, for it was hoped that from a new British line east of Neuve Chapelle, a further

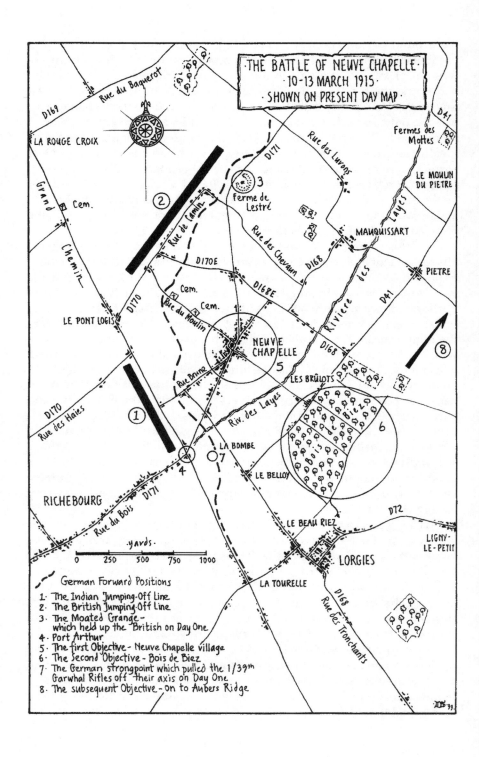

THE BATTLE OF NEUVE CHAPELLE·
·10-13 MARCH 1915·
·SHOWN ON PRESENT DAY MAP·

Rue du Baquerot
D169
LA ROUGE CROIX
Grand
Chemin
Cem.
②
Rue de Camin
Ferme de
Lestré
③
D170E
Cem.
D170
Cem.
LE PONT LOGIS
Rue du Moulin
Rue Brune
D170
Rue des Haies
①
Rue du Bois
D171
RICHEBOURG
Rue du Bois
D171
NEUVE
CHAPELLE
⑤
Rue des Chevaux
D168
D168E
Riviere
D168E
Rue des Layons
D171
Fermes des
Mottes
D41
LE MOULIN
DU PIETRE
MAUQUISSART
des
Layes
PIETRE
D41
D168
⑧
LES BRÛLOTS
Bois
Biez
⑥
LA BOMBE
⑦
LE BELLOY
Riv. des Layes
LE BEAU RIEZ
D72
LIGNY-
LE-PETIT
LORGIES
LA TOURELLE
Rue des Tronchants
D168

·yards·
0   250   500   750   1000

German Forward Positions
1· The Indian Jumping-Off Line
2· The British Jumping-Off Line
3· The Moated Grange -
   which held up the British on Day One
4· Port Arthur
5· The First Objective - Neuve Chapelle village
6· The Second Objective - Bois de Biez
7· The German strongpoint which pulled the 1/39th
   Garwhal Rifles off their axis on Day One
8· The subsequent Objective - on to Aubers Ridge

JOS '99

advance could be made to capture the high ground of the Aubers Ridge. In fact this latter phase was not attempted and the battle of Neuve Chapelle was fought out over three days in an area contained by six map squares.

In the case of IV British Corps the operation would be carried out by 8 Division, while the Indian Corps gave the task to the Meerut Division, with the Lahore Division remaining in Corps reserve. Haig had emphasised the importance of security prior to the attack, which was scheduled for 10 March, and in the weeks leading up to that date the Royal Flying Corps had made prodigious, and largely successful, efforts to keep German aviators away from the area. Aerial photography was by then well advanced, and pictures of the inevitable troop movements and stockpiling of stores and supplies would have given the Germans advance warning that a major operation was in preparation, allowing them, at the very least, to shell the concentration areas and dumps.

Lieutenant General Sir Charles Anderson DSO, commanding the Meerut Division, issued his Operation Order Number 21 on 9 March, the day before the attack was to begin. In it he gave an outline of the First Army plan and laid down that the Bareilly Brigade would hold the present front line, the Garhwal Brigade would assault following an artillery bombardment, and the Dehra Dun Brigade would follow up. He ordered that the Garhwal Brigade was to take the German trenches forward of the line running from Port Arthur north-west to the road junction of the Rue des Haies with the Estaires/La Bassée road (the D947), link up with the British 8 Division and then push on to the 'best available line'[1] to the east of the Port Arthur/Neuve Chapelle road. Subsequent objectives would be the east edge of the Bois de Biez and the high ground of the Aubers Ridge.

In detailing the Garhwal Brigade as the assaulting brigade, General Anderson placed particular emphasis on the need for the brigade to provide blocking parties to fill in the German trenches on the extreme right of the assault, to prevent the enemy infiltrating behind the attackers, and the importance of the right, exposed, flank. The Garhwal Brigade was to be closely followed up by a half company of Sappers and Miners and a company of the divisional pioneer battalion, 107th Pioneers, to assist in the preparation of a new line of trenches once the brigade had reached its first objective. The Bareilly Brigade was not only to hold the present line but was to assist the assault by rifle fire at the enemy line during the preliminary bombardment and on the flanks during the assault. This brigade was to watch the progress of 8 Division on the left so that no friendly fire fell on them. Finally the Bareilly Brigade was to be prepared to move forward to take up position on the eventual new line.

The supporting brigade, the Dehra Dun Brigade, was to form up along the Garhwal Brigade start line once the latter had vacated it. One company of the 2/8th Gurkhas was to act as prisoner of war escort. The role of divisional reserve was allocated to the 4th Cavalry, the divisional cavalry regiment (dismounted, and the equivalent therefore of about a company of infantry), the remainder of the 2/8th Gurkhas, a company of the 107th Pioneers and a company of Sappers and Miners, the whole under command of Lieutenant Colonel Stainforth, Commanding Officer 4th Cavalry. The Assistant Provost Marshal was instructed to stop all civilian traffic from entering the area.

Brigadier General CG Blackader DSO[*], commanding the Garhwal Brigade, extracted his brigade's mission from the divisional order and translated that into tasks for the units in his brigade. The Brigade was to line up on the start line in the order left to right, or north to south, 2/39th Garhwalis, 2/3rd Gurkhas, 2nd Leicesters, and 1/39th Garhwalis on the extreme right at Port Arthur. The 1/3rd Londons (a British Territorial battalion) would be in reserve, in breastworks built behind the present front line. Brigade headquarters would be in Des Lobes, about 8,000 yards to the west and on the face of it rather far away to be able to exercise any real influence on the battle.

Each battalion in the Garhwal Brigade was to take two machine-guns forward with them, while all other machine-guns in the Brigade (ten) were to be concentrated on the left flank where they could provide fire support in the assault. Trench mortars, or what were still described as bomb guns, were to be placed on the right flank in order to assist in preventing any interference from the German line not under attack. Each man in the assaulting battalions was to carry 150 rounds of ammunition, two sand bags, an emergency ration and the 'unexpired portion' of the day's ration. Each battalion was to take 192 bombs (mainly of the Battye and hairbrush variety but with a few jam pots as well), and the location of reserve ammunition dumps was specified.

Commanding officers of battalions could now issue their orders. Those of Lieutenant Colonel D H Drake-Brockman, commanding 2/39th Garhwalis which would be the left assault battalion, were issued verbally at 2000 hours on the 9th, the day before the attack, to all British and Garhwali officers and were confirmed in writing later that night. These orders laid down the route to the start line and in which order and formation companies were to line up for the attack. Men were to carry 200 rounds of ammunition, 50 more than the Brigade Commander had ordered, and every detail of how the attack was to be executed was spelt out. He ordered that:

Men in leading platoons whose kukris fit easily in their scabbards are to be told off to draw kukris to cut the hedge [which ran along

---

[*]   Blackader, who had arrived in France from India in command of the 2nd Leicesters, would eventually be promoted to Major General and be given command of a division.

148

the road in front of the start line] if necessary to clear a passage through.[2]

No one was to fall out to attend to wounded men, who were to be left for the stretcher bearers, and company commanders were to take periscopes, and pink coloured cloth to mark captured enemy trenches for the artillery observers.

The La Bassée/Estaires road, the start line for the attack, had a low hedge on the enemy side and a drainage ditch running along the home side. Just behind the ditch ran the line of trenches occupied by the Bareilly Brigade, and 100 yards behind them was a series of breastworks, built up because the water table prevented digging down. From the road the boggy, wet plough ran flat to Neuve Chapelle, a typical French hamlet of the period with a church conspicuous in the centre, the village square surrounded by small shops and cafés, and more substantial houses on the outskirts. Most of the buildings had suffered some damage in the previous fighting and were now to be virtually destroyed. The German forward entrenchments were protected by barbed wire, mainly wooden knife rests with coils of wire wrapped around them, and some low wire entanglements. From the left of the start line, where the Garhwal Brigade machine-guns would be, there was an excellent field of fire right across the front, not only in front of the assaulting battalions of the Indian Corps but also across the front of the British troops' line of advance and through the 600-yard gap that separated the right of the British start line from the left of the Indians.

During the reconnaissance on the days leading up to the attack it had been noted that the road to the Indian Corps' front was raised slightly above the surrounding countryside, and that the area of the ditch on the home side would offer a jumping off point under cover from view of the enemy side. If the ditch could be improved slightly, it would be under cover from fire as well. The Bareilly Brigade agreed to carry out the necessary work during the nights leading up to the attack and dug a shallow trench to the rear of the ditch as well as creating some gaps in the bank to allow the assaulting troops to move off quickly. Ladders were provided to allow those troops who could not be accommodated in the new trench or the ditch to leave the main trenches easily, and portable bridges were provided where the ditch could not be jumped. On the right flank, the dangers of which had been seen by army, divisional and brigade commanders, the Bareilly Brigade would mass its machine-guns to provide maximum fire against the German line which would otherwise enfilade the attack.

During the night of 9 March the assaulting troops moved into position. Marching up the Rue du Bois and the Rue des Haies the Garhwalis, Gurkhas and Leicesters turned right and left and filed into their positions alongside the men of the Bareilly Brigade. By 0515 hours on 10 March the assaulting companies were lining the ditch in their assault formations. Each battalion would advance with two companies in the first wave, each company with two platoons forward in extended line with the other two platoons 30 yards behind. Over the total brigade frontage of 800 yards there would be a man every five yards. The men had their greatcoats with them to guard against the cold during the long wait for Zero Hour at 0805 hours. As they would not take their greatcoats into the attack it had been agreed that they would be recovered and stored temporarily by the Bareilly Brigade, showing enormous trust in the quartermasters of another brigade. While this was going on the artillery of the Indian Corps was hauled into position for the opening bombardment, some of the guns being only 1,000 yards in rear of the start line. The artillery bombardment was to begin at 0730 hours, but at 0700, just as it had begun to get light, a German aeroplane appeared. The pilot, showing great courage and daring, flew very low—around 200 feet—over Port Arthur and, as we now know, was able to signal the presence of unusual amounts of men and equipment to his colleagues on the ground. This information drew the inevitable artillery and machine-gun fire on the 2nd Leicesters and the 1/39th Garhwalis, both of whom suffered some casualties. It was too late to prevent what was to come.

At 0730 the British bombardment began. It was the biggest British artillery operation of the war so far: 420^3 guns ranging from 18-pounders in the field batteries which fired on the German wire, to 6-inch, 9.2-inch and 15-inch howitzers which took on the enemy trenches and strongpoints in the village. Other targets for the artillery were German gun positions in rear and, to prevent enemy reinforcement coming up, the roads leading to the area. Although far shorter and of much less intensity than opening bombardments later in the war, the artillery efforts on the morning of 10 March were nevertheless impressive, and many soldiers stood up to watch the effects as shells burst on the German wire and in the village of Neuve Chapelle. The shells of the 18-pounders, being fired on a relatively flat trajectory, were passing only a few feet above the men of the Garhwal and Bareilly Brigades, and the howitzer shells could even be followed by the naked eye from their apogee until landing on their targets. Inevitably, all this instigated a reply from the German guns, which was relatively insignificant—relatively, but not entirely. The Commanding Officer of the 2/39th Garhwalis was sitting on the edge of the ditch with his adjutant, his orderly Rifleman Keshar Sing Rana and a sepoy of the 6th Jat Light Infantry, the battalion of the Bareilly Brigade manning that part of the line. An enemy shell burst a few yards in front of them, killing the orderly— who had won the IDSM at Festubert in November 1914—and the 6th Jat, but leaving colonel and adjutant unscathed. As if in retaliation, a few moments later the upper half of a German officer, cap still firmly fixed on the head, was blown into the ditch just beside the two officers.

While the bombardment was going on the men in the forward companies were able to come out of their ditch and trenches and lie down lining the edge of the road. At 0805 the assaulting companies were, in the words of the Commanding Officer 2/39th Garhwalis, 'up and away without a moment's hesitation, which was splendid'[4]. Over most of the line the artillery had done what it was intended to do and the German wire was very largely destroyed, providing no obstacle to the Indians. Dropping their greatcoats the lead companies doubled across the ground in front reaching the forward German trenches—which were in some cases less than 100 yards away—before the defenders had even realised that the bombardment had stopped. A few shots and the sepoys were on to the second line, pressing on yet farther until they reached the far side of a small orchard 500 yards from the start line. The battalions halted briefly and sorted themselves out, checking for any casualties. These were few and caused not by the defenders of the first two lines of entrenchments[*] but from enemy machine-gun fire from the flanks and from a few brave Germans who had stayed under cover as the first waves passed over them, emerging to engage the backs of the advancing sepoys. They were quickly dealt with.

On the left and centre of the Garhwal Brigade all had gone well so far. Not so on the right. The right assaulting battalion, attacking from Port Arthur, was the 1/39th Garhwalis, the sister battalion of the attackers on the left, and its officers and men were well aware of the risk posed by the German line which outflanked the attack start line and could enfilade it from the south. This threat had been well understood by all involved in the planning of the operation from Haig downwards, but despite the bomb guns and the massed machine-guns of the Bareilly Brigade, the 1/39th Garhwalis, whose axis of advance was towards the north-east, came under heavy fire from German strongpoints to the east of Port Arthur. Unable to ignore the fire being directed against them, which was starting to inflict casualties very early on, the Garhwalis had no option but to swing to their right to deal with the hostile fire. This created a gap between themselves and the 2nd Leicesters and brought them up against German wire which had escaped the bombardment and was uncut. The action on the right degenerated into a fire fight with very little cover for the attackers. Men crawled forward a few yards and attempted to cut or get through the wire, and the momentum of the battalion's advance slowed to a few hard won yards in the first hour. Two companies of the Leicesters fought their way along the German trench and built a strong point with sand bags, from where they and a party of Indian Sappers and Miners gave fire and bombing support to the Garhwalis. With the Sappers

---

[*] Most of the second line of trenches were flooded and only lightly held.

and Miners party was Lieutenant Percy Hobart who would be awarded the Military Cross for his bravery on this day, and who would, as Major General Sir Percy Hobart, be a leading exponent of armoured vehicle design and tactics prior to and during the Second World War.

Eventually the German stronghold was captured in the late afternoon by an attack by the 3rd Londons, the reserve battalion of the brigade, and what was left of the 1/39th Garhwalis, supported by a flank attack by the 4th Seaforths from the Dehra Dun Brigade. The position was finally won at a heavy cost. Every single British officer of the 1/39th Garhwalis, including the medical officer, became a casualty with seven of them killed and the Commanding Officer seriously wounded.* Immediately after the battle it was thought that 98 Indian Other Ranks had been killed with 22 missing, but it was later discovered that the missing, first assumed to have been taken prisoner, had in fact all been killed. The 2nd Leicesters too suffered grievously, but gloriously. Private William Buckingham dashed into no man's land on several occasions to rescue wounded sepoys and for his bravery on this occasion, and later in the battle on 12 March, he was awarded the Victoria Cross. He was killed during the battle and his body was never found.

Elsewhere all was going well. The 2/39th Garhwalis, the 2/3rd Gurkhas and the rest of the Leicesters paused on the outskirts of the village and sent parties back to clear any Germans still in the trenches which had been overrun. Many of the survivors were in a state of shocked disorientation from the effects of the artillery bombardment and there were many mangled German bodies. On the extreme left the 2/39th were responsible for clearing the trenches off to the north-west so as to link up with the British assaulting brigade. One party commanded by Rifleman Gobar Sing Negi† jumped into the German trench line and began to work their way along to the left. They were armed with a plentiful supply of Captain Battye's inventions and were bombing their way along from traverse to traverse when they came up against a section of the line which was still strongly held. Gobar Sing lit the fuse and hurled a bomb into a traverse, waited for it to explode and then led his small party round the corner, shooting and bayoneting the survivors before repeating the exercise against the next traverse. Showing leadership normally only expected from an officer or an NCO, he was making remarkable progress when the inevitable happened:

---

*   Lieutenant Colonel Swiney survived and returned to the Western Front but was eventually drowned on his way to India when the SS *Persia* was torpedoed and sunk in the Mediterranean on 30 December 1915.

†   No relation to Darwan Sing Negi, of the First Battalion of the same regiment, who had won the VC at Festubert in 1914. Negi is a clan name.

his luck ran out and he was killed. Gobar Sing's body was never found, or if it was found was never identified, the trench where it was lying being demolished later by German shelling. He received the posthumous award of the Victoria Cross and his name is engraved on the Indian Memorial at Port Arthur.

Many Germans had been killed or wounded by now, and those who were unable to withdraw into the village surrendered. The 2/39th Garhwalls alone sent 200 prisoners back to the start line to be taken away to the rear by the 2/8th Gurkhas. By now contact had been made with the British 25 Brigade attacking from the north-west and together they pressed on into the village, fighting from house to house using the street fighting techniques they had worked out beforehand. Street fighting, even in a small village such as Neuve Chapelle, is tiring, time consuming, wasteful of anummition and heavy on casualties. The procedure was to fight through the village house by house. While one group would bring down rifle fire on the windows, doors and any loopholes created by the defenders, another group would make an entry to the building, either by a window or through a shell hole. The doors were avoided as being certain to be covered by the occupants. Having made an entry the storming party would clear the house room by room and floor by floor, firing through the ceilings and using bombs on landings. Rifleman Gane Gurung, 2/3rd Gurkhas, apparently grew tired of following the laid down procedures and, seeing heavy fire coming from one house in the centre of the hamlet, rushed it alone. His comrades saw him burst through the door and disappear. They assumed they would see Gane no more. A few moments later eight burly Germans emerged in single file, their hands held above their heads, while behind them, bayonet aimed menacingly at the ample bottom of the last German, came Riflemen Gane Gurung, all five feet two inches of him, with a broad smile on his face. In the midst of battle the 2nd Rifle Brigade, the right-hand battalion of 25 Brigade and also fighting through the village, halted in their tracks and gave three rousing cheers. Gane Gurung, who had already been noted for showing great bravery, was awarded the Indian Order of Merit Second Class for his daring on this occasion.

By 0900 hours the village of Neuve Chapelle was secure, and the Garhwal Brigade swung right towards the south-east facing the Bois de Biez. Just short of the old Smith-Dorrien trench line[*] the brigade took cover with the 2/3rd Gurkhas on the left, half of the 2nd Leicesters on the right and the 2/39th Garhwalis in support in rear. To the Garhwal Brigade's left was the Rifle Brigade, the right-hand battalion of 25 Brigade. The men were in extended line and took cover where they could, those with entrenching

---

[*]   The Smith-Dorrien trench itself was flooded and could not be occupied.

tools digging themselves shell scrapes.* The 1/39th Garhwalis and the other half of the 2nd Leicesters were still fighting their own private battle in front of Port Arthur and were keeping the enemy so engaged that the rest of the brigade was not interfered with from that quarter.

It was now that the Dehra Dun Brigade should have been following up closely, ready to storm through and take the Bois de Biez, 800 yards in front of the Garhwal Brigade's new position. Unfortunately the very success of the initial attack had out-run the plan and there was now a long delay. During the night the Dehra Dun Brigade had been moved forward to what was named A1 Redoubt, about 800 yards south-west of Port Arthur on the D166, but it was not until 1100 hours on the 10th that the Dehra Dun Brigade arrived at Port Arthur and 1600 when they were ordered to advance through the Garhwal Brigade with their first objective as the Des Layes river, followed by the road on the far side of the Bois de Biez. It was this delay, the first of several, which was to play a large part in preventing the original plan from being a total success. Surprise had been an essential element of the attack and it had been difficult enough to conceal the presence of two brigades at the jumping off line. It would simply not have been possible for the Dehra Dun Brigade to have been accommodated in the firing line as well, but had that brigade been ordered to move up as soon as the bombardment began, they might have been nearer the action much sooner, and in a position to exploit the initial success.

The Layes is a tributary of the Lys and runs roughly south-west passing between Neuve Chapelle and the Bois de Biez, about 800 yards from the village and 400 yards from the wood. It is an insignificant feature in times of peace, being not much more than a drainage ditch which dries up completely in summer†, but to advancing infantry in the wet season it was a definite obstacle and a protective covering for the enemy, who had built some breastworks and dug trenches along it. In March 1915 the stream was about ten feet across from bank to bank, just too broad to be jumped by men carrying weapons and entrenching tools and with boots clogged with clay. The water was four feet deep and the surface of the water a further three to four feet below the bank.

The battalions of the Dehra Dun Brigade had already drawn portable bridges from the Sappers and Miners and the Brigade moved off in file with the 1/9th Gurkhas leading followed by the 2/2nd Gurkhas with the 4th Seaforths, who would be in support, bringing up the rear. They moved up towards Neuve Chapelle by the minor road that had been the

---

* Not a trench but literally a scrape 6" or so in depth and the length of a man, in which he could lie down facing the enemy and be able to fire his rifle.

† It may have originated as a man-made drainage ditch. The author was able to walk its complete length in August, with almost dry feet.

boundary between 1/39th Garhwalis and 2/3rd Gurkhas. They used the houses along the road as cover but movement was hindered by damaged buildings, shell holes and the remains of German wired knife rests. After about 300 yards they turned right, off the road, and as there was no longer cover from view, enemy shelling began to take a toll. Emerging from the orchards and gardens which lined the road the two lead battalions deployed into assault formation facing the Bois de Biez, with 1/9th Gurkhas on the left, 2/2nd Gurkhas on the right and 4th Seaforths in rear. Both forward battalions had two companies up and two in close support 50 yards behind.

By 1730 hours the lead battalions of the Dehra Dun Brigade had reached the old Smith-Dorrien trench and passed through the Garhwal Brigade. German machine-guns opened up from the Bois de Biez, but by now it was getting dark and the fire was largely ineffective. The right-hand forward company of the 1/9th Gurkhas should have kept in touch with the left-hand company of the 2/2nd Gurkhas, but in the scurrying necessary to avoid hostile fire a gap opened up and the 1/9th Gurkhas' Commanding Officer ordered his two rear companies forward to fill it. The Germans manning the defences along the Layes river had withdrawn into the wood and the stream was crossed with little difficulty. Farther right a company of the 2/2nd Gurkhas had pressed on over the stream and reached the edge of the wood, where they started to dig in, a number of Germans coming forward and surrendering.

To attack through the wood in the dark with an exposed flank, with no clear idea where the enemy was and with only three companies (two of the 2/2nd Gurkhas and one of the 1/9th Gurkhas), was clearly not a possibility. The forward battalions each sent an officer back to brigade headquarters of the Dehra Dun Brigade, now established in Neuve Chapelle. Once Brigadier General Jacob was apprised of the situation he ordered the two forward battalions to consolidate where they were, with the Seaforths sending two companies up to act as a reserve. This would have led to an untidy and tactically unsound situation when the morning light permitted enemy observation. Brigadier Jacob quickly thought better of it, sending a staff officer up to cancel his previous instructions and ordering the whole line to pull back to the Layes. At this stage the only means of communication between battalions and from battalions to Headquarters was by runner or personal visit, and it would not be until 1800 hours on 11 March that contact via telephone would be establjshed.

Both the 1/9th and the 2/2nd Gurkhas retired, companies and platoons covering each other rearward. The Layes was reached and men of both battalions began to dig in behind it, a task which was to occupy them for most of the night. Digging was not made easier by the lack of proper shovels and the men had to make do with the 'Sirhind' entrenching tool, adequate for scraping out an individual shelter in an emergency, but never

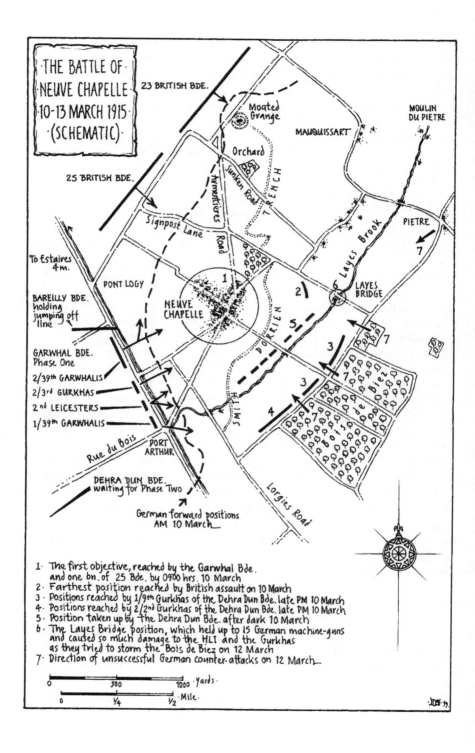

THE BATTLE OF
NEUVE CHAPELLE
10-13 MARCH 1915
(SCHEMATIC)

23 BRITISH BDE.

Moated Grange

MAUQUISSART

MOULIN DU PIETRE

Orchard

Sunken Road

25 BRITISH BDE.

Armentières Road

TRENCH

Signpost Lane

Layes Brook

PIETRE

7

To Estaires 4m.

PONT LOGY

1

NEUVE CHAPELLE

2

6 Layes Brook
LAYES BRIDGE

BAREILLY BDE.
holding jumping off line

5

7

GARWHAL BDE.
Phase One

2/39th GARWHALIS

2/3rd GURKHAS

2nd LEICESTERS

1/39th GARWHALIS

SMITH

DORRIEN

3

Bois de Biez

3

4

Rue du Bois

PORT ARTHUR

DEHRA DUN BDE.
waiting for Phase Two

German forward positions
AM 10 March

Lorgies Road

1 · The first objective, reached by the Garwhal Bde.
   and one bn. of 25 Bde. by 0900 hrs. 10 March
2 · Farthest position reached by British assault on 10 March
3 · Positions reached by 1/9th Gurkhas of the Dehra Dun Bde. late PM 10 March
4 · Positions reached by 2/2nd Gurkhas of the Dehra Dun Bde. late PM 10 March
5 · Position taken up by the Dehra Dun Bde. after dark 10 March
6 · The Layes Bridge position, which held up to 15 German machine-guns
   and caused so much damage to the HLI and the Gurkhas
   as they tried to storm the Bois de Biez on 12 March
7 · Direction of unsuccessful German counter-attacks on 12 March

0   500   1000 Yards.
0   1/4   1/2 Mile.

JDS·99

intended for the construction of a major line of defence. It was expected that the advance would be renewed on the morrow and more portable bridges were brought up and placed in position across the stream, ready for a jump off at first light. The situation now was that the 2/2nd Gurkhas held the river bank to the south, the 1/9th Gurkhas to the north. Farther north of them should have been the 2nd Rifle Brigade of 25 Brigade, but its men had made slower progress than the Dehra Dun Brigade, due to there being large amounts of uncut wire and collapsed buildings on their axis. The result was that the left, northern, flank of 1/9th Gurkhas was in the air, about 400 yards in advance of the right-hand man of the Rifle Brigade. The Commanding Officer of the 1/9th was well aware of the danger and he stationed his battalion's two machine-guns on the left of his line, under Lieutenant Murray. It was as well that he did so, for at 0200 hours a substantial party of enemy did try to get round the flank and into the gap between the two brigades. Murray had sited his guns well, however, and the enemy were driven off with considerable loss.

During the night orders arrived from Brigade Headquarters that the Dehra Dun Brigade was to attack the Bois de Biez at 0700 hours next morning, 11 March, with the proviso that there was to be no move forward until 25 Brigade, on the left, moved up too. The men of the 1/9th and 2/2nd Gurkhas crossed the Layes and laid down in assault formation on the open ground, but just before Zero Hour it was announced that the attack was postponed until 1200 hours and the Jullunder Brigade of the Lahore Division was ordered to move up short of Neuve Chapelle ready to assist. 25 Brigade had been held up by heavy machine-gun fire from Pietre, a group of houses about 1,200 yards north-east of Neuve Chapelle, and was unable to move. The morning of 11 March was foggy, but as dawn broke and the mist cleared, the men of the Garhwal Brigade could see that during the night the Germans had dug trenches and laid wire along the edge of the wood and in the open ground between the wood and the Layes, as well as having re-occupied the houses from which they had been ejected the evening before. The enemy line now reached the Layes, to the left of the 1/9th Gurkhas' open flank, and they had constructed a strongpoint around the small bridge where the Layes crossed what is now the D168E, and which runs south-east from the north of Neuve Chapelle. In this strongpoint were an estimated 15 German machine-guns. At around 0800 hours fatigue parties from both forward battalions, assisted by men of the 2/8th Gurkhas, hove into sight across open fields weighed down by huge boxes of army biscuits—the resupply of rations had arrived. The Germans lost no time in taking advantage of this slow moving target and some of the carriers were hit, although most managed to get through.

Mid-day came and went and there was still no movement from 25 Brigade. The Dehra Dun Brigade, now back in their hastily constructed trenches behind the Layes, continued to try to improve their positions.

Movement along the narrow and shallow trench was difficult, and some men were killed by enemy sniper fire passing through the parapet. Even when most German resistance had been suppressed or eliminated, sniping was a continual problem. On one occasion Havildar Ismail Khan, 21st Company Sappers and Miners, of the Lahore Division but lent to the Meerut Division for the Neuve Chapelle operation, was working on the forward defence line when a sniper shot him through both legs. While being tended to the havildar expressed professional admiration for an enemy who, so he assumed, had waited until both the havildar's legs were in line before firing, in order to conserve ammunition.

Some time after noon a message was received by the 2/2nd Gurkhas, but not by 1/9th Gurkhas, that 25 Brigade hoped to be able to move shortly and that the attack was now scheduled for 1415 hours. At 1400 the artillery of the Indian Corps began to shell the Bois de Biez. It was a ferocious bombardment and even today holes 20 feet across and four feet deep bear evidence to the plight of the Germans in the wood. Shrapnel or burst-on-contact rounds are particularly dangerous to the inhabitants of woods because the shells not only cause their own damage on impact, but also blow arboreal debris down into trenches and through the roofs of dugouts. A flying branch kills just as surely as a shell splinter. Still no movement from 25 Brigade materialised, and while an independent advance by the Dehra Dun Brigade might have secured a local tactical success, it would have left their flank completely exposed, and in any case they had been specifically ordered not to advance alone. The difficulty actually lay not with 25 Brigade, but farther north with the two brigades on 25 Brigade's left, 23 and 24 Brigades. These two brigades had met with very heavy German resistance and were making only slow progress. Without at least one of them to cover the northern flank, 25 Brigade could not move, so neither could the Indians. At about 1500 hours the Germans were seen evacuating their trenches and cottages along the edge of the Bois de Biez and their breastworks in front of it, and by dark all firing had ceased—the Germans had gone.

At 1800 hours telephone lines were at last laid to Brigade Headquarters in Neuve Chapelle. By now the hamlet had received the attention of both British and German artillery and, on top of the damage caused by the fighting of the previous year, resembled nothing more than the scene of a particularly devastating earthquake. The church, which had been clearly visible from the Garhwal Brigade's start line, was destroyed and on fire. Shells falling in the cemetery had burst open graves, exposing long dead bodies to the light of the flames. The largest building, a brewery, was still more or less intact and was taken over by the 107th Pioneers and the Sappers and Miners as the base for their night-time work of improving defences. Brigade Headquarters found a cellar still intact, in which they established a forward command post. Even with voice communication now established, orders being passed to battalions were far from clear.

The intention was to relieve the Dehra Dun Brigade by the Sirhind Brigade during the night of 11/12 March but cut telephone wires, lost runners and the general confusion of the night led to instructions for the relief being improperly relayed. The 1/9th Gurkhas were under the impression that they were to withdraw without relief once they had evacuated their casualties, while the 2/2nd Gurkhas thought that they were to be relieved but were unsure when. The 1/9th Gurkhas had 40 stretcher cases—defined as wounded men who were unable to walk—but had only eight stretchers, so men were evacuated on planks, doors and other men's backs. It was midnight before the 1/9th Gurkhas got all their casualties out, either to the brigade dressing station or, for less serious cases, to their own Regimental Aid Post which was down the Port Arthur road, and having got the wounded clear the battalion began to withdraw. Seeing the 1/9th withdraw the 2/2nd Gurkhas also began to pull back.

At this stage both the Jullunder and Sirhind Brigades were at Richebourg St Vaast, 3,000 yards to the west. The intention was for the Sirhind Brigade to relieve the Dehra Dun Brigade during the night, and then for the British 8th Division and both the Sirhind and Jullunder Brigades to attack the Bois de Biez and the area to the north of the wood on the morning of 12 March.

The Sirhind Brigade began to move the four miles from Vieille Chapelle to Neuve Chapelle at 2100 hours on the night of 11 March. Progress was slow and the roads were sporadically shelled, but casualties were fortunately light. Meanwhile the two forward battalions of the Dehra Dun Brigade had begun to withdraw. The 2/2nd Gurkhas withdrew first and managed to get through Neuve Chapelle and back to billets in Vieille Chapelle by 0130, but the 1/9th Gurkhas were unable to get clear of their positions until much later. They eventually passed through the Garhwal Brigade, still holding the Smith-Dorrien Line as outposts but also being withdrawn themselves, at around 0300 hours. Heading for Neuve Chapelle the 1/9th met the men of the Sirhind Brigade coming up to relieve them. Protests from the latter that the two Gurkha battalions should not have moved until relieved by the battalions of the Sirhind Brigade were to no avail—it was now far too late to reverse the movement in the darkness and under opportunist German shelling. In Neuve Chapelle itself all was confusion. The Sirhind Brigade coming up and the Dehra Dun Brigade going down, convoys of wounded, roads rendered impassable by shell holes, collapsed buildings and intermittent enemy shelling and the complete impossibility of runners establishing communications in a fluid situation, all contributed to utter chaos. The 1/9th Gurkhas did not manage to pick their way through and arrive in Vieille Chapelle until 0700 on the morning of 12 March. They had hardly tumbled into what sleeping accommodation they could find when at 0830 hours they were ordered to Richebourg St Vaast in preparation for the projected attack on the Bois de Biez by the Sirhind and Jullunder Brigades.

Despite the difficulties, the Sirhind Brigade managed to retain some form of cohesion. The battalions reached the Smith-Dorrien Line and moved on in the direction of the Layes, but due to the difficulties of moving through and out of Neuve Chapelle, the Highland Light Infantry and the 1/4th Gurkhas had changed places. The 1/4th now found themselves on the right of the brigade, instead of the left, and took up positions with their right-hand company along the southern portion of the Layes. The Gurkhas' left forward company was farther back from the river, linking up with the Highland Light Infantry whose line bent north-west away from the stream until their left was just short of Neuve Chapelle. Well before dawn the Sirhind Brigade was in position, and the brigade commander issued new orders to take into account the current deployments. Brigadier Walker was able to tell his commanding officers that there would be a 20-minute artillery bombardment of the Bois de Biez starting at 0700 on 12 March. Following this the 1/4th Gurkha Rifles and the Highland Light Infantry were to advance and storm the north-west edge of the wood, after which the 15th Sikhs and the 1/1st Gurkhas were to pass through and capture the south-eastern corner.

Unfortunately the delays of 10 and 11 March had enabled the Germans to move up reinforcements and this was to allow the enemy to pre-empt the attack on the Bois de Biez. Although the Indian Corps did not know it at the time, there were but two German infantry battalions in the Bois de Biez on 11 March. On the night of 11/12 March a further two Saxon and two Bavarian battalions came in and the entire 6th Bavarian division was approaching the battlefield. As daybreak on 12 March approached, the entire area was covered with a thick fog. Visibility was down to a few yards and with the first glimmerings of light at 0500 hours came a short but intense enemy artillery bombardment directed at the Highland Light Infantry and the 1/4th Gurkhas as well as on the Port Arthur area. The men of the Sirhind Brigade were lucky, however, as the German spotters had not realised that the Gurkhas and the Scots were as far forward as they were. Most of the shells fell behind the Indian lines, although some did fall on the Scinde Rifles, who were moving up to the north as part of the Jullunder Brigade.

As suddenly as it had started the German artillery fire ceased, and the men of the Sirhind Brigade peered anxiously through the mist. They could see nothing yet, but they could hear movement, shouting and cheering to their front. Suddenly massed ranks of men came into view 60 yards from the Indian trenches, co-ordinated with similar attacks on the Port Arthur area and from the Pietre direction. For a moment the sepoys thought they must be the Highlanders, for in the pre-dawn light the greatcoats worn by the attackers made them look as if they were wearing kilts. Then the spiked pickelhaubes could be seen and it was clear that a massive German attack was upon them. From the whole of the line, the Sirhind Brigade behind the Layes and the Bareilly Brigade around Port Arthur, belched a storm of rifle fire. At first it seemed as if nothing could stop the dense columns[5] more reminiscent of 1870 than of 1915 and with several officers on horseback, but the accurate rifle fire and the brigaded machine-guns of the Bareilly, Garhwal and Dehra Dun Brigades cut huge swathes through the leading columns. Soon the Indian Corps artillery opened up and this too began to reap a rich harvest. More and more Germans came on, but with no supporting fire they could not reach the Indian lines and the sepoys were able to stand up, some on top of the parapet, and fire accurately at the oncoming ranks. Just as full daylight broke the attack faded away and nothing could now be seen but dead and wounded Germans lying on the grass. The semi-official History records:

> Piles of wriggling, heaving bodies lay on the ground, and the air resounded with shrieks, groans and curses. The wounded tried to shelter themselves behind parapets formed of bodies of their own dead comrades, while some attempted to dig themselves in. For hours afterwards wounded Germans continued to crawl into our lines, where they received medical attention and were sent off in ambulances as soon as possible.[6]

The slaughter was truly horrendous. In front of the Bareilly Brigade, around Port Arthur alone, 600 dead were counted, and an estimated 3,000 dead and wounded lay along the whole Meerut Division front, from Neuve Chapelle to Port Arthur, to which must be added an unknown number killed and wounded by the shelling of the Bois de Biez.

What would have happened had the attack by the Sirhind and Jullunder Brigades gone in at 0700 hours on 12 March as planned is one of the innumerable and imponderable 'what ifs?' of military history. The German attack had been utterly routed at great loss. Those still alive were demoralised and may well have surrendered, whilst the sepoys were ready and raring to go. An immediate assault on the Bois de Biez might well have succeeded. 'Might well' it must remain however, for the bombardment due to begin at 0700 hours did not take place. In playing their part in repelling the German attack, the guns had fired off much of the ammunition stockpiled for use in the bombardment, and the persistent mist made it impossible for what ammunition was left to be used in close support of advancing infantry. Without artillery support neither the Corps nor the Divisional Commander was prepared to launch the battalions across open ground against the wood, the size and dispositions of whose garrison was unknown. In order to bring up more ammunition and allow the mist to clear, the assault on the Bois de Biez was postponed until 1100 with the preliminary bombardment to begin at 1030. At 1030 the guns did open fire on the wood, but visibility was still very poor and the artillery observers were not satisfied that they had been able to register their targets properly. The attack was further postponed until 1300.

At 1230 hours the guns began their bombardment and at first it looked as if the attack would be successful. On the Sirhind Brigade front the order had been for the advance to be made 'by the left', and when the bombardment stopped at 1300 hours the Highland Light Infantry moved forward as fast as they could. They quickly reached the Layes to find that the bridges which had been placed there by the Dehra Dun Brigade had been removed by the enemy during the night. The men jumped into the stream and began to pull themselves up the muddy and slippery bank on the far side. At this point fire was opened on them from the Layes bridge strongpoint, still held by the Germans and still with at least 12 machine-guns. Firing straight down the Layes the enemy had a perfect enfilade position and no sooner had a soldier begun to struggle up the bank than he was hit. The stream was said to have run red with blood and to have been full of the dead and dying. The Highland Light Infantry could go no farther. The 1/4th Gurkhas had also reached the Layes, where the bridges had not been removed, but as the order had been 'by the left', when the Highland Light Infantry had perforce to halt the 1/4th Gurkhas halted too.

Had the brigade commander known the situation he might have ordered the 1/4th to press on alone, but he did not know. Prior to the attack Brigadier Walker, commanding the Sirhind Brigade, had been placed in command of both his own brigade and the Jullunder Brigade, a logical arrangement which ensured that the attack was under the sole command of one man. The Jullunder Brigade had been detached from the Lahore Division and while General Anderson, the commander of the Meerut Division, could have commanded the attack himself, he had three other brigades—Bareilly, Garhwal and Dehra Dun—to worry about, and it was eminently sensible to delegate overall command of the operation to Brigadier Walker. What were not so sensible, however, were the command and control arrangements to effect this delegation. Brigadier Walker had to create a temporary divisional headquarters for the attack, and to do it he took with him the staff and signals section of the Sirhind Brigade headquarters. Command of the Sirhind Brigade now devolved upon the senior commanding officer, Lieutenant Colonel W C Anderson, normally commanding 1/1st Gurkhas. Because he now had to set up a new brigade headquarters, Anderson took with him the 1/1st's adjutant and most of the battalion's signallers. Command of 1/1st now fell to the senior company commander who had to make do the best he could, without an adjutant and with very few signallers. Neither the overall commander, Walker, in Neuve Chapelle, nor the acting brigade commander, Anderson, could see very much due to the mist which still hung around in patches, and their communications were sketchy at best.

On the Jullunder Brigade front the Manchesters moved forward intending to pass through the forward trenches held by the Garhwal Brigade, but no sooner did they reach them than they came under very heavy fire and the leading companies had to take shelter in the already crowded trenches of the 2/3rd Gurkhas. Behind them such communication and support trenches as had been dug became blocked as more and more men were forced to take cover in them. The 47th Sikhs in the centre also reached the forward Indian trenches, but they too found they could go no farther owing to fierce enemy fire, directed particularly at officers. During this move the acting Commanding Officer of the 47th Sikhs, Captain Combe, was wounded and could go no farther. He was replaced by Captain Hogge, until he too was shot down. Command now devolved upon Captain Talbot, and as two other British officers had been killed during the short advance, the 47th Sikhs had lost almost all their British officers. Subadar Harnam Singh was also killed, a particularly poignant loss as his only son, a sepoy in the same regiment, had been killed at Festubert in December 1914.

On the right the combined Suffolk/Scinde battalion fared no better, the Suffolks losing an officer and seven ORs killed and 77 wounded, or over half their strength, and the Scinde Rifles losing all their British officers and a large number of men.[*] The problem was that on the extreme left the British 25 Brigade were unable to get forward, and this allowed the enemy to enfilade the Jullunder Brigade battalion by battalion. As each unit was prevented from moving forward, the unit on its right became subject to enfilade fire, and so on down the line.

Despite unreliable communications, with telephone lines being cut by shell fire almost as soon as they had been laid, Brigadier Walker, in overall command of the attack, knew why the Highland Light Infantry had been held up. From his command post in Neuve Chapelle he could see the difficulties the Scotsmen faced, but the mist prevented him from seeing why the 1/4th Gurkhas were not moving forward—was it because of the 'by the left' instruction, or was it because they too had come under fire which they could not overcome? Assuming, wrongly but not unreasonably, the latter, Walker sent an order to Lieutenant Colonel Anderson, acting commander of the Sirhind Brigade, telling him to send the 1/1st Gurkhas forward in support of the 1/4th. This order did not reach Anderson until about 1400 hours, and being nearer to the 1/4th than was Walker, he had already worked out the real reason for the delay. Anderson had already sent Captain G S Kennedy, Adjutant 1/1st Gurkhas and now acting Brigade Major, forward to confirm that the 1/4th had halted because the Highland Light Infantry had, and to order them to press on independ-

---

[*] Since arriving in France five months before, the Scinde Rifles had now lost ten British officers killed and 19 wounded, from an establishment of 12 British officers.

ently. Having despatched Kennedy, Anderson now received Walker's order to send up the 1/1st Gurkhas, but he delayed implementing it until he had heard Kennedy's report. Unfortunately Kennedy was killed on his way up and, after waiting in vain for news, at around 1430 hours Anderson ordered the 1/1st to move up and attack on the left of the 1/4th. The 1/1st Gurkhas received the order and began to move. They came under intense artillery and machine-gun fire. A shell wiped out most of battalion headquarters, including the few signallers who remained, while the acting commanding officer was hit very shortly after the advance began. At 1700 hours the battalion reached the Layes, where they found all the footbridges had been removed. Now they began to come under fire from the Layes bridge strongpoint which had so devastated the Highland Light Infantry, and they too could progress no farther. The 1/4th Gurkhas attempted an advance in conformity with the 1/1st, but the enemy fire was such that this was quickly cancelled. Farther north neither the Jullunder Brigade nor the British 25 Brigade had made any progress. The enemy was now on the field in greater strength than the combined British and Indian force and the line was essentially still where it had been on the night of 10 March.

At around 1815 hours on 12 March the Germans attempted a counter-attack from the Bois de Biez. Again they came on in dense columns led by officers on horseback, and again they were easily beaten off.

The artillery had now fired 112,000 shells and the infantry in the region of 3,000,000 rounds. This expenditure simply could not be maintained at this stage in the war. There was now no chance of capturing either the Bois de Biez or the more ambitious objective of the Aubers Ridge, and at 2200 hours on the night of 12 March General Haig, the Army Commander, called a halt to any further attacks and instructed units to consolidate the ground already won.

Sir John French said in his despatches that 12,000 German wounded had been evacuated by train[7] and, while this is probably an exaggeration, around 2,000 dead had been counted on the Meerut Division front alone. To this last figure must be added the results of the shelling of the Bois de Biez and the casualties on the British front. In addition to the dead and wounded the Indian Corps alone recorded the capture of 12 German officers and 617 Other Ranks, out of a total of 30 officers and 1,657 Other Ranks captured in the whole battle. The small proportion of prisoners taken by the Indian Corps in relation to their having provided more than half the troops on the British side may be accounted for by the Germans' fear of the Indians. The enemy had been led to believe that should they fall into Indian hands they would be tortured or executed out of hand, and many Indian battalions record instances of prisoners on their knees, weeping and begging not to be killed. Given a choice, Germans preferred to surrender to British or French troops rather than

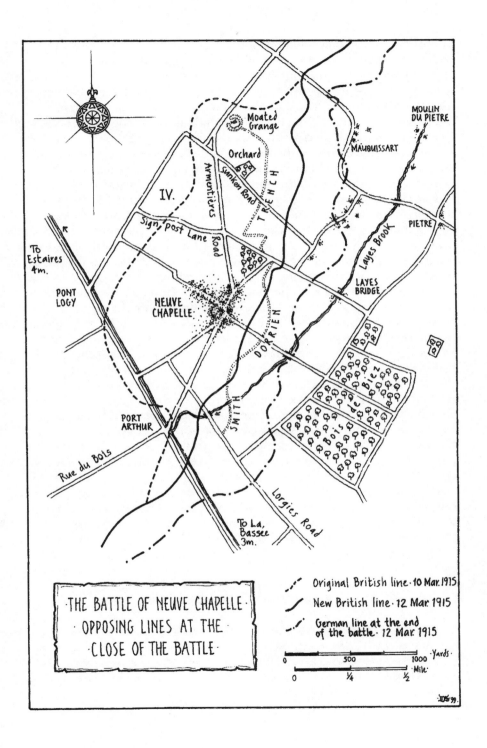

MOULIN DU PIETRE

Moated Grange

MAUQUISSART

Orchard

T R E N C H

Armentiers Road

Sunken Road

PIETRE

IV.

Sign Post Lane Road

Layes Brook

LAYES BRIDGE

To Estaires 4m.

PONT LOGY

NEUVE CHAPELLE

S M I T H   D O R R I E N

de Biez

PORT ARTHUR

Bois de

Rue du Bois

To La Bassee 3m.

Lorgies Road

·THE BATTLE OF NEUVE CHAPELLE·
·OPPOSING LINES AT THE·
·CLOSE OF THE BATTLE·

Original British line · 10 Mar. 1915

New British line · 12 Mar. 1915

German line at the end of the battle · 12 Mar. 1915

0   500   1000 ·Yards·
0   ¼   ½   ·Mile·

to Indians.* Altogether the total German casualties were probably in the region of 18,000. Most of the German dead and wounded were removed within a few days, but about 400 bodies remained between the lines for weeks, rotting as the weather got warmer and forcing the soldiers manning the Allied line to wear improvised masks against the foul smell.

The total casualties of the British and Indian forces engaged at Neuve Chapelle were 12,811, and as an attack is expected to produce more casualties amongst the attackers than the defenders, then in strict arithmetical terms the balance was well in the Allied favour. These figures disguise, however, the high rate of attrition amongst British officers of the Indian Corps, and the high percentage of casualties given that the Indian Corps was much smaller than a British corps. In all the Indian Corps lost around 20% of its strength at Neuve Chapelle, despite only five of the Corps' six brigades being involved, and while some of these were relatively lightly wounded and would return, a very great many would not, thus exacerbating the already thorny problem of reserves and replacements.

There can be little doubt that had the Dehra Dun Brigade been able to follow up the initial success of the Garhwal Brigade on the morning of 10 March, then the Bois de Biez would have been captured that day and an assault on the Aubers Ridge on 11 March might have been a real possibility. As we have seen, there was not room in the forward trenches for the Dehra Dun Brigade before the Garhwal Brigade crossed the start line on that first morning. The Dehra Dun Brigade was in fact positioned at the A1 Redoubt, only about 800 yards from the Garhwal Brigade start line. One may ask why the Divisional Commander did not move them forward much earlier than he did—they were not told to move up to the start line until 1100 hours and were then kept waiting until 1600 before being moved forward of that. It would seem that the reason for the delay was the side-show—a bloody side-show but a side-show for all that—on the right flank. Although the village of Neuve Chapelle had been captured by 0900 hours the position to the 1/39th Garhwalis' right was not taken until late in the afternoon, and the Divisional Commander did not wish to start Phase Two until Phase One had been completed.

The complete ineptitude displayed on the night of 11 March, when the Dehra Dun Brigade pulled back before being properly relieved, is hard to excuse. The result was that instead of the line being held along the Layes it was re-established farther back, allowing the enemy to remove

---

* Myths persist. In the Falklands War of 1982 Argentine officers, in order to stiffen their men's resolve, told them that if captured by Gurkhas they would be killed and eaten. The Argentine Army became a victim of its own propaganda as, on every occasion when the one Gurkha battalion present was put into the attack, the Argentines abandoned the position rather than stay and fight.

the footbridges and cause such carnage to the Highland Light Infantry. Information was vague, communications were difficult, both the 1/9th Gurkhas and the 2/2nd Gurkhas had lost key British officers, but the Brigade headquarters should have satisfied itself beyond doubt that both battalions knew they were to be relieved by the Sirhind Brigade and that they were to stay put until they were. Even with the shambles in Neuve Chapelle and the German artillery harassing fire, it must have been obvious to the remaining officers in both Gurkha battalions that a withdrawal was not in prospect, and yet they did withdraw in good order. Poor staff work at brigade and battalion level must take the blame for this, even if that blame is accompanied by sympathy for the appalling conditions under which officers had to take decisions.

The German attack on the morning of 12 March was devastatingly defeated by the Indian Corps, and the delays thereafter can be blamed on a shortage of artillery ammunition and the poor visibility, neither being a factor under the control of brigade, divisional or army commanders. The 'by the left' order, which prevented battalions pressing on independently, was to blame for the 1/4th Gurkhas halting prematurely on 12 March, but again this was a control mechanism imposed by the technology of the day—and particularly the artillery fire control technology—rather than any desire for tidiness. Later in the war matters would improve and a similar attack could be allowed to develop into a series of localised 'bite and hold' operations, but that time was not yet.

The fact remains that the Meerut Division did virtually nothing on 12 March but wait for attacks which never came off. It will be recalled that the Division had strict orders not to advance until 25 Brigade of 8 Division, IV Corps, advanced to the north, and this brigade was unable to make any progress forward. Sir John French said in his despatch of 5 April:

> I am of the opinion that this delay would not have occurred had the clearly expressed orders of the General Officer Commanding First Army [Haig] been more carefully observed. The difficulties above enumerated might have been overcome at an earlier period of the day if the General Officer Commanding IV Corps had been able to bring his reserve brigade more speedily into action.[8]

The artillery, at least on the Meerut Division front, had done all that it could be expected to do. Its opening bombardment on 10 March had achieved all its aims: the German wire had been cut, the defenders of the lines in front of Neuve Chapelle and those in the village itself had been killed or disorientated, and the subsequent artillery fire missions had been as competent and effective as visibility and the technology of the time would allow. Appreciating the lack of artillery ammunition for any more adventures, and that the Germans now outnumbered the British and

Indians between Neuve Chapelle and the Aubers Ridge, Haig was right to halt the battle when he did.

In calculating the profit and loss account of the Battle of Neuve Chapelle there can be no doubt that it was a victory, albeit a limited and expensive one. On the positive side the British line had been pushed forward 1,000 yards on a front of two miles; Neuve Chapelle had been captured*, severe losses had been inflicted on the Germans and the salient had been straightened out, removing the dangerous bend at Port Arthur. The Germans had certainly had a shock: later intelligence reported that there was panic in Lille, and that the main German hospital and much of their General Headquarters were moved to Tournai, 15 miles back. Politically too a great deal had been achieved. The French would complain no more about British tardiness, the Germans had taken more casualties than the British and Indians combined and, despite their very heavy losses, the Indian Corps had received a tremendous boost in morale after a wet and miserable winter, as is attested by the Censor of Indian Mails' reports.

That which had gone wrong—delay, communications failures, poor staff work—was very largely unavoidable at the time. Individual units had performed magnificently despite the losses of their British officers. Sir Douglas Haig said in his order of the day published after the battle:

> I desire to express to all ranks of First Army my great appreciation of the task accomplished by them in the past four days of severe fighting. The First Army has captured the German trenches on a front of two miles including the whole village of Neuve Chapelle, and some strongly defended works. Very serious losses have been inflicted on the enemy, nearly 2,000 prisoners are in our hands, and his casualties in killed and wounded are estimated at about 16,000. I wish also to thank all concerned for the careful preparation made for the assault ... The absolute success of the operation of breaking through the German lines on the first day is not only a tribute to the careful forethought and attention to detail on the part of the leaders, but it has proved beyond question that our forces can defeat the Germans where and when they choose, no matter what mechanical contrivances or elaborate defences are opposed to their advance.[9]

In the same order Haig went on to say:

> The losses sustained by the First Army, though heavy, are fully compensated for by the results achieved, which have brought us one step forward in our efforts to end the war; and the British soldier [he

---

*   It would remain in British hands until 1918, when it was lost by the Portuguese.

might have added 'and Indian soldier']* has once more given the Germans a proof of his superiority in a fight, as well as of his pluck and determination to conquer.[10]

Sir John French cabled the Viceroy of India:

I am glad to be able to inform your Excellency that the Indian troops under Sir James Willcocks fought with great gallantry and marked success in the capture of Neuve Chapelle and subsequent fighting which took place on 10th, 11th, 12th and 13th of this month. The fighting was very severe and the losses heavy, but nothing daunted them; their tenacity, courage and endurance were admirable, and worthy of the best traditions of the soldiers of India.[11]

On the night of 13/14 March 1915 the Lahore Division relieved the Meerut Division on the Indian Corps front, which now covered a distance of 3,500 yards running from Brewery Road, immediately east of Neuve Chapelle, to the south of Richebourg l'Avoue.

SOURCE NOTES

1. Operation Order reproduced in *The Royal Garhwal Rifles in the Great War 1914 – 1917*, DH Drake-Brockman, Charles Clarke Ltd, Haywards Heath, 1934 (privately published).
2. Ibid.
3. Sources vary as to the exact number of guns employed. The semi official *The Indian Corps in France* says 'Nearly 480' while others vary from 400 up. I have taken 420 as being the likely number.
4. *The Royal Garhwal Rifles in the Great War 1914 – 1917.*
5. It was later estimated that in all 16,000 men had taken part in the German counter-attack along the front of the Meerut Division, with ten battalions in front supported by a further four battalions, and with a further six battalions in reserve. (*Military Operations France and Belgium 1915*, JH Edmonds, Macmillan and Co, London, 1928)
6. *The Indian Corps in France*, Merewether and Smith, John Murray, London, 1919.

---

* Haig was sometimes prone to forget that a large portion of his Army was Indian. In his order of the day before the battle he exhorted the men to 'Fight for the honour of Old England'. Over half of those who would take part had never seen Old England, although it did not prevent them from fighting magnificently.

7. Despatch of 5 Apr 1915. Supplement to *London Gazette* dated April 1915.
8. Ibid.
9. Quoted in *The Indian Corps in France.*
10. Ibid.
11. Ibid.

VIII

Hospitals, Gas, Gallantry
and Desertion

The casualties sustained at the Battle of Neuve Chapelle were by far the largest so far incurred by the Indian Corps in such a short period. The arrangements employed for the evacuation and treatment of the Indian wounded were similar to those for the rest of the BEF. Under the command of the battalion Medical Officer were a number of military medical orderlies and a stretcher bearer party, the latter usually totalling 16 soldiers but which could be increased by drafting in men from companies prior to a major attack. The Medical Officer would aim to set up a Regimental Aid Post close to the line, but not so close that it would come under enemy fire—although many did. Eventually aid posts would be well dug in, revetted and under cover, but in the early stages of the war the doctor would establish himself where he could, preferably, but not always, under cover from the elements. The location of the Regimental Aid Post would always be promulgated so that every man knew where it was.

A wounded man would make his way back to the Regimental Aid Post by himself if he could walk, or be assisted by the stretcher bearers or his own comrades if he could not. The Medical Officer would assess the casualty and, where possible, patch him up and either return him to duty or order rest in billets for a period. If the man required attention beyond what could be provided by the Regimental Aid Post, further evacuation was from the rear and the responsibility of the Indian Field Ambulance, a military medical unit staffed by officers of the Indian Medical Services, Other Ranks of the Indian Hospital Corps and kahars, or civilian followers, whose task it was to carry the wounded back. The kahars often went much farther forward than they were supposed to, and the Corps Commander recalled cautioning one of their number about he danger he was in. The man replied cheerfully that he was a healing man, not a fighting man, and would be quite safe[1]. While it was unusual for either side to fire deliberately at a wearer of the red cross armband, artillery and mortar shells had no such discrimination and many kahars were killed or wounded in the performance of their duties.

The kahars carried the wounded man back to the Advanced Dressing Station, one or more being established for each brigade, either on stretchers or by horse-drawn or motor ambulance. At the Advanced Dressing Station medical staff applied further first aid, removed the man's weapon and military equipment and had him moved on back to the Casualty Clearing Station. From the Casualty Clearing Station the man was transferred to a field hospital or a base hospital. Initially the policy was for all British and Indian wounded to be evacuated to military hospitals in England. Later, hospitals were established in France, although the occupants of these were usually removed to England prior to a major attack in order to release beds for the expected casualties.

There were six Indian Military Hospitals established in England in late 1914 or early 1915: two at Brighton, one at Milford on Sea, one at New Milton, one at Bournemouth and one at Brockenhurst[*]. A further temporary hospital was opened in Netley but this closed in February 1915 and its 548 cases were transferred to Brighton. The main Indian hospital, and incidentally the largest military hospital in England, was the Kitchener Indian Hospital, opened on 13 January 1915 in the grounds of the Brighton Poor Law Guardians' Institution. The hospital was manned by combining the staffs of I, Y and Z Indian Military General Hospitals. In addition 75 NCOs and men of the Royal Army Medical Corps reserve and the Voluntary Aid Detachment were attached to the hospital as nurses, it being considered that females would be out of place in an Indian unit. These men had received no prior training other than St John's Ambulance courses and spoke not a word of any Indian dialect, but they were a great success and no language difficulties were apparent. As there were no ward orderlies supplied, general duty soldiers were trained for the task. Being detailed as a ward orderly was unpopular with the troops as there was no outlet for promotion, which could only be obtained with a battalion in the line.

The hospital accommodation was hutted with corrugated iron roofing and regulations demanded 40 square feet of floor space per man. Lavatories were adapted to the Indian style (continental or squatting type, and beds had springs for patients and boards for permanent staff. The hospital had operating theatres, X-ray, electrical and orthopaedic departments and a laboratory, and later employed a number of masseurs in an early form of physiotherapy. Water was plentiful, and so much was used—77 gallons per head per day in February 1915 rising to 111 gallons pet head per day in October—that the Brighton council remonstrated, after which consumption was reduced to 55 gallons per day by restricting the flushing of lavatories and the depths of baths.

The hospital was commanded by Colonel Sir Bruce Seaton Bt of the Indian Medical Services, a man of considerable drive who knew what he wanted for his hospital and generally got it. Initially he was unhappy with the standard of civilian followers. He considered that the dhobiwallas,

---

[*] Unlike others whose funding was a government responsibility, the Brokenhurst Hospital was funded by the Indian Soldiers Comforts Fund a staffed by retired members of the Indian Medical Services.

cooks, bhistis and sweepers had been too hastily recruited at the mobilisation centres and were 'the sweepings of Bombay'[2] and 'habitual drunks',
while the clerks and storekeepers were 'unqualified adventurers'. Colonel
Seaton was particularly concerned by the followers' seeming propensity
for conducting liaisons with the local inhabitants of Brighton and feared
that the 'ill advised conduct of the women of the town' would lead to
'grave scandals'. Seaton solved this difficulty simply and quickly: he
applied strict military discipline (probably illegally) to the followers who
were now banned from leaving the grounds of the hospital and subjected
to close order drill. In the Colonel's words 'military discipline soon converted a mob of bazaar coolies into an efficient body of men'.

Patients arrived at the hospital by train from Southampton, not in an orderly
flow but as battle dictated. Immediately after Neuve Chapelle in March 1915
a group of 647 arrived, with a further 1,135 being added after Second Ypres
in April and May. July produced 195, the battle of Loos provided 430 in
September and the last major intake of 387 reported in November. These
numbers were augmented by a steady trickle at other times. On arrival at the
hospital the first priority was to decide what treatment the man required and
then to clean him up ready for medical attention. Men arrived still with the
mud of the trenches on them and their uniforms in tatters. They were dirty,
most were infested with lice, and the long hair of the Sikhs was often verminous. Every man was given a hot bath on arrival and thereafter at least once a
week, while original uniforms were burnt and new ones issued. Burning of
clothing had to be carried out with circumspection after some men's pockets
were found to be stuffed with ammunition, although the discovery of an
officer's stolen revolver in the kit of one man led to the patient's court martial
and a sentence of two years' imprisonment.

Causes of admission to the Kitchener hospital were:

Gunshot wounds (including wounds caused by shells and grenades)	1,850
Bronchitis	399
Rheumatic afflictions	179
Frostbite and trench foot	121
Malaria	370
Tuberculosis	81
Leprosy	18
Leishmania affection*	3
Venereal Disease	164

* Leishmaniasis is caused by a tiny fly biting and laying its eggs under the skin. The eggs
hatch out and begin to eat away portions of the face, ears and nose. If not treated it leads
to permanent disfigurement. In 1978 the 6th Gurkha Rifles, in which the author was then
a company commander, were deployed in haste to Belize in response to Guatemalan sabre

The balance was made up by transfers from Netley and other hospitals and by 30 'Insanes', the Kitchener Hospital being responsible for all Indian Army psychiatric cases.

In the early days, before the trickle of patients became a flow, a comprehensive training programme was instituted for the staff. Officers with temporary commissions, sub assistant surgeons (warrant officers), Ward Orderlies and followers all had to complete a month-long course in stretcher and wagon drill and thereafter had to attend regular refresher periods. The enforcement of strict discipline, shortly to be extended to the patients as well as the staff, caused some umbrage, but was generally accepted except by one sub assistant surgeon, who tried to shoot Colonel Seaton in protest. He soon found himself facing a summary general court martial and a sentence of seven years' rigorous imprisonment.

One patient wrote home in Hindi:

The only fault is that there is no liberty, but that is all right or we would spend all our money in dissipation.[3]

All convalescent patients and staff wore uniform, and patients who were capable helped the ward orderlies and carried out fatigues. Although walking out was generally banned, patients were not entirely closeted from the outside world. Indian officer patients and Indian officers and warrant officers on the staff were allowed out of the grounds until dusk, after which they needed a pass. Every day three patients went out for a walk escorted by a private of the RAMC, 24 went out in a motor ambulance under a sub assistant surgeon and up to 100 went on a route march, designed as much to get them fit again for the trenches as to allow them to view the English countryside.

There were very few disciplinary problems with patients—amongst whom the smuggling in of drink was the most common offence—and in the nine months of the hospital's existence only 24 patients were charged under Indian military law. Most offences were minor, but two patients were arraigned by court martial accused of malingering—that is, claiming to be sick when they were not. Then, as now, this was a charge notoriously difficult to prove, not least because doctors are most reluctant to support

rattling. The battalion spent longer in the jungle than had any previous (British) garrison and men began to find portions of their faces being eaten away. They were evacuated to the UK for treatment, where the doctors were totally baffled, until one recalled reading an account of Leishmania affection in WWI. It was too late to prevent disfigurement for the first cases, but thereafter men were swiftly and effectively treated.

it in case they are subsequently shown to be wrong, and both men were found not guilty.

Although followers' discipline had improved enormously since Colonel Seaton had instituted his regime, there were a total of 565 charges preferred against them. Of these 377 were found guilty, of whom 209 were fined and 57 jailed for varying periods. The most prevalent transgressions amongst followers were loss of items of kit and equipment, smoking inside the wooden huts, gambling, 'quarrelling', leaving lights on and disobedience to orders. The erection of a barbed wire fence around the hospital grounds and the formation in April 1915 of a military police from amongst the fitter convalescents improved matters even more.

That the hospital was composed of a mixture of races and classes was not forgotten. A Caste Committee was formed, which advised the Commanding Officer on any matter which might affect religious or caste susceptibilities. There were three cookhouses, for Hindu meat-eaters, Hindu non-meat-eaters and Moslems, although Seaton complained that Dogra patients were suspicious of the caste of some of the kitchen staff, which he felt could be solved by the provision of more Brahmin cooks. The Moslem representatives on the Caste Committee advised as to which patients were fit enough to fast in daylight hours during Ramadan, the fasting month, and those who were told not to fast appear to have accepted the order. A slaughterhouse was built by the Royal Engineers beside the council abattoir, Indian rations were provided and the introduction of rolling pins and baking boards for the making of chapattis was considered a welcome advance.

Rooms within the grounds were found for the establishment of temples which the various religions could use, and the necessary books were provided by the Indian Soldiers Fund. Although there were few deaths in the Kitchener Indian Hospital, arrangements were made for the proper disposal of the bodies. Hindus were cremated on a burning ghat built on the Downs at Patcham, just outside Brighton,[*] and the bodies of Moslems were taken by motor hearse to a Moslem cemetery in Woking for burial.

Throughout its existence only 30 psychiatric cases—then termed insanes' or 'lunacy cases'—were referred to the hospital. As the Kitchener was the only Indian hospital which dealt with such patients the number seems very small. Nowhere in the surviving reports is there any mention of 'shell shock' and the causes of admission were diagnosed as being:

Mania (i.e. very mad indeed)	14 combatants	1 follower
Melancholia (i.e. depression)	4 combatants	1 follower
Hysteria (i.e. psychosomatic problems brought on by stress)	2 combatants	

---

[*] It is still there, albeit now unused.

Idiocy (i.e. educationally sub normal)		1 follower (the doctors considered that he should never have been enlisted in the first place)
Chronic Delusional Insanity (i.e. schizophrenia)	1 combatant	1 follower
Dementia (i.e. moderately mad)	2 combatants	1 follower
Undiagnosed	2 combatants	

The largest racial group amongst the 'insanes' were the Pathans, including six from the 129th Baluchis alone, but in a field of only 30 cases it is difficult to draw any conclusions which are statistically meaningful.* Medical opinion was that about half the total would recover in between six and 12 months.

Although the other Indian military hospitals were smaller than the Kitchener, they were all run on much the same lines, although perhaps not as rigidly. For the vast majority of the wounded evacuation to England was their first visit to that country. One Sikh NCO wrote home saying:

The hospital in which I am was formerly a big hotel. The arrangements are excellent and I am absolutely comfortable in every way. At first I was at Brockenhurst which was near Mr Lieutenant Governor Dane's † house. He used to come and see us and the King and Queen came. Lord Curzon came too and other officers of high estate came and they look after us very well.[4]

The Subadar Major of the 6th Jat Light Infantry, evacuated to England in January 1915, wrote:

'It [England] is a very fine country. The inhabitants are amiable and very kind to us.'[5]

That some hospital commanding officers held rather more liberal views than did Colonel Seaton of the Kitchener Hospital is indicated by a letter from Colonel Strachey of the India Office in London to Colonel Groves, Indian Medical Services, Conunanding Officer of the other Brighton hos-

---

* The Consultant Psychiatrist to the British Army, Brigadier Douglas Wickenden, has pointed out in a letter to the author that Pathans, because of their background in a society where personal security and stability were lacking, could be expected to be more susceptible to depression in the clinical sense than those races living a more settled existence in India proper.

† Ex Lt Governor of the Punjab.

pital, that located in the Brighton Pavilion. Strachey had doubts as to the wisdom of a medical officer taking a convalescent Lance Naik of Wilde's Rifles to the 1914 Christmas pantomime:

… where the Principal Boy was a very handsome young woman whose lower limbs, of which her costume allowed a complete view, were very symmetrical. I do not think I should have chosen the entertainment as one giving an example of English life, considering the character of the Indian nautch girl *, but I know that a visit to the Alhambra or to the Empire is always part of the programme in a personally conducted sightseeing visit of our gallant Indian troops.[6]

One letter which caused considerable disquiet when it was read by the censor was an anonymous missive sent to a lance naik of the 129th Baluchis from a patient in the Pavilion hospital:

For our medicine and treatment there are Englishmen and all the helpers are English soldiers of low caste. One day a colonel said to a Punjabi 'You are a malingerer.' After saying that he went away to his quarters. After that one or two accursed Christian ward orderlies beat that Indian soldier in such a fashion that blood ran from his fundament [rectum]. After that a native officer of India brought the sepoy before the colonel commanding and pointed out that he had been thus unjustly beaten by the ward orderlies. The colonel replied 'Subadar Saheb, I cannot say anything to a white man on account of a sepoy.' Now it is time to reflect. We took our oath to serve in Europe. We have crossed the seven seas and left our homes and our dear ones and our parents, and for the honour of such an unjust and false-promising King we have sacrificed our lives and now this is the honour that we get in his council. No doubt before them we are regarded as inarticulate animals, but who can say that to oppress us and dishonour us is good?[7]

The letter was brought to the attention of the Indian Corps Commander and subsequently placed before no less a personage than the Commander-in-Chief India himself. A thorough inquiry was ordered. Patients and staff were interviewed by Colonels Strachey and Groves and no one could be found who had been beaten or who had seen anyone else being beaten. Eventually the writer was identified. He turned out to be the lance naik who had been taken to the pantomime. He had a bullet lodged in his brain and despite a number of operations it could not be removed and he was

---

*   A nautch girl was a professional singer and dancer. Many engaged in prostitution as a
    sideline.

quite mad. No further action was taken but the letter was withheld by the Censors.

One of the difficulties faced by the staff of all the Indian military hospitals was that patients had to consent to being operated upon. Indians were suspicious of the knife, and being fatalists in the main, many refused consent until the last minute, hoping the condition would heal itself. Sometimes it was too late. Despite their problems the record of the Indian military hospitals was remarkable good. It must be remembered that the purpose of military medicine differs somewhat from that of its civilian counterpart. The first duty of army doctors is to return men to their units fit for duty in the shortest possible time, and this the Indian military hospitals certainly did. Of all the patients admitted to the Kitchener' Hospital 63% were returned to duty after an average stay of 63½ days—an excellent record by any standards. From January 1915 until the Kitchener Hospital closed on 22 November 1915 upon the transfer of the Indian Corps to Mesopotamia, 3,454 combatants wounded and 436 followers were dealt with. Only 26 combatants and 13 followers died. The statistics for the other hospitals were similar.

One of the criticisms of the Indian Corps on the Western Front, then and now,[*] was the allegation that they had a high proportion of self-inflicted wounds. The Corps Commander was naturally concerned, and in a letter written to the Commanding Officer of the 2/2nd Gurkhas on 10 November 1914, commiserating with the heavy losses recently sustained by that battalion, he added:

PS I look to you and your officers to carefully watch any cases of hand wounds and help me to eradicate this grave evil.[8]

On 16 November 1914 the Adjutant of the 59th Scinde Rifles noted:

Of 210 wounded, 98 were hit in the hand. Company commanders requested to take a statement from responsible persons whenever a man is hit in the hand.[9]

In May 1915 the 69th Punjabis arrived in France as a reinforcement from India. On 13 July Sepoy Mohammed Khan was arraigned before a court martial accused of rendering himself unfit for duty by shooting himself in the finger. He was found not guilty and acquitted.

The fact was that people did believe that sepoys of the Indian Corps were deliberately sustaining wounds to the hand. Self-inflicted wounds occur in all armies, although perhaps more so with conscripts than with

[*]   Most recently in *Facing Armageddon*, Cecil and Liddle (eds), Leo Cooper, London, 1996.

178

regular volunteers, and Sir James Willcocks was so concerned about the possibility of self-wounding—intended to allow the perpetrator an escape from the war—that he ordered an official inquiry. The officer appointed to conduct the inquiry was Colonel Sir Bruce Seaton, Commanding Officer of the Kitchener Indian Hospital Brighton. Colonel Seaton took as his sample the first 1,000 wounded to arrive at his hospital and classified them according to the cause of their wounds.

In his report[10] Colonel Seaton defined the most likely self-inflicted wounds as one incurred by a man shooting himself in the hand or wrist*, or getting another to shoot him, or holding his hand above the parapet until an enemy bullet did it for him. Seaton pointed out that self-inflicted wounds were generally to the left hand†, usually to a finger rather than to the palm, and that a glancing wound was probably not self-inflicted. If a hand was held above the parapet it would probably be the left, but the wound could be anywhere.

Seaton assumed that a wound to a part of the body which was inaccessible, or where the wound would be life-threatening, or where it was likely to cause permanent serious disablement, was not likely to be self-inflicted. On these grounds he excluded 206 wounds which were to the head, face, neck, chest, back and perineum. Similarly he excluded injuries caused by trench falls and the effects of gas (94) and bayonet wounds, of which there were three. This left 697 wounds which Seaton included in his study.

Having examined each of the 697 wounds carefully, Seaton now excluded those which could not have been self-inflicted because they were on parts of the body other than the hand and could only have been caused by shrapnel or grenade fragments. This left 280 wounds of the hand and wrist. Of these he now excluded 55 because they had been witnessed to have been caused by shell or bomb. A further 61 were eliminated because by the nature of the injury (direction of the entry wound, range from which the bullet had been fired) they could not have been self-inflicted nor the result of the hand held above the parapet. He eliminated a further two cases where the man had wounds in both hands caused by shrapnel.

Seaton was now left with 69 wounds which had definitely been caused by a bullet, and a further 93 which could not be positively identified as having being caused by either a bullet or a shell. Of this total of 162 hand wounds, 78 were to the right hand while 84 were to the left. As enemy

---

*   British self-inflicted wounds tended to be in the foot (hence the expression, now almost
     always incorrectly used, 'shooting yourself in the foot'). Indians went for the hand,
     presumably because public transport in India was rather less readily available than in
     Britain.

†   Most Indian children were forced to be right-handed, and in training the Army always
     assumed right-handedness. As in Britain until fairly recently, left-handedness was
     regarded as an affliction.

bullets did not discriminate, Seaton concluded that, on the assumption that the 78 wounds to the right hand were caused by the enemy, then statistically 78 of the left-hand wounds had also been so caused. There were therefore only six wounds to the left hand which could have been self-inflicted. Seaton explained that, while the normal expectation of hand wounds amongst survivors of a battle was 28% of the total, one 'most distinguished regiment'[11] had returned a figure of 46%, and this in open fighting where the wounds could not have been self-inflicted because if they had been they would have been witnessed.

What Seaton did not say, but which he might have done had he been an infantryman, was that both in the advance and in the firing position from a trench, the left hand is more exposed than the right. Soldiers advancing in the open carry the rifle in what is known as the 'port' position, that is canted forward at an angle of 45 degrees with the left hand forward gripping the stock and the right hand by the waist, gripping the small of the butt. In the firing position the butt is in the shoulder with the hands in much the same position. The left hand is always forward while the right is partially protected by the magazine of the rifle. This protection for the right hand is even more pronounced when firing from a trench, when the right hand is actually behind the parapet while the left hand is on top of it. One might therefore expect rather more injuries to the left hand than to the right.

Colonel Seaton's report concluded that it was unfair to assume that injuries to the left hand were self-inflicted. 'Others claim it', he wrote, 'it is not true.'[12]

Despite the losses at Neuve Chapelle, morale in the Indian Corps in France remained high. A Sikh wrote to his wife in the Punjab:

> Now I have seen the war I am very pleased. When we met the enemy hand to hand my heart exulted. The enemy suffered great loss and has now retreated. On our side there are six Kings. Against us there is but one. How then can the enemy win?'[13]

Which is not to say that the sepoys did not realise the scale of the fighting, as a Punjabi Mussalman did:

> It is terrible fighting. God have mercy. The Germans were very strong but as soon as the Indian troops arrived their strength was broken.[14]

And there were those who wished they had stayed at home, as did another Punjabi Mussalman, a cavalry sowar writing to his father:

> You told me not to join the Army, but I paid no heed to your words. Now I regret this bitterly.[15]

Despite the strictures on writing anything about operations, some news of Neuve Chapelle did filter out, and a Gurkha soldier serving in Singapore wrote to a friend serving in the 1/1st Gurkhas in the Sirhind Brigade:

I am very sorry that I could not stay in my beloved regiment the 1/9th Gurkhas. If I had not left it, by this time I too should have been joining in the battle, as our forefathers did. Keep your courage. We are Chettris and fighting is our business.[16]

A sepoy in 55th Coke's Rifles, writing to his brother in Wilde's Rifles, felt much the same:

And please God we shall soon come to take our part in the English war. We are all ready but must wait for the order.[17]

Howell, the Chief Censor, was perhaps over sensitive to indications of low morale, for on one occasion he reported that many of the soldiers were composing poetry, which he saw as a sign of a fatalistic acceptance of death. Of 220 letters from men from combat units in hospitals in England examined by him in early 1915, Howell thought that 28 showed the writer to be in the depths of despair and resigned to death, 15 showed admirable spirit, and the remainder showed fatalistic resignation.[18] One would be surprised if things were very different in the armies of any of the belligerents. A Garhwali patient wrote:

I have no confidence in being able to escape death. In this sinful country it rains very much and it also snows, and many men have been frost-bitten. Some of their hands and feet cannot be stretched out and those who stand up cannot sit down again. Some have died like this and some have been killed by bullets. In this way many have perished. In a few days you will hear that in our country only women will be left. All the men will be finished here. In the space of a few months how many men have fallen and how many have been wounded. The wounded are in England and those who have lost hands or feet are by way of recompense sent back to India.[19]

After Neuve Chapelle the Meerut Division continued to hold the line while the Jullunder Brigade and the Ferozepore Brigade were withdrawn back into corps reserve. The remainder of March was relatively quiet and allowed some reorganisation within the Corps to bring all brigades back to more or less equal strength. The two battalions of the Garhwal Rifles had each taken so many casualties that they were no longer viable as separate battalions and so were amalgamated into one battalion, henceforth known as The 39th Garhwal Rifles, and the two battalions of The

Connaught Rangers were also amalgamated. Some battalions moved brigades, the newly arrived territorial battalions were incorporated and the 40th Pathans arrived from China on 9 April.

Although the weather throughout March remained cold and wet, including a fall of snow on 18 March, all soldiers had now been issued with clothing suitable for wear in Europe. In addition to his recently acquired warm serge, each man carried a waterproof sheet, a blanket, a towel and soap. In the regimental transport was an extra blanket and an extra shirt per man. In December 1914 short sheepskin jackets had been issued, which were excellent for normal wear but could not be worn under belt, pouches and bandolier as the issue belt was too short to fit round it. New underwear began to be issued but there was insufficient for each man. The first battalion to arrive at a bath and laundry point would hand in their underwear and receive a new issue. The next battalion to arrive would receive the laundered underwear of the previous battalion and hand in their own. This was not popular with the troops and unacceptable to the Sikhs, whose drawers have religious significance, and was not persisted with.

On the night of 23/24 April the Lahore Division was again scheduled to take over the firing line from the Meerut Division. The Sirhind Brigade was to be first to take over, and on 23 April the units of the Brigade moved off towards the line. The 1/4th Gurkhas were ordered to Colonne with a view to moving into the trenches east of Neuve Chapelle. Arriving at Vieille Chapelle the battalion received a message telling them to go no farther, to bivouac for the night and to stand by to entrain for an undisclosed destination the following morning. It was a wet evening and all the houses in the area were already full of troops. The Gurkhas could find no shelter and had no option but to make the best they could in the sodden fields either side of the Vieille Chapelle Road. Their situation was not improved by the battalion transport continuing in the original direction, with the result that the men could obtain neither their waterproof sheets nor a hot meal. The battalion bought what food they could from local inhabitants and from the estaminets in the village, but French civilians had little enough for themselves and the Gurkhas spent a cold, wet and hungry night sheltering by the stunted hedgerows and in any relatively dry portion of ditch that they could find.

That night, and at 0600 the next morning when the battalion fell in on the road and waited to be told what to do, rumour in and around Vieille Chapelle was rife. The British officers and those Gurkhas who could understand English were being told that there had been a great battle at Ypres; that the British 2nd Army and the French had been defeated; that the Germans had used a gas which killed all who breathed it; that the whole of the BEF was in danger of being cut off and surrounded. The officers paid little attention to all this: by now they had learned to ignore the grapevine, and the riflemen shrugged their shoulders and continued to do what they were told. The officers had heard reports of gas before, indeed some intelligence reports had made mention of it, but, as one British officer put it, 'the reports made no mention of precautionary measures, therefore it was assumed that there was nothing in them.'[20]

In early April 1915 the British V Corps had taken over a large part of the Ypres Salient from the French. The total front held by the BEF was now 30 miles, running from Langemark on the Ypres Salient to south of the La Bassée canal. North of the British, and still on the salient, was a French Territorial division and an Algerian colonial division, between Steenstraate and Langemark. The recently arrived Canadian Division then carried the line on to Berlin Wood, about a mile west of Passchendaele, where they joined with the British 28 Division. The line was held by 28 Division as far as Polygon Wood, by 27 Division to Hill 60 near Zwarteleen, by 5 Division to half a mile east of St Eloi and by 3 Division to the southern end of the Salient.

What became known as the Second Battle of Ypres officially opened on 22 April, described by the Official History as 'a glorious spring day'. It began at 1700 hours when the Germans released large quantities of chlorine gas (their first use of it in the war) from cylinders brought up to their front line opposite the French-held portion of the Salient. Watchers on the Allied side could see the thick, yellow gas being carried slowly by the wind towards the French lines, and from even five miles away British observers could detect a peculiar smell accompanied by a tingling of the eyes, mouth and throat. Following up the gas came the German infantry, and the Algerians, with no protection or training against the effects of gas, fled in panic, as did most of the French Territorial Division with the exception of half a battalion which held on at the extreme left of their line. The collapse of the French front exposed the left flank of the Canadian Division, which had no alternative but to retreat to St Julien with their left flank thrown back. By nightfall the Germans had seized the French trenches, penetrated up to two miles into the Salient on a front of three miles and had captured the French guns. There was now a huge gap between the Canadian Division south-west of Poelkappelle and the British GHQ line, a reserve position which ran from the north of Wieltje round and down to Zillebeke. From the north of the GHQ line was another gap which extended west to the withdrawn French line south-east of Boesinghe.

The situation was now serious and on 23 April the Lahore Division, which had been intended to relieve the Meerut Division on the Indian Corps front, was ordered to stand by for a rapid move to an as yet undisclosed destination, a message which reached the detached Sirhind Brigade that evening. On the morning of 24 April the Lahore Division was ordered to move north in the direction of Ypres, the order being passed to the Sirhind Brigade at 0800 hours. The 1/4th Gurkhas, followed now by the rest of the Sirhind Brigade, moved off—no question of entraining now—and caught up with the remainder of the Division around midday. Many of the sepoys still suffered from frost-bitten feet and the after effects of trench foot. Marching over roads deeply rutted by the passage of towed artillery and motor lorries, the pave cracked and gaping with huge holes, each man carrying between 60 and 100 lbs weight[*] was bad enough by day but became worse as night fell. The Division had recently been issued with GS wagons, driven by British soldiers of the Army Service Corps who had little experience of horses and mules. On the narrow roads at night the carts were constantly slipping into the mud and most battalions had to detail off an entire company to pull wagons out of ditches and to lead the animals. Battalions told off an officer each to check the many estaminets on the route to ensure that no exhausted men were tempted to leave the line of march and seek warmth, light, shelter and food. Not a single man did.

Around midnight, after marching 23 miles, the Lahore Division arrived at La Manche on the Belgian border, where they were told to halt for the night. Billets were eventually found, but the sepoys had no sooner fallen into an exhausted slumber than orders arrived for the Division to push on a further nine miles to Ouderdom. Some soldiers had to be literally kicked awake, but all fell in once more and moved off. Most of the sepoys had not eaten since having a frugal breakfast the previous day, and in the 1/4th Gurkhas a British officer rode ahead and found a British artillery battery camped by the side of the road. The gunners turned to and dished out handfuls of biscuits to the riflemen as they marched by. At 0700 the head of the long column at last reached the outskirts of Ouderdom, where they were halted and told to wait in readiness. Over the next few hours men whose feet had not enabled them to keep up with the column limped in, and by mid-morning 25 April the Lahore Division was complete. Immediately upon arrival at Ouderdom groups of officers went forward on horseback to have a look at the ground over which they would have to operate. In the words of the regimental historian of the 4th Gurkha Rifles:

Ypres and all the roads leading to it were under heavy artillery fire and the confusion everywhere was indescribable. No one knew

---

[*] The weight of what the man was officially supposed to carry was 65 lbs, including his weapon, but items of personal kit, extra ammunition, bombs, sand bags, and signalling equipment which could not be carried in the battalion transport often put the load well over 100 lbs. This was no great hardship for Gurkha who were short and squat and accustomed to carrying weight, but it was a severe strain for some of the taller and more wiry races.

where were the enemy and where our own troops. One found parties of men, with and without officers, in bits of trench or ditch facing in every direction. Every individual gave a different account of what had happened and of what was happening. The heavy haze of smoke and gas that lay over the battlefield made map reading most difficult for newcomers. The few troops met were themselves new to the country; they had little idea where they were and had been too busy fighting to find out. Everyone seemed to have names for the farms etc, different from those given by everyone else. The only names that no one had heard were those on the map.[21]

The recce parties returned to Ouderdom little wiser than when they had left.

On the same day, a Sunday, a British counter-attack on St Julien failed to take the village, but it did prevent any further German advance in that direction, and the line behind the eastern gap was for the time being stabilised. The Lahore Division was now placed under command of the 2nd Army, whose commander, General Sir Horace Smith-Dorrien, decided upon an attack on the western gap, between the French and the end of the GHQ line. Early on the morning of 26 April Smith-Dorrien issued a warning order for an attack to be made that afternoon. The French would advance from their front in a north-easterly direction while on their right the Lahore Division would advance to the north. On the right of the Lahore Division would be units of the British V Corps. The Indian brigades moved off to get into their jumping off positions, the Ferozepore Brigade at 0530 to get to St Jean, the Jullunder Brigade at 0700 to Wieltje. The Sirhind Brigade would be in divisional reserve south east of St Jean.

The Jullunder Brigade had reached its forming up point, some open fields to the west of Wieltje, when they came under shell fire. Rather than the high explosive or shrapnel to which the sepoys had become accustomed, these shells released gas which made the men's eyes water severely. The gas was only effective at a range of 50 yards, however, and the effects wore off after a few minutes.

By 1230 hours all three brigades were in position and detailed orders were issued. The plan envisaged an artillery bombardment beginning at 1320 hours lasting 40 minutes, followed immediately by five minutes of intensive fire after which the infantry would assault the enemy positions to the north of St Jean, establishing a new line as far north as they could reach. The boundary between the Ferozepore Brigade and the French would be the Ypres/Langemark road. As no one was sure exactly where the enemy were, officers from the forward battalions were sent ahead to reconnoitre. They did not return.

As soon as the Allied artillery began their bombardment, the French and Indian infantry started to advance, in order to get to assaulting distance

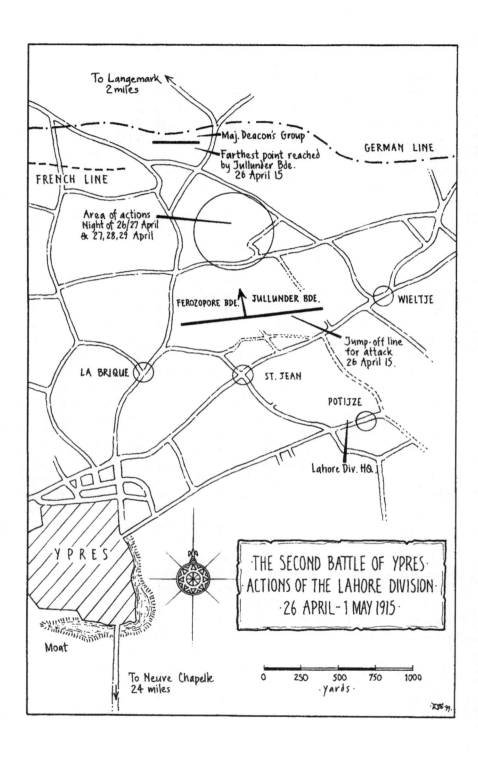

To Langemark
2 miles

Maj. Deacon's Group

Farthest point reached
by Jullunder Bde.
26 April 15

GERMAN LINE

FRENCH LINE

Area of actions
Night of 26/27 April
& 27, 28, 29 April

FEROZOPORE BDE.   JULLUNDER BDE.

WIELTJE

Jump-off line
for attack
26 April 15.

LA BRIQUE

ST. JEAN

POTIJZE

Lahore Div. HQ.

Y P R E S

Moat

THE SECOND BATTLE OF YPRES·
·ACTIONS OF THE LAHORE DIVISION·
·26 APRIL – 1 MAY 1915·

To Neuve Chapelle
24 miles

0   250   500   750   1000
·yards·

before the guns stopped firing. Whilst the French artillery support was reasonably efficient, that of the Lahore Division was not. Extra artillery in the shape of three 18-pounder field batteries (two of them Canadian) and two howitzer batteries (one of them Canadian) had been allocated for close support to the Ferozepore and Jullunder Brigades, in addition to the existing divisional artillery, but the gunners suffered from disadvantages not of their own making. The guns themselves were sited to the west of the Ypres canal, and the distance between them and the artillery observers—who would control the fire—was such that communications by telephone were unreliable or non-existent. The guns had not had an opportunity to register, partly because the attack was put together in a hurry, and partly because the exact positions of the enemy were not known. Finally, the Allied guns were subject to constant counter-battery fire from the German artillery, which put many of the guns out of action or forced the crews to take cover.

Although the infantry did not know it at the time, the German positions were between 1,500 and 2,000 yards away to the north. The ground from the Lahore Division's start line, which ran roughly east to west from St Jean to La Brique and across to the boundary road between Ferozepore Brigade and the French, sloped gently upwards for 500 yards to a crest line, from where knee-deep wheat fields divided by dry ditches and small hedgerows sloped down to a stream lined with pollarded willows. From the stream—which was not an obstacle—the ground was open and sloped up to Mauser Ridge* on which the Germans had entrenched themselves. The Lahore Division's supporting artillery being largely ineffective, the German infantry and artillery observers were not forced to take shelter in the bottom of their trenches and the Indians came under artillery fire almost as soon as they got up to advance. As the lines of men crossed the first crest line enemy rifle and machine-gun fire augmented the shelling and sepoys started to go down. The fire was particularly fierce on the Jullunder Brigade on the right, where units of the British V Corps were attempting, largely unsuccessfully, to provide covering fire. The Jullunder Brigade began to edge over to their left, crowding the Ferozepore Brigade who in turn pressed upon the French on the other side of the Ypres/Langemark road. German aircraft appeared overhead, and with a complete absence of French or British machines, were able to send accurate information to their artillery on the ground. As the men moved down the slope, some battalions now mixed in with others, and gas shells began to fall. The men of the Indian Corps had received no training or advice in anti-gas precautions, other than to tie a damp handkerchief or pagri end over the mouth, preferably urinating on it first. The other piece of advice given, and much

---

* Sometimes, wrongly, referred to as 'Pilkem Ridge', so difficult was it to map read with accuracy.

favoured in the Sappers and Miners, was to chew tobacco incessantly, an exhortation of little help to the Sikhs, to whom tobacco is an abomination. The shells were filled with a lachrymatory gas—tear gas—and, while they caused eye watering and some temporary blindness, they were unable to stop the advance, which continued albeit with mounting casualties over the open ground.

The 129th Baluchis, the right-hand battalion of the right-hand brigade, got to a farm 200 yards from the enemy line. By then they had one Indian officer and 11 IORs killed and seven British officers, six Indian officers and 171 IORs wounded. In the centre of the brigade 57th Wilde's Rifles got to within 80 yards of the enemy, by which time three British officers, three Indian officers and 36 IORs had been killed, and four British officers, seven Indian officers and 215 IORs wounded. The Connaught Rangers, on the brigade's left, got to about 120 yards of the enemy trenches and suffered three officers killed and 12 wounded (including the Commanding Officer) and 361 BORs killed and wounded.

In the Jullunder Brigade the Manchesters, the right-hand battalion, managed to get to within 60 yards of the objective with an officer and 15 ORs killed, 11 officers and 206 men wounded and 56 missing. In the centre the 40th Pathans had seen their Commanding Officer killed 300 yards from the start line, and all of their machine-gunners save one killed or wounded. They too stopped short, having had three British officers, two Indian officers and 23 IORs killed, and five British officers, ten Indian officers and 258 IORs wounded. On the extreme left of the attack the 47th Sikhs had become entangled with the French across the boundary to their left and with the 40th Pathans on their right. They could get no closer than 70 yards from the enemy positions and in doing so lost their Commanding Officer and most of battalion headquarters killed, every other British officer save one, and a total of 78 per cent of the battalion killed or wounded. Command of the battalion now devolved upon Lieutenant Drysdale, with just five years' service in the Army[*].

Battalions were now hopelessly intermingled. French, British and Indians under the command of whoever happened to be the most senior in the area began to dig themselves in where they were. They could not stand up and all that could be hoped for was a line of shell scrapes which wavered across the front, at some points 50 or 60 yards from the enemy, at others 200 yards away. There were many cases of individual gallantry. Major Holbrooke of the 129th Baluchis was seen lying out in the open, wounded and unable to move, while his men were trying to entrench themselves under fire from the enemy. Sepoy Ghulam Hussein

[*] The strength of the 47th Sikhs when the battalion crossed the start line on 26 April was 444 all ranks. The next day it numbered just two British officers, two Indian officers and 92 IORs.

got to his feet, ran out under fire to Holbrooke and carried the officer back to the dubious safety of his own shell scrape. During the advance by Wilde's Rifles Captain Banks, of the Guides and commanding the Guides company sent as reinforcements to Wilde's, was shot and killed and his orderly, Sepoy Bhal Singh, also from the Guides, severely wounded in the face. Despite his own wounds and still a target for the enemy, Bhal Singh attempted to carry the body of his officer to safety. Eventually he collapsed from exhaustion and loss of blood. He could carry Banks' body no farther but he removed the dead officer's equipment and personal possessions and brought them back to the battalion's position.

The advance could go no farther. All along the line the battalions, French, British and Indian, had been halted short of their objective. It was less than one hour from the beginning of the attack, but all they could do now was to try to hold on where they were.

At 1430 hours, as the French troops on the Indians' left attempted a further advance, clouds of gas began to issue from the German positions. The wind was blowing towards the south-south-west and the thick yellow clouds rolled slowly across the intervening space and enveloped the left of the Lahore Division line and the right of the French. The Sirhind Brigade, still at the rear watching, could see nothing in the cloud, and then suddenly men began to run from out of the haze of vapour, a few at first and then groups of six or seven and then more and more. The French had broken and the panic was infectious. The French and most of the Ferozepore Brigade, except for those incapacitated by the gas, recoiled leaving the dead and wounded lying behind them. Horses with guns, horses without guns, men of three armies, retching and screaming, poured back down the road. The Ferozepore Brigade were not rallied until they had reached La Brique, virtually where they had started from. In the van were French colonial troops who wore light blue-grey uniforms. The Jullunder Brigade, accustomed to French soldiers in blue jackets and red trousers*, initially mistook the Africans for Germans, and the watching Sirhind Brigade's machine-guns, now brigaded, opened up on them. The cry of 'Counter-Attack' went up and the men of the Jullunder Brigade too ran back to where they could find some dover to repel what they thought was a German attack.

Not all had fled. One party composed of men of the Manchesters, the H 47th Sikhs, the 40th Pathans, the 129th Baluchis, Wilde's Rifles and the Connaught Rangers held grimly on, pressing their faces into the ground until the gas passed over them. The Germans now followed up their

---

* The French had begun a programme of replacing the blue and red with a light grey uniform for all their troops but not all units had received it in April. To satisfy the traditionalists in the French Army some blue and red threads were woven into the new uniform.

devastating use of gas by an infantry counter-attack. The little group, commanded by Major Deacon of the Connaughts, gave up ground stubbornly, but were forced back 80 or 100 yards until turning at bay and stopping any further enemy advance. Despite repeated attempts to dislodge them, there they remained.

Throughout the day the Lahore Divisional Headquarters had remained at Potijze, in the centre of, and about 800 yards behind, the start line. Major General Keary spent most of the time in a wooden observation tower, but even from that vantage point the fog of war was such that he could see little. It was not until the Divisional Signal Company had managed to lay a line to the Jullunder Brigade Headquarters, some time after the German counter-attack, that Keary was fully aware that the Indian attack had failed. He now ordered the Sirhind Brigade to move to La Brique, and on discovering that Major Deacon and his mixed bag of officers and men were still holding on, at about 1500 hours he ordered the Sirhind Brigade to detach the Highland Light Infantry and the 1/4th Gurkhas to the Jullunder Brigade, with a view to their continuing the attack and making contact with Deacon. The two battalions duly reported to Brigadier General Strickland, commanding the Jullunder Brigade; Strickland was by now a seasoned campaigner on the Western Front, he had commanded the 1st Manchesters in the same brigade, and he well understood the futility of reinforcing failure. Two brigades and the French could not take the German positions: to throw in two more battalions now, when it was still light, would be a pointless waste of lives and Strickland told General Keary so. The attack was cancelled.

While a further attack in daylight could not succeed, one after dark just might. The 9th Bhopals had been in support during the operations of the Ferozepore Brigade during the afternoon, and had taken relatively few casualties. They, along with the 15th Sikhs and the 1/4th Gurkhas of the Sirhind Brigade, were now warned for a night attack with the aim of making contact with Deacon's force and then, if the opportunity arose, pressing on to the German lines and beyond. Just before 2000 hours the Sikhs and the Gurkhas, supported by the men of the 9th Bhopals, moved off towards the north. After a great deal of stumbling about in the dark, including finding themselves in a re-entrant overlooked on both sides by Germans—who were fortunately asleep—contact was made with Deacon's force. There was still no real idea as to the location of the enemy main positions, the only reliable report so far being that they were on a ridge somewhere to the front and protected by uncut wire. Armed with this information Lieutenant Colonel Hill, Commanding Officer 15th Sikhs and the senior officer present, made his way back to the headquarters of the Ferozepore Brigade and persuaded the Brigadier that the advance should not be pressed farther. The 15th Sikhs and the 1/4th Gurkhas began to dig in where they were, linking up with the French on their left.

There was one other, smaller, group which had stood its ground when the line had given way under attack by gas. Jemadar Mir Dast, a Pathan of 55th Coke's Rifles, attached as a reinforcement to Wilde's Rifles, stayed in his position close to the German trenches when all his British officers had been killed or wounded and the line had been routed. Mir Dast now gathered together what men were left around him, including those who had been only lightly gassed and were beginning to recover, and created a strongpoint from which he would not be shifted, despite determined efforts by the enemy. At intervals he organised the recovery to his position of wounded men and held on until he was ordered to retire after dark. On his way back to the Allied lines, he collected as many wounded as he could and brought them with him. Having delivered his men to relative safety, Mir Dast then spent the night scouring no man's land, bringing back a number of wounded officers and men. For his gallantry that day Jemadar Mir Dast was awarded the Victoria Cross, the fourth to a soldier of the Indian Army since its arrival in France.

Immediately after the Germans' first use of gas on 22 April an appeal was made to the women of Great Britain to manufacture gas masks, and on the morning of the 27th the first issues were made to the Indian Corps and to the British troops in the immediate area. These devices consisted of a pad of cotton waste, soaked in sal ammoniac and contained in a net made from ladies' veils. The men were instructed to moisten them with water and to tie them round the nose and face. Primitive though they were, they did provide some protection and demonstrated that at least something was being done. The only battalion to have any real protection before that was Wilde's Rifles, whose Quartermaster, Lieutenant Mein, managed to procure some tins of chloride of lime (where on earth from, one wonders?) into which the men dipped the ends of their pagris before tying them over their faces.

It was jointly decided that a further push north should be attempted on the afternoon of 27 April. A French Moroccan division would be on the left, while the Sirhind Brigade and the Ferozepore Brigade would be on the right, the boundary once again being the Ypres/Langemark road. The attack would be supported by French, British and Canadian artillery and by a British brigade which would co-operate to the right of the Sirhind Brigade. Within the Sirhind Brigade the 1/1st Gurkhas were on the extreme left, keeping in touch with the French, and the 1/4th Gurkhas on the right. In support were the Highland Light Infantry, less one company which had relieved Major Deacon and his band, and the 15th Sikhs The 4th King's Liverpool was in brigade reserve. To the right of the Sirhind Brigade the Ferozepore Brigade had the 4th Londons on the left, in touch with the right-hand battalion of the Sirhind Brigade, and the 9th Bhopals on the right. In support were the Connaught Rangers and the combined Wilde's Rifles and 129th Baluchis, as a result of the previous day both now reduced to a few hundred men between them, in brigade reserve.

The artillery bombardment began at 1230 hours on 27 April and the attacking troops moved off. As soon as the Indians came into view of the enemy, the machine-guns and the rifles added their contribution to the shelling which had started as soon as they had got up to move. It was clear that the Germans had worked out the range to every hedgerow, fold in the ground and bank, and once more casualties began to mount. Despite the supporting battalions being thrown in to the assault, and despite a few small groups of Gurkhas and men of the King's Liverpool getting close enough to the enemy trenches to fire into them, the advance stalled about 400 yards from the enemy firing line. The French too had failed to reach their objectives and, halting level with the Sirhind Brigade, formed a rough firing line. The advance by the British brigade never happened at all, because both the brigade commander and his brigade major were killed by an enemy shell while in the act of writing out the orders for it, and with their deaths nobody else in the brigade knew anything about what was intended. Further attempts to push forward this time augmented by the attachment of a British composite brigade to the Lahore division, came to nought.

All telephone wires had now been cut by shelling, and as fast as the signal companies repaired them, they were cut again. The Sirhind Brigade sent messages back by runner and were eventually told that a further advance must be tried, this time in conjunction with the French who would advance after a heavy artillery bombardment. At 1900 the French attack began, but once more the wind was favourable to the Germans and clouds of noxious gas issued from their trenches. The Moroccans retreated, the Indians could go no farther without support, and no more could be done that day save to try to turn the positions reached into something resembling a defensive line. The night was spent digging in, collecting the wounded, burying the dead and wondering what the morrow might bring.

Next day, 28 April, a planned French attack to be supported by the Sirhind Brigade never came off, and the day degenerated into an artillery duel, which the Germans must be said to have won. Another night was spent digging. There was no question of being able to bring up rations and more ammunition by day, and each night re-supply was carried out by the battalions' transport. It did at least have the advantage of forcing the drivers to learn to drive, for the wagons had to be brought up at a flat gallop, the stores unloaded, and the wagons sent back as fast as they had come before they became targets for German artillery.

On the 29th an attack was to be made by the French and again the Sirhind Brigade and the Ferozepore Brigade were ordered to assist. The Indian brigades stood to all day as the attack was postponed again and again, being finally cancelled altogether at 1800 hours. That night the Jullunder and Ferozepore Brigades were withdrawn back to Ouderdom, leaving the Sirhind Brigade to continue to participate in the battle. On

30 April a joint attack was once more ordered, and again postponed and finally cancelled when the Moroccan commander reported that he could not carry out any further advance without reinforcement. During the night more French units were fed into the battle area, and on 1 May yet another joint operation was planned, this time with the French attacking towards the north-east and the Sirhind Brigade attempting to seize the feature known as Hill 29, the highest point of the Mauser Ridge.

It was on this day, just before the battalions deployed for the attack, that the gas mask Mark II (called a 'smoke helmet') arrived in the firing line. This too had been made by the women of Britain and consisted of a flannel hood which covered the whole of the head and face, being tucked into the collar of the jacket. The flannel was impregnated with protective chemicals and the helmet had celluloid eyepieces. It was regarded as effective against chlorine gas, but the eye pieces tended to mist up.

The artillery supporting the advance opened up at 1450, and to minimise casualties the commanding officers of the two leading Gurkha battalions, the 1/1st and the 1/4th, decided to move as fast as possible down the open slope on the enemy side of the start line. Leaving all their equipment save weapons and ammunition, the leading battalions got to their feet and ran towards the enemy, being cheered by the 15th Sikhs as they passed over the forward friendly trenches. They got to within 150 yards of the enemy with remarkably light casualties, but by now the Germans had realised what was up and the guns, rifles and machine-guns opened up. The first wave could progress no farther, and when an enemy barrage prevented the King's Liverpool from reinforcing, the attack ground to a halt. Two platoons of the 1/4th Gurkhas did get as far as the German wire, which they found undamaged by the artillery. They tried to cut through the wire with kukris and wire cutters but were table to make any progress and were forced back into a ditch forward of the enemy trenches. There they spent the rest of the day keeping German local attacks at bay by throwing bombs at intervals.

Meanwhile the French on the left, having been subjected to severe artillery fire for most of the day, had not advanced at all. There was nothing further to be gained by prolonging the agony and the Lahore Divisional Commander ordered the Sirhind Brigade to hold where they were, wait until dark and then withdraw. As dusk fell the men of the Sirhind Brigade buried their dead, collected their wounded and retired, to be ordered back to Ouderdom. While the march back was not so harrowing as the march up, it was bad enough. The battalions' transport and the machine-gun mules were fully occupied in carrying wounded, and the sepoys had to carry the machine-guns, all the reserve, ammunition, shovels and the impedimenta which would normally have been the responsibility of the transport. After a trying march, made longer by the need to avoid areas of German shelling, the Sirhind Brigade reached Ouderdom at 0530 on 2

May. On 3 May the Lahore Division marched south to rejoin the Indian Corps. By its part in Second Ypres the Lahore Division had sustained 3,889 casualties, or 20% of the troops engaged, Wilde's Rifles alone had gone into the battle with eight British officers, 12 Indian officers and 560 IORs. They marched away with three British officers, three Indian officers and 216 IORs, but the German advance into the Salient had been stopped and pushed back a mile. The enemy would not capture Ypres.

The award of the Victoria Cross to Jemadar Mir Dast for his actions on the night of 26/27 April was of more than usual significance. Mir Dast had a brother, Mir Mast, who was a jemadar in Vaughan's Rifles in the Bareilly Brigade. On the night of 2/3 March 1915 Jemadar Mir Mast was in command of a section of the firing line in the Neuve Chapelle area when he deserted to the Germans, taking with him two havildars, two naiks and eight sepoys, all, like Mir Mast, Pathans. It was a major embarrassment for Vaughan's, and indeed for the Indian Corps as a whole, particularly when it was reported that Mir Mast had been awarded the Iron Cross by the Kaiser[*]. He and two sepoys accompanied a German mission to Afghanistan and in June 1915 were repatriated to the Tirah, well outside British jurisdiction. With the award of the Victoria Cross to his brother some of the family honour was restored, at least in British eyes, but the cynic might remark that whoever won the war, the Mir family were going to be all right.

Desertion was a problem that was to plague all the armies on the Western Front, French, British and German, as the war went on. A British, or French soldier could, if he was lucky, melt into the local population and remain undetected for weeks, sometimes months. An Indian soldier had no chance of surviving unquestioned in the French countryside.

During the 14 months that the Indian Corps served in France a very small number—38 men in all—did desert, mostly to the Germans[22]. They were all Pathans save for one naik in the 41st Dogras and two sepoys from the 35th Sikhs attached to the 47th Sikhs. The Dogra was under investigation, having been suspected of attacking a British officer, but no one ever worked out quite why the two Sikhs went. Pathans in India always did have a tendency to desert, being able to return home where they were out of British jurisdiction, and they were of course Moslem.

Of the 35 Pathans who deserted from the Western Front 11, a naik and ten sepoys, were from the 40th Pathans and with the exception of Mir Mast and his party, the remainder were all sepoys in ones and twos from other regiments with a Pathan content.

That Pathans were perfectly capable of dissembling to the detriment of the King's enemies is demonstrated by the strange case of Naik Ayub

---

[*]   I can find no evidence for this, but it was believed at the time and is mentioned in a
number of contemporaneous accounts.

Khan, of the 129th Baluchis. Ayub Khan was a member of a patrol sent out on the night of 21 June 1915 to reconnoitre the enemy trenches. After a series of adventures including being fired upon, the patrol returned and Ayub Khan was missing. As he was last seen near the German firing line it was assumed that he had been killed, wounded or taken prisoner. Brigade headquarters, sceptical staff officers as they were, suggested that it was far more likely that he had deserted to the Germans, an assertion vehemently denied by the British officers of the 129th Baluchis who insisted that Ayub Khan was a thoroughly good and loyal NCO.

Two nights later Ayub Khan came crawling over the parapet of his own firing line, unscratched and carrying his rifle and ammunition. He explained to his astonished Commanding Officer that while near the German wire it occurred to him that he might visit the enemy and see what information he could glean. Hiding his rifle and bandolier in no man's land, he stood up, raised his hands above his head and called out that he was a Mussalman. The German occupants of the trench invited him into it and he was taken to an officer, conducted along a communiation trench to the Bois de Biez and eventually to a divisional headquarters at Marquillies. Here the Germans managed to find an officer who spoke some Hindustani and Ayub was subjected to a long interrogation, mostly about morale in the Indian regiments and the iniquity of Moslem soldiers fighting Turkey's ally. Ayub told his interlocutors that many of the men in his regiment were ready to desert, and if the Germans would allow him to return to his own lines he could bring 20 men back with him (for a reward of 20 German marks a head). This was agreed, and on the night of 23 June Ayub Khan was taken by motor car to the Bois de Biez and then back to the point where he had entered the German trenches. Bidding au revoir to his new found friends he returned to his regiment. Ayub Khan was able to give the shoulder strap numbers of all the enemy soldiers that he had seen, describe accurately the paths through the wood, point out ammunition dumps and supply routes and—perhaps most significant of all—could say with certainty that there were no signs of any apparatus for the release of gas anywhere in the areas where he had been.

Initially Ayub's commanders were suspicious of this incredible tale, but as the information he gave began to be confirmed from other intelligence sources, it became clear that he had carried out a very brave, if foolhardy, act and that what he was able to report was of considerable help to the planners and to the intelligence staffs. Ayub Khan was promoted to jemadar and awarded the OBI Second Class.

Whether it was the attraction of Germany's ally, Turkey, as a Moslem nation, or German propaganda, that persuaded the genuine Pathan deserters is not known, but it is more likely that the natural Pathan propensity for seeking personal advantage was the chief motivating factor. Most

Pathan deserters were repatriated to Afghanistan by the Germans,[*] and as desertions from one tribe affected the balance of control over water and grazing around the villages, it tended to be followed by desertions from another tribe concerned that the first defectors would seize control at home. All in all the record of Indian troops was very good: the vast majority stayed loyal, whether in the line or as prisoners, and the Indian government's fears of mass desertions of Pathans and other Moslems were largely groundless.

SOURCE NOTES

1. *With the Indians in France*, Lt Gen Sir James Willcocks, Constable and Co, London, 1920.
2. 'Report on the King's Indian Hospital Brighton' by Col Sir Bruce Seaton Bt IMS, India Office Library and Records, L/MIL/17/5/2016
3. 'Report of the Censor of Indian Mails France 1914 – 1918 Vol I', India Office Library and Records, L/MIL/5/825.
4. Ibid.
5. Ibid.
6. Copies of correspondence in 'Printed Reports Censor of Indian Mails France Dec 1914 – Jun 1918', India Office Library and Records, L/MIL/5/828.
7. Ibid.
8. Quoted in *History of the 2nd King Edward's Own Goorkhas (The Sirmoor Rifle Regiment) Vol II 1911 – 1921*, LW Shakespear, Gale and Polden, Aldershot, 1962 (privately published).
9. War Diary 59th Scinde Rifles, Public Record Office, WO/95 3927.
10. 'An Analysis of 1000 Wounds and Injuries Received in Action With Special Reference to the Theory of the Prevalence of Self Infliction', India Office Library and Records, L/MIL/17/5/2402 (Secret)
11. Ibid.
12. Ibid.
13. 'Report of the Censor of Indian Mails France 1914 – 1918 Vol I'.
14. Ibid.
15. Ibid.
16. Ibid.
17. Ibid.
18. 'Printed Reports Censor of Indian Mails France Dec 1914 – Jun 1918.'
19. Ibid.

[*] Although some were sent to Mesopotamia later where they were used to try to turn Indian POWs. Their efforts were largely unsuccessful.

20. *A History of the 4th Prince of Wales' Own Gurkha Rifles 1857 – 1937*, MacDonell and Macaulay, Blackwood and Sons, Edinburgh and London, 1940 (privately published).
21. Ibid.
22. 'Nominal roll of Indian prisoners of war suspected of having deserted to the enemy or to have given information or to have otherwise assisted the enemy after capture', India Office Library and Records, L/MIL/17/5/2403 List A (Secret).

IX

Comforts, Religion, Aubers
and the Press

Whilst the Lahore Division was involved in the second battle of Ypres, the Meerut Division remained in the trenches around the Neuve Chapelle area. Although the Corps History[1] records that 'nothing of importance happened', the Division continued to take a steady toll of casualties on patrols and from German shelling. Reinforcements for the Corps continued to arrive, albeit in dribs and drabs, and a draft of 250 men from the Burma Military Police actually joined the 1/4th Gurkhas while the battalion were on the march down from Ypres. Most reinforcements were now from regiments other than the ones they were joining, with all the problems of assimilation that inevitably ensued. The 9th Bhopal Infantry was reorganised into a three-company battalion on 4 May. Number 1 Company was composed of Sikhs, of their own and of the 21st Punjabis, and Rajputs of the 4th and 16th Rajputs. Number 2 Company had Mohammadans of the 9th, 17th and 18th Infantry and 19th Punjabis, while Number 3 Company contained Brahmins and Rajputs from the 1 Brahmins, the 8th Infantry, 11th Rajputs, 89th Punjabis and 96th Berar Infantry. Like all the infantry battalions of the Indian Corps the Bhopals had very few men left who had landed in Marseilles six month before.

Despite the losses of the Corps, which the reinforcements could not keep up with, morale at this time was generally good. Neuve Chapelle was seen by the soldiers as a victory (although most modern histories regard it as a failure) and at last the weather improved. The cold, wet winter had persisted into the spring of 1915 but now the rain stopped the ground began to dry out, and the sun was occasionally seen. The welfare of the Indian troops in France had not been neglected and the Indian Soldiers' Comforts Fund had been founded in England to assist with matters not within the official purview of the Army.

The Indian Soldiers' Comforts Fund had been set up on 1 October 1914 with the aim of providing assistance to Indian soldiers serving at front and in hospitals. It was run by a committee under the chairmanship of Sir John Hewitt, one time Lieutenant Governor of the United Province (Oudh and Agra), and composed of people who had lived and worked in India in some capacity, and of representatives of the Indian community living in England. Lord Curzon, a former Viceroy, allowed the use of his

London residence, 1 Carlton House Terrace, as the Fund's headquarters. The Committee appealed for donations from the general public and the response was overwhelming. Pensioners, residents of a home for the blind, schoolchildren as well as those of more substantial means all sent in their contributions, and during the time the Indian Corps was in France over £150,000* was collected by public subscription. An appeal to firms in the City raised a further £45,000, and all this at a time when business and the public were already inundated by appeals for good causes in support of the Army and Navy.

In the first 12 months of its existence the Fund sent to the men of the Indian Corps and the Indian Cavalry Corps in France, amongst other items, 78,000 pairs of socks, 12,000 balaclava caps, 85,000 handkerchiefs and 850,000 envelopes. Recreation was not forgotten for the fund also despatched 40 gramophones, 130 footballs, 22,000,000 cigarettes and 125,000 pounds of sweets. Articles to help in the fighting were not excluded and the Fund had 2,000 trench periscopes made and sent out at its own expense.

The Fund also helped with spiritual welfare. In the British Army each battalion of infantry and regiment of cavalry had its own Christian chaplain who would be a minister of the religion of the majority of the soldiers in the unit. British units in the Indian Corps had their chaplains provided by the Indian Ecclesiastical Department. The Indian Army too had its religious representatives, depending upon the racial composition of the regiment. Unlike British chaplains these priests, pandits and maulvis were not enlisted into the Army but were civilians attached, paid a salary by the government. Neither then nor later were any of these spiritual mentors taken into the field by the regiments, all were left behind in India. Partly this was due to the Indian association of priests with death, and partly to the difficulties in administering them. A Hindu battalion had a Brahmin priest who, unlike his secular brethren, could not in any circumstances compromise the rules of caste. For a Hindu soldier to cross the kalo pani was bad enough, and entailed purification ceremonies when he returned to India; but for a priest to lose caste by travelling entailed long and expensive rites which might never reinstate him fully. The priests stayed at home.

That there was no official practitioner of religion with the Indian Corps was of no great importance. The dead were buried or burnt under the supervision of the subadar major, and if any religious ceremony had to be performed, there was always somebody with the knowledge and of the correct caste to do it. The Comforts Fund helped here too. For the Sikhs the Fund collected and sent to the Western Front 3,178 religious books and pamphlets, and for the Moslems copies of the Koran. In order that there

---

* More than £5 million at today's values—a staggering amount.

could be no suspicion of theological contamination, all religious items for the Sikhs were packed by the secretary of the Sikh temple in West Kent, and for the Moslems by members of the London branch of the All India Moslem League. In April the Corps Commander asked the Fund to send paperback, rather than bound, copies of books as the latter were difficult to carry away in a hurry.

The Sikh religion required each member to wear at all times a steel bracelet (kara), comb (kirpan) and dagger (khanda), and as the Army took religion seriously Sikh soldiers were required to wear these items in uniform. In the fighting daggers got lost, and combs and bracelets broke, so the Fund found a contractor in Sheffield who made them and had them shipped to France and delivered to hospitals, paid for by the Fund. The Sikhs also had their own prescribed design of underpants, and the fund had 4,000 pairs made for the troops in France. Even Brahminnical threads were supplied. Sir James Willcocks had doubts as to the wisdom of offering threads made in England to Brahmins, but he eventually agreed to their being sent out. Their arrival does not appear to have precipitated any difficulties.

If the religious requirements of the Indian Corps were satisfactorily discharged by the men themselves, with the assistance of the Indian Soldiers' Comforts Fund, the activities of some Christian organisations did give rise to disquiet. The last time proselytising amongst Indian soldiers had been tolerated, prior to 1857, there had been a mutiny and the Indian Army rule was absolute: no interference whatsoever with the religion of the sepoys was permitted. No soldier was allowed to change to another religion—to any other religion, not just to Christianity—and a soldier who insisted was instantly discharged.* German propaganda emphasised that its ally, Turkey, was a Moslem state, and claimed that the English intended forcibly to convert all Indian soldiers to Christianity. A number of letters from sepoys in France, written to relatives in India, emphasised that the writer had no intention of 'concluding an English marriage'[2]. The subject was therefore extremely sensitive and, while it was easy to prevent attempts at conversion in the battle areas, and there were in any case very few, men recuperating in hospitals in England were sometimes the subjects of well meaning but misguided attempts at conversion to Christianity.

The YMCA in particular got into trouble when they made a gift of headed notepaper to Indian patients in hospitals in England, and the censor's staff had to cut off the heading from each sheet of paper before forwarding the letter on. Captain Howell, the Chief Censor, wrote indignantly to the India Office:

---

* The same rule applies to the British Brigade of Gurkhas today, and Gurkha Christians (of whom there are a few) are not generally enlisted.

We should stop the manufacture of these items to prevent them falling into the hands of well meaning but ignorant persons who might conceivably cause really serious trouble by their present ill timed efforts at making converts.[3]

Occasionally English Christians would give the sepoys postcards with biblical quotations on them. The men, not understanding what the quotations said, would send the cards home and if not intercepted by the censor they could cause real worry in the villages.

Indian prisoners of war were not forgotten by the Comforts Fund. By the spring of 1915 names of prisoners of war were being submitted to the Swiss Red Cross by the captors, and passed on to the Indian government. In all it was known that there were around 500 Indian prisoners in German hands by May 1915. In general the Germans adhered to the international conventions regarding the treatment of prisoners, but life was by no means easy for men incarcerated in a country already short of food. Naik Bahadur Pun of the 2/8th Gurkhas wrote to Rifleman Sangraj Pun of the same battalion:

Your brother Bahadur Pun sends his greetings. If you have three or four rupees about you please send them, also things to eat and drink and clothes should be put in a parcel and sent. Dhaniram Pun and I are prisoners of war in Germany. Do not worry about us or grieve. Our address is Hormar Laagar, Zossen, Germany.[4]

As soon as it was known who the Indian prisoners were, the Fund sent a Red Cross parcel to each man, via the Swiss. In the parcel were items of food, underwear and warm clothing, and flour was sent for the Brahmins who could only eat food prepared by their own caste.

The Germans made strenuous efforts to persuade Indian prisoners to change their allegiance, and in the course of the war 54 Indian soldiers captured by the Germans, all NCOs or sepoys, were suspected of having been turned and of giving information to or otherwise helping the enemy.[5] As with the deserters the vast majority (48 of the 54) were Pathans, the others being five Sikhs and a Dogra. 28 of the Pathans were men of the 129th Baluchis, either of that regiment or attached to it, and 16 of those were embodied into a battalion of the Turkish Army in March 1916, although they do not appear ever to have seen action.

Unfortunately for those disloyal soldiers, amongst the prisoners was the Subadar Major of the 129th Baluchis, wounded and captured in France. Himself a Pathan, he kept careful notes on the activities of those who had broken their oath, notes which were never discovered by the Germans despite regular searches of prisoners and their accommodation. When the Subadar Major was eventually returned to his regiment, as part of an exchange of wounded prisoners, he handed in his notes. As the Germans repatriated the Pathan defectors to Afghanistan or to tribal territory, there was little that the Indian authorities could do about it, except to ensure that men from deserters' villages and families were not recruited in future.

In April 1915 German successes on the Eastern Front persuaded General Joffre that a major offensive should be launched with a view to taking advantage of the removal of some German formations from the west, and to take some of the pressure off the Russians. The French would attack towards Lens, and Sir John French agreed to support them with Haig's First Army on the French left. Unlike previous offensives by the BEF, this would not be a local affair but would try once more to capture the Aubers Ridge, a subsequent objective of the Neuve Chapelle battle in March but which had never been reached. Capture of the ridge would prevent the Germans being able to dominate the British front line, give the British a firm and dry new line, and would threaten German communications between La Bassée and Lille.

Haig decided to mount a pincer attack, with two prongs which would meet on the Aubers Ridge. His orders for what would become known as the Battle of Aubers, to be included as part of the Battle of Festubert 1915, were issued on 13 April. The British I Corps were to advance on the line Rue de Marais to Illies, with its right flank on Givenchy, while the Indian Corps would take the line Ligny le Grand to La Cliqueterie Farm. Meanwhile the British IV Corps was to turn the German defences on Aubers Ridge from the north-east and link up with the Indian Corps at La Cliqueterie. The British and Indian cavalry would be in rear, to exploit the breakthrough.

Second Ypres now caused all plans to be put on hold, and it was not until the Lahore Division had returned to the Corps on May that any serious attention could be devoted to Aubers Ridge. It was agreed that the joint attack should begin on 8 May. On the British and Indian side lessons had been learned from Neuve Chapelle, and ammunition was pre-dumped, approach roads were improved and breastworks to provide jumping off points were constructed or enlarged. Small portable bridges were placed in position across a drainage ditch in front of the Indian lines. The orders stressed the importance of reinforcing and reserve troops being as close up as possible, and that communication must be maintained. It was easy to say.

The weather, which in April had been showing a steady improvement allowing the mud to dry out and the water level in trenches to go down, now took a turn for the worse. On 4 May there was a violent thunderstorm accompanied by heavy rain, followed by several days of hot, humid weather interspersed with prolonged showers. The terrain reverted to its winter consistency of glutinous mud. At Zero Hour on 8 May there was a thick mist, reducing visibility to a few yards, and the attack was postponed, for 24 hours.

The 9th of May was a fine, bright day and it was decided to go ahead. The attack was to be preceded by a 40-minute artillery bombardment after which the Dehra Dun Brigade would assault the enemy front line trenches, followed up by the Bareilly Brigade. Because the plan envisaged a pincers movement, there would inevitably be enemy strongholds which the two arms of the pincer would bypass. Once the jaws of the pincers met and cut off the Germans from reinforcing these cut off positions, dedicated groups would deal with them.

At 0500 hours the artillery, whose guns had spent the previous days registering their targets, opened up. It seemed to the waiting Dehra Dun Brigade to be less effective than they had expected. Although the shells seemed to be cutting the German wire, the enemy parapet was untouched, and a large number of shells were seen to fall either well beyond the German trenches or in no man's land, worryingly close to the Indians' own positions. Shortly after the bombardment began the Dehra Dun Brigade climbed out of the forward trenches and lined up. As was now accepted practice each battalion had two companies forward and two behind, each battalion covering a frontage of about 200 yards. Within the companies the formation was 'column of platoons' which meant one platoon forward in extended line, followed at 25-yard intervals by the other three platoons, one behind the other, each platoon also in extended line.

It had been intended that the troops should begin their advance at 0525 hours, so as to get as close as possible to the enemy trenches before the artillery lifted, but the number of shells falling short meant that the sepoys could not advance until the bombardment stopped altogether. At 0540 hours the last British shell exploded and the men of the Dehra Dun Brigade jumped to their feet. Watchers saw that suddenly the German parapet was lined with men. Little damage had been done to them by the artillery and they had simply taken shelter in the bottom of their trenches until the fire and smoke had passed. For the Germans it was what the Americans, in a later conflict, would describe as a turkey shoot. With a clear, open field to shoot across, and with machine-guns carefully sited to fire about eight inches above the ground, the enemy were able to inflict huge casualties in the first few minutes. On the extreme right of the Dehra Dun Brigade, a company of the 6th Jats saw both their British officer and Indian officer killed almost as soon as they had got to their feet, and before they had crossed a hundred yards every man was either killed or wounded. The right-hand battalion, 2/2nd Gurkhas, had every single British officer and a high proportion of Gurkha officers and NCOs killed or wounded. The battalion struggled on, more men falling by the minute, until they reached a ditch 100 yards from their objective where they went to ground. A few groups of three or four men, each under junior NCOs and riflemen, did manage to get into the German trenches but all were shot or bayoneted. In the centre the 4th Seaforths had three officers and 62 BORs killed and 127 wounded before they too took shelter in the ditch. The 1st Seaforths, on the left, fared even worse, with seven officers and 131 BORs killed and ten officers and 346 BORs wounded before reaching the dubious safety of the ditch. By 0600 hours what was left of the Dehra Dun Brigade was 100 yards from the German line, unable to advance in the face of continuing heavy fire. Those who could withdrew to their original line; many had no option but to stay where they were, eventually rejoining the Brigade after dark.

Meanwhile the Bareilly Brigade, in support, had lined up in their assembly area north of the Rue de Bois and, although breastworks had been constructed to provide some protection, the Brigade now came under artillery fire, which caused heavy losses in the 41st Dogras. Not all the damage was caused by the Germans, for the 4th Black Watch took 14 casualties as the result of British shells falling short.

To the right of the Indian Corps the advance of the British I Division had also stopped short, unable to proceed because of uncut wire and heavy defensive fire. Major Boileau, commanding 2/2nd Gurkhas, struggled along the ditch and made contact with the Welsh Regiment; the right-hand battalion of I Division, and suggested that both battalions should attack together. The Welsh were in the process of being relieved after themselves taking heavy casualties, and were in no position to help.

On the left the British 8 Division of IV Corps had initially made good progress, capturing the first line of German trenches at Rouges Bancs, but enemy enfilade fire soon made its position untenable and it too was forced to retire.

A further bombardment was now planned for 0745 hours, when the Dehra Dun Brigade would make another attempt using its supporting battalions and what was left of battalions still in the ditch to the front. This was cancelled when the British 1 Division was unable to get through the uncut wire. Further discussions between the divisional commanders took place and it was agreed that a co-ordinated attack would be made by the Bareilly Brigade and 1 Division at 1400, later postponed to 1600. Despite the experiences of Neuve Chapelle, the movement of the Bareilly Brigade to a position from where it could assault was carried out under extreme difficulty. The communication trenches had been heavily shelled and were full of wounded, stretcher bearers trying to get down and reinforcements trying to get up. When the Bareilly Brigade did get into the front line trenches and relieve the mauled remnants of the Dehra Dun Brigade, Brigadier General Southey was able to assess the situation. It was clear to him that his chances of success were no greater than those of the Dehra Dun Brigade, and given the casualties his battalions had already taken and that the Germans had reinforced their line, probably a great deal less. Southey reported his misgivings to the Divisional Commander, but when this was reported to the Corps Commander, Sir James Willcocks ordered that the assault was to proceed, again using the chilling phrase 'at all costs.'[6]

The artillery opened up on time and the men of the Bareilly Brigade scrambled out of their trenches to line up ready for the advance. As soon as heads began to appear above the Indian parapet, rifle and machine-gun fire from the German line began. Many of the British shells were falling short, others were sinking into the mud and failing to explode. The advance got as far as a drainage ditch 30 yards from their own lines and there it stopped, with only a few small parties able to get more than 100 yards from the start line. Over this short stretch of ground the Black Watch took 270 casualties out of a strength of 450 all ranks, Vaughan's Rifles 252 out of about 400, and the 41st Dogras 401 (including every British and Indian officer save one subadar) out of 645 engaged.

It was clear to all on the ground that any further attempts on the German line would lead only to yet more deaths and maiming to no avail. On the right and left of the Indian Corps the story was the same: no ground had been taken. Despite this the Garhwal Brigade was ordered up to relieve the Bareilly Brigade, with a view to trying one more time. The relief was completed by 0100 on the night of 9/10 May and the remainder of the night was spent in trying to bring back the wounded of the other two brigades. At daylight on 10 May battalions were told of striking French successes to the south: three lines of trenches on a frontage of three miles had been taken and 3,000 prisoners and some guns captured. The French attack had been preceded by the heaviest artillery bombardment yet seen on the Western Front, which had not only cut the German wire but virtually demolished the enemy front line and support trenches. It was to be a long time before the BEF would have the luxury of unlimited guns and ammunition. Further orders were issued for a renewal of the attack by the Meerut Division and by the British divisions on the left and right on 10 May, but were later cancelled. The Battle of Aubers Ridge had lasted one day, produced over 2,000 casualties in the Indian Corps alone, and had achieved nothing.

If the British had learned valuable lessons from Neuve Chapelle, so had the Germans. In March the German front line trenches had been lightly held and had been in better condition, but only just, than those occupied by the BEF. Now they held their front lines in strength with machine-gun nests placed farther back to deal with any penetration. The Germans had paid far closer attention to trench construction than had the British or Indians, the latter still inhibited by a philosophy which held that occupation of defensive positions was a temporary phenomenon to be endured only until the march on Berlin could resume. German trenches were well revetted, drained, and provided with firesteps both front and rear. Their communication trenches were constructed so that they could be used for fighting from if necessary. The Germans were, after all, occupying someone else's territory and could afford simply to stay on the defensive and wait for the Allies to attack them. The French on the other hand, wanted to remove the invader from French soil as soon as possible. As they were very much the senior partner in the Alliance, this attitude perforce infected the British too, much as Kitchener might have preferred to have the BEF simply hold a sector of the Western Front until his New Armies were ready for decisive intervention. Haig had seen his Army break through the German lines at Neuve Chapelle, he knew it could be done and he saw no reason why a breakthrough at Aubers could not lead to much greater things. He had not reckoned with the vastly improved and determined German capability to resist—but to be fair, neither had anyone else.

The British artillery had been generally successful at Neuve Chapelle until it ran out of shells, but it had only had to support a limited attack by two divisions over a relatively short length of front. At Aubers there were three divisions in the first phase and more to come, and that over a much more widely dispersed area. Despite Sir John French's appeals there was still insufficient artillery ammunition, and insufficient guns from which to fire it, reaching the Front from England. British industry was not yet structured to produce what was needed, and would not be until the 'Shell Scandal' forced the government to intervene directly in a way that the Asquithian Liberals would never have done without extreme pressure. The artillery did not have enough high explosive shells, far more effective against earthworks than the shrapnel designed for an open war of manoeuvre, and some of the guns were relics of the Boer War and incapable of the accuracy needed to support troops moving across open ground against a well dug in enemy.

The offensive would not end with the failure of 9 and 10 May however. Rain continued on 11 and 12 May and, despite what even the least aware soldier must have seen as a less than hopeful situation, there were individual acts of great gallantry. On 12 May Rifleman Dhanraj Thapa of the 2/8th Gurkhas had one hand blown off by a German shell. Hasty first aid was applied by his comrades and Dhanraj was waiting resignedly in his trench for the order to make his way back to the Regimental Aid Post. Looking out over no man's land he saw the body of a British officer. Who the British officer was and whether he was alive or dead Dhanraj had no idea, but he suddenly left his position, went out into the open and succeeded in bringing back the dead body of an officer of the 2nd Leicesters, also of the Garhwal Brigade. It was an utterly pointless act, but something that Indian soldiers regularly did, the frontier ethos of always recovering bodies, and particularly the bodies of British officers, being deeply ingrained. Rifleman Dhanraj Thapa was subsequently awarded the Russian Order of Saint George, a medal which was widely bestowed on soldiers of the British and Indian Armies. Unlike the British the Russians had a medal which could be awarded not only to their own men but to members of the Allied forces as well, and they had given the French and the British a quota. As British decorations were awarded sparingly, a Russian medal was the next best thing. There were a number of British officers and civil servants who felt that the British too should have an order which could be awarded to foreigners, and indeed to civilians, for meritorious service and it was this view that eventually led to the creation of The Most Excellent Order of The British Empire.

On the morning of 13 May orders arrived for a further attack on the German line on the 14th. This time there would be a night attack by the Meerut Division, with the Sirhind Brigade under command in place of the badly mauled Dehra Dun Brigade, and the British 1 Division. On the 13th and 14th more rain fell, this time so heavily that not only were the artillery observation officers unable to see enough to register the targets properly, but many of the ranging shells dug deep into the mud and did not detonate. The attack was postponed for 24 hours, and as so little had been achieved by the artillery, they were instructed to keep on registering and bombarding the German position throughout the day of 15 May. Instead of the rather optimistic objectives laid down for 9 May, this time the two divisions would capture a limited objective, consolidate and then press on to the next objective. Initially the Meerut Division was to advance south-east and establish a new line along the Festubert to La Tourelle road, about 1,000 yards from their own lines. Once there battalions would reorganise, issue fresh ammunition and establish communications with their respective brigade headquarters. During the reorganisation phase a further bombardment would be directed onto the line between Rue d'Ouvert and Rue de Marais, and the division would then make a further 1,000-yard advance and seize that line. Subsequent exploitation would be limited, owing to darkness, but the men were to press on if the circumstances permitted. The circumstances would not permit.

After dark on the night of 15 May the Garhwal Brigade, which would be the assault brigade of the Indian Corps' contribution to the affair, sorted itself out ready to advance after a preliminary artillery bombardment. Sufficient machine-guns had been obtained from within the Corps to allow each battalion to carry six in the advance. Men crept out to place bridges over the drainage ditch about ten feet wide and three to five feet deep just in front of their own trenches and breastworks, and although some men of the carrying parties were shot or hit by shellfire, the bridges were at last in position.

At 2330 hours the artillery bombardment ceased and the leading battalions, the 2nd Leicesters and the 39th Garhwalis, got to their feet and began to advance. Instantly a hail of fire erupted from the German lines, including trench mortars firing high explosive and illuminating shells. These latter, along with enemy flares and searchlights, gave the Germans clear targets to fire at while preventing the Indian Corps from seeing anything. As the lead companies pushed on over the little bridges, successive lines of platoons found them blocked with dead and wounded men. Existing shell holes, blown down trees and the incessant enemy machine-gun fire created barriers against which no one could advance more than a few yards.

By midnight on 15 May it was obvious that no progress could be made and the Leicesters and the Garhwalis, having suffered 228 and 154 casualties respectively, were pulled out of the line and replaced by the 2/3rd Gurkhas and the 3rd Londons. At 0245 on 16 May, after a half-hour artillery bombardment, the Gurkhas and the Londons struggled across the few remaining bridges and, keeping level with the British 1 Division on their right, moved towards the German lines. Once more the enemy were ready and once more small arms and artillery fire stopped the attack in its tracks, with 76 casualties in the 2/3rd Gurkhas and 104 in the Londons.

It was now quite clear that to attempt any further attacks on this portion of the line, whether by day or by night, would be futile, but it was possible that something might be done on the extreme right of the Indian Corps line, and to this end the Sirhind Brigade, the 107th Pioneers Number 4 Company Sappers and Miners were placed under command of the British 2 Division. It was intended that 2 Division should attempt the capture of the German lines to their front and, should further advance then be possible, for the Indian Corps to extend to its right and occupy and hold the captured trenches. At 0600 hours on the morning of 16 May all troops were withdrawn from the forward trenches in order to allow the British artillery to make a determined attempt to break up and breach the German front line parapets. Once this bombardment had finished, 2 Division advanced and did make some small gains, while the Bareilly Brigade relieved the Garhwal Brigade in the Indian Corps sector. In the small hours of 17 May the Sirhind Brigade took over from the British Brigade in a portion of the enemy line which had now been captured by 2 Division. As the communication trenches were by now almost obliterated and as heavy shelling had made the ground difficult to cross, the relief was not finished until well after first light, and it was fortunate that a German attack on the position being taken over by the 15th Sikhs was not pressed home and was easily beaten off. The dawn displayed a scene of complete desolation. Bodies—British, Indian and German—lay sprawled in the mud, trenches had collapsed and where they had not, parapets had been blown down or dug away. The carnage was made worse by British shelling having unearthed German make-shift graves. Bodies and bits of bodies in varying stages of decomposition added their cloying smell to that of the rotten, over-manured mud, burnt lyddite and overflowing latrine pits. One company of The Highland Light Infantry alone buried 104 bodies of a variety of nationalities and regiments during the night of 18 May.

By mid-day on 18 May the Bareilly Brigade and the 2/8th Gurkhas were holding the original line from the La Bassée road to the Rue du Bois, while the Sirhind Brigade had the 15th Sikhs and one company of the Highland Light Infantry in the captured trench, with the 4th King's Liverpool to the west in the old British line. In support farther back were the 1/1st and 1/4th Gurkhas. The Garhwal Brigade was in billets and in reserve trenches around Croix Barbée and the Debra Dun Brigade was in Meerut divisional reserve.

The 15th Sikhs had two companies forward in the old German front line. The left-hand company was particularly isolated as the trenches which they held connected with the remainder of the uncaptured German line. During the day of 18 May the enemy repeatedly tried to drive out the Sikhs by attacking down the line of trenches. All these attempts failed, thanks to the Sikhs having a plentiful supply of bombs, until in the early afternoon supplies began to run short. Lieutenant J G Smyth, who was in the Sikhs' support line, was ordered to organise a replenishment of bombs to the forward company. He asked for volunteers and selected a lance naik and nine sepoys. Taking with them two boxes, each containing 48 bombs, the group, led by Smyth, crawled up a sap which reached out about 50 yards forward of their position. Emerging from the sap they at once came under heavy shrapnel fire from the enemy artillery, forcing them to crawl into a small stream which was full of water. It was during his manoeuvre that men began to be hit. Pulling the boxes behind them with pagris tied to the handles, the party crawled from shell hole to shell hole inching ever closer to the Sikhs' left forward company. By the time Smyth had got to about 50 yards from his objective, he had only three men left and they were no longer enough to drag the heavy boxes behind them. Smyth ordered the boxes to be opened and intended to carry up bombs by hand. Now a further sepoy was shot through the head, being killed instantly.

There was nothing that Smyth could do but wait until dark to ferry the bombs up, and he and the two survivors, the lance naik and a sepoy, did eventually manage to crawl into the beleaguered company's position and get the bombs to them. For his gallant actions and leadership shown throughout that day, Smyth was awarded the Victoria Cross. 27 years later, Major General J G Smyth VC, in command of a division, would be abruptly reduced to the rank of brigadier and sacked.*

---

* Smyth was commanding a division during the Japanese invasion of Burma in 1942. His instructions were to delay the Japanese as long as possible and to maintain the strength of his division for the defence of Rangoon—conflicting aims. Withdrawing over the Sittang river in February 1942 by the one bridge still standing but which had been prepared for demolition, and still in contact with the enemy, one brigade had reached the 'friendly' bank while the other brigade was still to cross. During the night Smyth received intelligence reports which indicated that the Japanese were building up to a major attack on the bridge at first light. Knowing that he could not afford to allow the bridge to fall in Japanese hands Smyth ordered it to be blown. The brigade trapped on the far side had to abandon its heavy equipment and many of the soldiers—mainly Gurkhas and Sikhs—were drowned as they tried to cross the river on makeshift rafts. The Japanese attack did not materialise. Smyth took the blame and was never to command troops again.

Orders now arrived for yet another attempt to press forward, this time with bombing parties of the Sirhind Brigade assaulting the Ferme du 4 Bois in conjunction with the British Guards Brigade which would attack at Cour D'Avoue with the aim of seizing the line of the road from La Tourelle to Quinque Rue. The attack would be preceded by an artillery bombardment and the infantry would advance at 1630 hours. At 1620 Brigadier General Walker VC, commanding the Sirhind Brigade, reported by telephone that he saw no possibility of his men being able to advance against the very heavy German shelling which was making the whole area between his lines and the Ferme impassable. Walker's thoughts went to the Divisional and then to the Corps Commander and once again the words 'at all costs' came back down the telephone wires. At 1800 hour Walker reported that, despite three attempts by his bombing parties to reach the Ferme, all had been either killed or wounded and the task was impossible. As the Guards had made some little progress, Sir James Willcocks ordered that a further attempt should be made at night. At 2200 hours Walker again advised that he saw no prospect of success, further attacks would achieve nothing and merely waste lives. Willcocks, according to his own account, said 'While again reminding the division that it was most desirable the attack should be made, I left it to the judgement of General Walker, an experienced officer, on the spot, to decide'[7]. There was no attack.

On 19 May the small gains made by the British 2 and 7 Divisions had been consolidated and orders arrived for further attacks all along the line on that day. Walker again demurred. The 15th Sikhs and the King's Liverpool had taken heavy casualties, the Sikhs now mustering only about 250 men; throughout the Brigade no one had had any rest for 48 hours and he saw no prospect of them being able to do anything other than hold their present positions until at least 20 May. This Willcocks reluctantly agreed to, and during the night of 19 May the 15th Sikhs were relieved by the 1/1st Gurkhas. About 1800 hours, shortly before they were due to be relieved, the 15th Sikhs faced a determined German attempt to bomb their left-hand company out of its trenches, but a dogged resistance saw the enemy eventually withdraw. At about the same time orders arrived from Haig's First Army that the Indian Corps was to capture the Ferme du Bois by the morning of 22 May—'at all costs'[8]. They were to do it in conjunction with the Canadian and Highland Divisions, who would attack Cour D'Avoue farther south.

As a preliminary for the main attack on the morning of 22 May, the Meerut Division was instructed to probe forward on the night of 21/22 May, to establish themselves near the Ferme du Bois and its supporting defensive positions, and to dig trenches which would be used as forming up places for the main attack. This probe would in effect be three attacks, supporting one another, beginning from a start line at right angles to the trenches now held by the 1/4th Gurkhas. The Highland Light Infantry on the left would capture the area of the road running north-west from the Ferme du Bois, the 1/1st Gurkhas in the centre would get as close as they could to the Ferme itself while on the right the 1/4th Gurkhas would take the road running south-east from the Ferme. To the north-west the 15th Sikhs' machine-guns would be established where they could provide fire support. Mindful that the Cour D'Avoue (which would not be attacked until daylight by the British divisions) was only 100 yards south of the 1/4th Gurkhas' line of advance and was heavily fortified, the machine-guns of the King's Liverpool would follow up the rear company of the 1/4th. Running roughly south-west past the southerly corner of the Ferme du Bois was a German sap which was used by enemy patrols, so the main attack would be preceded by a bombing party of the 1/1st Gurkhas who would rush the head of the sap and seize it by coup de main.

The British artillery were bombarding the enemy lines when the troops moved off at midnight. They had 400 yards to go before reaching their objectives and, after they had covered half that distance, the guns, as had been arranged, lifted from the German forward positions and switched to the enemy rear in order to prevent reinforcement. As soon as the shelling ceased the whole of the German line erupted in rifle and machine-gun fire. The progress of the Sirhind Brigade was slow owing to the dark and the need to keep direction and maintain contact with battalions on either side, and the 1/4th Gurkhas were particularly singled out by enemy machine-guns to their right at the Cour D'Avoue.

Running just on the Indian side of the roads entering and leaving the Ferme du Bois was a drainage ditch, about six feet deep and with three feet of water in it and at some points only 20 yards from the German trenches. While not an insuperable obstacle in daylight it caused a very real difficulty at night. On the left of the Sirhind Brigade the Highland Light Infantry came under heavy enfilade machine-gun fire from the north, got to the ditch and could proceed no farther. In the centre the 1/1st Gurkhas' bombing party succeeded in their attack on the head of the communication trench and the rest of the battalion pressed on and managed to reach the Ferme, which itself gave them some cover from the enemy positions beyond it, and found that the wire between the buildings and the German trenches had been cut by the artillery. Unwisely, at this point the men began to cheer and the Germans, suddenly realising that they were about to be discommoded, opened up with rifles and machine-guns. Despite this the Gurkhas stormed through the Ferme and beyond it into the enemy trenches. Firing at almost point blank range and slashing with bayonet and kukri they managed to establish themselves in a portion of the German line and began to barricade themselves in from counter-attack from the right and left. By now all the British officers accompanying the attack had been killed or wounded and command devolved upon Subadar Jitsing Gurung. All communication with the Sirhind Brigade headquarters had been lost and the 1/1st Gurkhas' local success was not known about until it was too late to reinforce it.

On the right the 1/4th Gurkhas, more than half of whose men were now composed of reinforcements from their own 2nd Battalion and the Burma Military Police, were coming under increasingly heavy fire from the Cour D'Avoue as they encountered the ditch, here only yards from the German firing line. The wire between the ditch and the enemy was uncut. It was unfortunate that the brave but imprudent machine-gun officer of the King's Liverpool had ignored his orders to follow the rear company of the 1/4th and had insisted on pressing on to the front, for he and all his men were killed or wounded and his guns rendered useless. Two British officers and a handful of Gurkhas did manage to force a way through the wire and into the German trenches. They were seen no more.

By 0300 the 1/1st Gurkhas, under extreme pressure from their front and from both flanks had been forced to pull back into the Ferme du Bois and, with casualties mounting and still no reinforcement, Subadar Jitsing Gurung's position was precarious. On the left and right of the 1/1st Gurkhas the Highland Light Infantry and the 1/4th Gurkhas still clung to the ditch but could not move forward. Of the whole attacking force only two British officers, both subalterns, were still alive and unwounded. The officers now commanding the three forward battalions consulted. In view of the inability of the right and the left to get beyond the ditch, the heavy casualties so far sustained, and the impossible position in which they would be once dawn broke, they decided to retire their men to their original positions while they could still do so under cover of darkness. This they did, and Brigadier General Walker wisely decided that a further assault that morning was out of the question. The Battle of Festubert 1915 was officially considered to have ended on 22 May with gains of 600 yards on a four-mile front, 800 German prisoners and ten machine-guns captured and an unknown number of Germans killed—almost certainly fewer than the combined British and Indian losses. In the Sirhind Brigade the casualties amounted to 126 in the Highland Light Infantry, 121 in the 1/1st Gurkhas and 102, out of 300 engaged, in the 1/4th Gurkhas. On 23 May the Sirhind Brigade was relieved in the front line by the Dehra Dun Brigade and moved into billets in Colonne. They had been in action constantly for a month, since taking part in the Second Battle of Ypres in April.

It was fortunate that the next few weeks were relatively quiet in the Indian Corps sector, for most of the regiments were sorely in need of reorganisation and retraining, to say nothing of rest. Since arriving on the Western Front in October the butcher's bill had now passed the 25,000 mark which included 772 British officers, or the equivalent of the entire officer strength of 64 Indian battalions. Wilde's Rifles now mustered 446 all ranks from six different regiments, the 129th Baluchis 263 from seven regiments, and the 9th Bhopals 409 from 11 different regiments. The 39th Garhwalis, despite being an amalgamation of two battalions, were short of ten Indian officers and 64 NCOs and as this was the only regiment into which Garhwalis were enlisted, there was no other unit from which they could be reinforced. Eventually men from the Teri Garhwal Sappers and Miners, a States Forces unit from 'Foreign Garhwal' which had volunteered for service in France, were drafted into the 39th Garhwalis as being the only source of trained men of that race.

Now the first of the original Indian Corps battalions was to leave France. Turkey had turned out to be a far more formidable opponent than anyone had calculated, and more troops were required for Egypt. The 9th Bhopals and Napier's Rifles departed for that theatre in early June. The situation in France was therefore only marginally improved by the arrival of the 89th Punjabis and the 69th Punjabis, two fresh battalions from India, on 4 and 5 June. The 69th had a particularly unfortunate introduction to trench warfare when the Second-in-Command and the Adjutant were both killed by a shell on their first visit to the trenches the day after their arrival. The composition of the infantry of the Indian Corps was now only around 2,000 more Indians than British, and the British strength increased as the Highland, 8 and 49 Divisions were attached to the Corps at various times and for various periods.

The weather throughout the month of June was hot and sultry, giving rise to fears that an outbreak of typhus which had appeared amongst the French civilians living in the battle area might spread to the troops. Thanks to rigid health discipline and the enforcement of strict hygiene standards by the Indian Medical Services this did not happen, but even without any military activity of any significance during the month, casualties were still inflicted from sniping, shelling or on patrols. In the month of June 1915 the Corps still had ten British officers, 14 Indian officers and 59 IORs killed, and 30 British officers, 14 Indian officers and 635 IORs wounded.

By the end of June it was apparent that the Indian units of the corps must be withdrawn from the line for reorganisation. With battalions now composed of men from up to 11 different regiments, and with nearly all the original regular British and Indian officers gone, many of the officers and men hardly knew each other, and the recently arrived reinforcements had perforce been sent straight into the trenches without any training in European warfare. As the Corps as a whole could not be released from front line duty, Sir James Willcocks effected a temporary reorganisation which saw all the British units grouped in the Lahore Division, which continued to hold the line, and all the Indian units in the Meerut Division which was now withdrawn for rest and re-training. This period was supposed to last for a month, but on 19 July the Lahore Division was given three days' notice to extend its sector to take over that portion of the line south of the Fauquissart to Aubers road, previously held by the Highland

Division. The Lahore Division had therefore to be reinforced by units of the Meerut Division and for most of the Indian battalions the period of recuperation came to an end.

The line remained relatively quiet, but still the steady drain of killed and wounded went on. An officer and a rifleman of the 1/4th Gurkha were blown up by a bomb which malfunctioned, and men still forgot to keep their heads below the parapet, or were lost in the aggressive patrolling of no man's land. Even the logisticians were not spared. Lieutenant E G Bullard, of the Indian Postal Service, was being driven in a car laden with letters and packages for members of the Corps when a shell hit his car near Croix Barbée, killing both officer and driver. On 2 August, with the whole of the Corps now effectively back in the line, another re-shuffle of units took place as both the Lahore and Meerut Divisions reverted to their normal composition.

During August there was further depletion of the Corps by the removal of the 6th Jats and the 41st Dogras who left for the Middle East. Yet more depredation occurred when Kitchener asked Sir James Willcocks personally whether he could provide four companies of Gurkhas, four of the Gurkha regiments to provide a company each, to go to Gallipoli. Sir Ian Hamilton, commanding in that ill-fated campaign, was convinced that more Gurkhas were the answer to the problems of geography and a tenacious enemy* and had appealed to the War Minister direct. Sir James felt that a complete formed battallon was a better answer, and the 1/4th Gurkhas were made up to full strength by drafting men from the 2/2nd and the 1/9th, and were duly sent off to Marseilles. The loss of three battalions was not compensated for by the arrival of the 33rd Punjabis from the Suez Canal and the 93rd Burma Infantry later in September.

The Corps Commander found time to make an inspection of the Indian Corps base at Marseilles. Complaints about reservists were still flooding in to his headquarters and what Willcocks found did nothing to reassure him. He described[9] how he found one complete draft as being 'utterly valueless', another as 'particularly poor', while of another draft of 35 men, ten were plague victims who had not yet fully recovered. One boy was only 14 years old, while a draft sent for the 129th Baluchis, an entirely Moslem regiment, was made up of Hindus.

A committee set up by the Corps Commander to report on the situation found that of 212 men examined, only five or six were fit for service. Clearly, while the efforts of the Adjutant General's Department in India was having some effect in recruiting regular soldiers, the hopelessly anti-

---

*   He was probably right—the only battalion actually to reach its objective in the attack on Sari Bair Ridge was a Gurkha battalion, albeit with none of its British officers and having taken 30% casualties overall. Hamilton maintained to the end of his days that if he had had more Gurkhas he would have captured the peninsula.

quated reserve system was still failing. Sir James was also concerned about the practice of sending to Marseilles wounded men who had finished their convalescence but were not yet sufficiently recovered to return to the front line. Lines of men in bandages and walking sticks was not the most cheering sight to greet regiments and reinforcements arriving from India, and these wounded were eventually formed into a composite battalion behind the lines where they could be usefully employed without as yet being subjected to the full rigours of war.

All was not doom, gloom and work. The 4th Cavalry, the Meerut divisional cavalry regiment with a squadron each of Rajputana and Hindustani Mussalmans, Sikhs and Jats, held its regimental sports which included tent pegging and show jumping; the Pipes and Drums of the 40th Pathans beat retreat in the village where they were billeted, and the Gurkhas all played football where they could, with astonishing energy if not always great skill.

The postal system was now working well with both incoming and outgoing mail increasing by the month. Newspapers from India and England were arriving regularly and reasonably quickly, albeit that there was little news of the doings of the Indian Corps in the former. At the beginning of the war the authorities had tried to prevent news of operations getting into the press, and correspondents were kept under tight control, with cameras, whether of reporters or of officers and soldiers, forbidden in the front line.

It soon became clear that, as far as the British troops were concerned, this was counter-productive and had an adverse effect on recruiting and on the morale of the troops and of those at home. It was also almost impossible to enforce, and restrictions on the British press were quickly relaxed. The Indian government, however, had far stricter laws in regard to what could be published and what could not and there is absolutely no doubt that the publication of long lists of casualties with no news of what the Indian units were doing in France had an adverse effect on the war effort in India.

British reporting of the activities of the Indian Corps varied from the wildly fantastic to the non-existent. Most of the British public regarded the Indian Army as national pets. Apart from the existence of the Bengal Lancers, Sikhs and Gurkhas, who were exotic, Middle England knew little of the composition of the Indian Army. Reporters wrote what they thought they already knew, coloured by their perception of the Indian Army as brought to them in a diet of Boys' Own Paper-style accounts imbibed as schoolboys. The *Illustrated London News* of 7 November under a headline 'A surprise Visit by the Gurkhas to a German Trench' claims:

The Gurkhas attacked one of the enemy trenches on the left wing surprised and utterly routed them with their famous 'Cookers'. After the fight many dragged those whom they had killed back to the lines to show their British comrades how successful they had been.

It is probably unnecessary to observe that this account bears no relation to anything in any of the Gurkha battalions' war diaries, and that no Gurkha would waste time and energy in bringing a dead enemy back to his own position.* The same issue of the *Illustrated London News* carries a drawing by the magazine's artist at the Front showing British and Indian soldiers charging side by side, with fixed bayonets against a line of thuggish looking Germans. The caption says:

Our brave Indian troops working shoulder to shoulder with the thin khaki line: Upholders of the Izzat of the British Raj attacking Germans with the bayonet.

That the artist did not himself witness this action is obvious from his depiction of British and Sikhs wearing greatcoats, an item which was not available to any Sikh until late December. The article accompanying the drawing tells us:

Then the Indians charged with the bayonet, there was a fierce scrimmage for a moment, after which the Germans all turned and ran with the Indians in the thick of them slaying them right and left. Pursuit did not cease until well within the German main position. An officer serving with them said, 'They behaved splendidly well and, I think, thought the shells were fireworks let off for their benefit. They shouted with glee when they saw a German, and let him know what good shots they are.'

It might be thought churlish to remark that nobody in the Indian Corps was a very good shot in early 1914, but the fact is that most of the regiments had received only one day's firing practice on the range with the new rifle—some none at all—before being thrown into the trenches. This sort of journalistic hyperbole annoyed the British officers of the Corps because what the sepoys genuinely had done well was missed, and it gave the impression that the Indian soldiers were supermen, which they were not. A report which particularly exasperated the Corps Commander was one which described the Indian troops as 'slaughtering the Germans like cattle'[10]. The point that a very large proportion of the Indian Corps would have regarded the killing of cattle as a mortal sin must have got through

---

* Although they had been known to bring back ears and heads, but not of Germans, having been warned that such was unsporting against European enemies.

to the reporter, for the next edition referred to Germans being slaughtered like sheep.

By Boxing Day 1914 reports of First Ypres were being printed and the *Illustrated London News* of 26 December carried a drawing of a line of Sikhs driving the enemy back from the outskirts of an Ypres in flames, led by an Indian officer waving a drawn sword. Once again the artist cannot have been present. In the same edition we find a description of Gurkhas 'hurling kukris with deadly accuracy': not a way in which the Gurkha has ever used his kukri.

The daily press were not much better. The *Daily Mail* of 4 March 1915 carried a story of a Pathan sepoy who was alleged to have reported to the Regimental Aid Post wearing a blanket draped around his shoulders and with a cigarette in his mouth. When the Medical Officer entered the dugout he asked the Pathan why he had not removed the cigarette from his mouth in the presence of an officer. The Pathan is alleged to have grinned and said casually that he was unable to lift his hand to his mouth. Asked what was wrong with him he replied that he was 'sick outside'. Shrugging off the blanket he is reported to have exhibited both arms broken and lacerated by German machine-gun bullets.

If tall stories were carried when there was little basis of fact to support them, then there was often complete silence when Indian soldiers had done something highly creditable. The *Daily Mail* of March 11, 1915 reported briefly the capture of Neuve Chapelle, without any mention of the Indian Corps, despite the fact that it had been they who had captured the village and they who had done most of the fighting. The next day the *Mail* reported baldly: 'The 4th and Indian Corps have advanced 4000 yards yesterday'. The *Mail* carried its version of the full story of the Battle of Neuve Chapelle on March 16 under the headline 'The Capture of Neuve Chapelle. Magnificent Dash of British'. The story, by C Valentine Williams, the *Daily Mail's* special correspondent, reads:

> Another marked feature of the fighting was the splendid gallantry of all the British troops engaged. I believe I should not be incorrect in stating that some apprehension existed here least [sic] our troops after long months of sitting in trenches engaged in the siege operations into which the war developed during the winter should have proved themselves, in military slang, 'sticky'—that is to say, slow in the assault.
>
> Our troops however showed that the winter in the trenches had deprived them of none of their customary dash. They even exceeded the high hopes which their commanders have learned to place in them.
>
> When the moment came for them to attack, though the German fire, particularly from Machine Guns, was murderous, they

clambered out of their trenches and despite their heavy packs, the hail of bullets from machine-guns and shrapnel, yellow amid balls of white smoke, dashed forward at a run yelling like a football crowd.

The next day the *Daily Mail* listed the British casualties from the battle, with no mention of any Indian losses, and the back page was given up to photographs of individual soldiers under the headline of 'The Victors of Neuve Chapelle'. All are British; not a sepoy is to be seen.

The final major battle in which the Indian Corps would participate was to be the Battle of Loos (or 'Lens' to the French) in which they would have a peripheral role. Before that, however, something happened which hit the Indian soldiers as a cataclysmic bolt from the blue: their corps commander was taken from them. On 3 September 1915 Sir James Willcocks attended a conference of the First Army corps commanders presided over by Haig at the château at Hinges, Willcocks' own first headquarters in France. At the end of the conference Willcocks abruptly, and rather ungenerously, was sacked—officially ordered to proceed on leave forthwith—by the Army Commander. It was a terrible blow to Willcocks; only three weeks previously he had been invested with the GCMG by the King and told what a splendid job the Indian Corps was doing. He had no thought that he would not see the war out in command of his corps. Willcocks keeps silent in his memoirs, although promising to reveal all in due time, but it seems that Haig considered him to be 'lacking in initiative and tactical skill'[11]. Even if that was true, and Willcocks conceded that it might be, it did not detract from the feelings that the sepoys had for him. Despite a gammy leg he spent hours and days of every week on horseback visiting his units, and was often in the front line trenches. He cared about the sepoys and he knew them, and they reciprocated. Certainly Willcocks had his enemies: he was an officer of the old school and, in a parody of the accolade bestowed upon English kings he was known to some as 'James, by the grace of God', or to those less well disposed as 'God, by the grace of James'. If he was more of a figurehead than an operational commander then this is not necessarily to denigrate him. At that time of the war and on that sector of the front it was a war fought by divisions, brigades and individual battalions with the corps headquarters fulfilling a loose co-ordinating role. Willcocks had done well by the Indian Corps. He had also done well by the BEF, and he deserved better from it.

Haig had never been over impressed by the leadership of the Indian Corps. He later said[12] of an Italian general that he was reminded of 'the Indian Corps under General Willcocks, who, when I asked him to act vigorously had a thousand and more reasons for doing nothing'. Haig never understood, or if he did he ignored, the fact that the size of the Indian Corps (and therefore the tasks it could take on) never approached that of a British corps, nor did he appreciate the almost insuperable difficulties in replacing Indian casualties.

Haig also thought that the leaders of the Indian Corps were too old, and in this he may have had a point. Willcocks himself, at 58, was four years older than Haig in 1915, and commanding officers of battalions were certainly past the first flush of youthful vigour. In 1914, when the Indian Corps arrived in France, the oldest infantry commanding officers were Lieutenant Colonel W G Walker of the 1/4th Gurkhas, Lieutenant Colonel C F Dobbie of the 9th Bhopals and Lieutenant Colonel E R R Swiney of the 1/39th Garhwalis who were all 51, and the youngest were Lieutenant Colonel C W Tribe of the 41st Dogras and Lieutenant Colonel Drake-Brockman of the 2/39th Garhwalis, who were 46. Of the other 13 officers in command of Indian infantry battalions two were aged 50, three were 49, five were 48 and three were 47. The two cavalry regiments were similarly in the hands of mature men, both 49 years old in 1914.[13]

Promotion in peacetime, when officers joined intending to spend their working lives in the service, was inevitably slow. Promotion was by time, although acting rank might be granted for vacancies caused by promotion out of the regiment, retirement or death. Even the subaltern ranks of the Indian regiments contained men of considerable experience, and in October 1914 the oldest lieutenant in the infantry of the Indian Corps was 28, having had ten years' service, and the youngest 24 with six years. It took experience to know Indian soldiers well enough to command them, and while the commanding officers were perhaps past doing too much dashing about at the head of their men, they did their jobs well enough and all held their battalions together even under the most difficult circumstances. The British Army too started the war with its battalions and regiments commanded by men elderly by modern standards, but as time went on the average age of commanding officers became younger and younger, until by 1917 many were in their mid twenties. As virtually the whole of the British Army was on the Western Front there was no reserve of more senior officers to replace commanding officers as they were killed, wounded or promoted. (Although the oldest man to be killed at Loos was a 61-year-old commanding officer of a British militia battalion.) The Indian Army, on the other hand, had only one corps in France, the remainder being in theatres where the rate of attrition was less, or in India guarding the frontiers. Indian commanding officers killed in France were replaced temporarily by younger men, but the peacetime rules of promotion by seniority tempered by merit held, and these temporary commanders were in turn superseded by more senior officers posted in from India, or by the return of a wounded but patched up commanding officer. In October 1915, despite the British officer casualties in the past year, the oldest commanding officers were now Lieutenant Colonels HL Richardson 47th Silchs and CA Ormsby 2/3rd. Gurkhas who were both 50, while the youngest was Lieutenant Colonel BU Nicolay 1/4th Gurkhas, who was but 42: Even Nicolay, a temporary lieutenant colonel, would be replaced by one of substantive rank from the 9th Gurkhas when the 1/4th left France for Gallipoli.

Age does not necessarily indicate feebleness, nor lack of milltary prowess nor ardour, but whether Haig was right or wrong in thinking the leadership of the Indian Corps to be past it, he was the Army Commander and Willcocks had to go, so quickly that he did not even have an opportunity to say goodbye to the units which had served under him. The only consolation from this distasteful episode was that Willcocks' successor in command of the Indian Corps was Lieutenant General Sir Charles Anderson, until then commander of the Meerut Division, who in turn was replaced by Brigadier General Claud Jacob from the Dehra Dun Brigade. Command of the Dehra Dun Brigade passed to Lieutenant Colonel WJ Harvey, 2nd Black Watch. If Sir James Willcocks had to go then 'Paddy' Anderson was the obvious, and ideal, choice to succeed him. He* was an artilleryman who had spent long years in India and knew the sepoys well. His tactful assumption of command of the Corps did much to lessen the impact of his predecessor's rude dismissal.

SOURCE NOTES

1. *The Indian Corps in France*, Merewether and Smith, John Murray, London, 1919.
2. 'Report of the Censor of Indian Mails France 1914 – 1918 Vol I', India Office Library and Records, L/MIL/5/825.
3. 'Printed Reports Censor of Indian Mails France Dec 1914 – Jun 1918', India Office Library and Records, L/MIL/5/828.
4. 'Report of the Censor of Indian Mails France 1914 – 1918 Vol I', India Office Library and Records, L/MIL/5/825. Despite having the same last name and the salutation 'Brother', they were not related. Pun is the tribal name and Gurkhas address each other as 'brother' regardless of actual kinship.
5. 'Nominal Rolls of Indian Prisoners of War suspected of having deserted to the enemy or of giving information to the enemy', List A (Secret), India Office Library and Records, L/MIL/17/5/2403.
6. *The Indian Corps in France*.
7. *With the Indians in France*, Lt Gen Sir James Willcocks, Constable and Co, London, 1920.
8. Ibid.

---

* He would be given command of a British corps when the Indian Corps left the Western Front.

9. Ibid.
10. Ibid.
11. Ibid.
12. *The Private Papers of Sir Douglas Haig 1914 – 1919*, R Blake, Eyre & Spottiswoode, London, 1952.
13. Information taken from the Indian Army Lists of Oct 1914 and Oct 1915, Superintendent of Government Printing, Calcutta. These lists include dates of birth, promotion, appointment, etc. of all officers of the Indian Army.

X

Diversions at Loos and Departure

In August 1915 General Joffre, the French Commander-in-Chief, saw an opportunity to make a major break in the German line which if successful would not necessarily bring victory, but might create the conditions which would lead to an armistice and eventual peace. As we shall see, this was not to be, but had the operation succeeded, Loos and the associated French attacks could well have been the decisive battle of the war, and might have ended the fighting three years early. Certainly the plan was ambitious, far more so than anything planned for Aubers or Festubert—one allotted cavalry objective was 50 miles to the east—but looked at from the overall perspective it did look feasible. Joffre's plan was for the French First and Tenth Armies to attack in the area of Lens and Arras, with a parallel thrust by the French Second and Fourth Armies in Champagne. Simultaneously the British First Army would attack south of the La Bassée canal, in the Loos area which had now been taken over from the French.

Feasible from the overall perspective the proposition may have been, but looked at purely from the point of view of the BEF, Sir John French had severe reservations about its wisdom. He was still desperately short of artillery ammunition, and the ground over which his troops would have to advance was overlooked by the enemy. Kitchener nevertheless ordered the Commander-in-Chief to co-operate fully with the French proposal. Normally cautious in the extreme, Kitchener did of course have his own, British, reasons for concurring with Joffre's plans. Anything which might divert attention from the Gallipoli disaster was to be encouraged[*], and a major attack on the Western Front would take some of the pressure off Russia, where things were not going well for the Allies.

The British contribution would come from Haig's First Army, and specifically from Rawlinson's IV Corps which held the line running from the La Bassée Canal south to Sud Maroc, two miles north-west of Lens. In front of IV Corps the ground was flat and undulating, with little cover between the opposing lines which were between 200 and 400 yards apart. Just north of the centre of the area over which the British would attack

---

[*] There were 17,000 French troops at Galhpoli too, but it was the British who were considered to have failed.

was the Hohenzollern Redoubt, a German strongpoint which linked up with chalk pits, piles of spoil from the mines in the area, slag heaps and quarries, all of which gave the enemy excellent observation and fields of fire. Haig too had grave doubts as to the prudence of a major British attack in this area, but had no choice but to concur: it was all part of a grander design and any advance on a broad front will always have some stretches which are difficult. It was the British misfortune that they happened to hold the sector least well suited to an infantry attack. In order to try to even the chances somewhat, it was decided that the British would give the Germans a taste of their own frightfulness and use gas. While the Germans knew full well that a major attack was in the offing—they put up notices in the trenches asking when it would start—they do not appear to have had any idea that the British possessed large quantities of gas, and the ferrying up to the front line of thousands of cylinders containing a total of 150 tons of chlorine seems to have been completed in total secrecy.

After a number of changes and postponements it was decided that the attack would begin with an artillery bombardment and release of gas at 0550 hours on 25 September 1915, with Zero Hour for the assault at 0630. To the left of the main attack, north of the La Bassée canal, the Indian Corps would put in a diversionary attack beginning two hours (later changed to 30 minutes) before the main assault, with the aim of drawing off German reserves and preventing the enemy from reinforcing those parts of his line threatened by the main attack. Whatever the result of the Indian Corps' efforts might be, they could only be a diversion, as the bulk of the artillery ammunition must perforce be allocated to the divisions carrying out the main assault. The Indian Corps had in any case no reserves with which to reinforce any success the sepoys might achieve.

The Indian Corps was now allocated a third division, the British 19 Division, and held its sector with all three divisions in the line. To the south was 19 Division, linking up with the British I Corps on its right at a point opposite Le Plantin. The Lahore Division was in the centre, while to the north the Meerut Division held the front as far as the Winchester Road, which ran roughly north-west from Mauquissart to the Rue Tilleloy, where the Indian Corps joined with the British III Corps. The whole front-age held by the Indian Corps was about five and a half miles.

The warning order for what would become known as the Battle of Loos was issued on 30 August 1915 and the full orders were given out on 20 September. The Indian Corps diversion would involve the Lahore Division and 19 Division holding the present line, while the Meerut Division car-ried out the attack. From the village of Mauquissart was a road which ran south-west for 400 yards before it cut the German front line. The road then ran for a further 350 yards where it met the 'Duck's Bill', a fortified sap which ran south-east for 200 yards from the Indian line and was held by the 3rd Londons, of the Garhwal Brigade. The plan was for the attack to pivot on the Duck's Bill and swing south east, through the area between Winchester Road and Sunken Road, and establish a line running north-east to south-west, taking in Mauquissart and the road from there to the Duck's Bill. This projected new line was between 700 yards behind, and 200 yards in front of, the German firing line. From this new line the Meerut Division was to press on to the high ground around Haut Pommereau and La Cliqueterie, from where the Division would try to turn the La Bassée defences from the north. All this presupposed that, although the main attack on the Indian Corps' right would begin later than the diversionary attack, it would nevertheless have advanced sufficiently to ensure that the Indian Corps would not be interfered with by the Germans to their right. On the left of the Meerut Division's advance, the 12th Battalion The Rifle Brigade, from the British 60 Brigade, would protect the Indians' left flank.

The Meerut Division planned to attack with two brigades forward, the Bareilly Brigade left and the Garhwal Brigade right, with the Dehra Dun Brigade in divisional reserve. The Bareilly Brigade would have the 2nd Black Watch on the left, the 69th Punjabis in the centre and the 4th Black Watch on the right, while Vaughan's Rifles and the 33rd Punjabis would be in reserve. In the Garhwal Brigade the 2/8th Gurkhas would be on the left, the 2nd Leicesters in the centre and the 2/3rd Gurkhas on the right. The 3rd Londons would hold the Duck's Bill pivot on the extreme right and the 39th Garhwalis would be in reserve. Although described in the operation orders as being in reserve, the battalions so detailed should more properly be described as in support, for their role was to follow up the leading battalions ready to resupply them with ammunition, provide bombing parties and reinforce them if needed. There was therefore no brigade reserve, the distinction being that a reserve is held under the personal control of the brigade commander, and is only employed on his orders.

The entire operation would be preceded by four days of bombardment, including both artillery and the newly arrived Stokes trench mortar, much more accurate than the home-made contraptions produced by the Sappers and Miners. Shelling would necessarily be sparse on the Indian Corps front, in order to put maximum effort into the main attack, but some guns would be manhandled into the front line to smash down the enemy parapet and knock out machine-guns. The Meerut Division would be assisted by gas and by the explosion of a mine which the Sappers and Miners had positioned under a small German salient beside the Winchester Road, on the left flank of the Division's line of advance.

On 22 September the Lahore Division engaged in subterfuge. The artillery fired for five minutes on the German front line, switching to the enemy support line. The 47th Sikhs then waved their bayonets in the air and pushed dummies on poles over their own parapet, after which the artillery again concentrated on the German firing line with shrapnel. The idea was to make the Germans think an attack was in the offing and cause them to come out of their dugouts and line their parapet. The ruse had little effect, probably because the dummies had been sent up the previous day and the carrying parties had made little attempt to hide what they considered a pointless burden.

This would be the first time that the British used gas, and with what little was known about its properties, the Meerut Division staff had calculated that if all likely permutations of wind direction were to be catered for, 1,100 cylinders would be needed. In the event only 160 cylinders could be delivered, and the plans now had to be recast allowing for various options for their use depending upon the wind on the day. The cylinders were delivered to the firing line on the night of 23/24 September by the Royal Engineers, and were placed under cover to ensure that a German shell could not cause premature initiation. In addition to such artillery and gas as could be made available, the attack would be covered by smoke candles placed in no man's land, phosphorus bombs fired by catapult, the Sappers and Miners version of which could now reach out to 350 yards; and smoke shells fired by trench mortar. This was all very well, but it would not only be the German view that was restricted, but that of the friendly artillery observers too.

During the night the troops moved up to their positions for the attack. It was a slow process as heavily laden men followed one another up the narrow communication trenches, but by 2230 hours all the troops had managed to get into their assigned positions for the attack, Most were in trenches: some already being used, some previously abandoned and now recycled, and some specially prepared. In addition to his rifle and leather equipment each man carried 200 rounds of ammunition, an emergency ration and the day's pre-cooked ration in his haversack, two sand bags and a waterproof sheet. Each company of the battalions in support, who would follow up the first wave, carried 53 shovels, 16 picks, an illuminating pistol and extra supplies of anti-gas spray and bottles of solution for re-impregnating smoke helmets. Every man, attack or support, wore a balaclava and had two smoke helmets, one in the haversack as a spare and the rolled up on the top of his head ready to be pulled down when required. Flags in distinguishing brigade colours were carried to indicate limits of advance and signallers took not only telephone and line but heliograph equipment as well. In the battalions each company was ordered to detail 'one intelligent man' to move with battalion headquarters as a runner.

During the 24th the wind had been blowing from the west, directly towards the German lines at three to four miles per hour, ideal for the use of gas. During the night the wind changed, veering to coming from the south, and then from the south-west until at around 0300 hours it again appeared to be blowing from the desired, westerly, direction. At 0440 a German shell burst in the Duck's Bill, damaging the store of gas cylinders there, and at once gas began billowing forth. The Royal Engineers officer in charge of the gas detachment was incapacitated, as were one officer and 18 soldiers of the Londons and a bombing party from the Manchesters who were in the same trench. Fortunately the majority of the men quickly donned their smoke helmets and earth was shovelled onto the leaking cylinders before any further damage could ensue.

At 0548 the mine under the German position on the left flank was detonated. It went off with a tremendous bang which was heard miles away, and left a crater 92 feet wide and very little trace of the former occupants. At 0550 the artillery began an intense bombardment of the enemy front line. One of the three guns which had been positioned in the firing line discharged no fewer than 46 rounds in under five minutes, before being forced to cease fire when the opposing parapet was obscured by the smoke screen. At, this time too the gas was due to be released.

It was unfortunate that the Royal Engineers detachments manning the cylinders had been given no discretion as to whether or not to turn the cylinder taps on. They had been told to discharge gas at 0550 and, despite the demurral of a number of the infantry officers who had noticed that the wind no longer blew towards the enemy but was now blowing back towards the Indians' own trenches, the taps were turned to 'on'. Some of the gas simply stayed where it was, filling up the Indian trenches and moving slowly along them; some blew back towards the supporting battalions. After a certain amount of arguing the detachment commanders were prevailed upon to turn the cylinders off before too much damage had been done to their own side, but not before the smell had permeated right along and behind the line, necessitating everyone having to wear their smoke helmets with the consequent difficulties in hearing shouted orders and in seeing what was happening.

Despite the nonsense with the gas, the smoke screen was thickening up nicely and at 0600 the infantry assault began. The leading companies of the 2nd Leicesters and the 2/3rd Gurkhas reached the German wire with few casualties, and found that the only gaps in it were in the area where the two battalions joined. Men of both battalions rushed for these gaps, and despite the thick smoke which prevented anyone from seeing farther than a few yards, the Germans were alerted to the fact that their enemy was at the wire. Firing into the smoke the range was so short that the Germans could not help but begin to cause casualties as the Gurkhas and the Leicesters bunched together trying to get through the gaps. One company of the 2/3rd Gurkhas commanded by Brevet Lieutenant Colonel Brakspear with Lieutenant Tyson-Tyson as Company Officer, veered to its right and came up against uncut wire. There are no clear accounts of exactly what happened to them, but both British officers and many of their men were shot dead without ever penetrating the wire. A few individuals did manage to get through the wire and into the German trench, including

Lieutenant Wood of Number 4 Company, who got in with four men, all being killed except one rifleman.

The one survivor of Wood's party was a singular soldier indeed. Rifleman Kulbir Thapa, of the Magar clan came from Palpa[1] in West Nepal. According to his documents he was born in 1888, and even if in accordance with the common Gurkha practice he had added a couple of years to his real age in order to qualify for enlistment[*], he was an experienced soldier by 1915. Originally in the 1/3rd Gurkhas he had been transferred to the 2nd Battalion on the outbreak of war. Having forced his way through the wire Kulbir got into the German trenches where he was wounded. Finding himself the only survivor of Wood's little group he scrambled out of the trench on to the enemy side and began to take up a fire position. He then saw a badly wounded soldier of the 2nd Leicesters. Kulbir stayed with that soldier all day and all night, comforting him in what little English he had, and shooting any German who approached. On the morning of 26 September there was a thick fog and Kulbir picked up the wounded Leicester and carried him across the German trench, through the wire, and put him in a shell hole where he would be under cover. Kulbir then crossed back to the enemy side of the trench and, looking around, found two wounded Gurkhas of his own regiment who were unable to move. He picked up one of the Gurkhas and carried him back to the 39th Garhwalis, who were farther back in support. He returned and brought in the other wounded Gurkha. By now it was broad daylight and Kulbir, unable to move very fast nor to take cover, returned once more to the German trench and brought in the wounded Leicester, under enemy fire the while. For outstanding gallantry to be recognised officially it must be witnessed by a superior, and fortunately Kulbir's actions had been seen by an officer of the Leicesters and by several British officers of the Garhwalis. On 18 November 1915 the *London Gazette* carried the announcement of the award of the Victoria Cross to 2129 Rifleman Kulbir Thapa, 2nd Battalion 3rd Queen Alexandra's Own Gurkha Rifles.

Kulbir survived the war, returned with his battalion to India and eventually retired as a havildar. He died at his home in Nepal on 3 October 1958 aged 68[†].

While Kulbir was fighting his way through the German wire on the morning of 25 September, all was a mystery as far as the brigade and leading battalions' headquarters were concerned. The smoke prevented anyone from seeing what was going on at the point of the attack and

---

[*]   As they still do. In 1997 the author, then commanding the Gurkha recruit training centre, estimated that 20% of the recruits were under age on enlistment.

[†]   Or so it was claimed when he died. His 'Army age' was two years older.

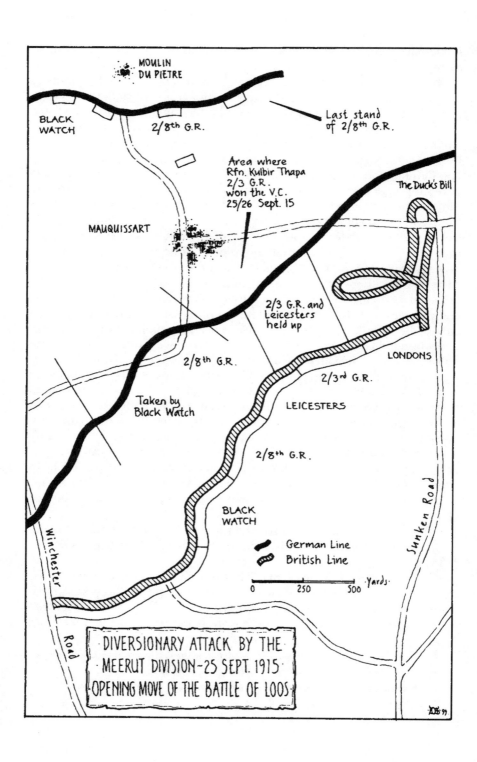

MOULIN DU PIETRE

BLACK WATCH

2/8th G.R.

Last stand of 2/8th G.R.

Area where
Rfn. Kulbir Thapa
2/3 G.R.
won the V.C.
25/26 Sept. 15

The Duck's Bill

MAUQUISSART

2/3 G.R. and Leicesters held up

2/8th G.R.

LONDONS

Taken by Black Watch

2/3rd G.R.

LEICESTERS

2/8th G.R.

BLACK WATCH

German Line
British Line

Sunken Road

Winchester

Road

Yards
0   250   500

DIVERSIONARY ATTACK BY THE
MEERUT DIVISION – 25 SEPT. 1915
OPENING MOVE OF THE BATTLE OF LOOS

nobody had yet been able to lay a telephone line. A third company of the 2/3rd Gurkhas was now sent forward at about 0630 hours. These men too hit the uncut wire and were shot down as they tried to get through it. The company disintegrated into a few groups of unwounded taking what cover they could in shell holes and folds in the ground. The only information which came back was a report that there was now a gap between the 2nd Leicesters and the 2/3rd, and to fill this gap half of the remaining company of the 2/3rd, under Subadar Bhimsing Thapa, was sent forward at about 0730 hours. Bhimsing and his men disappeared into the smoke and nothing was heard of them for four hours. Battalion headquarters sent patrols up to make contact with Bhimsing and bring back a report of the situation, but none of them ever returned. What was actually happening, but unknown to the battalion headquarters at the time, was that as the lines of men emerged from the smoke they were still on the wrong side of the enemy lines. Concentrated fire stopped them in their tracks.

Eventually, well after 1100 hours, a report came back from Subadar Bhimsing to the effect that the wire was uncut, the Germans still held their trenches and both the 2/3rd Gurkhas and the 2nd Leicesters were now coming under enfilade fire from both flanks. There was now only half a company of the 2/3rd not already committed and pinned down, and brigade headquarters issued instructions for those men to be placed under command of the 39th Garhwalis who were ordered to prepare to advance and reinforce the original attack.

The doings of the extreme left-hand battalion, the 2/8th Gurkhas, were unknown to anyone else in the Garhwal Brigade at this stage, but they had in fact made remarkable progress. During the previous night the Gurkhas had realised that the enemy line to their front was less heavily defended than was the rest of the sector, and they sent patrols out under cover of darkness to cut gaps in the German wire. Lieutenant Moran, in command of the wire cutting parties, and some of his men were killed and a number wounded, but they did manage to create lanes through the wire. When they advanced in the morning the 2/8th, pushing companies forward one after the other, were able to cross the obstacle belt and take the first line of German trenches. They swept through Mauquissart and attacked towards the German second, support, line and it was here that the casualties began to mount. The 2/8th had now lost all contact with the 2nd Leicesters on the right, that battalion having been held up on the wire protecting the enemy firing line, and thus were open to enfilade fire from untouched German positions to their right. The Gurkhas were, however, in contact with the right-hand battalion of the Bareilly Brigade, the 4th Black Watch, which was also making headway. By 0830 the 2/8th were in possession of a portion of the German support line about 300 yards south-east of Mauquissart and just short of Moulin du Pietre. The battalion had advanced 800 yards, but had only one British officer left.

By 1130 hours a runner from the Garhwal Brigade headquarters had reached the 2/8th with orders for the senior officer of that battalion to return to the brigade headquarters, report the situation and then exercise command from the original front line trenches. Here was a conflict: the need for the brigade headquarters to know what the up-to-date situation was, in order that they could influence the battle by the use of reserves, balanced against the need to command the battalion, which in this case could only be done from the front. Whatever his thoughts may have been, Captain Buckland—not just the senior but the only British officer left to the 2/8th Gurkhas—did return. The brigade headquarters now knew the situation facing the 2nd Leicesters and the 2/3rd Gurkhas, and of the achievements of the 2/8th Gurkhas. The mission given to the Garhwalis was now changed: they would exploit the successes of the 2/8th and try to extend those gains to the right.

Meanwhile the Bareilly Brigade, on the left of the Meerut Division's attack, had suffered mixed fortunes. At first all appeared to be going to plan: the mine had exploded on the left flank of the 2nd Black Watch, the left-hand battalion of the brigade, and had left the enemy occupants of that portion of their trench dead or unable to offer any resistance. As soon as the gas was turned on, however, it blew back amongst the soldiers waiting to advance. A number were incapacitated, but once the battalion had advanced under the command of Major Wauchope* they were able to get clear of the gas and press on. As the three leading battalions reached the German wire they found it had been well cut by the artillery and they were able to fight their way across it with relatively few casualties. After a hasty search of the German positions—too hasty as it transpired—the 2nd Black Watch, the 60th Punjabis and the 4th Black Watch moved on past Mauquissart and reached the German second line in front of Moulin du Pietre. Because of the unsettling effects of their own gas, the thick smoke and the casualties caused by the German defenders of the second line, many of the companies and battalions were mixed in with each other, but the right-hand battalion, the 4th Black Watch, managed to make contact with the 2/8th Gurkhas. The Highianders went firm behind and in support of the Gurkhas.

Also amongst the groups which got through the German firing line and on to the second line in front of the Moulin was a group of Vaughan's Rifles, who had no business to be there at all.

Vaughan's Rifles were in support but their orders had been clear: they were to occupy the trenches vacated by the 2nd Black Watch when the latter started to advance, and were on no account to move forward until

---

* A member of a famous Scottish family. An ancestor was at Waterloo and another was killed commanding the Highland Brigade at Maegersfontein.

ordered by the Brigade Commander, unless the Scots were in extreme difficulties—which they were not at this point—or unless there were no communications with brigade headquarters. In the inquiry after the attack the Brigade Commander, Norie of the 2nd Gurkhas in lieu of Southey, was adamant that telephone communications to his headquarters were working and that no orders to advance had been given to Vaughan's Rifles. As the Commanding Officer of Vaughan's, Lieutenant Colonel Davidson-Houston, was killed, and his orderly who was also the telephone operator wounded and captured, we shall never know why the battalion did advance. Davidson-Houston, although the youngest of the battalion commanders in the Indian Corps, was a very experienced officer, and he would have had sound reasons for ignoring orders. Whatever the rationale, Vaughan's Rifles duly occupied the 2nd Black Watch trenches at Zero Hour, and at 0615 two companies advanced and crossed the German front line trenches where they began to dig shell scrapes. The battalion's other two companies passed through and reached the German second line, where they placed themselves under the orders of the 2nd Black Watch.

By mid-day, when the Garhwal Brigade Headquarters was trying to launch a reinforcing attack by the 39th Garhwalis, the Debra Dun Brigade should have been well forward and ready for action. In fact they were only now arriving in the Garhwali trenches, adding to the confusion caused by gassed and wounded men, the smoke and the ever present mud and water. As happened so often in this war, the need for reserves and reinforcements to be well forward so that they could act quickly and decisively was fully recognised. The practicalities of getting large numbers of men near enough to the battle area to be able to deploy rapidly, while at the same time keeping them protected from fire until they were needed, would not be solved until the invention of the tank and the armoured personnel carrier, a form of mobile protection not available in 1915.

The Meerut Division had achieved its objectives, but the situation was serious. There was a narrow and tenuous corridor reaching out from the Division's front line as far as the Moulin du Pietre, but the left flank of the Bareilly Brigade was in the air. Some men of the 12th Rifle Brigade, which should have been protecting that flank, had appeared but of the rest of the battalion there was no sign. The two companies of Vaughan's Rifles, which should not have been there at all, took up positions to protect the left flank of the 2nd Black Watch as best they could. The Germans were now attacking on the Bareilly Brigade left flank with bombing parties supported by machine-guns.

To the right of the Meerut Division the main British attack should by now have reached and gone beyond the Indian objectives. Unfortunately there were problems. The British were to attack on a five-mile front between La Bassée and Lens, using six divisions in the first assault. Despite the Indian Corps' use of gas earlier, the information does not seem to have been passed to the Germans farther south. The failure by the Germans to pass information was of little consequence, however, for only in the southern portion of the front was the British gas reasonably successful; elsewhere it either blew back towards the British, hung about where it was released, or moved towards the enemy lines so slowly that the advancing British troops caught it up and suffered accordingly. On the 2 Division front, immediately to the right of the Meerut Division, the gas had harmed no one but the British, and the enemy line was stoutly defended. After an initial advance 2 Division was thrown back to its original lines with heavy casualties.

The Meerut Division now became a victim of its own success. By creating a narrow salient in the German positions, but with no corresponding advance by the 2nd Division to cover the right flank, and the failure of 60 British Brigade to protect the left, the Indians came under increasing pressure on both flanks from an enemy determined to snip off this inconvenient intrusion. Casualties, already serious, began to mount.

At the point of the Indian lodgement, along the German second line by the Moulin du Pietre, the detachment of Vaughan's Rifles was trying to hold the left of the captured German line. Next to Vaughan's, and opposite the mill by the road running to Mauquissart, was the 2nd Black Watch while the 2/8th Gurkhas held the right of the captured area. Behind the Black Watch were the remainder of the Vaughan's, who had now come up, and the 69th and 33rd Punjabis, while the 4th Black Watch were behind the 2/8th. To call any of these units battalions is a misnomer. Most by now had only 50% of the numbers with which they had started the day, although the 2/8th Gurkhas had commandeered a platoon-sized carrying party of the 39th Garhwalis which had been sent up with resupplies of bombs and ammunition. All were now subjected to constant probing attacks by German infantry and bombing parties, and under heavy fire from the ubiquitous machine-guns. Back in the original front line both the Garhwalis' Commanding Officer and the Commander of the newly arrived Dehra Dun Brigade were trying to organise attacks, but the chaos caused by four battalions crowding into communication trenches and a firing line designed for one, to say nothing of the congestion caused by stretcher bearers and ammunition carrying parties, made this a difficult business until the two commanders agreed to move the Dehra Dun Brigade farther back to where they could spread out. Drake-Brockman, commanding the Garhwalis, agreed with Harvey, commanding the Dehra Dun Brigade, that there was little point in them both attempting an attack and that it should be a joint effort. As the afternoon wore on and the smoke began to clear, both commanders began to have increasing doubts as to whether anything could usefully be achieved, and these doubts were emphasised when it became known that there would be no artillery to support any attack.

One company of the Garhwalis and one of the 2/2nd Gurkhas were sent forward mid-afternoon. The Garhwali company was led by Lieutenant Jodha Jang Bahadur Rana, a nephew of the Rajah of 'Foreign Garhwal' and a relation of the hereditary Prime Minister of Nepal, attached to the 39th Garhwal Rifles from his own state's forces. The two companies got 40 yards from their own position and no farther—some only as far as their own parapet. Those few not killed or wounded could do nothing but take cover and wait for dark. Conspicuous for his bravery and sound military sense during that day was Lieutenant Jodha, who was subsequently awarded the Military Cross.

Up near the Moulin a major German counter-attack now materialised and it was clear that no more could be achieved. The Indian Corps had done what it had been ordered to do and had tied down considerable numbers of Germans. To try to remain in possession of a narrow salient under increasing danger of being cut off would achieve nothing and only waste lives unnecessarily. The Meerut Division was instructed to retire to its original trenches. As dusk approached the remains of the battalions pulled back in stages, groups covering each other by fire and then retreating themselves in short rushes. It was now that the enthusiasm which encouraged the Bareilly Brigade to press on beyond the German first line without thoroughly clearing its bunkers and dugouts began to exact its toll. German soldiers who had concealed themselves from the first rush emerged and began to fire at the withdrawing sepoys. The retirement degenerated into a series of scrappy and confused local fights as the men pulled back under fire from in front and behind. By last light, however, the Indian Corps was back in its original trenches. The total casualties of the two Indian divisions of the Corps in their one-day participation in the battle of Loos amounted to 3,973, including the alarming total of 156 British officers. Vaughan's Rifles alone, never ordered forward but very useful when they did join in, lost eight British officers killed, wounded or missing, out of an establishment of 12, and 251 Indian officers and other ranks. The 69th Punjabis started the day with 11 British officers and ended it with three, a major, a lieutenant and a second lieutenant, five of the others being killed and three wounded.

Haig's report of 26 September 1915 includes the words: 'The GOC is very pleased with the manner in which the I, III and Indian Corps carried out the role assigned to them of retaining the enemy on their front.'[2] Sir John French, in his despatch of 15 October 1915 said:

The Indian Corps attacked the Moulin du Pietre while the III Corps was directed against the trenches at Le Bridoux. These attacks started at daybreak and were at first successful all along the line. Later in the day the enemy brought up strong reserves, and after hard fighting and variable fortunes, the troops engaged in this part of the line reoccupied the original trenches at nightfall. They succeeded admirably, however, in fulfilling the role allotted to them, and in holding large numbers of the enemy away from the main attack.[3]

The diversionary attack on the first day of the Battle of Loos was the last major operation undertaken by the Indian Corps on the Western Front. The battle itself would grind on for another fortnight, and is generally agreed to have been a disaster for the British. The concept had been imaginative, and had it worked might have achieved great things, but the failure to commit the two reserve divisions until 24 hours after they were needed contributed to Loos being classified as a bloody 'might have been'.

The Indian Corps now continued to hold the same sector of the front where they had been for so long, virtually since arriving in France. After Loos the Indian front, including that portion held by the British 19 Division, stretched for six and a half miles, from north of Neuve Chapelle to the La Bassée canal. Patrolling, sapping and tunnelling continued, and on 8 October and 27 October German attacks on the Indian firing line were beaten off, the latter being preceded by the explosion of a German mine, once again under the Duck's Bill sap. Reinforcements were still arriving, but they were never enough and could not in any way keep pace with the casualties—indeed the men who had so far been sent as reinforcements outnumbered the entire corps strength on its arrival in France. Most battalions now had fewer than 100 men who had been with them throughout and there were hardly any of the original officers left. In the 47th Sikhs there were no British or Indian officers and only 28 sepoys who had been with the regiment since arriving at the front and who had not been away due to wounds or sickness. In the Scinde Rifles, before they departed for Egypt, the figures were no British officers, four Indian officers and 75 sepoys.

Individual actions continued to be fought. On 2 October a patrol of one NCO and six sepoys from the 47th Sikhs was sent out to attack a German listening post which was in no man's land. It was in a low-lying bit of ground and could not be seen from the 47th Sikhs' own trenches, but its presence allowed the enemy to detect patrols leaving the Indian lines and to call down fire on them by telephone. The Sikh patrol went out during the night and managed to surround the listening post before it was detected. A bombing fight ensued and the patrol withdrew with no casualties. On return to his own lines the patrol commander discovered that one young sepoy, only recently arrived in France and sent out with the patrol as part of his education, had left his rifle behind. This was still regarded by the Sikhs as a terrible disgrace, and two havildars and a lance naik volunteered to go out and retrieve the lost weapon. By now it was daylight but the three crawled out and got to the rifle, when they were attacked by a 12-man strong enemy patrol. The naik was shot and killed and the two havildars attempted to withdraw with the naik's body and the rifle. Unable to do so one of the havildars stayed with the body while the other got back to his company trench and asked for help. The company commander refused to allow any more men to risk their lives for a body and a rifle. The havildar returned to his comrade and the pair managed to withdraw unscathed, with the rifle but without the body. The dead man, Lance Naik Buta Singh, was an honoured member of the regiment. He had been awarded the IDSM for gallantry on 26 October 1914, had been wounded at Second Ypres and had a reputation for sneaking over to the enemy lines and removing flags and propaganda notices which were posted there. Eventually, on 30 October, a patrol from the 47th Sikhs did recover his body. It was by then in a state of putrefaction, but honour was satisfied.

Ever since March and the heavy losses at Neuve Chapelle, the possibility of moving the Indian Corps from the Western Front had been mooted. It was not because they could not cope with the requirements of modern war—far from it—but simply because, smaller than a British corps to begin with, their strength continued to dwindle. The reinforcement system, as we have seen, did not work, and the wider involvement of the Indian Army in other theatres—the Middle East, Gallipoli and Africa being the major commitments—made it increasingly difficult to sustain the force on the Western Front while still maintaining all the other expeditionary forces and retaining sufficient troops in India to ensure law and order and the defence of the frontiers. Originally the presence of the Indian Corps had been vital to the British effort in France—in 1914 they were the only source of trained reinforcement. Now the Canadians had started to arrive in force and the New Army divisions were almost ready—indeed the first two to be sent overseas had participated in the Battle of Loos. It was felt that the Indian Corps could now be spared from the Western Front and redeployed to Mesopotamia where, so opinion ran, they could more easily be supported from home and where they would adapt to the climatic conditions and the nature of the terrain more easily than would British troops. As it happened, the Indian Corps exchanged a bad situation for another far worse. Administration in Mesopotamia broke down and an overextended and ill supplied force suffered dreadfully from disease and the over-optimism of Generals Nixon and Townshend. But that, as they say, is another story.

An announcement that the Indian Corps would embark at Marseilles for an unknown destination was made on 31 October. The British 19 Division would remain in France, as would the British territorial battalions in the Lahore and Meerut Divisions. The announcement was not universally welcomed. Some of the Indian officers and sepoys thought that the removal of the Corps from the Western Front was a slight on their prowess; others felt that as the war had not been won, the Indian Army should not leave until it was. The British officers understood this feeling, and sympathised with it, but the stark facts were that the Corps could not be maintained at its former strength or level of efficiency and it now could, and should, be transferred to another front. On 4 November 1915 the Indian Corps began to be relieved in the front line by the British XI Corps, and the units of the original two divisions were withdrawn to billets prior to entraining for Marseilles. By 10 November 1915 the last unit of the Indian Corps had left the Front.

In reviewing the actions of the Indian Army during its 15 months in the trenches of France and Flanders, it is relevant to examine what effect residence in Europe had on the sepoys. Many senior British officers and officials of the Indian and British governments had been concerned that taking part in a European war might politicise the Army. The sepoys would see how the Europeans lived and went about their lives, and they might contrast that with conditions back home, to the detriment of the latter. The experiences of the soldiers might bolster the fledgling political movements in India, some of which sought a cessation of British rule and independence. It was these concerns that caused so much attention to be paid to the Censor of Indian Mails' reports, but in fact none of the worries seem to have been realised. Certainly the Indians were impressed by aspects of France. They generally liked the French and admired the French way of doing things. Many, particularly the Sikhs and Pathans, learned enough French to buy small luxuries in the shops and enjoy a glass of wine in the estaminets, but any ideas of Liberty, Equality and Brotherhood which might have been supposed to rub off were very largely ignored, unnoticed or not considered to be valid for military men. The soldiers were enlisted from the most loyal, and politically inert, part of the Indian population. Their careers and livelihoods depended upon the British, and while the men themselves had no experience of alternative employers, enough had been handed down from their elders for them to accept implicitly that the British were better masters than the Moghuls or the Maharajahs, and the British were at least fair and untouched by prejudices of caste or religion.

The French liked the Indians and got on well with them. Initially fearful of these wild-looking men who spoke no known language, and reluctant to billet them in their homes, they soon came to appreciate the natural good manners and self-disciplined ways of the Indian soldier, and to prefer them to other Allied troops as lodgers. Mostly farmers themselves, the sepoys understood the problems faced by civilians living in a war zone, and often helped with harvesting and gathering of crops. In the mid 1970s the author met an old lady in Neuve Chapelle who had lived in Richebourg as a child during the Great War. Asked if she remembered the Indian Army in the area, her son interjected 'Ah, the Pakistanis!'. 'Non,' snapped the old lady, 'Les Hindoues. Très bon, très bon, très civilatricé'.

England had less influence on the Indians. Other than some Indian officers who visited on leave from the Front for short periods, it was only the recuperating wounded and the staffs of the hospitals who spent any length of time in England. The largest Indian military community was in Brighton, where there were two Indian military hospitals, and relations appear to have been excellent. The *Brighton Herald and Hove Chronicle* of 2 January 1915 reported the arrival of a train-load of Indian wounded:

It would have to be admitted that Brighton could not have made a favourable first impression on these gallant warriors from sunny India. It was a dreadful day of howling wind and drenching rain. All the same, people gave the Indians a warm enough greeting. The station was very busy with the Christmas traffic and there was a large gathering under cover to cheer the khaki motor ambulances as they passed out into Queen's Road. The best greeting of all came from a company of the blue-clad soldiers of Kitchener's Army who happened to be forming up in Queen's Road at the time. These young soldiers who have their battles yet to fight gave to these men who have fought the heartiest of cheers.

The other local paper, the *Brighton Advertiser and Sussex County Herald*, said: 'It was a distinct compliment to Brighton when the powers that be decided to send wounded Indian soldiers to that town'.

A perusal of the local papers of 1915 shows that the Indians were popular members of the community. The activities of the wounded, and of the Indian Corps in France, got much wider coverage locally than they did in the national press. Both Brighton papers took a great interest in Havildar Ganga Singh of Wilde's Rifles, the gymnast who had so effectively disposed of a number of Germans in the confused fighting of First Ypres. Ganga had been evacuated to Brighton where he was recovering from his wounds, and bulletins on his health were regularly carried. The *Herald* had erroneously reported that Ganga had been awarded the Victoria Cross, and then later had to explain that he had not, while insisting that he should certainly receive some recognition for his conduct. He was, of course, awarded the IOM.

A common thread throughout the reports in the Brighton papers during the year when soldiers of the Indian Army lived there was the typical, for the time, attitude towards them as loveable pets. The *Herald* carried an article in January 1915 headlined 'Indians in our Street' and asked 'Is this really our old Brighton?' The text refers to the Indians as being visitors who 'ever manifest the friendliest disposition' and goes on to relate the tale of an Indian doctor who entered a local restaurant for lunch. As it was bitterly cold he was invited by gesture to sit by the fire, and the customer who made way for him noted that 'he had the most beautiful teeth'. The waitress was so amazed at the doctor's wishing her 'good morning' in English that 'the salutation nearly made her drop a dish'. The other customers engaged the doctor in conversation and he is quoted as asking 'Is this really Brighton weather? And yet you call Brighton a health resort!' The paper admonishes:

> We desire to assure our Indian visitor that it does not always rain in Brighton so pitilessly through December—sometimes it snows. We hope that he will remain until the Spring. Then he will know that Brighton can be very gracious and very charming to a degree not to be imagined in these dark days of cold winds, drenching rain, gales and frowning skies.

Many editions of the Brighton newspapers refer to the concern felt by residents about the deterioration in standards of behaviour brought about by the war. 'Lewes is the most immoral town in England, and the Brighton area generally,' thundered one published letter. This was at a time when the readers of the Brighton papers could follow avidly the trial of the Reverend Elliot, a local vicar accused of fathering a bastard child on one of his servants (he got off), and when crime of all sorts was considered to be rife. The crime rate in the Brighton area was actually pretty small beer by modern standards, the chief offence seemingly driving a motor vehicle without a licence or without lights at night (officers mostly), or fraudulently collecting money for charity. There was much concern about sexual liaisons between British soldiers and local girls, so much so that Lewes Council introduced a bye-law which placed a curfew on young women out alone after 8pm. Although never explicitly stated, there is allusion to prostitution, and to affairs conducted by women whose husbands were away at the Front. Prostitution inevitably flourishes, then as now, wherever soldiers are stationed, but the impression given by the local newspapers is that the soldiers were unwary victims of predatory females and that it was all the fault of the women.

In all the court reports, fulmination against immorality and stories of indiscipline, there is never a reference to any Indian involvement. British soldiers got into trouble, were arrested and hauled before the magistrates and their cases reported, but either the sepoys were paragons of virtue, the press was not aware of any misdemeanours by them, or the Army hushed up any incidents. It was probably a combination of all three. Indian soldiers were generally well behaved; discipline in the Indian hospitals was strict; the local population seem to have welcomed the Indian presence in their towns and the Indian Army was very concerned to retain its good name. The only passing reference to any sort of Indian connection with crime was when one William Francis Vidler, of 1 Guardswell Place, Lewes, was sentenced to six months hard labour for attempting to seduce two West Indian soldiers from their allegiance by telling them in a public house that they should not be involving themselves in a white man's war. The reported evidence mentioned that there were two sepoys present, but that they left when the argument started and had not been traced.

Indian soldiers in England did contract venereal disease*, as the sick returns show, and they did have liaisons with local women. A storekeeper in the Kitchener Hospital wrote:

> This place is very picturesque and the Indians are liked very much here. The girls of this place are notorious and are very fond of accosting Indians and fooling with them, they are ever ready for any purpose, and in truth are no better than the girls of Adda bazaar in Indore.[4]

Whether the sepoys with venereal disease had been involved with prostitutes or with enthusiastic amateurs is unknown, but it may be that at a time when cross-race sexual frolics would have been regarded with disapproval, such matters were deliberately not reported so as not to besmirch British womanhood.

Despite the weather, Indians liked being in England and nearly all their letters speak approvingly of the country and the people. The more intelligent made the connection between wealth and education, considering that the latter led to the former. One civilian postal worker saw the dangers of copying the appearance of British ways without absorbing the substance. He wrote to a friend in Rawlpindi in November 1915:

> Our people copy the faults of the British nation and leave its good qualities alone. We shall never advance ourselves merely by wearing trousers and hats and smoking cigarettes and drinking wine. In fact they have a real moral superiority. They are energetic. We are poor and hunger for ease. They limit their leisure, do their work justly and do it well. They do not follow their own inclinations but obey their superior officers and masters. They avoid idle chatter ... they delight in cleanliness ... never under any circumstances do they tell lies ... they do not marry until they have reached maturity. For a lad of 16 to marry and beget children is looked upon with disapproval ...'[5]

A Mahratta sub assistant surgeon wrote in the same month a perceptive description of the different mores found in England:

> The fear that you entertain about my falling in love with a girl here is

---

* Although the incidence of sexually transmitted diseases among Indian troops was much lower than that for the British.

not without foundation, but my poor circumstances are in my way. The girls of this part are so anxious to marry that even I met one. She said, 'no matter how poor you may be I am quite ready to live openly with you'. Such is the position of all my friends here, but my friends are all married, so their condition is different. Nevertheless in one case although a plurality of wives is not allowed here a girl said to one of my friends that she was quite happy to marry him and live with his Indian wife without any argument ... many of the [British] men here are opposed to marriage because the girls are more numerous than the men and when I ask some of the girls why they do not marry they reply 'With whom am I to marry? If you are ready then come, for I am.' Here the men procure women without having to marry them, why should they therefore marry?

... Once married the men are not allowed to go with other girls because of the control the wife exercises, so the men come to the conclusion that it is best not to marry ... Ultimately there is the Government old age pension so the idea is to enjoy themselves while they can ... [6]

In general, then, the effect of an influx of Indians upon the French and British populations was minimal. Conversely, any ideas that the Indians might have picked up from their exposure to the west were largely forgotten on return to India, where the old conservative attitudes still held. It would be another generation that would take British ideas of liberalism and self-determination and adapt them to an Indian context.

The departure of the Indian Corps from the Western Front is an apposite point in this account to examine some of the criticisms made about it, then and later. It had long been said that the British Army was not an army at all but a collection of regiments. Every regiment had its own peculiarities of dress, drill, tradition and custom. The name of the regiment had to be preserved at all costs, which is why British regimental histories in isolation make unreliable sources for controversial facts, and most regular British officers and soldiers believed that their particular battalion was better than any other. All this had its strengths, and it did reinforce fighting spirit in adverse situations, but it could also lead to unhelpful sniping and uninformed criticism of other regiments which happened to do things in a different way. It is perhaps unsurprising, therefore, that the deeds of the Indian Army on the Western Front were not viewed with total admiration by all other components of the BEF. People generally accept that which they know and are suspicious of that which is different. The Indian Army, with its unfamiliar forms of dress, religious and dietary differences and plethora of languages, was an easy target for the ignorant or the malicious, and the Indians' cause was not assisted by the wildly exaggerated accounts of their doings which appeared in some sections of the British press. The Indian Corps was (sometimes) reported as doing its share of killing Germans, but the implication that the British units were not rankled with the latter.

We have already disposed of the accusation that Indian troops had an unusually high rate of self-inflicted wounds, but a far more damaging, and lasting, canard was that they behaved in a cowardly fashion during their early days on the Western Front. This suggestion comes from an account written by Private Frank Richards DCM MM[7] and has been repeated by a number of subsequent writers. Richards was a regular soldier of the Royal Welsh Fusiliers who wrote a number of books in his latter years. His tales have the ring of authenticity, and he became something of a cult figure. That the Foreword to *Old Soldiers Never Die* was written by Robert Graves was no doubt taken as confirmation of what was in the body of the text.

Richards was not, of course, an historian, nor would he have claimed to be. He was an old soldier, of the type common in the pre-war regular army, and he was telling his tale as he remembered it. Like all old soldiers' tales his will have improved with age, and *Old Soldiers Never Die* was first published 19 years after the events which it relates. As Richards' memoirs are frequently cited as a source, his allegations bear examination.

Richards says that his battalion left the Aisne to march north 'in the first week of October 1914' and that passing through St Omer, Ballieul and Laventie the 2nd Royal Welsh Fusiliers took up a position on the far side of Fromelles. He says that two days later the battalion moved back through Fromelles and dug trenches 400 yards west of that village. According to Richards a 'Battalion of Indian Native Infantry' was on the Royal Welsh Fusiliers' right and that on the third day in that position the left-hand platoon of the Indian battalion 'had lost its white officer, and the enemy shelling had put the wind up them'. Richards says that a German attack was met by fire from his battalion but that the Indian sepoys would not show their heads above the parapet and merely fired in the air. Every evening after that 'until the native infantry were relieved by a British battalion' 12 men of the Royal Welsh Fusiliers are said to have been sent over to the Indian trenches and to have stayed there all night. These men are claimed to have found the Indians 'weeping and wailing, with no sentry out and they had not bothered to remove their own dead from the trenches'. The Fusiliers 'cursed them in Hindustani' and finding that of no avail kicked and threatened the sepoys 'as they might have hopped it in the dark. Native Infantry were no good in France,' says Richards, 'some writers in the Press said that they couldn't stand the cold weather but the truth was that they suffered from cold feet and a few enemy shells exploding round their trenches were enough to demoralise the majority of them.'

Although Richards is vague about dates, the facts, taken from the Official History, are that 19 Brigade, of which the 2nd Battalion The Royal Welsh Fusiliers was a part, moved into position east of Fromelles at first light on 21 October 1914 and were pushed back on 22 October when they took up a new defensive position 2,000 yards north-west of the village. On 15 November the brigade was relieved and did not return to that area. On the night of 24 October the Jullunder Brigade took post to the right of 19 Brigade, so Richards' account can only refer to the period 24 October to 15 November. The 19 Brigade war diary[8] tells us however that the 2nd Royal Welsh Fusiliers were never the right-hand battalion of the brigade, but were in the centre, and never contiguous to a battalion of the Indian Corps. It was the 1st Battalion The Royal Fusiliers which was ordered by 19 Brigade to take over the right-hand sector from French dismounted cavalry and to make contact with the Indian Corps. The war diary of the 2nd Royal Welsh Fusiliers for the period agrees with the brigade diary and contains nothing to support Richards' account.

The Royal Fusthers war diary[9] for 24 October says: 'We had been asked to take up a line protecting the RWF right, but found that the Indian troops had also had the same orders and were there first'. The situation was sorted out and the Royal Fusiliers took up a position on the right of 19 Brigade. To their right again was the Jullunder Brigade. The left-hand battalion of the Jullunder Brigade was the Scinde Rifles with one company of the 34th Sikh Pioneers. In front of both 19 Brigade and the left-hand portion of the Jullunder Brigade line was a French cyclist battalion and a French cavalry brigade (dismounted) until they were removed once the British/Indian line was established. On the night of 24/25 October 16 men of the 34th Sikh Pioneers were wounded, mostly in the hands and upper body due to firing over the parapet. The Royal Fusiliers war diary for 26 October says: 'The Sikhs kept up a goodly fire all night', and on 27th we read: 'Another attack at 1am on the Sikhs, but none on us.' There is no further reference to Indian units in the war diaries of 19 Brigade, the Welsh Fusiliers or the Royal Fusiliers, and on 1 November the 47th Sikhs took over from the Scinde Rifles and the company of the 34th Sikh Pioneers until relieved by the Scinde Rifles once again on 10 November. There was never a relief by a British battalion as Richards alleges. During the entire period all three Indian battalions sustained considerable casualties—which would indicate that they were certainly not sheltering at the bottom of their trenches—but at no stage were any so short of British officers as not to have supervision of their entire frontage. All three battalions were congratulated by name by both the Divisional and the Corps Commander for their actions during the period and, as we have seen earlier, all displayed aggression and dogged determination to hold their portion of the line.

Richards, like many pre-war regular British Other Ranks who had served in India, did not like Indians. Much of this was simple xenophobia. The British working class of 1914, being at the bottom of the heap in their own country, disliked non-white peoples—and indeed any foreigners—because they had to find someone to despise and ridicule. Some of it was jealousy: Indian solders performed better in the Indian climate than did their British counterparts, and Indian regiments won most of the sporting competitions, with the possible exception of football. It would appear that Richards was simply making up the story in an attempt to justify his hatred of anything not English (or Welsh), although there is another possibility.

At the time of Richards' account there were French colonial troops in the area and it is just conceivable that, if the incident took place at all, Richards is actually referring to them, which would explain the inability of the 'Native troops' to understand Hindustani. Richards and his friends would have been unlikely to have distinguished between coloured troops in the French service and those in the British. In any event it may reasonably be assumed that Richards' memory was failing him when he wrote his book and that this excoriation can be considered to be without foundation.

SOURCE NOTES

1. See Chapter VII for comments on the over-recruitment of Gurkhas from Palpa.
2. Quoted in *The Indian Corps in France*, Merewether and Smith, John Murray, London, 1919.
3. Supplement to *London Gazette*, Oct 1915, HMSO.
4. 'Report of the Censor of Indian Mails France 1914 – 1918 Vol I', India Office Library and Records, L/MIL/5/825.
5. Ibid.
6. Ibid.
7. *Old Soldiers Never Die*, Frank Richards with Foreword by Robert Graves, Faber & Faber, 1933. The uncharitable (who include this author) might be forgiven for suspecting that the whole thing was written by Graves, drawing on Richards as a source.
8. War Diary 19 Brigade 1914, Public Record Office London, WO/95/1364.
9. War Diary 1st Bn Royal Fusiliers 1914, Public Record Office London, WO/95/1613.

Epilogue

The Indian Army had not been organised or intended for high intensity warfare against a first-class enemy. If it raised its sights at all from frontier skirmishes and punitive expeditions it was towards Russia, and although the threat from that quarter had receded by 1914—if indeed it ever existed—Indian Army thinking was largely directed to a delaying battle against an army of reluctant conscripts with little technical backing. An accurate rifle, a few machine-guns and fit, hardy and well motivated soldiery could hold the Russian hordes long enough for help to arrive, and might even beat them without it. Some officers of the Indian Army had given consideration to war in Europe and they had the tacit backing of the British Army. When the call came in August 1914 no one, in either the British or the Indian Armies, had any idea what the war would be like. The British Army was trained and equipped for a war of manoeuvre and few had predicted that the fighting would quickly develop into a succession of assaults on static and increasingly fortified lines of trenchworks, interspersed with long periods in defence.

Nobody in pre-war India had given much thought to the maintenance of a large force in the field for long periods. At 2,333 British officers and 159,134 Indian ranks the pre-war Indian Army was only slightly smaller than the British, and it considered that it got the best officer material emerging from Sandhurst and Woolwich. There was no Indian equivalent of the Territorial Force and no reserve system worthy of the name, but if the Indian Army was to have any influence in matters of imperial defence, and if its officers were to retain credibility with their British counterparts, the Indian Army had to fight in the main theatre of their war, and that meant the Western Front.

Despite the varying quality of the sea transport provided for the Corps, it arrived in Marseilles complete and with high morale. It was a pity that the Sirhind Brigade had been retained in Egypt for a time, but even so had First Ypres not intervened the Corps could have been given time to retrain on the new rifle and get used to the new four-company organisation. That they could not be given that time meant that they could not at first produce that fast and accurate marksmanship which was a hallmark of the British regular battalions of the BEF. The Indians were given no winter uniforms until late December 1914, but British soldiers of the New Armies had none either. British industry was not yet ready to supply mass armies and would not be as long as the officially stated 'business as usual' policy held good.

The dispersal of the Indian Corps during First Ypres came as a sudden shock. It was bad enough trying to adjust to a completely foreign country, the weather and the intensity of the fighting, but to be thrown in as they were in battalions, half battalions and even single companies under command of, and flanked by, people whom they did not know and with whom only the British officers could communicate, was to disorient and confuse them. While many of the sepoys had been under fire before, it had been from frontier tribesmen armed with rifles and without machine-guns of any sort. Shelling was a totally new experience. Given all this, it is frankly amazing that the Indian regiments and battalions did so well at First Ypres. Their presence, blocking up gaps in the already desperately thin and stretched Allied line, was just enough and just in time to prevent German breakthrough, a breakthrough which if it did not reach the Channel ports and finish the war, could certainly have captured Ypres and reached well beyond.

Just prior to taking over their own sector of Front the Indian Corps succeeded in recapturing the village of Neuve Chapelle in October 1914 after it had been lost by the British, albeit that they could not hold it. The sepoys fought doggedly at Festubert and Givenchy in 1914, and while no ground was gained neither was any of significance lost. At Neuve Chapelle in 1915 the Indian Corps were the first troops of the BEF to break the German line and to hold what they had captured. That no further progress was made towards Aubers Ridge was due to the lack of artillery ammunition and the inability of the British 8 Division to make progress on the Indians' left.[*] At Second Ypres the Lahore Division was moved up into the Salient and arrived just in time to stem the German advance and to push them back. We now know that the Germans were not seeking a major breakthrough— they did not have the reserves to exploit it—but were concerned solely with Ypres. That said, the situation was serious enough, involving as it did the first use of gas. The Germans regarded Second Ypres as a defeat and awarded no battle honours for it. At Aubers Ridge and at Festubert 1915, which overlapped with Second Ypres, the battalions of the Indian Corps attacked with great gallantry and determination but initial successes could not be exploited and the wire and the machine-guns prevented any meaningful gains. At Loos the Corps implemented the first British use of gas, and did all that was asked of it. It was the failure of the main attack to advance on the Indians' right that prevented further success.

---

[*]   Rawlinson, the Corps Commander, wanted to sack the divisional commander, Maj Gen Davies, but was eventually persuaded not to.

Throughout its 15 months on the Western Front the Indian Corps lived up to the highest traditions of the old Indian Army, despite horrific casualties and in particular the casualties in British officers. British and French battalions had casualties too, and these were numerically no less than those of the Indians, but it was the loss of so many of the leaders which was to be significant in the Indian units. It is difficult to be precise as to the numbers of casualties suffered by the Indian Corps. The semi-official history gives the figures for the Indian units of the Corps as being:

Killed: 153 British officers, 109 Indian officers and 2,345 Indian Other Ranks (including deaths other than by direct enemy action).

Wounded: 294 British officers, 336 Indian officers and 14,221 Indian Other Ranks.

Missing: 3,247 all ranks.[1]

These figures are almost certainly on the low side, because of the 'Missing' many were subsequently found to have been killed. Even so, the British officer casualties were the equivalent of 12 battalions' worth killed and a further 23 battalions' worth wounded. Most of those killed were in the infantry, and at any one time the Corps only had 18 battalions of Indian infantry. When the casualties of the British units which formed a permanent part of the Indian Corps—12,807—and those suffered by the staff of Corps Headquarters are added, we see that the total casualties of the Indian Corps in France amounted to 34,252, or considerably more than the entire strength of the Corps on arrival. There is no doubt that as casualties mounted, and as battalions were diluted by reinforcements not of their own cap badge, and as experienced British officers were killed or wounded and evacuated, the standards of the Indian units did decline. The wonder is that they continued to function at all, and that as late as Loos men were still willing to risk all in a cause which was never their own anyway. It says much for the old Indian Army that the sepoys and the sowars, the riflemen and the sappers still fought true to their oath when all that was familiar to them had been taken away.

Many of the lessons which the Indian Corps took away with them from the Western Front were common to the whole BEF: the need for reserves and reinforcements to be close up but still to be protected until needed, a dichotomy that was never resolved; the difficulties in passing information forward and back, not solved until the invention of portable and reliable radios in the next war; the fact that the farther an attacker advanced the thinner his supporting and administrative link became, while the defender was pushed back on his own reserves and supplies; the need for commanders to be far enough forward to know what was happening and to be able to influence the battle, but not so far forward as to become caught up in the local fighting. All these points would be pondered and practised before the next major war, but there were two lessons which emerged which were specific to the Indian Army. One was the position of staff officers and the other was the matter of reinforcement.

Modern mythology about the Great War tells us that staff officers moved about in a scented world of their own making, oblivious to what was really happening and sending men to their deaths with no idea of what they faced. Much of this is false, but those who were critical of the way in which the British Army fought the war were literate and it was they who wrote down their perorations for later generations to read. By the end of 1914 most staff officers had themselves experienced regimental service in the trenches and were trying to do a thankless job in circumstances for which many of them had never been properly trained. Prior to 1914 there had been no permanent headquarters above divisional level. During the war British corps changed their composition frequently, and the staff officers in a corps headquarters could not possibly get to know all the regimental officers whose units were—often temporarily—assigned to that corps. There were misunderstandings and mistakes, disasters even, but these rarely happened because the staff did not care, or did not know, but were brought about by the development of the conflict into a war that nobody had planned for, trained for, or even imagined. The technology of the attack had lagged behind that of the defence and, until the invention of the tank, the machine-gun and barbed wire were supreme, however con- scientiously staff officers tried to devise plans to defeat them. In the Indian Corps the situation was very different. Apart from brief attachments of a single British division or a couple of brigades for short periods, the Indian Corps retained much the same components throughout. There were few enough British officers in the Corps for each to know nearly every other, at least to begin with, and the staff officers knew, and were known by, the regiments whose activities they directed. The staff officers of the Indian Army came out of the conflict with their reputations unsullied.

Reinforcements were another matter. Here the system had manifestly failed, and it became clear early on that an army which consisted for the most part of single-battalion regiments, each with its own class composi- tion, was totally unsuitable for high intensity warfare. Try as the Adjutant General's Department did to recruit sufficient men of the right racial mix, it could never keep up with the drain of dead and wounded. A bet- ter system had to be found, and in 1922, after much discussion and soul searching, it was.

The Indian infantry would undergo yet another change of title. Instead of single-battalion regiments there would now be 20 regiments only, each of which would have between four and seven battalions. The exception would be the Gurkhas whose organisation into ten regiments, each of two

247

battalions, would remain unaltered. Thus the 129th Baluchis became the 4th Battalion 10th Baluch Regiment, the other battalions being formed from the 124th and 126th Infantry, the 127th Light Infantry and the 130th Baluchis. The 15th Sikhs and the 47th Sikhs became the 2nd and 5th Battalions of the 11th Sikh Regiment, the other battalions coming from the 14th, 35th, 36th and 45th Sikhs. 57th Wilde's Rifles, 58th Vaughan's Rifles and the 59th Scinde Rifles became the 4th, 5th and 6th Battalions of the 13th Frontier Force Rifles; the 40th Pathans the 5th Battalion the 14th Punjab Regiment, and the 6th Jat Light Infantry the 1st Battalion 9th Jat Regiment. As only one regiment recruited Garhwalis the 39th Garhwal Rifles became the 18th Garhwal Rifles, but the two pre-war battalions, amalgamated into one after Neuve Chapelle, would be expanded into four battalions.

Each regiment was formed from pre-war regiments which recruited either the same races, or at least races which were compatible. The overall racial balance of the infantry was little changed except for a reduction in the number of Pathans and Brahmins and some slight concessions to the Adjutant General's recommendation that as many races as possible should be represented in the Army. It was still largely to be an army of Punjabi Mussalmans, Sikhs, Gurkhas, Rajputs, Jats and men from the north. Instead of each battalion training its own recruits, each regiment would have a Regimental Centre which would train recruits for all the battalions in the group. All battalions in a regiment would wear the same cap badge, and uniforms were to be standardised. Regimental peculiarities of dress are held dear by the British and, inevitably perhaps, old battalion idiosyncrasies crept back in, with whistle cords, cummerbunds and titles in brackets reflecting the old allegiances. The 129th Baluchis, now part of the 10th Baluch Regiment, very quickly became the 4th Battalion (Duke of Connaught's Own), and the 125th Napiers' Rifles the 5th Battalion (Napier's) 6th Rajputana Rifles. This resistance to total uniformity, which included the re-emergence of the old forms of ceremonial dress and officers' mess dress, did no harm: the sepoys all carried out recruit training together and so knew at least some of the men in other battalions. The reinforcement of a battalion from others in the same large regiment became a relatively easy proposition, and that was the main rationale behind the reorganisation.

All these amalgamations and groupings into large regiments were designed to ensure that in a future war the Indian Army would not find itself unable to sustain a large force in full-scale conflict, and in that sense it worked. The Indian Army had modernised by 1918 and had the same weapons, the same number of machine-guns and approximately the same motor transport scale as its British counterpart. At the end of the war, however, there were other priorities for the Indian government and defence spending was cut back to the minimum consistent with the old roles of the Indian Army—law and order and the security of the frontiers. The Indian Army which would take the field in the Second World War was a very different creature to that which had mobilised in 1914. It had Indians holding the King's commission, it had a Territorial Force of sorts, it had a large Indian Army Reserve of Officers, and very few British officers now thought that the Raj would last for ever*, but in some ways things had not changed. The 1st Battalion 2nd Gurkha Rifles was ordered to Meerut from its lines in Dehra Dun for mobilisation in 1940. It marched out of Dehra Dun with the British officers on horseback and the men on their feet. It had no motor transport, no radios and no light machine-guns†.

Despite reversion to pre-1914 fiscal policies, the Indian Army added to its high reputation in the Second War. The British campaign in the Far East fell almost entirely to the Indian Army and Indian regiments fought in North Africa, the Middle East and Italy. In the post-war rush to independence and partition the Indian Army was divided between the armies of India and Pakistan, and the regiments which shed their blood so uncomplainingly on the Western Front serve on today, still with the same battle honours, with very much the same forms of dress and with their traditions unchanged. The Gurkhas, not being citizens of India or Pakistan, were divided between the Indian Army and the British Army in 1948, with four regiments each of two battalions transferring to Britain and the remaining six regiments staying in India. Today the Indian Army has 42 battalions of Gurkhas. It is not within the scope of this account to describe the fortunes of the eight battalions of Gurkha Rifles which transferred to the British Army. Suffice it to say that, after winning the Malaya and Borneo campaigns for the British, garrisoning Hong Kong and playing their part in the Falklands and the Gulf, the defence cuts of the 1990s hit the Gurkhas far harder than any other part of the British Army. The treatment of the Gurkhas is a sad story of betrayal, exploitation, politicking and self-seeking by senior officers; jealousy on the part of the British infantry and poor thanks for all those dead Magars and Gurungs, Rais and Limbus and Chettris who lay in the mud of Neuve Chapelle, on the hills of Gallipoli and on the banks of the Tigris. It says little for the word of an Englishman. There are now but 3,000 Gurkhas left in the British Army, and in an age where Britain seems to have a penchant for toadying to her enemies and betraying her friends, their future can only be viewed with uncertainty.

The Indian Army has passed from Europe, but its graves remain. The Indian cemetery at Zelobes, north of Bethune, is a quiet, dignified place, kept tidy by the Commonwealth War Graves Commission. The rows

---

* Although few British, and very few Indians, thought it would come to an end as quickly as it did.

† The Indian Army did not have a single tank at the outbreak of WW II.

of white headstones stand in the shade of the trees which surround the graveyard and there are few visitors. Each stone is carved with a name, a number and a regiment, with an epitaph in the language of the soldier who lies there. Not all the dead are soldiers, for saddest of all are the graves of the followers. Muleteers, cooks, sweepers, mess servants, stretcher bearers, orderlies, civilians all, they served their masters with honour and loyalty for a few rupees a month. They cannot have known for what they died.

Near Neuve Chapelle, at the road junction known in 1915 as Port Arthur, is the Indian Memorial designed by Sir Herbert Baker. It was opened on 7 October 1927 by Lord Birkenhead, then Secretary of State for India and some time Recording Officer of the Indian Corps. Marshal Foch and Rudyard Kipling came to the ceremony, as did a representative party of Indian Army veterans. The Indian Corps lost about 20% of its strength at Neuve Chapelle and the memorial looks out over the fields across which the sepoys advanced on that morning in March 1915. A tall column, surmounted by the star of India and flanked by two lions, dominates the memorial. On the column is carved 'God is One' in Punjabi, Hindi, Gurkhali, Urdu, Gurumukhia and all the languages of the Indian Corps. The memorial itself is laid out in the form of a garden surrounded by carved screens in the Moghul style. Inside are two platforms representing burning ghats, and on the marble walls are carved the names of all those of the Indian Army who were killed in France but whose bodies were never found or which could not be identified. They include that of Rifleman Gobar Sing Negi VC, 2nd Battalion 39th Garhwal Rifles, killed at Neuve Chapelle. There are 5,015 names carved on the walls. It is a peaceful place, far removed now from the noise and the screaming horror and the mud and the blood and the maimed and dying and dead men from far away that it commemorates. Those who know and love the Indian and the Gurkha are not ashamed to shed a tear in the presence of their memory.[2]

In England few outward signs of the presence of the Indian Army remain. There is a memorial in Brighton, its presence unknown and unremarked, and the old burning chatta, used to cremate the bodies of the Hindus who died in hospitals, is still there on the Downs.

There were very few Indians living in England before the Great War, and those who did were mainly of the nobility or the occasional bearer brought home by a retired officer. Now there are many, and nearly every community of any size has an Indian or Pakistani presence. Working quietly in the professions or as small businessmen, they work hard, do not engage in crime and are not in any way a drain on our economy. They add colour and dignity to our national life and many, perhaps most, are descendants of those sepoys who fought and died for this nation in its hour of greatest need. They deserve better of us than the abuse and violence so often directed against them by the loutish elements in British society, louts who are free to behave as they do because their forebears fought with the ancestors of those 'Pakis' against whom they fulminate, in a common cause all those years ago.

When the Indian Corps left France they were visited by the Prince of Wales, who read out to them a message from his father, the King:

Officers, Non Commissioned Officers and men of the Indian Army Corps.

More than a year ago I summoned you from India to fight for the safety of my Empire and the honour of my pledged word on the battlefields of Belgium and France. The confidence which I then expressed in your sense of duty, your courage and your chivalry you have since then nobly justified.

I now require your services in another field of action but before you leave France I send my dear and gallant son, the Prince of Wales, who has shared with my Armies the dangers and hardships of the campaign*, to thank you in my name for your services and to express to you my satisfaction.

British and Indian comrades-in-arms, yours has been a fellowship in toils and hardships, in courage and endurance often against great odds, in deeds nobly done and days of memorable conflict. In a warfare waged under new conditions and in particularly trying circumstances, you have worthily upheld the honour of the empire and the great traditions of my Army in India.

I have followed your fortunes with the deepest interest and watched your gallant actions with pride and satisfaction. I mourn with you the loss of many gallant officers and men. Let it be your consolation, as it was their pride, that they gave their lives in a just cause for the honour of their sovereign and the safety of my Empire. They died as gallant soldiers, and I shall ever hold their sacrifice in grateful remembrance. You leave France with a just pride in honourable deeds already achieved and with my assured confidence that your proved valour and experience will contribute to further victories in the new fields of action to which you go.

I pray God to bless and guard you, and to bring you back safely, when the final victory is won, each to his own home—there to be welcomed with honour among his own people.[3]

---

* Hardly. The Prince of Wales was an ADC to Sir John French and did not want for good food and a feather mattress. Still, the thought was there.

In the visitors' book at the Indian Memorial at Neuve Chapelle an anonymous hand has written: 'One dead for every kilometre home'. Perhaps that poignant line is the most fitting epitaph to the contribution of the Indian Army on the Western Front.

SOURCE NOTES

1. *The Indian Corps in France,* Merewether and Smith, John Murray, London, 1919. I have found it difficult to get exact figures. Sources vary, almost certainly because of the 'Missing'. A tally of the units' war diaries roughly agrees with the figures I have quoted.

2. Details of the opening ceremony, who attended and what they said are in the official memorial booklet issued shortly after the opening, India Office Library and Records L/MIL/17/5/2419. Casualty figures are given in the booklet but they do not distinguish between those of the Indian Corps and those of the two Indian cavalry divisions which remained on the Western Front until 1918.

3. *The Indian Corps in France.*

APPENDIX I

Sources

PUBLISHED SOURCES

The Daily Mail, 1914/15.
The Illustrated London News, 1914/15.
The Brighton Advertiser and Sussex County Herald, 1915.
The Brighton Herald and Hove Chronicle, 1915.
Statistics of the Military Efforts of the British Empire in the Great War 1914–1920, HMSO, London, 1922.
India's Contribution to the Great War, Government of India, Calcutta, 1923.
The History of The 1st King George V's Own Gurkha Rifles (The Malaun Regt) Vol I, Gale & Polden, Aldershot, 1925.
History of the 59th Rifles 1884–1923, Gale & Polden, Aldershot, 1926.
47th Sikhs War Record in the Great War 1914–1918, Picton Publishing, Chippenham, 1992.
Aitchison G, *Unknown Brighton*, The Bodley Head, London, 1926.
Baker A, *Battle Honours of the British and Commonwealth Armies*, Ian Allan, London, 1987.
Blake R, *The Private Papers of Sir Douglas Haig 1914–1919*, Eyre & Spottiswoode, London, 1952.
Bristow A, *A Serious Disappointment*, Leo Cooper, London, 1995.
Brown M, *The Imperial War Museum Book of the Western Front*, Sidgwick & Jackson, London, 1993.
Chevenix Trench C, *The Indian Army and the King's Enemies 1900–1947*, Thames & Hudson 1988.
Condon WEH, *The Frontier Force Rifles*, Gale & Polden, Aldershot, 1953.
Condon WEH, *The Frontier Force Regiment*, Gale & Polden, Aldershot, 1962.
Drake-Brockman DH, *The Royal Garhwal Rifles in the Great War 1914–17*, Charles Clarke Ltd, Haywards Heath (privately published), 1934.
Edmonds JE, *Military Operations in France and Belgium 1914, 1915*, Macmillan & Co, London, 1928.
Gaylor J, *Sons of John Company*, Spellmount Publishers, Staplehurst, 1992.
Grimshaw, Captain Roly (Ed Wakefield and Weippert), *Indian Cavalry Officer 1914–15*, Costello, Tonbridge Wells, 1986.

Harfield A, *The Indian Army of the Queen Empress 1861–1903*, Spellmount Publishers, Staplehurst, 1990.

Haythornthwaite PJ, *The World War One Source Book*, Arms & Armour Press, London 1994.

Heathcote TA, *The Indian Army*, David & Charles, Newton Abbot, 1974.

Hudson H, *History of the 19th King George's Own Lancers 1858–1921*, Gale & Polden, Aldershot, 1937.

Huxford HJ, *The 8th Gurkha Rifles 1824–1940*, Gale & Polden, Aldershot, 1952.

Jaipur, HH Maharajha of, *History of the Indian States Forces*, New Dehli, 1967.

Lawford JP and Catto WE, *Solah Punjab*, Gale & Polden, Aldershot, 1962.

Lucas, *The Empire at War Vol V, India*, Oxford University Press, 1926.

MacDonell and Macaulay, *A History of the 4th Prince of Wales' Own Gurkha Rifles 1857–1937*, Blackwood & Sons, Edinburgh and London (privately published), 1940.

MacMunn G, *The Armies of India*, Sampson Low, Marston & Co Ltd, 1911.

MacMunn G, *The Martial Races of India*, Sampson Low, Marston & Co Ltd, 1930.

MacMunn G, *The History of the Sikh Pioneers*, Sampson Low, Marston & Co Ltd, 1932.

Mason P, *A Matter of Honour*, Jonathan Cape, London, 1974.

Merewether and Smith, *The Indian Corps in France*, John Murray, London, 1919.

Mollo, Boris, *The Indian Army*, Blandford Press, Dorset, 1981.

Poynder FS, *The 9th Gurkha Rifles 1817–1936*, RUSI, London, 1937.

Roberts, FM Earl, *41 Years in India*, Macmillan, London, 1914.

Robson, *Roberts in India*, Army Records Society, 1993.

Royle T, *The Kitchener Enigma*, Michael Joseph, London, 1985.

Sandes EWC, *The Indian Sappers and Miners*, Institute of Royal Engineers, Chatham, 1948.

Shakespear LW, *History of the 2nd King Edward's Own Goorkhas (The Sirmoor Rifle Regt) Vol II 1911–1921*, Gale & Polden, Aldershot (privately published), 1962.

Sixsmith EKG, *Douglas Haig*, Weidenfield & Nicholson, London, 1976.

Terraine J, *The First World War*, Leo Cooper, London, 1983.

Vadgama, Kusoom, *India in Britain*, Robert Royce, London, 1984.

Warner P, *The Battle of Loos*, Purnell, 1976.

Willcocks J, *With the Indians in France*, Constable & Co, London, 1920.

Woodyatt NG, *History of the 3rd Queen Alexandra's Own Gurkha Rifles 1815–1927*, Philip Allan & Co, London, 1929.

Wylly HC, *History of the 3rd Bn 13th Frontier Force Rifles 1849–1926*, Gale & Polden, Aldershot, 1929.

OTHER SOURCES

Author's Interviews Nepal and India 1970 to 1996, Much background material and anecdotal evidence.

Gurkha Museum and Archives Winchester, Letter 2 Jan 15 to Maj Edwards 1/3GR, 3GR/303.

Gurkha Museum and Archives, Winchester, Villiers-Stuart Papers, Gurkha Museum and Archives, Winchester, Regimental Records 2nd Gurkha Rifles,

India Office Library and Records (TOL), 'Recruiting in India Before and During 1914–18', L/MIL/17/5/2152.

IOL Adjutant General's Department, 'Report on the Kitchener Indian Hospital Brighton', L/MIL/17/5/2016.

IOL, 'Report of the Censor of Indian Mails France 1914–1918 Vol I', L/MIL/ 5/825.

IOL, 'Printed Reports Censor of Indian Mails France Dec 1914—Jun 1918', LI MIL/5/828.

IOL, *Manual of Indian Military Law 1911*, L/MIL/17/5/709, This was the law as applicable in 1914/15.

IOL, 'Analysis of 1000 Wounds and Injuries received in action, with special reference to the theory of the prevalence of self-infliction', L/MIL/17/5/2402, Report by Col Sir Bruce Seaton Bart, Commanding Officer KIH Brighton.

IOL, 'Casualties by units, brigades of the Indian Corps', L/MIL/5/82 et seq.

IOL, 'Nominal rolls of Indian prisoners of war suspected of having deserted to the enemy or of giving information to the enemy. List A (Secret)', L/MIL/17/5/2403.

IOL, 'Native Regiments – Insubordination and Misconduct 1886–1938', L/MIL/7/7266 – 7284.

Lieutenant Colonel MH Broadway, Letter from widow of Pte Harold Wand, 1st Bn Seaforth Highlanders, Survivor of Indian Corps action at Loos.

Public Records Office, Kew, London (PRO), War Diaries 20, 21 Coys Sappers and Miners, Div Sigs Coy, 34th Sikh Pnrs, WO 95/3919.

PRO, War Diary Ferozepore Bde HQ, WO 95/3822.

PRO, War Diaries 1 Connaught Rngrs, 1/4 London, 9th Bhopal Inf, 57th Wilde's Rifles, WO 95/3923.

PRO, War Diaries 89th Punjabis, 125th Napier's Rifles, 129th Baluchis, WO 95/3924.

PRO, War Diary 129th Baluchis (Cont), WO 95/3925.

PRO, War Diary Jullunder Bde HQ, WO 95/3926.

PRO, War Diaries 1 Manchester, 4 Suffolk, 40th Pathans, 47th Sikhs, 59th Scinde Rifles, WO 95/3927

PRO, War Diary Sirhind Bde HQ, WO 95/3928.

PRO, War Diaries 1 Highland Light Infantry, 4 King's Liverpool, 1/1 GR, 1/4 GR, 15th Sikhs, 27th Punjabis, WO 95/3929.

PRO, War Diary Meerut Division HQ (GS), WO 95/3930/31.

PRO, War Diary 4th Cavalry, WO 95/3936.

PRO, War Diaries 3, 4 Coys Sappers and Miners, Div Sigs Coy, 107th Pnrs, WO 95/3938.

PRO, War Diary Dehra Dun Bde HQ, WO 95/3940.

PRO, War Diaries 1 Seaforth, 4 Seaforth, 1/9 CR, WO 95/3941.

PRO, War Diaries 2/2 GR, 6th Jat LI, 93rd Burma Inf, WO 95/3942.

PRO, War Diary Garhwal Bde HQ, WO 95/3943/44.

PRO, War Diaries 1/3 London, 2 Leics, 39th Carwhal Rifles, WO 95/3945.

PRO, War Diaries 2/3 GR, 2/8 GR, WO 95/3946.

PRO, War Diary Bareilly Bde HQ, WO 95/3947.

PRO, War diaries 2 BW, 1/4 BW, 41st Dogras, 58th Vaughan's Rifles, 33rd Punjabis, 69th Punjabis, WO 95/3948.

PRO, War Diary 19 (British) Bde HQ, WO 95/1364.

PRO, War Diaries 1 RF, 2 RWF, WO 95/1613.

PRO, War Diary 15 Lancers, WO 95/3918.

Note:

The sources listed above have all been consulted. Specific references are shown in the source notes to each chapter.

Class Composition of the Indian Corps on the Western Front

INFANTRY BY COMPANIES

UNIT	SIKH	DOCRA	JAT	PATHAN	PENJABI MUSSALMAN	GURKHA	GARHWALI	RAJPUT	MAHRATTA	BRAHMIN	HINDU PUNJABI
6th JAT LI		4									
9th BHOPAL INFANTRY	1							1		1	
15th SIKHS	4										
33rd PUNJABIS	1			1	2						
39th GARHWAL (1ST BN)							4				
39th GARHWAL (2ND BN)							4				
41st DOGRAS		4									
40th PATHANS				4							
47th SIKHS	4										
57th RIFLES	1			1	1						
58th RIFLES	1			1	1						
59th RIFLES	1			1	1						
69th PUNJABIS	1				2						
89th PUNJABIS	1½				1½			½		½	1
93rd BURMA INFANTRY	2			2							
125th RIFLES								3	1		
129th BALUCHIS				3	1						
1/1st GURKHA RIFLES						4					
2/2nd GURKHA RIFLES						4					
2/3rd GURKCHA RIFLES						4					
1/4th GURKCHA RIFLES						4					
2/8th GURKHA RIFLES						4					
1/9th GURICELA RIFLES						4					
TOTALS	17½	7	4	11	12½	24	8	4½	1	1½	1

258

DIVISIONAL CAVALRY AND SECUNDERABAD CAVALRY BRIGADE BY SQUADRONS

UNIT	SIKH	JAT	MULTANI PATHAN	PUNJABI MUSSALMAN	RAJPUT	DEKHANI MUSSALMAN	BORDER MUSLIMS	RAJPUTANA MUSLIMS	HINDUSTANI MUSLIMS	KHAIMKHANIS
15th LANCERS							2	1		
4th CAVALRY	1	1	2				1	1		1
34th POONA HORSE				1	2					
20th DECCAN HORSE	1		2			1				
JODHPUR LANCERS					4					

PIONEERS BY COMPANIES

UNIT	SIKH	PATHAN	RAJPUTANA MUSSALMAN	MAHRATA
1/34th SUCH PIONEERS	4			
107th PIONEERS	1	1	1	1

SAPPERS AND MINERS

UNIT	SIKH	PUNJABI MUSSALMAN	HUNDUSTANI HINDU	HINIDUSTANI MUSSALMAN	MAHRATTA
NO 2 COY 1ST KGO SAPPERS AND MINERS	½	½			
NO 3 COY 1ST KGO SAPPERS AND MINERS	¼	¼	½	¼	
NO 20 COY 3RD SAPPERS AND MINERS	¼	½		¼	
NO 21 COY 3RD SAPPERS AND MINERS	¼	½		¼	

259

Genealogy of the Regiments of the Indian Corps

INFANTRY

PRE 1903 REORG	TITLE IN 1914	POST 1922 REORG
6th Bengal Infantry	6th Jat Light Infantry	1st Royal Bn (Light Infantry) 9th Jat Regt
Bhopal Levy	9th Bhopal Infantry	4th Bn (Bhopal) 16th Punjab Infantry
15th Bengal Infantry	15th Ludhiana Sikhs	2nd Bn (Ludhiana Sikhs) 11th Sikh Regt
33rd Bengal Infantry	33rd Punjabis	3rd Bn 16th Punjab Regt
34th Bengal Infantry	34th Sikh Pioneers	34th Royal Sikh Pioneers (1921) 3rd Royal Bn 3rd Sikh Pioneers (1922)
39th Bengal Infantry	39th Garhwal Rifles	18th Garhwal Rifles
40th Bengal Infantry	40th Pathans	5th Bn 14th Punjab Regt
41st Bengal Infantry	41st Dogras	3rd Bn 17th Dogra Regt
47th Bengal Infantry	47th Sikhs	47th Duke of Connaught's Own Sikhs (1921) 5th Bn (Duke of Connaught's Own) 11th Sikh Regt (1922)
4th Punjab Infantry	57th Wilde's Rifles (Frontier Force)	4th Bn (Wilde's) 13th Frontier Force Rifles
5th Punjab Infantry	58th Vaughan's Rifles (Frontier Force)	5th Bn 13th Frontier Force Rifles
6th Punjab Infantry	59th Scinde Rifles (Frontier Force)	59th Royal Scinde Rifles (Frontier Force) (1921) 6th Royal Battalion

		13th Frontier Force Rifles (1922)
9th Madras Infantry	69th Punjabis	2nd Bn 2nd Punjab Regt
29th Madras Infantry	89th Punjabis	1st Bn 8th Punjab Regt
33rd Madras Infantry	93rd Burma Infantry	5th (Burma) Bn 8th Punjab Regt
7th Bombay Infantry	107th Pioneers	1st Bn 2nd Bombay Pioneers
25th Bombay infantry	125th Napier's Rifles	5th Bn (Napier's) 6th Rajputana Rifles
29th Bombay Infantry	129th Duke of Connaught's Own Baluchis	4th Bn (Duke of Connaught's Own) 10th Baluch Regt
1st Gurkha Rifles (The Malaun Regt)	1st King George's Own Gurkha Rifles (The Malaun Regt)	No change
2nd (Prince of Wales's Own) Gurkha Regiment (The Sirmoor Rifles)	2nd King Edward's Own Gurkha Rifles (The Sirmoor Rifles)	No change
3rd Gurkha Rifles	3rd Queen Alexandra's Own Gurkha Rifles	No change
4th Gurkha Rifles	No change	No change
8th Gurkha Rifles	No change	No change
9th Gurkha Rifles	No change	No change

CAVALRY

PRE 1903 REORG	TITLE IN 1914	POST 1922 REORG
4th Bengal Cavalry	4th Cavalry	2nd Lancers (Gardner's Horse)
15th Bengal Cavalry	15th Lancers (Cureton's Multanis)	20th Lancers
1st Hyderabad Cavalry	20th Deccan Horse	9th Royal Deccan Horse
4th Bombay Cavalry	34th Prince Albert Victor's Own Poona Horse	17th Queen Victoria's Own Poona Horse

Index

Khan, Sepoy Zaman, Wildes
Rifles: 2
Kipling, Rudyard: 250
Kitchener, Field Marshall Lord: 3,
172-3, 205, 214, 222, 237
Kitchener Indian Hospital. *See*
Hospitals
Klein Zillebeck: 57
Kotdwara: 29
Kumaon: 28
Kumasi: 41

La Bassée: 0, 67, 77-8, 110, 119,
144-5, 147, 144-5, 147, 149, 183,
202, 208, 222-4, 231, 234
La Brique: 187, 189, 190
La Cliqueterie: 202, 224
La Cliqueterie Farm: 202
Lacouture: 101
La Gorgue: 32
La Manche: 184
Langemark: 183, 185, 187, 191
Lansdowne: 28
La Quinque Rue: 78-9, 114, 117,
121
La Tourelle: 207, 210
La Valentine: 39
Laventie: 64, 78, 241
Layes, River: 154-5, 157, 160-2,
164, 166
Le Bridoux: 234
Le Havre: 1
Lembernesse: 53
Lemprière, Lieutenant Colonel,
7DG: 119
Lens: 202, 218, 222, 231
Le Plantin: 120, 123, 223
Les Facons: 74
Les Fontaines: 103
Les Glatignes: 74
Les Lobes: 108
Les Rouges Bancs: 75, 77
Le Touquet: 113

Lewes: 238-9
Ligny le Grand: 202
Lille: 52, 74, 145, 168, 202
Lillers: 47, 74
Locon: 64, 96
Loharu: 140
London Gazette: 227
Loos: 173, 218-9, 222-3, 233-5,
245-6
Lucas, Lieutenant, 2/2 Gurkha
Rifles: 83, 88
Lushai Hills Military Police: 128,
130-1
Lys, River: 50, 154

MacKenzie, Major General CJ, CB:
69
MacMunn, Lieutenant General Sir
George: 4-7, 61, 66, 101
Macpherson, Major, 2/2 Gurkha
Rifles: 84
McBean, Major General F CVO
DSO: 25, 119-20, 133
McCleverty, Captain, 47th Sikhs:
McCleverty, Captain, 2/2 Gurkha
Rifles: 68, 70
McLintock, Brevet Major RL,
Sappers & Miners: 32
McSwiney, Lieutenant, 2/3
Gurkha Rifles: 95
Madras: x, 4, 8-9, 31, 38
Mahratta: Third War: 110
Maler Kotla Sappers & Miners.
See Sappers & Miners
Malwa SS. See Ships
Marne: 51, 73, 145
Marquillies: 195
Marseilles: 1-2, 14, 38-41, 45-6,
74-5, 93, 109, 131, 198, 214-5,
235-6, 244
Mary, Queen: 125, 139, 176
Mauquissart: 223-4, 229-32
Mauser Ridge: 187, 193